OXFORD STUDIES IN PC

Oxford Studies in Political Philosophy

Volume 3

Edited by
DAVID SOBEL, PETER VALLENTYNE,
AND STEVEN WALL

OXFORD
UNIVERSITY PRESS

OXFORD
UNIVERSITY PRESS

Great Clarendon Street, Oxford, OX2 6DP,
United Kingdom

Oxford University Press is a department of the University of Oxford.
It furthers the University's objective of excellence in research, scholarship,
and education by publishing worldwide. Oxford is a registered trade mark of
Oxford University Press in the UK and in certain other countries

Published in the United States of America by Oxford University Press
198 Madison Avenue, New York, NY 10016, United States of America

Library of Congress Cataloging in Publication Data
Data available

ISBN 978–0–19–880122–1 (Hbk.)
ISBN 978–0–19–880123–8 (Pbk.)

Printed and bound by
CPI Group (UK) Ltd, Croydon, CR0 4YY

Acknowledgements

The chapters assembled here were, mostly, first presented as papers at the Workshop for Oxford Studies in Political Philosophy at Syracuse University. We would like to thank all those that attended this event, with special thanks to Teresa Bruno Nino and Nikki Fortier for helping with the conference web pages, providing amazing artwork for the conference, and handling details on the ground in Syracuse. As always, Rosie Johnson's expert work on behalf of the workshop and this volume is most greatly appreciated. All of the chapters in this volume were referred. We mostly call on our editorial board to do this refereeing. We are, as always, most grateful to them for doing this important work. Travel by editor Steven Wall was made possible through the support of a grant from the John Templeton Foundation. The opinions expressed in this publication are those of the authors and do not necessarily reflect the views of the John Templeton Foundation.

Contents

List of Contributors

Elizabeth Anderson, University of Michigan
Ralf Bader, University of Oxford
David Enoch, Hebrew University, Jerusalem
Keith Hyams, University of Warwick
Seth Lazar, Australian National University
Serena Olsaretti, ICREA-Universitat Pompeu Fabra, Barcelona
Michael Otsuka, London School of Economics
Jonathan Parry, University of Birmingham
George Sher, Rice University
Seana Valentine Shiffrin, University of California, Los Angeles
Laura Valentini, London School of Economics

Introduction

David Sobel

Peter Vallentyne, Steve Wall, and I are pleased that Oxford Studies in Political Philosophy has so quickly become a fixture in the political philosophy landscape and that its associated workshop provides a useful regular gathering for the subfield.

With Volume 3 we are able to introduce a new feature of OSPP: The Sanders Prize in Political Philosophy (funded every two years by The Marc Sanders Foundation). We are most grateful to the Foundation for its generosity. The first winner of the prize is Keith Hyams. The award-winning paper is "On the Contribution of *Ex Ante* Equality to *Ex Post* Fairness."

EQUALITY AND JUSTICE

The thought that justice requires that we treat people as equals in some sense is so irresistible as to risk being trivial. The substantive issue involves determining in what dimension or dimensions we will insist on equality, as well as what we mean by equality, and in which dimensions we will tolerate or welcome inequality.

Hyams's paper, and several others in this volume (as well as a good deal of contemporary political philosophy), addresses issues concerning inequality, justice, and luck. Brute luck in life prospects is ubiquitous, concerning, and naturally draws the critical attention of egalitarians. "Luck egalitarians" have maintained that unequal outcomes that result from brute luck are, to that extent, unfair. If I am better off than you merely because I won the natural lottery in my genetic make-up, such views claim, the resulting inequality is unfair. But it also seems that we think that the equality of *ex ante* chances is relevant to fairness as well. We think justice sometimes speaks in favor of distributing windfall benefits or burdens via lotteries, such as when it seems recommended to draw straws to see who will have to perform some necessary but unpleasant task that is no one's assignable job. The intuition here is that, as Hyams says, "brute luck *ex post* inequalities are less unfair when they emerge from a less unequal *ex ante* distribution of chances than when they emerge from a more unequal *ex ante* distribution."

The attractions of combining the above set of intuitions have led a variety of influential philosophers to maintain that both *ex ante* equal chances and *ex post* equal distributions are relevant to the fairness of a situation. Because such views give weight both to *ex post* inequality and *ex ante* inequality, Hyams calls such views "egalitarian mixed views." Such views are contrasted with views that maintain that only *ex post* or only *ex ante* chances are relevant in determining fairness.

Hyams aims to show us that there are problems for egalitarian mixed views. He argues that the mixed view must be either unmotivated or incoherent. He concludes that we should not use up scarce resources to provide people more equal chances at benefit—letting the worse off eat chances—if this comes at the cost of more equal or better outcomes.

The concern to provide the best interpretation of the political goal of equality continues in Elizabeth Anderson's paper "The Problem of Equality from a Political Economy Perspective." She provides a broad overview of her influential take on the best understanding of egalitarian principles.

Anderson offers a sharp contrast to traditional philosophical accounts of egalitarian justice, which she labels "distributive egalitarianism." Such views maintain "justice consists in an equal distribution of some particular good or goods across individuals." But "such conceptions of equality, defined in terms of bare patterns of distribution of nonrelational goods that have no particular connection with the ways people treat and regard each other are detached from the welfare or interests of the people who figure in these patterns."

Rather than such understandings, Anderson argues the proper understanding of egalitarianism comes into view only when we see what the object of the "egalitarian impulse" has been throughout the ages. What we learn when we take this approach is that "what egalitarianism opposes is *social hierarchy*—that is, institutionalized social relations of superiors to inferiors." She offers a variety of ways in which this understanding is quite different from, and superior to, the traditional distributional understanding.

Anderson's focus in the paper is on providing a sweeping history of the human impulse towards domination, as well as towards resenting and resisting such domination. By understanding these, she hopes to explicate both what the key challenges to an egalitarian society are and what resources and strategies humans have developed to resist domination.

Serena Olsaretti, in "Liberal Equality and the Moral Status of Parent-Child Relationships," considers two ways in which ordinary parenting practices can seem problematic or at least in need of justification. First, how is it that parents in particular are entitled to make important decisions over their children's lives? Second, why is it permissible to show partiality towards one's child in ways that will exacerbate morally troubling inequalities? Olsaretti seeks a defense of these common features of parenthood but argues that existing defenses of such practices are insufficient. For example, the instrumentalist view, which maintains that parental rights and partiality are explained by the good that they cause, is too precarious, Olsaretti maintains, to be plausible. It is implausible to think that if a slightly more efficient system could be devised, such parental rights and permissions would disappear. Another rival view to Olsaretti's, the "Relationship" justification of the status quo, maintains that parent-child relationships are both instrumentally and intrinsically valuable and thus that some, but not all, partiality is justified as a cost worth paying to maintain such relationships. But this view cannot explain, she argues, why parents are obligated to enter into such relationships with their children in the first place. Additionally, such views have a hard time explaining why parents, rather than someone else, ought to especially start up such relationships.

These criticisms of existing views pave the way to Olsaretti's own favored approach. The status quo is justified in virtue of the existence of relationships between parents and children, as the Relationship view maintains, but parents have an obligation to enter into such relationships with their children. Provided one has become a parent in a fully voluntary way, one is obliged to enter into the sort of loving relationship children need if they are to thrive. This explains why the existence of such relationships is not optional for parents and why parents are especially the ones who should enter into them with their children.

George Sher, in "Doing Justice to Desert," considers the question of whether and to what extent justice requires that goods be distributed in accordance with desert. Sher sets aside several traditional philosophical grounds for skepticism about the significance of desert and develops his own novel ground for such skepticism. Sher maintains that there is a mismatch between the grounds of justice and the grounds of desert. "That we all have futures, that we all have likes, dislikes, and plans, and that we all have points of view from which things matter to us: these are the sorts of facts that are standardly taken to establish that we ourselves matter, and thus to undergird whichever principles of justice govern the distribution of goods among us. Because these are facts that hold of the deserving and undeserving alike, there is no reason to expect whatever principles they undergird to make any reference to desert."

Yet while Sher concludes that justice cannot simply involve giving to each person what she deserves, this does not mean that desert is irrelevant to justice. Even if we are subjects of justice due to features we all have in common, still, he maintains, the principles of justice might broadly reflect and match agents' different bases of desert. "We can simultaneously accommodate both the parties' moral equality and whatever case there is for honoring their particular deserts."

STATE LEGITIMACY

Another central issue in political philosophy concerns the justification for the state's use of coercive force. It can appear puzzling why the state should have permissions to do so beyond the extent that a mere assembly of individuals would have such permissions. Certainly if all had authentically consented to be ruled by the state, the resulting state exerting the powers characteristic of modern states would seem clearly in good order. But such consent cannot justify modern states and so the puzzle remains.

Ralf Bader's paper, "Counterfactual Justifications of the State," starts with an interpretive puzzle about Nozick's justification of the minimal state. Nozick's story about the development of a dominant protection agency at best seems to explain how a legitimate minimal state could have come about without violating rights. But given Nozick's deep commitment to the justificatory power of actual historical processes and the possibility of unanimous consent giving rise to a more than minimal state, it is hard to see the justificatory relevance of Nozick's counterfactual tale of the development of the dominant protection agency.

Bader urges us to recall that counterfactual considerations can be relevant for Nozick in determining what justice in rectification requires. He interprets Nozick's story about the dominant protection agency as a part of justice in rectification. "In the same way that counterfactual considerations become relevant in justifying distributions of holdings in non-ideal circumstances, they also become relevant in justifying political institutions in such circumstances...Nozick's justification of the state can be understood as a rectificationist justification of the minimal state." Having unearthed this notion of a rectificationist justification for the state, Bader goes on, no longer merely within Nozick's framework, to consider the prospects and problems for such an attempt to understand state legitimacy.

Public reason theorists, following Rawls, insist that the state must restrict its justifications for its actions and requirements to reasons all reasonable citizens can share. To the extent that the state fails to do this, and instead acts in ways that cannot be justified to all reasonable citizens, the requirements of the state are not binding.

David Enoch, in "Political Philosophy and Epistemology," suggests that part of the justification for the public reason theorists' restriction is the epistemic difficulty of justifying our commitment to our more fundamental and idiosyncratic doctrines. But of course the public reason theorist wants to allow that we may remain committed to our private comprehensive doctrines and presumably they would want to allow that we could sometimes be justified in doing so. It was, after all, in part the existence of reasonable pluralism that motivated this project.

Enoch considers the plight of someone who is committed to a comprehensive doctrine, who thinks it true, who is coherent, yet who finds good epistemic reason to not rely on their comprehensive doctrine in their political activities. What, Enoch asks, is the public reason theorist asking us to believe about her epistemic situation and how is it supposed to result in her maintaining but not relying on for some purposes her comprehensive doctrine? Enoch concludes, "I've been highlighting the following dilemma: the public reason theorist must fill in the details of the reasonable person—in particular, her beliefs about other reasonable people, who don't share her comprehensive doctrine—in a way that, first, renders her coherent (and plausibly reasonable), and second, that can justify the requirement not to rely in the political sphere on considerations that are controversial (in the relevant way) among the reasonable. And the results have been rather pessimistic: It's relatively easy to satisfy any one of these two conditions, but we have yet to see a plausible way of satisfying both."

Seth Lazar and Laura Valentini, in "Proxy Battles in Just War Theory," distinguish between different understandings of the "site of justice." "Political" approaches maintain that principles of justice apply primarily to institutions and only secondarily or derivatively to individuals. "Non-political" approaches, by contrast, maintain that principles of justice apply directly to individuals.

Lazar and Valentini argue that we can understand a good deal of disagreement in the just war literature, especially on the topic of *jus in bello*, as masking different commitments concerning the appropriate site of justice. Orthodox approaches to *jus in bello*, which maintain an equality in the rights and prohibitions of those who fight on the side of justice with those that do not, and which maintain that non-combatants enjoy immunity from hostilities, look easier to defend if one was already attracted to the political (state-based) conception of the site of justice. If one were attracted to a non-political conception, then it would be difficult to understand why those fighting on the side of justice lose any of their moral protections against those who are fighting an unjust war.

Lazar and Valentini hope that bringing out explicitly this backgrounded debate about the site of justice will allow us to make progress on first-order just war issues and motivate a recognition of the strengths of each side of the debate. They go on to examine the costs and benefits of orthodox and revisionist approaches when we keep in mind the two different sites of justice at play and point to the possibility of a motivated middle ground in these debates.

FURTHER TOPICS

The boundaries of political philosophy are being pushed outwards to include more applied pressing issues. Further, as we understand Oxford Studies in Political Philosophy, it is intended to include social issues that discuss structural aspects of a fully just society that are not easily understood in terms of personal morality, yet which need not centrally involve the state. Several of the papers in this volume make contributions in this direction.

Seana Valentine Shiffrin's paper, "The Moral Neglect of Negligence," is a meditation on the nature and significance of negligence, as well as a plea to stop ignoring its importance. Shiffrin understands the difference between negligence and malice in terms of different motives that animate such acts. As Shiffrin understands it, negligent agents fail to take due care to avoid harm to others but do not aim at or deliberately allow such harm as an end in itself or as a means to an end. Shiffrin maintains that traditionally malice is seen as worse than negligence. She does not aspire to turn that judgment on its head but rather aims to complicate the ranking in ways that highlight the largely ignored and underestimated moral seriousness of negligence. Negligence "involves a failure to take and exercise appropriate responsibility for one's agency" and this can be very morally serious indeed.

Shiffrin offers an extended discussion of the case of Edward Snowden to highlight various aspects of negligence. Snowden, Shiffrin argues, acted hastily and consulted few before he released sensitive information. The injustice of what Snowden was fighting, Shiffrin argues, did not insulate him from the requirement to aspire to think through the implications of his actions collaboratively with others, rather than just seek out like-minded people to break his story. His failure to find some structure to work within, rather than acting mainly alone, was negligent, Shiffrin argues. She also explores to what extent the thought that malice is generally morally worse than negligence might be due to supposing that that distinction lines up with either the act/omission distinction or the doctrine of double effect.

Michael Otsuka, in "How to Guard against the Risk of Living Too Long," argues for the preferability of retirement plans known as "collective defined contribution." Such plans are attractive from the point of view of employers as they are predictable and no more expensive to them than traditional defined contribution plans. They are attractive from the point of view of employees because they collectivize over generations the risks of living longer than expected and sharp downturns in the market. As is, prudent investors will curb the aggressiveness of their investments as they age to guard against downturns that they lack the time to recover from. While individually rational, such actions tend to be collectively sub-optimal in the long term compared to staying more fully and aggressively invested. Such costs might be individually rational to bear, much like buying insurance. But Otsuka points to a way for us all to do better. By remaining invested in ways that are long-term return maximizing and collectivizing risk we can all do better.

Further, Otsuka argues, such a scheme can be justified both to the right and to the left. It need not involve any involuntary taking from some for the sake of others. Further, it can be seen as grounded in a Rawlsian principle of reciprocity.

Jonathan Parry, in "Authority and Harm," considers the interaction between moral requirements to avoid harming and the moral authority to issue commands. A common view, which Parry resists, maintains that we lose our moral reason to avoid inflicting harm only when either 1) the person we would harm has in some way waived their right against being harmed or 2) the harm we inflict is outweighed by weightier moral reasons. A second view Parry resists maintains that, if I am justified in infringing your right against harm, you cannot be justified in resisting.

Parry thinks that both of the above views are false and we can see their falsity by thinking about commands from a legitimate authority. He argues that in some cases authority's commands can legitimately give us reasons to impose harms that would have been impermissible but for the command, which transgresses rights, even in situations in which the good brought about does not outweigh the transgression. Additionally, Parry maintains, thinking about the interactions between authority and harm can lead us to see that we may sometimes legitimately resist someone despite the fact that they are justified in attempting to harm us.

PART I
EQUALITY AND JUSTICE

1

On the Contribution of *Ex Ante* Equality to *Ex Post* Fairness

Keith Hyams

I

On 19 April 1841 the *William Brown* hit an iceberg off the coast of Newfoundland. Thirty-one of the passengers went down with the ship, while another fifty-one passengers and crewmen made it into one of two lifeboats. When one of the lifeboats began to take on water in adverse conditions, the first mate ordered the crewmen in the boat to throw overboard any male passengers who were not accompanied by their wives, in order to save the crewmen and the female passengers, who remained in the boat. Sixteen of the passengers were thrown overboard, while all of the crewmen and a number of remaining passengers, mostly women, survived. Only one of the crewmen, Alexander Holmes, was ever brought to trial. He was convicted of manslaughter and sentenced to six months in jail and a fine of 20 dollars.

In court, Holmes claimed the defence of necessity to self-preservation. In response, the district attorney made two key arguments. First, he argued that seamen are 'to undergo whatever hazard is necessary to preserve the boat and the passengers', even if such hazard calls for the sacrifice of their own life over that of the passengers. Second, he argued that, even if the seamen were not obliged to give their lives to save the passengers, nevertheless they should have held a lottery to decide who lived and who died:

If the source of the danger have been obvious, and destruction ascertained to be certainly about to arrive, though at a future time, there should be consultation, and some mode of selection fixed, by which those in equal relations may have equal chance for their life. By what mode, then, should selection be made?...When the ship is in no danger of sinking, but all sustenance is exhausted, and a sacrifice of one person is necessary to appease the hunger of others, the selection is by lot. This mode is resorted to as the fairest mode, and, in some sort, as an appeal to God, for selection of the victim.... For ourselves, we can conceive of no mode so consonant both to humanity and to justice... If time have existed to cast lots, and to select the victims, then, as we have said, sortition should be adopted.[1]

When distributing an indivisible harm or benefit between multiple individuals, all of whom have an equal claim to avoid the harm or receive the benefit, it is commonly thought that one should hold a lottery that gives each claimant an equal chance of avoiding the harm or receiving the benefit.[2] We might question whether the individuals in the lifeboat did have an equal claim to stay in the boat. Perhaps, we might think, any children on board had a stronger claim than the adults. Or we might think that the district attorney was right in his first argument, that the crewmen had a weaker claim than the passengers. But to the extent that the individuals in the boat did have an equal claim, it seems clear that they should indeed have held a lottery.[3]

Why should we hold lotteries in cases like the above? One familiar explanation is that, by giving each claimant an equal chance of getting the harm or benefit, you make the resultant outcome inequality less unfair than it would otherwise have been. According to this view, which I will call the *egalitarian mixed view*, brute luck *ex post* inequalities are less unfair when they emerge from a less unequal *ex ante* distribution of chances than when they emerge from a more unequal *ex ante* distribution.[4] The view is 'mixed' in the sense that it claims that the unfairness of a brute luck *ex post* distribution is a function of both the degree of inequality in the *ex post* distribution

---

[1] *United States v. Holmes.* Circuit Court, E. D. Pennsylvania. 26 F.Cas. 360 (1842).

[2] I assume that it is all things considered better to give the good to some agents but not others, rather than to level down and deny all agents the good, even though it may be more unfair, from the point of view of equality, that some agents will end up with the good whilst others will not. I also assume that it would either be unreasonable or impossible to decide between the two claimants on the basis of an auction. For discussion, see Kornhauser and Sager (1988: 508–9), Saunders (2008: 362–3).

[3] Some authors have argued that, where agents have unequal claims to a good, we should hold a lottery that gives each agent a chance of winning the good that is proportional to the strength of her claim to that good. If this is right, then one might think that they should have held a lottery, albeit a weighted one, even if the individuals had unequal claims. This claim is, however, more contentious than the claim that, when agents have equal claims, one should hold a lottery that gives each agent an equal chance of getting the good. It is more contentious because others have thought that, when agents have unequal claims, the good should go to the agent with the strongest claim. The present paper focuses only on cases in which agents have an equal claim to some good, since it is these cases in which we are most strongly inclined to recommend lotteries.

[4] By *ex ante* distribution of chance, I mean the distribution of unchosen (by those affected by the outcome) risk that obtains prior to resolution of that risk. By brute luck *ex post* inequality, I mean the inequality of outcome that emerges from unchosen (by those affected by the outcome) risk.

itself, and the degree of inequality in the *ex ante* distribution of chances from which it is derived. Versions of the egalitarian mixed view have been prominently endorsed by a number of authors, including Diamond (1967: 765–6), Broome (1990: 95), Arneson (1997: 238–41), Temkin (2001: 338–9), Lang (2005: 321–51), Otsuka (unpublished).[5] Parfit (2012) has also recently endorsed a prioritarian variant of the view in order to defend prioritarianism against the objection, put by Otsuka and Voorhoeve (2009), that prioritarianism cannot adequately accommodate intuitions about the moral relevance of the separateness of persons.[6]

The popularity of the egalitarian mixed view is perhaps largely the result of its promise to steer a middle course between opposed intuitions which, Scylla and Charybdis-like, have been thought to threaten views which link the fairness of a brute luck outcome either solely to the *ex ante* distribution or solely to the *ex post* distribution. On the one hand, a view which links the fairness of an outcome solely to the *ex ante* distribution of chances (the pure *ex ante* view) cannot accommodate widely endorsed intuitions about the badness of brute luck outcome inequality (e.g. Lippert-Rasmussen (1999: 482–3), Arneson (1999: 489–90), Dworkin (2000: 87–8)[7]). On the other hand, a view which links the fairness of an outcome solely to the *ex post* distribution (the pure *ex post* view) provides no explanation in itself of the intuition that we should hold a lottery. Voorhoeve and Fleurbaey (2012)

---

[5] The egalitarian mixed view applies both to straightforward lottery cases, in which the allocation of a scarce and indivisible good is at stake, and to other cases, in which the benefit to be allocated is not scarce and/or indivisible. One might attempt to explain the intuition that we should hold a lottery in cases like the above by appeal to a more restricted view, according to which lotteries render unequal outcomes less unfair only when it was not possible to reduce or avoid the outcome inequality itself, because the good in question was scarce and indivisible. Saunders (2008: 360–1), for example, seems to endorse such a view. The restricted view requires the claim that reductions in *ex post* inequality make a contribution to fairness that is lexically prior to reductions in *ex ante* inequality, such that the concern with *ex ante* inequality kicks in only when nothing can be done about *ex post* inequality. But it seems intuitively implausible that a concern with *ex ante* equality should be muted when the slightest improvement in *ex post* inequality is possible, even if such improvement comes at great expense to *ex ante* inequality—as in the example of INITIAL *EX ANTE* CHOICE below.

[6] See also Bovens (2015). Prioritarianism is the view that benefitting people matters more the worse off they are: see Parfit (2002: 101). Note that deontic egalitarians might also endorse a version of the egalitarian mixed view which makes no claims about fairness, but which insists nevertheless that the deontic strength of the reason against causing or allowing an *ex post* inequality to unfold or remain is diminished to the extent that the *ex post* inequality emerged or would emerge from a less unequal *ex ante* distribution of chances.

[7] Although elsewhere Dworkin appears to endorse the pure *ex ante* view: for discussion, see Otsuka (2004: 157 n. 17). For a response to some of these objections on behalf of *ex ante* egalitarianism, see Vallentyne (2002: 543–9).

have also recently charged that egalitarians who are solely concerned with the *ex post* distribution cannot accommodate intuitions about the moral relevance of the separateness of persons (for a response to this charge on behalf of the pure *ex post* view, see Hyams (2015)). The egalitarian mixed view promises to accommodate all of these intuitions, and thereby recommends itself over both the pure *ex ante* view and the pure *ex post* view.[8]

Clearly it matters greatly to a number of central areas of public policy whether the egalitarian mixed view is correct, since the view will make very different recommendations to both the pure *ex ante* view and the pure *ex post* view about the nature of socially just distributive arrangements. These policy consequences extend not only to cases that involve overt lotteries, such as military draft lotteries and the green card lottery, but also to broader political issues. Such issues include, for example, fair healthcare provision, and, as discussed below, the proper interpretation of fair equality of opportunity.[9]

In this paper I shall argue that the egalitarian mixed view is mistaken. I shall argue that the unfairness of *ex post* inequality is in no way diminished by the former presence of *ex ante* equality. Although I frame my argument as an argument against the more popular egalitarian mixed view, the argument also implies that we should reject the pure *ex ante* view. The paper proceeds as follows. I begin by showing how the view has distinct deontic implications, requiring those who hold the view to make choices that others would regard as morally impermissible. My main objection to the view is described in sections III and IV. I argue that, while the view imbues a distinction

[8] Another commonly mentioned reason for endorsing the egalitarian mixed view is the thought that the chance of a benefit (or the chance to avoid a disadvantage) is of genuine value to those who enjoy such chances, and/or that the chance of a benefit offers some sort of actual or surrogate satisfaction of an entitlement or claim to the benefit (e.g. Broome (1990: 98); Otsuka (unpublished)). Certainly it is true that agents are better off with the chance of a benefit than without the chance of a benefit. But notice that from the point of view of an agent's interest, the value of a chance evaporates in the event that the benefit does not obtain. In order to argue that the *ex ante* distribution makes a contribution to the fairness of an outcome, one would, therefore, require the additional claim that, from the point of view of fairness, the value of a chance does *not* similarly evaporate. Proponents of the mixed view certainly do make this additional claim, often explicitly. But it is precisely this additional claim that is controversial, and which those who endorse the pure *ex post* view would deny. Without it, the appeal to the value of an equal chance provides no argument in favour of the mixed view. For example, Sher (1980: 213–14) and Kornhauser and Sager (1988: 496), both recognize the value of an equal chance to its holder, but do not endorse the egalitarian mixed view.

[9] See the conclusion of this paper for further discussion of the latter question. On the relevance of lotteries to healthcare provision, see, for example, Daniels (2008: 107–8). For an extensive survey of the actual use of lotteries in matters of contemporary public policy, as well as a range of intriguing historical cases, see Elster (1988). For further examples and proposals, see Goodwin (2005, especially ch. 10).

between outcomes and changes to probabilities with central moral importance, that distinction looks morally arbitrary at best and incoherent at worst. Section V considers a way in which the view might be revised to avoid the objection, concluding that the revised version of the view runs up against alternative, equally damaging, objections. Section VI ends with some comments on the relevance of the conclusion for public policy.

II

In order to make the case against the egalitarian mixed view, it will be helpful to illustrate what is distinctive about the egalitarian mixed view at the deontic level. That is, it will be helpful to show how it requires us to make choices that those who endorse the pure *ex post* view would regard as morally impermissible. Consider, then, the case of INITIAL *EX ANTE* CHOICE.

In INITIAL *EX ANTE* CHOICE, you are charged with allocating one dose of a medicine to which two agents, call them Annie and Betty, each have an equal claim. Annie and Betty, who are strangers to you, both suffer from the same debilitating disease that would be fully cured by the medicine. Suppose that the dose takes the form of a single pill. You now face the following choice. Either you can hold a lottery that will, with equal probability, nominate either Annie or Betty as the winner of the medicine. Or you can split the pill in half and give one half to Annie and one half to Betty. Whereas it is known that a full dose of the medicine would fully cure either agent, it is also known that a half dose would have a different effect on each agent, as a result of their different physiological reactions to a less than full dose of the medicine. A half dose administered to Annie would have the effect of resolving the worst of Annie's symptoms, but would nevertheless leave a few unpleasant symptoms unresolved. A half dose administered to Betty, on the other hand, would resolve only a few of Betty's symptoms, leaving the worst of them unresolved. Table 1.1 shows the effect of the various possible outcomes on each agent's utility.[10]

How ought you to allocate the medicine, if your aim is to bring about the least bad outcome by minimizing the unfairness of any *ex post* inequality that results from your choice (I assume that Annie and Betty are unable to express their own views about how you should choose)? At first pass, those

---

[10] I use 'utility' to refer to that metric with which judgements about the fairness of distributions ought to be concerned, on a cardinal scale. I make no claims about the substantive nature of that metric, be it preference-satisfaction, objective well-being, or some other good or goods. I only assume that, if individuals have an interest in being treated fairly, or in fair outcomes, then this interest does not itself contribute to their utility.

Table 1.1 INITIAL *EX ANTE* CHOICE between LOTTERY and SPLIT PILL

Option	Claimant	Equiprobable Outcomes	
		Outcome 1	Outcome 2
LOTTERY	Annie	10	0
	Betty	0	10
SPLIT PILL	Annie	9	9
	Betty	1	1

who endorse the pure *ex post* view ought to have little trouble in deciding how to allocate the medicine. All other things being equal, proponents of the pure *ex post* view will recommend choosing SPLIT PILL since, on their view, it matters to fairness only that SPLIT PILL will result in less *ex post* inequality than LOTTERY. But the choice is less obvious for proponents of the egalitarian mixed view, since the scenario forces a trade-off between *ex ante* inequality and *ex post* inequality, and the egalitarian mixed view claims that both types of inequality increase the unfairness of the outcome.[11] If the decrease in *ex post* inequality under SPLIT PILL is not too great, relative to LOTTERY, then the egalitarian mixed view, unlike the pure *ex post* view, will recommend choosing LOTTERY over SPLIT PILL in order to minimize the unfairness of the outcome.

The preceding example suggests that, unlike the pure *ex post* view, the egalitarian mixed view is sometimes prepared to tolerate more *ex post* inequality if doing so will reduce *ex ante* inequality. But, one might object, proponents of the pure *ex post* view might in fact also endorse the choice of LOTTERY over SPLIT PILL, if the decrease in *ex post* inequality under SPLIT PILL is low enough. They will not do so in order to reduce the unfairness of the outcome inequality, but they might do so for some other reason. In particular, it is open to proponents of the pure *ex post* view to choose LOTTERY over SPLIT PILL for the sake of impartiality, or some similar reason such as

---

[11] One might object that there is no trade-off between *ex ante* and *ex post* inequality, because split pill is no less *ex ante* unequal than LOTTERY: the world could just as likely have been such that the pay-offs for Annie and Betty under SPLIT PILL were reversed. (It is sometimes argued on similar grounds that all *ex post* inequalities are less unfair than they would have been—or even, on the pure *ex ante* view, that they are entirely fair—because random processes led to the allocation of each individual's lot in life.) This objection points to a genuine difficulty for the egalitarian mixed view, insofar as it fails to give a clear account of why prior probabilities of the world being this way or that should not bear on fairness, in the same way that it claims that more immediate probabilities do bear on fairness. This issue is discussed in Spiekermann and Voorhoeve (unpublished). I shall not engage with this issue herein, since I shall in any case reject the egalitarian mixed view on entirely independent grounds.

equal concern. Sher (1980), Goodin (1988), Wasserman (1996), and Stone (2007) have all endorsed impartiality-based explanations of the intuition that we ought sometimes to hold lotteries, as alternatives to the egalitarian mixed view.[12] If impartiality, or similar, is valuable, then it is reasonable to suppose that this value should be weighed against the unfairness of outcome inequality when deciding how to choose, even if this unfairness would not be diminished by the equal-chance lottery.[13]

A proponent of the pure *ex post* view could, then, endorse the choice of LOTTERY over SPLIT PILL for the sake of impartiality. But there are nevertheless other cases in which the deontic recommendations of the pure *ex post* view, or what we might call the 'pure *ex post* plus impartiality view', will more reliably diverge from those of the egalitarian mixed view. First, in cases where *ex post* inequality emerges from unchosen *ex ante* equal *natural* lotteries, the egalitarian mixed view will regard the *ex post* inequalities as less unfair than inequalities that do not result from such lotteries, and so will prioritize efforts to remedy the latter over the former. The pure *ex post* plus impartiality view, on the other hand, will not distinguish between the two types of *ex post* inequality, because unchosen natural lotteries involving no human agency are not exercises of impartiality. Second, most accounts of impartiality allow that there are ways to be impartial other than to hold a lottery. To act impartially, one need only avoid choosing or intending to choose on the basis of a preference for a particular agent, and most authors have thought that one can do so without giving each agent an equal chance of winning the good (e.g. Kornhauser and Sager (1988: 489–90)).[14] Indeed, on some accounts of impartiality, even the choice of SPLIT PILL over LOTTERY could be impartial, if one chooses SPLIT PILL in order to reduce *ex post* inequality rather than to benefit Annie.[15] Third, perhaps the clearest

---

[12] See also Eyal (2015: 102). Relatedly, Elster (1988: 165–9) argues that lotteries are justified by their incentive effects, which derive largely from their impartiality. Notice that proponents of impartiality-type views—or as Wasserman calls them, 'prophylactic' views—often claim that the lottery itself is fair. But by this is meant a procedural kind of fairness, which is entirely compatible with the claim that a lottery does not diminish the substantive distributive unfairness of outcome inequality.

[13] Voorhoeve and Fleurbaey (2012: 396) assume that the impartiality view cannot motivate such a choice, since, they claim, the impartiality view implies that 'one should not care about the distribution of mere chances'. But if one has a reason to be impartial, then it is hard to see why this reason should not be weighed against one's reason to avoid the unfairness of *ex post* inequality, such that the choice of LOTTERY over SPLIT PILL could indeed be licensed by the impartiality view.

[14] Against this claim, Stone (2007: 287) argues that only fair lotteries can satisfy the requirement that one must intend to be impartial, because one cannot so intend when one knows to whom one will allocate the good.

[15] To make the choice *publicly* impartial, in the sense that others are able to verify that SPLIT PILL was not chosen only in order to benefit Annie, one might adopt the following

illustration of the difference between the deontic recommendations of the egalitarian mixed view and those of the pure *ex post* view, with or without an additional commitment to impartiality, is their differential willingness to tolerate overall costs in order to avoid *ex post* inequality that emerges from an *ex ante* equal distribution of chances. Consider the following example, INITIAL *EX ANTE* CHOICE II.

Suppose that there is a second alternative to LOTTERY, which involves not splitting the pill but completely crushing the pill and then administering a suspension of the crushed pill to each agent. By crushing the pill, you are able to administer unequal quantities of the medicine, so that you can give just enough of the medicine to each agent so as to completely offset the unequalizing effects of their different physiological reactions to a less than full dose of the medicine. Assuming that you divide the crushed pill in this way, the CRUSHED PILL scenario will therefore generate an outcome in which both agents are partially cured of their symptoms to exactly the same extent, both ending up as well off as the other in terms of utility. CRUSHED PILL, unlike SPLIT PILL, is therefore unambiguously as impartial as LOTTERY.[16] There is, however, an overall cost to crushing the pill, since the medicine is rendered less effective upon being crushed. As a result, if you crush the pill, the total gain in utility aggregated across both agents will be less than it would have been if you had instead held a lottery for the uncrushed pill (or split the pill). Table 1.2 shows the possible outcomes in terms of utility for LOTTERY and CRUSHED PILL.

What ought you to do when faced with a choice between LOTTERY and CRUSHED PILL (assuming, once again, that Annie and Betty are unable to express their own views about how you should choose)? Consider first what course of action the pure *ex post* view would recommend. Since CRUSHED PILL will have the effect of eliminating all *ex post* inequality, the pure *ex post* view would clearly regard it as preferable to LOTTERY from the point of view of equality alone. But the badness of an outcome need not depend exclusively on its unfairness, and when deciding how to choose, the question you face is, which option will generate the *overall* least bad outcome? Impartiality is not at stake here, but there is a difference in the total aggregated utility of each option. You should therefore ask, is it worth the cost of crushing the

policy. One might announce, in advance of knowing the specifics of the case, that one intends to apply a general policy of always choosing the least *ex post* unequal option, or a policy of choosing the option that is all things considered best once considerations of impartiality are excluded.

[16] Assuming that partiality is about favouring the promotion of one agent's utility rather than another's, and not about giving more resources to one agent rather than another, independently of the effect of those resources on each agent's utility. The example could easily be adjusted if this assumption does not hold.

Table 1.2 INITIAL *EX ANTE* CHOICE II between LOTTERY and CRUSHED PILL

Option	Claimant	Equiprobable Outcomes	
		Outcome 1	Outcome 2
LOTTERY	Annie	10	0
	Betty	0	10
CRUSHED PILL	Annie	4	4
	Betty	4	4

pill to avoid the unfair *ex post* inequality that would result from LOTTERY? The answer is that this is not obvious, and will depend on the relative disvalue that one attaches to the loss of overall utility under CRUSHED PILL versus the *ex post* unfairness of LOTTERY. But for the purpose of the argument that follows, let us suppose that the cost of crushing the pill is such that, on the pure *ex post* view, it would be *just* better overall to crush the pill than to suffer the unfair *ex post* inequality of LOTTERY.

Consider now what course of action the egalitarian mixed view would recommend. That is, what should you do if the *ex ante* equality of LOTTERY *does* diminish the unfairness of its unequal outcome? The unequal outcome that would emerge under LOTTERY would, on this view, be *less unfair* than it would have been had there not been a lottery, or had, on the pure *ex post* view, the lottery made no difference to the fairness of the outcome. As such, proponents of the egalitarian mixed view should be unwilling to bear the cost of crushing the pill in order to avoid the *ex post* inequality of LOTTERY. If the cost of crushing the pill is only just small enough so as to be preferable, on the pure *ex post* view, to the *undiminished* unfairness of the *ex post* inequality of LOTTERY, then it must be too great to be preferable, on the egalitarian mixed view, to the *diminished* unfairness of the *ex post* inequality of LOTTERY.

Proponents of the egalitarian mixed view, unlike proponents of the pure *ex post* view, should prefer LOTTERY over CRUSHED PILL, because they should be less willing to tolerate overall costs in order to avoid *ex post* inequality that emerges from an *ex ante* equal distribution of chances (cf. Wasserman (1996: 49)). This is true whether or not a proponent of the pure *ex post* view also endorses a commitment to impartiality. But this deontic difference does not in itself allow us to decide between the views, because it is not at all intuitively obvious what the right option to choose is. In order to make progress, we need to draw in some further intuitions, and to look deeper, to ask whether proponents of the egalitarian mixed view can explain the intuitions that they claim to have in a manner that situates them within an internally coherent framework. In what follows I shall introduce two further intuitions that provide the starting point for an argument to the effect that the egalitarian mixed view struggles to do so.

III

Consider two further scenarios, EX POST CHOICE and INTERIM EX ANTE CHOICE, both of which assume that you have previously chosen LOTTERY over CRUSHED PILL in INITIAL EX ANTE CHOICE II. EX POST CHOICE occurs immediately after the lottery machine has announced its result. You must now decide whether to give the medicine to the winner of the lottery—let us suppose that the winner is Annie, although it would make no difference to the argument if the winner was Betty—or whether to switch to CRUSHED PILL. It seems clear that, *if you should choose LOTTERY in the first place*, then you should also respect the result of the lottery once it is announced, and give the medicine to the winner. The egalitarian mixed view therefore seems committed not only to choosing LOTTERY in INITIAL EX ANTE CHOICE II, but also to choosing what I will call LOTTERY RESULT in EX POST CHOICE. It would be odd to think otherwise—to think that you should initially start up the lottery machine rather than pursue CRUSHED PILL, but then later ignore the result of the lottery and choose CRUSHED PILL after all.

Consider now the case of INTERIM EX ANTE CHOICE. In INTERIM EX ANTE CHOICE you discover, shortly before the lottery machine announces its result, that the randomizing function of the machine is broken, and has in fact been broken all along. As a result, the machine is, and always has been, certain to award the medicine to Annie (again, it would make no difference to the argument if the machine was instead certain to award the medicine to Betty). I assume that the discovery comes as a complete surprise: you did not previously assign a probability to the likelihood of your making such a discovery, and given the lack of relevant information could not have done so.[17] Suppose that, with the lottery machine broken, you have no other

---

[17] Without this assumption, it seems less clear whether or not you should stick with the broken lottery. If you did previously assign a probability to the likelihood of your making such a discovery, then some might be inclined to see the discovery of the breakdown as itself the outcome of a different lottery, a 'lottery for breakdown'. If the probability of the lottery breaking down in favour of Annie or Betty was equal, such readers might be inclined to stick with the result of the broken lottery on the ground that Annie and Betty did have an equal prior chance of winning the 'lottery for breakdown' (cf. Kornhauser and Sager (1988: 486)). Notice that this move highlights further the problem discussed in n. 11, namely, the apparent inability of the egalitarian mixed view to explain how far back to go: why stop at the lottery for breakdown rather than go all the way back to the great lottery of life? In any case, for the purpose of the argument that

means at your disposal to run a new lottery for the medicine. What should you do in INTERIM *EX ANTE* CHOICE, once you discover that the machine is broken and certain to award the medicine to Annie? Should you leave the machine to run its course and award the pill to the agent whom it announces as the winner, knowing full well that this will be Annie? Call this option BROKEN LOTTERY. Or should you disregard the machine and instead opt for CRUSHED PILL? Quite clearly, the possible outcomes in terms of utility for each agent in INTERIM *EX ANTE* CHOICE are the same as the possible outcomes in *EX POST* CHOICE, as illustrated in Table 1.3.

Many will share the intuition that, even if it was right to choose LOTTERY in the first place, nevertheless once you discover that the lottery machine is broken in INTERIM *EX ANTE* CHOICE your previous belief that Annie and Betty were equally likely to win the lottery is no longer relevant to your present decision. You should, according to this intuition, base your decision only on what you now believe to be true: that the lottery machine is broken and certain to award the medicine to Annie. You should therefore switch to CRUSHED PILL. Some readers, I grant, may not share this intuition. In section V, I shall argue that it does not in any case ultimately help the egalitarian mixed view to reject the intuition. For the time being, however, let us

Table 1.3 *EX POST* CHOICE and INTERIM *EX ANTE* CHOICE

Option	Claimant	Possible Outcome
	EX POST CHOICE	
LOTTERY RESULT	Annie	10
	Betty	0
CRUSHED PILL	Annie	4
	Betty	4
	INTERIM *EX ANTE* CHOICE	
BROKEN LOTTERY	Annie	10
	Betty	0
CRUSHED PILL	Annie	4
	Betty	4

follows, we need a case in which there was no prior probability of discovering the breakdown. (I note that on a classical interpretation of probability one would be licensed to assign a probability of 0.5 to the possibility of discovering the breakdown merely by virtue of there being two possibilities: discover a breakdown or don't discover a breakdown. But the classical interpretation is now rather less popular than the subjective and objective interpretations summarized below, and I assume does not therefore pose a significant challenge to the present argument.)

examine the difficulty that arises for those proponents of the egalitarian mixed view who do endorse the intuition that you should switch to CRUSHED PILL in INTERIM *EX ANTE* CHOICE.[18]

There is a tension between a commitment to sticking with LOTTERY RESULT in *EX POST* CHOICE and the intuition that you should switch to CRUSHED PILL in INTERIM *EX ANTE* CHOICE. The egalitarian mixed view, I shall argue, cannot resolve this tension. It arises for the following reason. A commitment to sticking with LOTTERY RESULT in *EX POST* CHOICE suggests a commitment to not revising one's original choice in the light of new information about how the lottery has turned out. But the intuition that we should switch to CRUSHED PILL in INTERIM *EX ANTE* CHOICE suggests a *prima facie* contradictory commitment to revising one's original choice in the light of new information about how the lottery will turn out. If the new information is relevant to one's decision in the latter case, why not also in the former? In the face of this *prima facie* similarity between the two cases, anyone who endorses the view that we should choose LOTTERY in the first place needs to be able to resolve this tension by pointing to some salient difference between the new information in each case. Moreover, they need to explain why—not merely to stipulate that—we should respond differently to each case because of that difference. The problem with the egalitarian mixed view, I shall argue, is that it lacks the resources to do so.

IV

In order to show why the egalitarian mixed view struggles to explain the difference between LOTTERY RESULT and INTERIM *EX ANTE* CHOICE, it will be helpful to distinguish two versions of the view, since each version has different explanatory resources available to it. The distinction depends on whether one interprets the egalitarian mixed view as fixing the *ex ante* distribution, for the purpose of making judgements about fairness, by reference to subjective probabilities, or by reference to objective probabilities. Subjective

---

[18] Notice that the intuition does not depend on the timing of the discovery, but on the content of the discovery. The intuition can be elicited just as effectively by imagining a scenario in which you discover, *after* the outcome has been announced, that the lottery was in fact broken all along. Under such circumstances, it still seems intuitive to switch to CRUSHED PILL, if it is not now too late to do so. What matters to the intuition is that one has discovered new information about the probabilities of various outcomes eventuating, not that the discovery takes place before the outcome. This observation does not, however, weaken the force of the objection that follows, since my objection will be that the egalitarian mixed view cannot justify the claim that we should respond differently to new information about probabilities and new information about outcomes, not that the egalitarian mixed view cannot justify the claim that we should respond differently to new information learnt before the outcome and new information learnt after the outcome.

probabilities are, roughly, probabilitics based on the degree of rational belief that a particular outcome will eventuate, held by some particular agent or group of agents. Objective probabilities are, roughly, probabilities based on statistical frequency or propensities.[19] Call a version of the egalitarian mixed view that fixes the *ex ante* distribution by reference to subjective probabilities the *subjective egalitarian mixed view*, and a version that refers to objective probabilities the *objective egalitarian mixed view*.

Consider, first, how the subjective egalitarian mixed view might attempt to explain the difference between INTERIM EX ANTE CHOICE and EX POST CHOICE. In INTERIM EX ANTE CHOICE, the view might claim, the new information that you learn causes you to assign new subjective probabilities to the likelihood of either agent winning, such that BROKEN LOTTERY is now more *ex ante* unequal than LOTTERY previously was. The *ex post* inequality that would eventuate from BROKEN LOTTERY will therefore, it claims, be more unfair than the *ex post* inequality that would have eventuated from LOTTERY. Hence a switch to CRUSHED PILL is justified. In EX POST CHOICE, on the other hand, the new information that you learn—information about what the outcome actually is rather than information about what the outcome might be—does not cause you to assign new subjective probabilities to the likelihood of either agent winning, and as such has no bearing on the *ex ante* distribution or its contribution to the fairness of the outcome. Hence there is no justification for a switch to CRUSHED PILL in EX POST CHOICE. In short, the subjective egalitarian mixed view claims that we should respond differently to the two cases because, in INTERIM EX ANTE CHOICE, the new information causes you to assign new probabilities, whereas in *ex post* CHOICE, the new information causes you merely to learn what the outcome is but not to assign new probabilities.

At first sight, the account provided by the subjective egalitarian mixed view might seem to offer an adequate resolution of the tension between EX POST CHOICE and INTERIM EX ANTE CHOICE. But a closer look reveals that the resolution that it offers is anything but adequate. The justification relies on imbuing the difference between changes to subjective probability and

[19] Within these broad characterizations, different interpretations have been proposed. For example, in the case of subjective probability, there is disagreement about what it ought to mean for a degree of credence to be *rational*. There are further, though less popular, interpretations of probability that are not captured by the rough characterization that I have given. These include so-called 'best system' interpretations of objective probability, classical probability, and logical probability. For the most part it will not matter for the purpose of the argument herein which exact interpretation of probability one adopts, beyond the broad distinction between subjective and objective probabilities. I have noted where particular interpretations would have a bearing on the argument, in n. 17, and in the discussion of the relation between subjective probabilities and beliefs about objective probabilities below.

the eventuation of an outcome with central moral significance. Yet such reliance is problematic, for two reasons. First, because those who do not endorse the egalitarian mixed view might reasonably deny that the distinction has moral significance, and it looks as though proponents of the egalitarian mixed view will not be able to say anything in defence of their claim to the contrary without appealing to the egalitarian mixed view itself.[20] For it is only by virtue of the subjective egalitarian mixed view's insistence that subjective probabilities make a difference to the fairness of an outcome—which the pure *ex post* view denies—that the distinction appears to proponents of the subjective egalitarian mixed view to have moral significance. The justification appeals to no new intuitions or deeper distinctions that might resonate with a wider audience. Of course, this observation does not in itself provide grounds to reject the intuitions of proponents of the subjective egalitarian mixed view, but it does mean that the putative justification will have no traction with those who do not already experience intuitions in support of the view. Being so tightly bound up with the egalitarian mixed view itself, the justification amounts, in effect, to little more than a restatement of the view.[21]

Second, and more problematically still, the supposedly relevant difference between the two cases is not even a genuine difference. The explanation claims that what distinguishes the two cases is that in INTERIM *EX ANTE* CHOICE, the new information causes you to assign new subjective probabilities to the likelihood of each agent's winning the lottery, whereas in *ex post* CHOICE it does not. But it is simply not true that we do not assign subjective probabilities to outcomes that have already occurred. It is commonplace in probability theory, when we know that an outcome has or has not occurred, to assign a probability to it. Where there is certainty what the outcome is, the probability assigned will be 1 or 0. Where there is uncertainty what the

---

[20] Or at least the sort of *sui generis* moral significance that the putative justification assumes. For discussion of how the impartiality view might imbue the distinction with non-*sui generis* moral significance, see n. 26. To be sure, as noted above, the egalitarian mixed finds support in its ability to accommodate intuitions about the badness of brute luck outcome inequality, the case for holding a lottery, and the separateness of persons. But there are other plausible views that can also accommodate all these intuitions, such as a version of the pure *ex post* plus impartiality view that claims that hypothetical choices matter to the badness of outcome inequality (see Hyams (2015)).

[21] Cf. the claim that it is permissible to experiment on non-human animals even when it would not, in a comparable situation, be permissible to experiment on human animals. In order to justify the differential treatment, one might appeal to the claim that the distinction between human and non-human animals is in itself morally salient. Such a justification can be endorsed by those who find such a claim intuitive, but has no traction with those who do not. In both the human/non-human animal case, and the change to probability/eventuation of outcome case, a justification that would apply to a wider audience would need to point to differences in the underlying features possessed by each side of the distinction which, even detractors will be compelled to agree, are morally salient.

outcome is, the subjective probability assigned may be any number between 1 and 0. Since we do assign subjective probabilities to outcomes that have eventuated, we cannot therefore distinguish between INTERIM *EX ANTE* CHOICE and *EX POST* CHOICE on the ground that in the former case subjective probabilities have changed, whereas in the latter case they have not. That is not to say that no relevant difference exists between the two cases, but merely that, if it does, the subjective egalitarian mixed view does not appear to identify it, and is, in that respect, deeply deficient.

Does the objective probability version of the egalitarian mixed view fare any better? Unlike the subjective egalitarian mixed view, the objective egalitarian mixed view can offer the following explanation of the difference between the INTERIM *EX ANTE* CHOICE and *EX POST* CHOICE. In the case of INTERIM *EX ANTE* CHOICE, the new information that comes to light reveals that the lottery in fact never did involve an equal distribution of objective chances, and so cannot after all contribute in the envisaged way to the fairness of the outcome.[22] But the new information that comes to light in *EX POST* CHOICE, about the actual outcome of the fair lottery, does not in the same way change our conception of the nature of the lottery, and so should make no difference to our judgement about the fairness of the outcome that would be produced by it. At the core of this explanation is a distinction between revising one's beliefs about an unchanged state of affairs (INTERIM *EX ANTE* CHOICE) and revising one's beliefs in response to a change in the state of affairs (*EX POST* CHOICE). We should switch in INTERIM *EX ANTE* CHOICE, the explanation claims, in order not to make distributive decisions based on former beliefs about unchanged objective probabilities that we now know to be false. But since this reason does not apply in the case of *EX POST* CHOICE, there is no reason to switch in that case.

Should we endorse an objective probability version of the egalitarian mixed view? One initial worry about endorsing the objective version is that it requires that, in order to reach a judgement about fairness, one must have a belief about objective probabilities. But in many cases, even when one is able to assign subjective probabilities, one may not have a belief about objective probabilities. For notice that assigning a subjective probability is not the same as, and need not require, having a belief about objective probabilities. To be sure, as David Lewis's (1986) widely endorsed Principal Principle tells us, rational agents who have beliefs about objective probabilities will align subjective probabilities to those beliefs. But it does not follow

---

[22] One might worry that, if determinism is true, then there could never be an equal objective chance lottery. But on a statistical frequency interpretation of objective probability at least, the existence of objective chances other than 0 or 1 would be compatible with determinism. For further discussion, see Glynn (2010).

from Lewis's principle that rational agents who assign subjective probabilities will *always* do so on the basis of beliefs about objective probabilities. Quite how close one thinks that the relation between subjective probabilities and beliefs about objective probabilities is will depend partly on the precise interpretation that one adopts of each. There is a lively debate about the connection between the two (e.g. Hall (2004)). But it is generally thought that the two need not always coincide, that subjective probabilities need not always be based on beliefs about objective probabilities.

If, then, subjective probabilities need not always be based on beliefs about objective probabilities, proponents of the objective egalitarian mixed view are faced with swallowing a bitter pill. On those occasions when agents have no beliefs about objective probabilities, they will not be able to reach judgements about the fairness of possible outcomes, even if they can assign subjective probabilities. This observation does not amount to a knock-down objection against the objective egalitarian mixed view, but it is nevertheless a significant concession. For it has seemed intuitive to many that we can make judgements about fairness in cases where we assign subjective probabilities other than on the basis of beliefs about objective probabilities.[23] Yet the objective egalitarian mixed view will require us to repudiate this intuition and conclude instead that we should withhold judgements about fairness when we have no beliefs about objective probabilities.

A second and more damaging objection is that, even if the objective egalitarian mixed view is able to resolve the tension between intuitions about EX POST CHOICE and INTERIM EX ANTE CHOICE, nevertheless it remains unable to resolve a similar tension between EX POST *choice* and a modified version of INTERIM EX ANTE CHOICE. In the modified version, you do not merely learn that the machine has in fact been broken all along. Rather, you learn that the objective probability of Annie winning the lottery has just been magically transformed from 0.5 to 1. There was previously an equal

[23] Perhaps for this reason, most who have discussed lotteries have claimed, on intuitive grounds, that subjective probabilities do indeed matter in their own right, either alongside, or, more commonly, instead of, objective probabilities. For example, Sher (1980), Wasserman (1996: 34), and Saunders (2008: 363) all claim that subjective probabilities matter in their own right. Otsuka (unpublished) claims that both subjective and objective probabilities matter in their own right. Kornhauser and Sager (1988: 485) claim that equal objective probabilities make things fairer than equal subjective probabilities, but that subjective probabilities might nevertheless also matter in their own right, depending on the underlying reason for thinking that lotteries contribute to fairness. (All of these authors endorse the claim that lotteries are in some sense fair, but not all endorse the egalitarian mixed view: their various commitments are described elsewhere in this paper.) Notice that a version of the egalitarian mixed view that claims that both objective and subjective probabilities matter in their own right will still encounter the stated objection. In the absence of beliefs about objective probabilities, subjective probabilities alone will not on this view suffice to reach a judgement about fairness.

objective chance of either agent winning, but now, as a result of the trans-formation, Annie is objectively guaranteed to win the lottery. There was, moreover, no prior objective probability that such a transformation would occur.[24] As in the original version of INTERIM *EX ANTE* CHOICE, it seems clear that, after the transformation, you should not continue with the lottery, but should instead switch to CRUSHED PILL. What now matters to fairness is only that Annie is objectively certain to win the lottery. That she previously had an objective 0.5 chance of winning now seems irrelevant.[25]

The objective egalitarian mixed view struggles to explain the difference between the modified version of INTERIM *EX ANTE* CHOICE and *EX POST* CHOICE. In the modified version, you do not simply update a previously false belief about objective probabilities in order to render your belief more accurate. In the modified version, the objective probabilities actually change, so that your updated belief reflects a change in the world, just as it does in *EX POST* CHOICE. The distinction that the objective egalitarian mixed view sought to draw between the original version of INTERIM *EX ANTE* CHOICE and *EX POST* CHOICE—between revising one's beliefs about an unchanged state of affairs and revising one's beliefs in response to a change in the state of affairs—does not apply when we compare *EX POST* CHOICE with the modified version of INTERIM *EX ANTE* CHOICE.Nor can the objective mixed view explain the dif-ference by saying that objective probabilities change in the modified INTERIM *EX ANTE* CHOICE, whereas in *EX POST* CHOICE an outcome eventuates. Such an explanation would run into just the same two difficulties that the subjective egalitarian mixed view ran into when it tried to distinguish the original cases by saying that in INTERIM *EX ANTE* CHOICE subjective probabil-ities change whereas in *EX POST* CHOICE an outcome eventuated. First, such an explanation offers nothing to those who do not already experience intu-itions in support of the egalitarian mixed view, because the explanation appeals to no new intuitions or considerations that might persuade detract-ors of the moral salience of the difference between changes to probability and eventuation of outcomes. Second, the justification again relies on the false claim that probabilities do not change when an outcome eventuates. Even in the case of objective probabilities, it is standard practice in

---

[24] This assumption is required for the reason described in n. 17. It is not unreasonable to assume that such 'probability gaps' are possible. See for example Hajek (2003 and unpublished).

[25] Otsuka (unpublished: 14–15), one of the few proponents of the egalitarian mixed view who has explicitly claimed that objective probabilities, and not only subjective prob-abilities, matter to fairness, seems to agree. He asks us to imagine that the situation of two individuals 'is transformed from one in which one is fated to die and the other is fated to live into a situation in which each has an objective 50% chance of living and dying'. This transformation, he writes, 'appears to be of genuine value because it gives rise to a fairer because more equal distribution of burdens'.

probability theory to attach a probability—1 or 0—to outcomes that have or have not eventuated. Objective probabilities do change in EX POST CHOICE, just as they do in the modified version of INTERIM EX ANTE CHOICE.

That the objective egalitarian mixed view cannot point to any morally salient difference between the change to objective probability in the modified version of INTERIM EX ANTE CHOICE and the eventuation of outcomes in EX POST CHOICE does not mean that there are no differences between the cases. The two cases can, in fact, be distinguished on the ground that there is a prior objective probability of the outcome eventuating in EX POST CHOICE but no prior objective probability of the objective probability changing in the modified version of INTERIM EX ANTE CHOICE. They can also be distinguished on the ground that the outcome in EX POST CHOICE is unalterable, whereas the objective probability in INTERIM EX ANTE CHOICE might yet change again. The problem for the objective egalitarian mixed view is not that there are no differences between the cases, but that the view gives us no reason to treat any of these differences as morally salient, and therefore no reason to choose differently in the two cases.[26]

---

[26] Might a proponent of the pure *ex post* view who rejects the thought that we should sometimes choose lotteries for the sake of impartiality offer a similar objection to what I called the pure *ex post* plus impartiality view? Suppose that the overall loss of utility in CRUSHED PILL is sufficiently large such that even the pure *ex post* plus impartiality view will prefer lottery to crushed pill in initial *ex ante* choice II (or suppose instead that the alternative to LOTTERY/BROKEN LOTTERY/LOTTERY OUTCOME is not CRUSHED PILL but SPLIT PILL). Can a proponent of the pure *ex post* plus impartiality view explain, using this revised example, why we should switch in the interim case but not the *ex post* case? It seems to me that, unlike a proponent of the egalitarian mixed view, a proponent of the impartiality view can offer the following persuasive justification for the difference: 'In order to express and/or demonstrate my impartiality, I committed to a particular process, which involved both choosing an equal chances lottery in the first place, and honouring the result of the lottery once it was announced. The former without the latter would not have been sufficient to demonstrate my impartiality, and that explains why I should not switch in EX POST CHOICE. But in INTERIM EX ANTE CHOICE, the process to which I committed no longer exists, and as such I am required to switch. For even though I neither knew that the lottery would break down nor had control over the manner in which it broke down, nevertheless I did not commit in advance to pursuing the result of a broken lottery. As such, if I were to choose to stick with BROKEN LOTTERY rather than switch to CRUSHED PILL, there would be no way for others (and myself?) to know whether or not I was doing so in order to favour Annie for the sorts of impermissible reasons that impartial processes aim to exclude.' This seems to me the most plausible justification for treating INTERIM EX ANTE CHOICE differently to EX POST CHOICE. But it is a justification that is available only to the impartiality view and not to the egalitarian mixed view, because the latter, unlike the former, does not ground the relevance of the *ex ante* distribution of chances in one's having committed to a particular process (indeed, as previously noted, the egalitarian mixed view ought even to treat unchosen natural lotteries that involve no human agency as bearing on *ex post* fairness).

V

I have thus far argued that the egalitarian mixed view, both in its subjective probability form and in its objective probability form, is unable to explain why we should respond differently to (one or both versions of) INTERIM *EX ANTE* CHOICE and *EX POST* CHOICE. When we look more closely, it becomes apparent that the cases are on a par in all but some minor respects, and even proponents of the egalitarian mixed view will be forced to admit that these minor differences provide no reason to attach the central moral significance to the distinction that the egalitarian mixed view requires. But the case against the egalitarian mixed view is thus far not yet decisive. The option once again to bite the bullet, this time by rejecting the intuition that we should switch to CRUSHED PILL in INTERIM *EX ANTE* CHOICE, remains open to proponents of the view. Some readers, as I noted above, might not even experience the intuition in the first place. Proponents of the egalitarian mixed view could therefore claim that we should stick to our guns and refuse to update our decision in the light of the change in INTERIM *EX ANTE* CHOICE. Any tension between *EX POST* CHOICE and INTERIM *EX ANTE* CHOICE would thereby evaporate.

   In the present section, I shall argue that, if we reject the intuition that we should switch in INTERIM *EX ANTE* CHOICE, then we end up with a version of the egalitarian mixed view that even the most enthusiastic supporters of the view would, on closer inspection, find rather unattractive. My argument applies in equal measure to the subjective egalitarian mixed view and the objective egalitarian mixed view. Where I refer to INTERIM *EX ANTE* CHOICE in what follows, the reader may wish to select between the original scenario and the modified scenario depending on whether she thinks that the subjective probability version or the objective probability version of the egalitarian mixed view is the more plausible.[27]

   In order to understand the difference between a version of the egalitarian mixed view that endorses the intuition that we should switch to CRUSHED PILL in INTERIM *EX ANTE* CHOICE, and a version of the egalitarian mixed view that rejects the intuition, we need to return to the question, which probabilities count? As we saw above, answers to this question might vary insofar as they claim that either subjective or objective probabilities are (ultimately) relevant to the fairness of the outcome. But there is another dimension in which answers to the question might vary, which cuts across the subjective–objective divide. For a proponent of the egalitarian mixed view is required

---

[27] Alternatively, the reader might simply use the modified scenario to test whichever of the two versions she finds more plausible, since both the objective probability *and* the subjective probability change in that scenario.

to tell us not only which type of probabilities are relevant to the fairness of the outcome, but also when the census of probabilities should be taken, for the purpose of deciding the fairness of the outcome.

When should the census of probabilities be taken? I have thus far assumed that a proponent of the egalitarian mixed view will want to say that what renders *ex post* inequality more or less unfair than it would otherwise have been is the distribution of chances that obtains *at the moment immediately before the outcome eventuates*. If called upon to make a distributive decision before the outcome eventuates, the proponent of the mixed view would say that one should therefore base one's predictions about the fairness of possible outcomes on the most up-to-date beliefs that one has about the probabilities that will obtain at the moment immediately before the outcome eventuates. These beliefs are reflected in the probabilities that one currently assigns to different outcomes (unless one has reason to believe that one's assignments are fallacious, or that they will change before the outcome eventuates[28]). Proponents of the egalitarian mixed view who endorse this assumption will want to endorse the intuition that we should switch to CRUSHED PILL in INTERIM *EX ANTE* CHOICE. But by doing so, as I argued in the previous two sections, they encounter an irresolvable tension with their commitment to not switching to CRUSHED PILL in *EX POST* CHOICE.

In order to reject the intuition that we should switch to CRUSHED PILL in INTERIM *EX ANTE* CHOICE, and thereby avoid the tension with their commitment to not switching in *EX POST* CHOICE, proponents of the egalitarian mixed view must take an alternative view about when the census of probabilities should be taken. In particular, they must claim something like the following. What renders *ex post* inequality more or less unfair than it would otherwise have been is not the distribution of chances that obtains at the point at which the outcome eventuates, but the distribution of chances that obtains *at some earlier initial starting point*. They must claim that this is so even if those chances subsequently change prior to the eventuation of the outcome, and even if they have already changed prior to one's being called upon to make a distributive decision, as in INTERIM *EX ANTE* CHOICE. Yet such a claim is, I shall argue, imprecise, unmotivated, and implausible.

The claim that what matters to fairness is the distribution of chances at some initial starting point is, first, imprecise. It is imprecise because it leaves open what the initial starting point is. To be sure, in cases like those

---

[28] One might think that such a qualification is unnecessary, because such beliefs should already be incorporated into the probabilities that one currently assigns to different outcomes.

described above, there might seem to be an obvious point in time to take as the initial starting point: the point at which the agent decides to hold a lottery. But it is less clear when we should take as the initial starting point when making judgements about fairness—and when deciding whether to intervene—in cases in which no agency is involved in fixing the distribution of chances. Imagine, for example, that for as long as you or anyone else can remember, there has been a risk that an earthquake will hit somewhere in a particular region. In due course, some houses are built in the region, and some people move in. You (and others) have, at different times, rationally assigned different probabilities to the likelihood that an earthquake will affect different parts of the region. Suppose that an earthquake eventually hits in one part of the region, destroying houses in that part of the region but not in others. On a subjective probability version of the mixed view (we could adjust the example to suit an objective probability version), it is not at all clear how to decide which probability you should look to in order to assess the extent of the unfairness of the resultant *ex post* inequality. The probability that you assigned at the time the houses were built? At the time the present occupants moved in? At the time you first became aware of the risk of an earthquake?

Suppose, nevertheless, that the imprecision in the view can, one way or another, be addressed. Still, the view looks unmotivated. It provides no reason at all why we should fixate on initial probabilities even when those probabilities change. Rather, the view simply stipulates that we should so fixate, without giving any rationale for doing so, except the *ad hoc* rationale that by doing so we can avoid a conflict between INTERIM *EX ANTE* CHOICE and *EX POST* CHOICE. It remains in principle possible that a rationale could be provided, but it is hard to imagine what such a rationale would look like. For recall that we are considering here cases where there was no prior probability of the probability changing, so we cannot justify fixing on the initial probabilities on something like the ground that the change in probability is itself the outcome of a fair equal-chance lottery.[29] More problematically still, the view looks quite implausible. If, on the subjective egalitarian mixed view, we learn new information that allows us to improve the subjective probabilities that we assign to events, or if, on the objective egalitarian mixed view, objective probabilities actually change, then it seems quite counter-intuitive not to take this new information or change into account, if we are still able to do so. We should, when making decisions about fairness, appeal to the best information presently available to us, and not merely to the best information available to us at some earlier time, if that information

---

[29] See n. 11 and n. 17 for further discussion of this point.

has now been superseded. This is, surely, the underlying reason why to many readers it will seem right to switch to CRUSHED PILL in INTERIM *EX ANTE* CHOICE.[30]

VI

We can summarize the overall argument of the paper as follows. Whether or not a proponent of the egalitarian mixed view endorses the intuition that we should switch from LOTTERY to CRUSHED PILL in INTERIM *EX ANTE* CHOICE, she will face difficulties. On the one hand, if she endorses the intuition that we should switch, then she will be unable to explain why we should respond differently in INTERIM *EX ANTE* CHOICE and *EX POST* CHOICE. When she tries to do so, she will find herself relying on a distinction between changes to probability and eventuation of outcomes that looks morally arbitrary at best, and incoherent at worst. She will encounter this problem whether she claims that the probabilities in question are subjective probabilities, or that the probabilities in question are objective probabilities. On the other hand, as I argued in section V, if she rejects the intuition that we should switch in INTERIM *EX ANTE* CHOICE, then she must claim that the relevant probabilities are not those that obtain immediately before the outcome eventuates, but those that obtain at some initial starting point. This version of the egalitarian mixed view invites the objection that it is, for the reasons described, imprecise, unmotivated, and implausible.

The apparent inability of the egalitarian mixed view to justify its claims has important consequences for public policy. It does not mean that we should abandon the practice of holding lotteries altogether because, as noted, there might be other reasons such as impartiality to choose lotteries on particular occasions, albeit not as frequently as the egalitarian mixed view would recommend.[31] But to the extent that governments are concerned

---

[30] Again, a version of the impartiality account might do a better job than the egalitarian mixed view of accommodating the intuitions of those readers who think otherwise. On the impartiality account, one might argue that you should not switch because, even though there was—*ex hypothesi*—no prior probability of a breakdown, nevertheless the mere fact that you had no idea that the lottery machine would break down means that BROKEN LOTTERY is an impartial method of allocation. This explanation will only work on certain understandings of what impartiality requires: in n. 26, for example, I describe a different understanding of what impartiality requires (namely, precommitment to a particular process), which would not be compatible with the present explanation.

[31] In addition to the impartiality justification, is sometimes said that the pure *ex post* view can provide an instrumental case for choosing lotteries over laissez-faire when the following conditions are met: (1) an indivisible good must be allocated on multiple occasions to a subset of the claimant pool; (2) under laissez-faire, the goods will repeatedly

to ensure fair equality of opportunity, the failure of the egalitarian mixed view does suggest that no gains to fairness are to be made by expending resources on policies that merely seek to redistribute more equally the chances that any particular individual will be able to achieve a position of privilege, if doing so will do nothing to alter the limited supply of such positions.[32] Rather, they should focus their efforts on policies designed to ensure the greater availability of positions of privilege, or to lessen the gap between more and less privileged positions, at least insofar as it is a matter of chance rather than choice who gets to fill which position.[33] They should aim to ensure that all are able to achieve similarly good outcomes, and not allow a lucky few to enjoy privilege whilst leaving the rest, as Wasserman (1996) aptly puts it, to eat chances.

Acknowledgments

For helpful written comments I thank Matthew Clayton, Iskra Fileva, Dan Hausman, Seth Lazar, Andy Mason, Adam Swift, Patrick Tomlin, Peter Vallentyne, and two anonymous referees. The paper benefitted from valuable feedback from audiences at the universities of Oxford and Reading, at the Workshop for Oxford Studies in Political Philosophy 2015 in Syracuse, the Society for Applied Philosophy

---

find their way into the hands of the same claimants, thereby increasing *ex post* inequality. But notice that the following allocative procedure does an even better job of reducing *ex post* inequality than the multiple lottery procedure: use hand-outs, but don't give the good to an agent who has already received the good on a previous occasion, at least until all agents have received the good once (and so on for further rounds).

[32] Such interventions might have the virtue of eliminating certain unjust forms of discrimination, for example against women or particular ethnic groups. But the goal of eliminating unjust discrimination is as well served by reducing inequalities in the outcome schedule as it is served by reducing inequalities in chances, and the former also has the virtue of reducing the unfairness of the outcome.

[33] It is a reasonable assumption that this latter condition obtains in most if not all states, since it is reasonable to suppose that the present supply of such positions is smaller than the number of people who make reasonable choices aimed at achieving such a position. I claim only that the conclusion of the present paper suggests that we should endorse a conception of equality of opportunity of this broad type. The present paper does not in itself give us a fully fleshed out conception of equality of opportunity, since the relationship between the concerns of the present paper and equality of opportunity is not straightforward. For one thing, opportunities are about option sets and choices as much as they are about chances and/or outcomes. For another, acquiring a position of privilege is not the only way to achieve gains in utility. For rich discussions of the relationship between the concerns of the present paper and broader questions about equality of opportunity, see Arneson (1999) and Mason (2006). Both Arneson and Mason defend a conception of fair equality of opportunity that falls under the latter of my broad characterizations, that which I claim is suggested by the present paper.

Conference 2014 in Oxford, and the 5th Meeting on Ethics and Political Philosophy 2014 in Minho. The research was partly funded by an AHRC research grant on equality, AH/F018878.

References

Arneson, Richard J. (1997), 'Postscript to "Equality and Equal Opportunity for Welfare"', in Louis Pojman and Robert Westmoreland, eds, *Equality: Selected Readings* (Oxford: Oxford University Press): 229–42.

Arneson, Richard J. (1999), 'Equality of Opportunity for Welfare Defended and Recanted', *Journal of Political Philosophy* 7: 488–97.

Bovens, Luc (2015), 'Concerns for the Poorly Off in Ordering Risky Prospects', *Economics and Philosophy* 31: 397–429.

Broome, John (1990), 'Fairness', *Proceedings of the Aristotelian Society* 91: 87–101.

Daniels, Norman (2008), *Just Health: Meeting Health Needs Fairly* (Cambridge: Cambridge University Press).

Diamond, Peter (1967), 'Cardinal Welfare, Individualistic Ethics, and Interpersonal Comparison of Utility: Comment', *Journal of Political Economy* 75: 765–6.

Dworkin, Ronald (2000), *Sovereign Virtue* (Cambridge, MA: Harvard University Press).

Elster, Jon (1988), 'Taming Chance: Randomization in Individual and Social Decisions', in S. McMurrin, ed., *The Tanner Lectures on Human Values IX* (Utah: Utah University Press): 105–80.

Eyal, Nir (2015), 'Concentrated Risk, the Coventry Blitz, Chamberlain's Cancer', in Glenn Cohen, Norman Daniels, and Nir Eyal, eds, *Identified versus Statistical Lives: An Interdisciplinary Perspective* (Oxford: Oxford University Press): 94–107.

Glynn, Luke (2010), 'Deterministic Chance', *British Journal for the Philosophy of Science* 61: 51–80.

Goodin, Robert E. (1988), *Reasons for Welfare: The Political Theory of the Welfare State* (Princeton, NJ: Princeton University Press).

Goodwin, Barbara (2005), *Justice by Lottery*, 2nd edn (Exeter: Imprint).

Hajek, Alan (2003), 'What Conditional Probability Could Not Be', *Synthese* 137: 273–323.

Hajek, Alan (unpublished), 'Staying Regular?'

Hall, Ned (2004), 'Two Mistakes about Credence and Chance', *Australasian Journal of Philosophy* 82: 93–111.

Hyams, Keith (2015), 'Hypothetical Choice, Egalitarianism, and the Separateness of Persons', *Utilitas* 27: 217–39.

Kornhauser, Lewis A., and Sager, Lawrence G. (1988), 'Just Lotteries', *Social Science Information* 27: 483–516.

Lang, Gerald (2005), 'Fairness in Life and Death Cases', *Erkenntnis* 62: 321–51.

Lewis, David (1986), 'A Subjectivist's Guide to Objective Chance', in his *Philosophical Papers*, Vol. 2 (Oxford: Oxford University Press): 83–132.

Lippert-Rasmussen, Kasper (1999), 'Arneson on Equality of Opportunity for Welfare', *Journal of Political Philosophy* 7: 478–87.

Mason, Andrew (2006), *Levelling the Playing Field: The Idea of Equal Opportunity and Its Place in Egalitarian Thought* (Oxford: Oxford University Press).

Otsuka, Michael (2004), 'Equality, Ambition, and Insurance', *Proceedings of the Aristotelian Society* supplementary volume 78: 151–66.

Otsuka, Michael (unpublished), 'The Fairness of Equal Chances'.

Otsuka, Michael, and Voorhoeve, Alex (2009), 'Why It Matters That Some Are Worse Off Than Others: An Argument against the Priority View', *Philosophy and Public Affairs* 37: 171–99.

Parfit, Derek (2002), 'Equality or Priority?', in Matthew Clayton and Andrew Williams, eds, *The Ideal of Equality* (Basingstoke: Palgrave): 81–125, originally published in *The Lindley Lecture* (Lawrence, KS: University of Kansas, 1991).

Parfit, Derek (2012), 'Another Defense of the Priority View', *Utilitas* 24: 399–440.

Saunders, Ben (2008), 'The Equality of Lotteries', *Philosophy* 83: 359–72.

Sher, George (1980), 'What Makes a Lottery Fair?', *Noûs* 14: 203–16.

Spiekermann, Kai, and Voorhoeve, Alex (unpublished), 'Reversal of Fortunes'.

Stone, Peter (2007), 'Why Lotteries Are Just', *The Journal of Political Philosophy* 15: 276–95.

Temkin, Larry (2001), 'Inequality: A Complex, Individualistic, and Comparative Notion', *Philosophical Issues* 11: 327–53.

Vallentyne, Peter (2002), 'Brute Luck, Option Luck, and Equality of Initial Opportunities', *Ethics* 112: 529–57.

Voorhoeve, Alex, and Fleurbaey, Marc (2012), 'Egalitarianism and the Separateness of Persons', *Utilitas* 24: 381–98.

Wasserman, David (1996), 'Let Them Eat Chances: Probability and Distributive Justice', *Economics and Philosophy* 12: 29–49.

2

The Problem of Equality from a Political Economy Perspective

The Long View of History

Elizabeth Anderson

1. WHAT IS AN EGALITARIAN SOCIETY?

My aim in this paper is to outline some key institutional and motivational challenges to the creation of an egalitarian society, given what we know about human nature and history. To do this, I must first clarify what an egalitarian society is. I shall do so indirectly, by defining it as the object of egalitarian social movements in modern history, and of what I shall call "the egalitarian impulse" in the history of the human species. That is, egalitarian society is what people have sought, when motivated by the egalitarian impulse and sometimes organized in egalitarian social movements. An indirect definition is apt for two reasons. First, the actual or aspirational institutional infrastructure of egalitarian societies has changed over time, depending on the scale of the society in question, its technology, ideological resources, extant social institutions, and other social conditions. Second, egalitarian social movements, and the egalitarian impulse, have always been *oppositional* forces in human history: they have been defined more sharply by what they oppose than by what they embrace. These two reasons go hand in hand: as fundamentally oppositional, egalitarianism has historically been open to a variety of proposed alternative institutional embodiments, each promising to defeat or hold at bay what it opposes. Egalitarianism is therefore a *creative* impulse, constantly generating new institutional forms in response to opposition, as well as to flaws exposed in experiments in living according to egalitarian ideals, and opportunities posed by new ideas and technologies.

What egalitarianism opposes is *social hierarchy*—that is, institutionalized social relations of superiors to inferiors. Social hierarchy consists in durable group inequality sustained by social structures such as laws, organizations, and social norms. Such institutions define distinctive, unequal social positions into which different individuals are placed, often but not always due to ascribed social identities, as of race, ethnicity, class, gender, caste, religion, and sexual orientation. At different times and places, such hierarchical relations have included that of the monarch over his subjects, masters over slaves, lords over serfs, aristocrats over commoners, colonizers over colonized, higher castes over lower, creditors over debtors, patrons over clients, bosses over workers, patriarchs over wives, whites over persons of color, heterosexuals over LGBTQ persons, members of established religions over dissenting, subordinate, or suppressed religions, and so forth. Egalitarians of various movements aim to dismantle or at least tame social hierarchies, and replace them with relations of social equality. For example, democratic activists have aimed to replace the ruler/subject relation with the official/citizen relation, in which citizens are equals, and officials relate to them as agents to principals. Feminists have aimed to replace the patriarch/wife relation with one in which spouses relate to each other as legal and social equals in companionate marriages. Radical abolitionists aimed to replace the system of racialized slavery with free labor and equal citizenship for blacks. And so forth.

In other work (Anderson 2012), I have distinguished three types or dimensions of social hierarchy that are objects of egalitarian critique. (1) Hierarchies of authority are defined by relations of domination and subordination. In such hierarchies, occupants of higher social positions hold arbitrary, unaccountable power over their inferiors: they may order them around, subject them to violence, and/or radically constrain their freedom across one or more domains of social life. (2) Hierarchies of esteem are defined by relations of honor and contempt. Occupants of higher social positions enjoy high regard on account of their positions, and may exact tokens of honor, such as bowing, flattery, and obsequiousness, from those beneath. They hold their inferiors in contempt. Occupants of inferior positions also often suffer stigmatization in society at large, even from others of low rank. (3) Hierarchies of standing are defined by the unequal consideration members of different groups enjoy in the deliberations of other agents (including the state). Such hierarchies implicate at least two types of unequal consideration: with respect to interests, and with respect to inquiry. In a hierarchy of unequal consideration of interests, agents, including policymakers, pay close attention and assign great weight to the interests of the higher ranked, and ignore, neglect, or discount the interests of the lower ranked. Possession of greater material resources typically goes hand in hand with superior standing, although it is far from the only way to gain it. Hence, from the perspective of relational equality, concerns about distributive justice fall under concerns about unequal standing. Hierarchies of unequal consideration with respect to inquiry encompass all concerns of epistemic injustice (Fricker 2007). In such hierarchies, lower-ranked persons may be excluded from inquiry or relegated to subordinate roles, their testimony discounted or systematically misconstrued, their perspectives not consulted in the framing of questions and concepts, and so forth.

Typically, these three dimensions of hierarchy are joined: the same groups that wield arbitrary power over inferiors also enjoy high esteem and standing. However, these dimensions are analytically distinct. In addition, actual societies have sometimes separated them. In some despotic regimes, such as imperial China and Byzantium, eunuch slaves wielded enormous arbitrary power as imperial officeholders. Despots have often preferred to appoint slaves to administer their states because, as socially dead individuals lacking any relations to anyone other than their master, slaves were totally dependent on their master for their position, and incapable of forming alliances with aristocrats or other high-ranking free persons who might seek to challenge imperial power. Despite their power, even the most high-ranking eunuch slaves were despised as filthy, disgusting, degraded beings (Patterson 1982, 303–6, 314–19). And of course they were powerless in relation to their masters. Wives of wealthy men under the law of coverture often enjoyed high esteem and standing, but were powerless in relation to their husbands—vulnerable to domestic violence and rape, legally ineligible to acquire property or make contracts in their own names. Some economically successful minority groups in capitalist countries, such as ethnic Chinese in Malaysia, enjoy high standing of interests in virtue of their wealth, but suffer stigmatization on the basis of their ethnic identity. Similarly, many Jews in Germany and Austria before Hitler came to power enjoyed high epistemic standing in academic circles, but suffered stigmatization in the wider society.

The understanding of egalitarianism advanced here differs from dominant conceptions of egalitarianism in contemporary philosophy. *Telic egalitarianism* is the view that it is intrinsically bad if some morally considerable beings are worse off than others. This purely moral notion could apply across people who share no social institutions and have no interactions or even knowledge of one another (Parfit 1991, 4, 6–7). It could even apply across animal species (Vallentyne 2007). *Distributive egalitarianism* comprises a large family of views according to which justice consists in an equal distribution of some particular good or goods across individuals (Sen 1980), or in which such a distribution constitutes the normative baseline against which all deviations must be justified. For example, *luck egalitarianism* is a distributive egalitarian view according to which deviations from equality can only be justified by considerations of moral desert or voluntary choice (Dworkin 1981;

Temkin 2003). Such conceptions of equality, defined in terms of bare patterns of distribution of nonrelational goods that have no particular connection with the ways people treat and regard each other, are detached from the welfare or interests of the people who figure in these patterns.

The object of egalitarian social movements and the egalitarian impulse differs in several respects from such philosophical conceptions of equality. First, it is political, not purely moral: it is focused on institutions, not abstract moral principles that might be realized by accident. Second, its scope is social, not cosmic. It concerns the terms in which people actually interact in society, not the realization of distributive patterns among people or other beings who share no social institutions. Third, it is essentially relational, not distributive. Equality characterizes forms of social relations—the enduring terms in which people interact in society. While relational equality has important implications for the distribution of goods, the quest for equality is not reducible to particular distributions of nonrelational goods. Relational equality is a sociologically complex ideal that has implications for numerous institutional arrangements beyond purely distributive ones. Finally, it has direct implications for the welfare and interests of individuals who stand in relations of equality to each other. Social hierarchy is *bad* for people. To be systematically vulnerable to others' violence, subject to their arbitrary and unaccountable power, despised, insulted, or ostracized by others; to be excluded from participation in inquiry and other valuable social practices, or reduced to marginalized positions within such practices, or confined to drudgery; to not be believed when one speaks, to not be counted in the deliberations of others regarding decisions that affect one's interests—all such ways of occupying inferior positions in social hierarchies undermine people's welfare. No wonder, then, that egalitarian movements have historically been directed toward social equality.

That the egalitarian impulse and egalitarian social movements aim at more than distributive equality is demonstrated by the fact that both existed before the idea of distributive justice was conceived. The latter took place at the end of the eighteenth century (Fleischacker 2004). The egalitarian impulse was present among our hunter-gather ancestors, at a time when sustained material inequality was impossible, because everyone was living at subsistence. The Levellers of seventeenth-century England formed one of the earliest egalitarian social movements, yet they explicitly disavowed any claims to redistribute property. Their agenda included a nearly universal male franchise, and abolition of the lords' legal privileges (such as their special representation in the House of Lords, entitlement to a separate set of laws, and immunity from commoners' lawsuits) (Lilburne et al. 1649 [2003]). Many egalitarian movements today also focus on issues beyond distributive equality. Feminists campaign for women's reproductive freedom and against sexual harassment, domestic violence, and rape; LGBTQ activists campaign against the stigmatization of people with alternative sexualities; antiracist activists campaign against police brutality and harassment. These are movements against hierarchies of authority and esteem, not only of standing, where concerns of distributive justice lie.

The negative, oppositional aim of egalitarianism is to dismantle or at least tame social hierarchy. This aim explains the group-based focus of egalitarian social movements—their concern with inequalities defined along collective social identities as of race, caste, class, and gender. This focus reflects the fact that social hierarchies either constitute group identities in themselves, as in the case of class, or use group identities to assign people to different ranks in an enduring social hierarchy, as when a society uses gender or race as a basis for assigning women and people of color to low-paid, menial occupations. The focus is group-based because it addresses the hierarchical rankings of groups. It is fully compatible with moral individualism—with the idea that the fundamental bearers of moral considerability are individuals, not groups.

The positive aim of egalitarianism is to establish a free society of equals. One might question why freedom should be represented as a constitutive aim of egalitarianism. After all, some egalitarians have advanced equality at the expense of freedom. "Gracchus" Babeuf, the first advocate of revolutionary state communism, who was executed by the Directory in 1797, advocated strict material equality. He recognized that, under modern conditions, this required a totalitarian state (Buonarroti 1836; Babeuf 1967). Such are the perils of detaching the concern with distributive justice from the wider relational egalitarian agenda. A totalitarian state institutes an extreme hierarchy of domination between state officeholders and citizens, and hence is inherently incompatible with relational egalitarianism. A society of equals exists only when its social structures institute the republican freedom of all adults (Pettit 1997)—that is, when society's institutions do not make anyone subject to anyone else's arbitrary, unaccountable power, and secure everyone against such subjection. Hence, the ideals of equality and freedom, far from being opposed, are joined tightly together in the egalitarian impulse and social movements motivated by that impulse, even if not in all philosophical conceptions of equality.

2. WHY DOES SOCIAL HIERARCHY EXIST?
A POLITICAL ECONOMY PERSPECTIVE

The fact that egalitarianism is fundamentally oppositional reflects a deep challenge for humanity: it appears that human societies contain systematic tendencies to generate social hierarchy. Of course, they also contain tendencies to resist hierarchy, which are embodied in the egalitarian impulse, which egalitarian social movements mobilize and organize into collective action. To come to grips with the challenges to and prospects for creating a society of equals, we need to understand how hierarchical tendencies work, and what institutions might counteract these tendencies. We also need to evaluate different institutional arrangements. Such needs call for a political economy perspective on egalitarianism.

Political economy is the study of collective action problems and institutional designs to solve these problems. Collective action problems arise when individuals acting on their own or in accordance with certain customs, norms, or institutions generate aggregate outcomes with undesirable features, or where the institutions coordinating their behavior have undesirable features, and where there is reason to believe that an alteration in the institutional or organizational context of behavior would yield better results or be a more fair or free or legitimate way to coordinate people's behavior. Political economy incorporates three dimensions of study: normative, analytical, and empirical. The normative dimension supplies standards for evaluating outcomes, institutions, social relations, and social processes, and principles for adjudicating interpersonal conflicts and claims. The analytical dimension models the underlying motives, cognition, and behavioral tendencies of actors, as well as their institutionally and environmentally determined constraints, options, and payoffs, to identify the key causal mechanisms generating problematic aggregate outcomes, and alternative institutional arrangements and coordinated actions that could generate better outcomes or better satisfy other normative criteria, as of fairness. The empirical dimension provides parameters for and tests the causal models, focusing especially on whether collective experiments in living deliver the predicted outcomes of alternatives. The outcomes of these experiments in living feed back not only on the analytical models but on normative standards and principles (Anderson 1991; 2014).

Our first task is to analyze the fundamental motives and mechanisms that drive the creation and reproduction of social hierarchy. Christopher Boehm traces these to the fact that humans, from an evolutionary point of view, are a despotic species. In biology, species are classified as despotic if they engage in social dominance behaviors (such as direct interpersonal competition for resources and mates, interpersonal violence, and dominance displays), organize into social hierarchies, and (optionally) form political coalitions (Boehm 1999, Kindle loc. 66–71). It is evident that human beings engage in all three types of behavior. *In*egalitarian impulses—drives to dominate others—appear to be deeply rooted in human nature.

Yet this leads to a puzzle, for all nomadic hunter-gatherer societies are egalitarian. As *Homo sapiens* evolved in nomadic hunter-gatherer bands, it follows that originally, all humans lived in societies of equals. They did not begin to form social hierarchies until about 12,000 years ago (Boehm 1999, Kindle loc. 95–6). Boehm solves the puzzle by arguing that humans evolved an egalitarian impulse that opposes domination. This egalitarian motive is the desire for personal autonomy—what Philip Pettit (1997) calls "republican freedom." It is the desire to avoid subjection to a dominator, so that one can be self-governing. The egalitarian impulse leads people to resent submission and seek ways to avoid it. Taking advantage of their capacities to form political coalitions and coordinate their behavior around shared under-standings of morality, they manage to avoid domination by means of an egalitarian social contract. Among nomadic hunter-gatherers, this amounts to a small-scale version of Rousseau's (1762 [1988]) social contract. In it, everyone agrees to jointly enforce norms of equality and personal autonomy by sanctioning anyone who attempts to dominate others or displays other tendencies that threaten social equality. Boehm argues that thousands of generations of egalitarian living led humans to evolve capacities for altruism, generalized reciprocity inclusive of non-kin, and social insurance.

The result is what Boehm (1999, Kindle loc. 81–3, 2185–94) calls an "ambivalence" model of the possibility of egalitarian society. Humans are motivated both to dominate others and to resent domination. Depending on environmental conditions and institutional arrangements, human societies may either organize around social hierarchy, or constitute a society of free and equal individuals. However, humans can achieve an egalitarian society only by collectively organizing to maintain constant vigilance against potential dominators, and to control them when they arise. In game-theoretic terms, we face two types of equilibria. In a hierarchical equilibrium, dominators arrange the payoffs to make subordination the optimal strategy for social inferiors. In an egalitarian equilibrium, nearly everyone agrees to jointly sanction dominators, so as to make the risks of seeking a dominant position too great to justify the rewards. The result is a free society of equals. This representation is of course highly simplified, and omits the ideological apparatus necessary to legitimate and reconcile people to inequality, on the one hand, or to sustain solidarity in upholding egalitarian institutions, on the other. But it captures one vital aspect of the problem.

Boehm's ambivalence model explains four features of relational egalitarian-ism described in the introductory section of this paper. First, it explains why egalitarian social movements have always had a fundamentally oppositional character. Since human nature includes motives to domination, which lead to social hierarchy, egalitarian society does not come automatically to us, but only in virtue of opposing the will to dominate. Second, it explains why egalitarians have always been much sharper in articulating their critiques of what they oppose than in describing in concrete terms what they positively seek to institute. What it takes to dismantle hierarchy is always a work in progress, because dominant groups are always inventing new ways to maintain their dominance, and because we won't fully know what a society of equals amounts to until we experience it concretely. This accounts for the sketchy, aspirational quality of so many egalitarian social programs. Third, it explains why egalitarianism requires organized social movements to become effective. Individual moral persuasion is not enough. Only some kind of social contract or agreement to control dominators can dismantle hierarchy. Fourth, it explains why relational equality, the object of egalitarian social movements, ties social equality to individual freedom. The only society of equals worthy of that name is a society of free persons. Anything else fails to satisfy the core motive underlying the egalitarian impulse, which is the desire for personal autonomy.

3. PREMODERN EGALITARIAN SOCIETIES AND THE EMERGENCE OF SOCIAL HIERARCHY

This paper asks, in the broadest terms, how is egalitarian society possible? What are the key challenges it faces? To answer this question, it helps to consider how human beings managed to create egalitarian societies in the beginning, and how hierarchy emerged from them. Such investigation may help identify some of the fundamental causes of hierarchy and challenges to the creation of egalitarian society today. Although it is possible to imagine innumerable types of basic social organization, about five or six types appear to have been so successful that they were independently created multiple times across the world in premodern times (Flannery and Marcus 2012, 562). Two of these types of society are egalitarian: nomadic hunter-gatherer society, and tribal society.

Nomadic hunter-gatherer societies were the original society of Anatomically Modern Humans, emerging perhaps 100,000 years ago (Boehm 1999, Kindle loc. 2646–7). They are small, consisting of bands of typically twenty-five to fifty individuals, which may include non-kin. For certain purposes, hunter-gatherers may organize into groups of several hundred. These societies are egalitarian along all three dimensions of social relation. With respect to authority, they recognize no chiefs. When a decision must be made that concerns the whole group, such as where to migrate, all adults, men and women alike, participate in decision-making on terms of equality. Decisions are authorized by consensus. While some participants may enjoy greater influence due to persuasive reasoning or a reputation for sound judgment, they are never entitled to issue orders to others. With respect to standing, everyone's interests count equally. Various norms ensure a broad material equality for all, including those who are ill or less skilled. Big game must be shared among all members of the band, regardless of who made the kill. Hoarding is forbidden, ensuring that any temporary surpluses are distributed across members of the band. Bands practice generalized reciprocity, helping even non-kin without expectation of a specific return from those helped. Rather, they observe a norm of helping, in the expectation of being helped by someone or other should they need help in the future. In effect, these sharing norms institutionalize a form of social insurance. With respect to esteem, nomadic hunter-gatherers engage in practices that sharply limit opportunities for boasting. Many such societies have independently instituted weapon-sharing, so that the hunter who makes the kill must share credit with the individual who made the weapon (Boehm 1999, Kindle loc. 675–6; Flannery and Marcus 2012, 32).

Nomadic hunter-gatherers sustain their egalitarianism by enforcing a rigorous egalitarian ethos (Boehm 1999, Kindle loc. 621–7). These societies praise a common set of virtues: generosity, kindness, modesty, gentleness, equanimity. They are constantly on guard against anyone who threatens to disturb egalitarian social relations by exalting themselves above others. Hence, they have developed a range of sanctions against narcissists, bullies, and anyone who shows signs of arrogance, greed, anger, or aggressiveness. Initially, they deter and restrain such people with gossip and ridicule. If words don't work, they ostracize upstarts, allowing them to live only on the social periphery. Recalcitrant bullies may wake up to find themselves abandoned, because the group has secretly met and decided to quietly decamp overnight. The pathologically dangerous may be killed. Such executions are a group project, involving every adult member of the band (Boehm 1999, Kindle loc. 1037–137).

The second type of egalitarian society that emerged in premodern times is tribal society. Most humans belonged to tribal societies by the Neolithic era, around 12,000 years ago. Such societies are contrasted with hunter-gatherer societies by their practice of domestication. They are also organized on a larger scale, in groups of hundreds, and sometimes join confederations of several thousand. Each tribe is autonomous. Like hunter-gatherers, they observe egalitarian norms along all three dimensions of social relation. With respect to authority, they recognize no chiefs. All adults, or at least all men, participate in decision-making that affects the entire tribe. Decisions are authorized by consensus (Boehm 1999, Kindle loc. 1255–63, 1566). With respect to standing, domestication and a wider scope for trade create opportunities for unequal accumulation. However, norms of generosity prevent such material inequality from lasting. Anyone who acquires more wealth through more successful farming or herding, or sharp trading, is expected to distribute the surplus across the tribe, typically by providing public feasts (Boehm 1999, Kindle loc. 1550–1, 1543–6).

From an egalitarian perspective, the greatest contrast between the tribal ethos and the hunter-gatherer ethos arises with respect to esteem. Because intertribal warfare is endemic to tribal societies, tribes cultivate aggression among their male members, and honor the more successful warriors with higher esteem. Esteem competition in tribal societies also extends to other domains of achievement, including mastery of ritual, skill in mediating conflicts, bearing up under an ordeal of suffering, and providing big feasts. The latter constitute competitive displays of generosity. One "Big Man" can humiliate his rivals by giving them gifts larger than they could ever reciprocate (Boehm 1999, Kindle loc. 1322–8; Flannery and Marcus 2012, 55, 71, 94, 96).

The fact that the first institutional inequalities in human societies beyond the family arose with respect to esteem supports Rousseau's (1754) hypothesis that the origin of social inequality lies in the motive to obtain superior recognition from others. However, tribal societies have devised several norms to prevent esteem competition from leading to wider inequality. They forbid the conversion of esteem into authority. Even the most renowned of Big Men are not entitled to order others around. Norms also temper esteem inequality. The economy of esteem in tribal societies is not zero-sum. As many individuals as can master the rituals, display courage in battle, supply big feasts, endure ordeals, and perform other meritorious actions may claim honor for themselves. Tribal societies practice equality of opportunity. Competition for esteem is open to everyone. All receive training in honorable activities such as rituals, although women usually compete in different and less-regarded domains of achievement, and rarely engage in battle. Recognition is allocated on a meritocratic basis, solely on grounds of individual achievement. Highly esteemed fathers cannot pass their honor to their children (Boehm 1999, Kindle loc. 1322–8, 1604–8; Flannery and Marcus 2012, 102).

Inegalitarian social forms began around 7,000 years ago, with the rise of rank society (Flannery and Marcus 2012, 206). Rank society has two defining characteristics. First, opportunities to gain certain kinds of esteem or high status are limited in number. They are not open to everyone who performs up to some level. Second, unequal status can be inherited along family or clan lines. In rank society, those with inherited prestige typically also exercise authority. However, they do not monopolize material resources (Fried 1967, 109–10, 183). Hence, the second type of inequality to arise at the society-wide level was of authority.

In the simplest case, there are two social ranks, aristocrats and commoners. In some cases, as among the Apa Tani in the Himalayas, the highest ranked clan forms an oligarchy (Flannery and Marcus 2012, 257–8). However, most rank societies are ruled by chiefs. These societies are characterized by centralized authority over numerous villages, and hence tend to be larger in scale than tribes, although not necessarily larger than tribal confederations. Chiefdoms often arise from intertribal warfare. Intertribal competition creates an incentive for societies to enlarge their populations and capacity for warfare. Such competition may also shift the incentives for engaging in war: instead of simply taking heads for the sheer honor, winners in battle may now allow their rivals to live, but subordinate them to the winning tribe's authority, force them to pay tribute, or enslave them, so as to increase their material accumulation and hence their war-making capacity (Flannery and Marcus 2012, 206, 218). The expanded society now includes some kinship groups that are superior to others, thereby making inequality hereditary. Within the head village, different lineages also become ranked, differentiating at least between the chief's lineage, from which all future chiefs must descend, and commoners. Esteem thereby becomes inherited and not only achieved. Chiefs also exercise authority, although their despotic tendencies may be held in check by council elders. In the order of standing, the chief and his kin enjoy greater consideration and wealth. However, they are still expected to redistribute goods through feasts, patronage, and provision of public goods.

The next step after rank society in the spectrum of inequality is stratification. Stratification tends to accompany state formation, with formalized offices, centralized multilevel bureaucratic administration, law, and a monopoly of legitimate force over the territory. In a stratified society, the highest groups close their ranks to outsiders. They practice endogamy, only marrying members of their own rank, preventing lower ranked individuals from moving up by marrying those of higher rank (Flannery and Marcus 2012, 313). Nor can lower-ranked individuals rise to the top through achievement. Ethnocentric ideologies of descent group inequality may rigidify into caste or caste-like identities. The highest groups also monopolize resources and opportunities critical for gaining authority, standing, and prestige in that society (Tilly 1999). For example, they may limit access to ownership of land through inheritance rules such as primogeniture and entail, or limit access to the priesthood to a certain lineage.

In their magisterial survey of the rise of social hierarchy in human history, Kent Flannery and Joyce Marcus stress that material factors alone do not explain inequality. Tribal societies, which are egalitarian by definition, show that neither domestication nor settlement is sufficient for hierarchy. Nor is domestication necessary, as some settled hunter-gatherer groups, such as the Chumash of California, formed rank societies. Without any changes in their technology or mode of production, some groups continuously cycle between egalitarian and rank society (Flannery and Marcus 2012, ch. 5, 10). Cycling confirms Boehm's ambivalence model of egalitarianism: upstarts are always trying to establish hierarchy, but often meeting concerted resistance. If they cannot consolidate permanent supremacy, they will be periodically overthrown and the group will restore equality.

Beyond material circumstances, some kind of ideological shift is always needed to get people to accept hereditary inequality (Flannery and Marcus 2012, 191). A chiefly lineage may claim to be descended from a higher god; an emperor may claim to *be* a god. Rousseau (1754) argued that some kind of fraud or trickery is involved in persuading the propertyless to go along with claims to private property. Such cases have been observed: the Maliyaw subclan of the community of Avatip in Papua New Guinea attempted to monopolize ritual offices by claiming exclusive intellectual property rights to names, on the basis of manipulated genealogical memories (Flannery and Marcus 2012, 187–90). More generally, it is evident to us moderns that some kind of fraud underlies attempts to justify hereditary inequality. The bald idea that certain people are superior to others simply in virtue of their ancestry, while still *de facto* powerful in racism and forms of bigotry, no longer enjoys legitimacy. Nevertheless, a thousand rationalizations of *de facto* hereditary inequality remain even in modern democratic societies, often based on fraudulent misrepresentations of the structure of opportunities, and the greater admiration and sympathy accorded to the rich and powerful (Smith 1759 [1976], I.3.2.2, I.3.3.1–4). To overthrow hierarchies, the people must critique the ideologies that legitimate them and replace them with alternative egalitarian ideologies.

In the long view of history, from an egalitarian perspective it was mostly downhill for humanity from the rise of rank society until the modern era. Egalitarian hunter-gatherers were pushed to areas too poorly resourced to sustain surplus production. Most tribal societies either met the same fate in competition with larger, more hierarchically organized societies, were conquered by them, or else became hierarchical themselves. The same dynamics of inter-society rivalry, intensification of production, and growth of military capacity that generated chiefdoms led to kingdoms and empires—larger-scale state-based societies with additional ranks of administrative authority, more despotic rulers, greater social distance between the top and bottom ranks or castes, greater material inequality, and harsher inegalitarian ideologies. Not until the rise of democratic social movements, starting around the sixteenth to seventeenth centuries, do we observe egalitarianism making a comeback.

In this highly compressed account, five factors appear to be critical to the emergence, consolidation, and intensification of social hierarchy:

(1) *In*egalitarian impulses—drives to assert superiority over others. Rousseau appears to be on strong ground in arguing that the quest for superior esteem lies at the root of socially instituted inequality. However, Boehm's evolutionary account, according to which humans inherited their despotic tendencies from the last common ancestor with chimps, suggests that the will to dominate others may have evolved prior to the desire for esteem, as it probably ascribes too much self-consciousness to ascribe narcissistic tendencies to such remote ancestors. To put the point another way, inequality is driven not only by narcissists, but by bullies—the evolutionary inheritance of aggressiveness from the alpha individuals of the remote past.

(2) Ethnocentric opportunity hoarding. This is the manipulation of institutions by identity groups to enable them to monopolize resources and opportunities critical for gaining esteem, authority, and standing.

(3) Identity group closure or segregation by elites. This prevents outsiders from joining the superior groups or sharing their privileges.

(4) Large scale. Intersocial rivalry brings competitive advantages to scale, enabling larger societies to either conquer smaller societies or drive them to marginal territories. The administration of larger-scale societies almost always involves organizational complexity, with a multiplication of ranks of authority. State-based top-down commands replace participatory democracy and consensus decision-making. Only in rare cases, such as the Iroquois Confederacy, have tribal societies managed to scale up for a long period of time.

(5) Inegalitarian ideology. Raw power is not enough to stabilize hierarchy. People need to be persuaded that it is legitimate.

4. PROBLEMS WITH PREMODERN EGALITARIAN SOCIETIES AND THE VALUE OF HIERARCHY

The anthropological record demonstrates the deep-rootedness of the egalitarian impulse in human nature, and offers proof of the possibility of egalitarian society. However, examination of the normative limitations of premodern egalitarian societies offers lessons to us today. These limitations can be divided into two types: (1) failures to live up to fully egalitarian norms; and (2) failures to realize other important goods.

Consider first the failures of full egalitarianism. Both Flannery and Marcus and Boehm argue that even the most egalitarian societies ever realized still involve hierarchies of some sort. Flannery and Marcus stress the inegalitarianism embedded in hunter-gatherer cosmologies. From foragers' point of view, humans were mere gammas in a cosmic order that placed invisible supernatural spirits in alpha positions, and ancestors in beta positions. These beliefs do not disturb egalitarian social relations among living humans. But they do suggest the readiness of human minds to be persuaded by inegalitarian ideologies that could reassign unequal ranks to living humans (Flannery and Marcus 2012, 59).

Boehm argues that all societies have a dominance hierarchy, only that in egalitarian societies, the hierarchy is reversed: the betas (nonaggressive, modest, mild-mannered individuals) collectively dominate the alphas (bullies and narcissists) (Boehm 1999, Kindle loc. 920–30). To the extent that all he means is that authority relations are inescapable in every human society, his claim is correct. Yet it is misleading to suggest that egalitarianism is the equivalent of some kind of group-based reverse discrimination. Nomadic hunter-gatherer societies and tribal societies offer the same opportunities to bullies and narcissists as to everyone else, on the same conditions—that they respect the rights and personal independence of others.

More substantively, neither type of premodern egalitarian society avoids group-based inequality among living humans altogether. All vest greater esteem and authority in elders. Given the realities of human development, some age-based inequalities are inevitable in all societies. This does not violate equality of opportunity, since everyone gets access to the age-based privileges over time. More problematic is the fact that among clan-based societies, clans that can claim an older lineage enjoy higher standing (Flannery and Marcus 2012, 54).

Far more troubling is gender inequality. No premodern society practices full gender equality. Within bands and tribes, there are no significant gender-based inequalities in access to material resources. Men and women also have equal authority at the band and sometimes at the tribe level, particularly if the tribe is matrilineal, and in the rare cases where women engage in hunting or warfare. However, men more often attempt and attain positions of influence in group deliberation. Furthermore, male foragers enjoy more prestige than women due to their role in killing big game. Tribesmen enjoy more prestige due to their military role. Ideologically, men are considered more virtuous (Flannery and Marcus 2012, 54, 94–5). They also engage more intensively in esteem competition, including competitive feasts, and take credit for providing the pigs that were in fact raised by their wives (Boehm 1999, 345–6; Flannery and Marcus 2012, 96, 116). At the family level in both bands and tribes, men dominate their wives. Domestic violence is common and unregulated. Although the extent of male domination varies widely in these societies, and is mild in some cases, it is never absent (Boehm 1999, Kindle loc. 892–8, 1227, 1294–5).

Premodern egalitarian societies suffer from two major additional defects. One is a low level of economic development. Because these societies are small in scale and employ primitive technology, the scope of cooperation is low, and opportunities for gains from trade and a sophisticated division of labor are limited. Low economic development not only limits consumption possibilities; it also severely limits the variety of ways of life open for individual choice.

Premodern egalitarian societies also suffer from shockingly high levels of violence, including violent death. I have already mentioned the high rates of domestic violence. Among hunter-gatherers, men also frequently kill other men, often in jealous conflicts over women. Because no one has authority over others, it is difficult for outsiders to intervene in such situations. Among tribesmen, intertribal raiding and feuding are endemic. The archaeological and anthropological records show that among tribal societies, headhunting is widely practiced, based on the belief that bringing home enemy heads increases the life force of the tribe. It is a primary focus of esteem competition among tribesmen, and a major source of excitement in tribal villages. Steven Pinker (2011, Kindle loc. 1405–30) estimates that the rate of violent death (by warfare or homicide) averages 14–15% among hunter-gatherers, about 24% among tribes, 5% among subjects of premodern states, and less than 1% for citizens of states in the twentieth century. Homicide rates even in the least violent nonstate societies are dramatically higher than in modern states (Pinker 2011, figs 2–4).

These defects of premodern egalitarian societies in contrast with hierarchical state societies suggest that social hierarchy is not only an expression of bullying and narcissistic impulses in human beings. It has some uses for everyone. Two are primary: suppression of violence, and economic development, which offers not only greater material consumption, but also options over a much richer variety of ways of life.

Hierarchy, as established in state authority, has turned out to be by far the most effective institution ever invented for suppressing interpersonal violence, whether organized or individual. This may seem surprising, given the vast scale of slaughter inflicted by modern states in pursuit of colonialism, ethnic cleansing, conquest of neighbors, and consolidation of power. Yet the most comprehensive studies provide compelling evidence that a major consequence of large-scale state formation is massive suppression of violent conflict within state borders. In the long run, this effect far outweighs the violence states inflict in expanding and consolidating their power— activities that virtually always involve warfare (Gat 2006; Morris 2014). The state is the only organization that has effectively asserted a monopoly of violence over a large-scale territory. Scale is important, for violent conflict is endemic between smaller-scale societies such as tribes and bands. Peace within borders is generally more secure than between them, so long as national identity is strong enough to motivate people to support a common government.

Large scale almost invariably makes hierarchy, in the form of multilevel bureaucratic administration, necessary. Bureaucratic administration invariably shifts authority away from the governed to higher officeholders. Rousseau (1762 [1988]) tried to avoid this conclusion through an ingenious constitutional design for preserving participatory democracy under modern conditions, and scaling up by means of confederations of small republics. The Iroquois Confederacy perhaps came closest to realizing his ideal. The rarity of this model in history suggests that there are severe obstacles to realizing it. In any event, Rousseau's model is not up to the administrative tasks demanded of large-scale modern states.

The second value of hierarchy is economic. Economies of scale have turned out to be gigantic. If, as I have argued, administration of large-scale organizations requires bureaucratic hierarchy, then we owe the immense prosperity of the modern era, with its attendant benefits of longer, healthier lives, massively expanded knowledge, diversification of occupations and opportunities, high technology, comfort, and convenience, to hierarchy as well.

Yet, as already noted, social hierarchy also imposes grave costs in human welfare, particularly for those relegated to inferior ranks. Arguably, it also deprives superiors of certain goods of relating to others as equals, and corrupts their characters by inflaming arrogance, vanity, and greed. The great challenge for us moderns, then, is how to achieve a free society of equals—a society in which everyone enjoys personal independence from the domination of others, universal respect, equal opportunity for esteem, and equal standing for all—consistently with the two great benefits of scale and hierarchy: massive reduction of violence, and prosperity with all its dramatic increases in real freedom.

5. PROSPECTS FOR AND CHALLENGES TO EGALITARIANISM IN MODERN SOCIETIES

The political economy of egalitarian thought has two great branches, corresponding to two general ideas about the institutional conditions for a free society of equals: individualist and democratic. The individualist branch aims to minimize the scope of interpersonal authority so as maximize the room for each individual to decide how to live, without having to follow anyone else's orders, ask others' permission to act, or even to consult other people. The democratic branch aims to ensure that, wherever people must be subject to hierarchy—to organized, asymmetrical authority—those occupying authoritative positions are accountable to those they govern, and exercise their authority in the interests of the governed. Democracy is a way of effecting Boehm's "reverse dominance hierarchy," by reversing the principal-agent relationship: instead of governors being the principals, and subjects the agents commanded to serve them, governors are turned into agents of the citizens.

Some egalitarian theorists have argued that one or the other branch must be applied across the board to all social domains. Thus, we have individualist anarchists on one side, and communalist participatory democrats on the other side. Reflection on the limitations of the original egalitarian societies, along with the fundamental causes of social hierarchy revealed in human history, exposes the weaknesses of both approaches. Anarchists have no credible answer to the bullies of the world. If everyone were wholly moved by the egalitarian impulse—gentle, modest, cooperative, and reasonable, as Godwin (1793) and Kropotkin (1917) supposed—individuals could solve most of their conflicts peacefully, without centralized authority. But, as Boehm argues, the egalitarian impulse is *oppositional*, and requires collective organization to keep the bullies in line.

Still close to the individualist end lie libertarian advocates of a minimal state. Their strategy recognizes the need for government—for hierarchical administration—for one purpose only: the suppression of violence and coercion. In light of the argument of the last section, this appears to leave out the other great use of hierarchical administration, in the sphere of production. The vast bulk of production in advanced economies is carried out under the administration of little governments—mostly corporations—with nearly all other legal types of productive enterprise also instituting hierarchical administration whenever they have employees. It is to no avail to argue that they are consistent with freedom on the ground that most of these little governments are not operated by the state and are joined by consent. They all exercise coercive, hierarchical authority, and do so in the same way, whether they are run by the state, by private for-profit enterprises, or by private non-profit enterprises (Bromley and Meyer 2014; Anderson 2015b).

Libertarians are of three minds about this state of affairs. A tiny minority, leaning toward the anarchist end, is highly skeptical of the authority relations in the modern productive organization (Carson 2008). They keep alive the original libertarian vision, which was arguably the first model of egalitarianism for modern times that approached realization. It drew on Adam Smith's economics, but was mainly promulgated by Americans from

Thomas Paine through Lincoln and the Republican Party (Anderson 2015b). This model of a free society of equals combines a minimal state with nearly universal self-employment. In this model, productive enterprises are very small and numerous. Hence markets are free and perfectly competitive, and all economic transactions are effected by arms-length market transactions among independent proprietors, rather than administered by the internal authority relations of firms. This model came close to realization in the free states and territories of the United States from the War of Independence to the Civil War, an era in which about 90% of white men were self-employed, and opportunities for self-employment seemed unlimited in the territories.

To many egalitarians of the day, the free (nonslave) states and territories of America were the promised land. That average white Americans were also more prosperous than people anywhere else who had to work for a living seemed to demonstrate that the libertarian model of egalitarianism could deliver both great goods that premodern egalitarian societies could not deliver: peace and prosperity. This turned out to be an illusion, for several reasons. First, the model was predicated on the availability of free land, which was obtained by mass violence—ethnic cleansing of Native Americans. Second, even within the white community for which this libertarian model was designed, levels of interpersonal violence were high, and private orderings in the territories proved incapable of controlling them (Clowney 2014). Third, just as for premodern egalitarian societies, the modern American model accepted male supremacy within the family: wives suffered from domestic violence, and husbands exploited their wives' labor no less than the Big Men of tribal society, who took all the credit for the pigs their wives raised. Finally, the model was twice doomed. The inevitable closing of the frontier would eventually raise the price of land and close off opportunities for self-employment. The Industrial Revolution, too, destroyed most opportunities for self-employment by employing huge concentrations of indivisible capital such as railroads. These could only be operated by large multilevel bureaucratic organizations in which managers minutely controlled the labor of masses of propertyless workers. Large organizations, with their immense economies of scale, crushed sole proprietorships in market competition.

Most libertarians have quietly abandoned the dream of universal self-employment, while continuing to pretend that productive relations in modern economies are dominated by free markets, rather than by hierarchical organizations in which workers are subject to arbitrary, unaccountable power. This is simply to fail to face up to the problems of modern government, which extend far beyond the state (Anderson 2015b). The final libertarian response is to ground rights to rule others on property rights. This at least acknowledges modern economic realities. But the principle of legitimate government thereby embraced is not that of republican freedom. It is feudalism (Freeman 2001; Anderson 2015a).

At the other extreme of the spectrum, some egalitarians have embraced participatory democracy across the board (Albert and Hahnel 1991). This revives the political form of premodern band and tribal societies, with membership on a voluntaristic basis as in bands, rather than by family or clan, as in tribes. As numerous modern communal experiments—from utopian socialists to kibbutzim to hippie communes—have shown, such formations tend to be short-lived in free societies. The costs of free riding, monitoring, and collective deliberation, along with the lack of privacy and scope for individuality when the unit of production is also the unit of domestic life, overwhelm the benefits of democratic participation. In addition, fully participatory models have never managed to scale up, even though the two key benefits of modern societies—peace and prosperity—are achieved through scale.

These difficulties are well known within democratic theory. The mainstream democratic egalitarian response, from Madison and Paine on, has been to move toward representative forms of democracy. This is generally the right direction to take for managing problems that large organizations—multilevel administrations requiring close coordination of many individuals' activities—are needed to solve. Nevertheless, achieving egalitarian relations even within organizations that are democratic in form poses a large, messy set of problems for egalitarians to solve, more than a solution in itself.

If Boehm is right, then humanity faces a serious problem. The very people most motivated to seek higher offices within organizations are bullies and narcissists, who are attracted to them by opportunities to seek superior power and esteem. But these are the people egalitarians least want to be serving in those offices. In addition, the very occupation of such offices may corrupt, by activating arrogant and narcissistic impulses in individuals who, in other circumstances, would adopt an egalitarian ethos. Without elaborate formal and cultural constraints, and institutionalized opportunities for voice from and accountability to the governed, hierarchical administration tends to attract the worst and corrupt the rest.

One essential institution of modern democratic orders is the person/office distinction: individuals may exercise greater power only in virtue of their office, not in virtue of who they are; and only over the domains needed for solving the coordination problem their office is authorized to solve (Anderson 2008). Special dignity attaches to the office, not the person. Adam Smith reminds us of how extraordinarily difficult it is for human beings to pull this off. As he noted (1759 [1976], I.3.3.1), "the disposition to admire, and almost to worship, the rich and the powerful, and to despise, or, at least, to neglect, persons of poor and mean condition,...is...the great and most universal cause of the corruption of our moral sentiments." It takes a powerful egalitarian ethos to counteract this bias.

Moreover, identity groups already asymmetrically positioned in the highest offices are constantly aiming to convert them into their *de facto* heritable private property. It takes elaborate institutional arrangements and egalitarian pressure to dismantle the identity group segregation and opportunity hoarding that Charles Tilly (1999) has argued are the linchpins of group-based inequality. Nor can egalitarian innovation end, for the inegalitarian, reactionary impulse is at least as creative in getting around egalitarian institutional constraints as egalitarians have been in devising them. Current plutocratic trends do not bode well for representative democracy (Bartels 2008; Gilens and Page 2014; Piketty 2014).

By placing egalitarianism in the very long view of history and political economy, my aim has not been to offer answers, but to gain clarity on some of the fundamental challenges to realizing a free society of equals. Human beings have both egalitarian and inegalitarian tendencies, which are in constant opposition. It was easier to maintain an egalitarian equilibrium in premodern times, when human societies were small in scale. But this success was limited, for premodern egalitarian societies failed to achieve gender equality. They also suffered from high levels of interpersonal violence and low levels of development. Moreover, intersocial competition gave a decisive advantage to large-scale state-based societies that could only be administered through social hierarchy. An inegalitarian equilibrium overtook almost all human beings from the rise of states until the early modern era. At that point, egalitarian ideologies and social movements began to push back against centuries of hierarchy.

But modern egalitarians face a fundamentally different problem from their foraging and tribal predecessors. Hierarchy is oppressive, but it is needed to secure the scale of cooperation needed to generate peace, prosperity, and its attendant real freedoms. The challenge for moderns is to undo the dominance hierarchy of large-scale organizations: to force the occupants of higher office to serve the governed, to select for those eager to serve others, to block the opportunity hoarding and group closure whereby identity groups seek to exalt themselves above everyone else and monopolize offices, resources, and prestige for themselves at others' expense. This is a very complex problem of political economy, requiring the resources of all the social sciences as well as sustained normative inquiry. We cannot hope to make progress on it by elaborating ever more elaborate arguments for abstract, cosmic, asocial *a priori* principles of distributive justice.

References

Albert, Michael, and Robin Hahnel. 1991. *The Political Economy of Participatory Economics*. Princeton: Princeton University Press.

Anderson, Elizabeth. 1991. "John Stuart Mill and Experiments in Living." *Ethics* 102: 4–26.

Anderson, Elizabeth. 2008. "Expanding the Egalitarian Toolbox: Equality and Bureaucracy." *Proceedings of the Aristotelian Society* Supplementary Volume 82: 139–60.

Anderson, Elizabeth. 2012. "Equality." In *Oxford Handbook in Political Philosophy*, ed. David Estlund. New York: Oxford University Press, 40–57.

Anderson, Elizabeth. 2014. The Quest for Free Labor. Lecture 9. Amherst Lecture in Philosophy. Amherst College, http://www.amherstlecture.org/anderson2014/index.html.

Anderson, Elizabeth. 2015a. "Equality and Freedom in the Workplace: Recovering Republican Insights." *Social Philosophy and Policy* 31(2): 48–69.

Anderson, Elizabeth. 2015b. "Liberty, Equality, and Private Government." Tanner Lectures in Human Values. Princeton University. http://tannerlectures.utah.edu/Anderson%20manuscript.pdf.

Babeuf, Gracchus. 1967. *The Defense of Gracchus Babeuf before the High Court of Vendôme*. Ed. and trans. John Anthony Scott. Amherst: University of Massachusetts Press.

Bartels, Larry. 2008. *Unequal Democracy: The Political Economy of the New Gilded Age*. New York, Princeton: Russell Sage Foundation, Princeton University Press.

Boehm, Christopher. 1999. *Hierarchy in the Forest: The Evolution of Egalitarian Behavior*. Cambridge, MA: Harvard University Press.

Bromley, Patricia, and John Meyer. 2014. "'They Are All Organizations': The Cultural Roots of Blurring Between the Nonprofit, Business, and Government Sectors." *Administration & Society*, DOI: 10.1177/0095399714548268.

Buonarroti, Philippe. 1836. *Buonarroti's History of Babeuf's Conspiracy for Equality*. Bronterre [pseud.]. London: H. Hetherington.

Carson, Kevin. 2008. *Organization Theory: A Libertarian Perspective*. Charleston, SC: BookSurge Publishing.

Clowney, Stephen. 2014. "Rule of Flesh and Bone: The Dark Side of Informal Property Rights." *University of Illinois Law Review*, http://ssrn.com/abstract=2485526.

Dworkin, Ronald. 1981. "What is Equality? Part 2: Equality of Resources." *Philosophy and Public Affairs* 10(4): 283–345.

Flannery, Kent, and Joyce Marcus. 2012. *The Creation of Inequality: How Our Prehistoric Ancestors Set the Stage for Monarchy, Slavery, and Empire*. Cambridge, MA: Harvard University Press.

Fleischacker, Samuel. 2004. *A Short History of Distributive Justice*. Cambridge, MA: Harvard University Press.

Freeman, Samuel. 2001. "Illiberal Libertarians: Why Libertarianism Is Not a Liberal View." *Philosophy and Public Affairs* 30(2): 105–51.

Fricker, Miranda. 2007. *Epistemic Injustice: Power and the Ethics of Knowing*. Oxford: Oxford University Press.

Fried, Morton H. 1967. *The Evolution of Political Society: An Essay in Political Anthropology*. New York: Random House.

Gat, Azar. 2006. *War in Human Civilization*. Oxford and New York: Oxford University Press.

Gilens, Martin, and Benjamin Page. 2014. "Testing Theories of American Politics: Elites, Interest Groups, and Average Citizens." *Perspectives on Politics*, https://www.princeton.edu/~mgilens/Gilens%20homepage%20materials/Gilens%20and%20Page/Gilens%20and%20Page%202014-Testing%20Theories%203-7-14.pdf.

Godwin, William. 1793. *An Enquiry Concerning Political Justice, and Its Influence on General Virtue and Happiness*. London: G.G.J. and J. Robinson.

Kropotkin, Peter. 1917. *Mutual Aid: A Factor of Evolution*. New York: Knopf.

Lilburne, John, William Walwyn, Thomas Prince, and Richard Overton. 1649. "An Agreement of the Free People of England, 1 May 1649." In *The Levellers: Miscellaneous Writings*: Vol. 4, *James Otteson, The Levellers: Overton, Walwyn and Lilburne*. Bristol: Thoemmes Press, 215–25.

Morris, Ian. 2014. *War! What Is It Good For? Conflict and the Progress of Civilization from Primates to Robots*. New York: Farrar, Strauss, and Giroux.

Parfit, Derek. 1991. "Equality or Priority?" Lindley Lecture. Lawrence, KS: University of Kansas, Department of Philosophy, http://kuscholarworks.ku.edu/handle/1808/12405.

Patterson, Orlando. 1982. *Slavery and Social Death*. Cambridge, MA: Harvard University Press.

Pettit, Philip. 1997. *Republicanism: A Theory of Freedom and Government*. New York: Oxford University Press.

Piketty, Thomas. 2014. *Capital in the Twenty-First Century*. Trans. Arthur Goldhammer. Cambridge, MA: Belknap Press of Harvard University Press.

Pinker, Steven. 2011. *The Better Angels of Our Nature: Why Violence Has Declined*. New York: Viking.

Rousseau, Jean-Jacques. 1754. *What Is the Origin of Inequality among Men, and Is It Authorized by Natural Law?* G. D. H. Cole, http://www.constitution.org/jjr/ineq.htm.

Rousseau, Jean-Jacques. 1762. *The Social Contract*. G. D. H. Cole. Amherst, NY: Prometheus Books, http://www.constitution.org/jjr/socon.htm.

Sen, Amartya. 1980. "Equality of What?" ed. S. M. McMurrin. In *Tanner Lectures in Human Values*, vol. 1. Salt Lake City: University of Utah Press, 197–220.

Smith, Adam. 1759. *The Theory of Moral Sentiments*. Ed. D. D. Raphael and A. L. Macfie. Glasgow Edition of the Works and Correspondence of Adam Smith. Oxford: Oxford University Press.

Temkin, Larry. 2003. "Egalitarianism Defended." *Ethics* 113: 764–82.

Tilly, Charles. 1999. *Durable Inequality*. Berkeley and Los Angeles: University of California Press.

Vallentyne, Peter. 2007. "Of Mice and Men: Equality and Animals." In *Egalitarianism: New Essays on the Nature and Value of Equality*, ed. Nils Holtug and Kasper Lippert-Rasmussen. Oxford: Clarendon Press, 211–37.

3

Liberal Equality and the Moral Status of Parent-Child Relationships

Serena Olsaretti

INTRODUCTION

The family, and in particular the parent-child relationship that constitutes its core, is attracting increasing attention among political philosophers. Contemporary theorists of justice, who, until a couple of decades ago, either neglected the family or saw its relevance mostly in light of its being a site of gender injustice, are now addressing a host of questions about the structure and role of the family in a just society (Macleod 2002; Clayton 2006; Archard 2010a; Brighouse and Swift 2014).

One such question is whether and why in a just society there should be parent-child relationships (or the family) at all. Tackling it head on, a few liberal egalitarian philosophers now defend the family by appealing to the non-instrumental value of the parent-child relationship for both parents and children alike (Macleod 2002, 2010; Brighouse and Swift 2009, 2014). They claim that this defense of the family accounts for some of the prerogatives and responsibilities that are often seen to characterize the parent-child relationship, while at the same time showing others to be unwarranted. In particular, this "relationship view" aims to give support to parents' having rights over their children, including the right to exercise some discretion about how to raise them (compatibly with their respecting children's claims). It also aims to show that some parental partiality is justified—namely, the kind of partiality that is integral to the valuable parent-child relationship.

The relationship view thus addresses two challenges that the justification of the family raises for liberal egalitarians: the problem of authority and the problem of partiality. These two challenges point, respectively, to the burdens of justifying *to children* their parents' having rights over them, and *to third parties* parents' favoring of their children in ways that disrupt equality. This paper asks whether the relationship view succeeds in meeting these challenges. It suggests that it does not fully do that: the relationship view does not capture some important convictions about the moral status of the parent-child relationship and, as a result, it does not fully address the two stated challenges. The paper also offers an alternative basis for justifying the parent-child relationship on which parents, by virtue of being morally responsible for their children's existence, have an obligation to enter a relationship with them. Section 1 outlines the challenges of authority and of partiality in more detail. Sections 2 and 3 introduce the main claims of the relationship view, by contrasting it with those made by the instrumental view of the family, and identify its main shortcomings. Section 4 presents my alternative view, on which those who are morally responsible for a child's existence have an obligation to enter and sustain a caring relationship with that child.

1. LIBERAL EGALITARIANISM AND THE BURDENS OF JUSTIFYING THE FAMILY

In justifying the family, liberal egalitarians face two specific challenges—that of authority and of partiality—reflecting their liberal and their egalitarian commitments.

The problem of authority is the problem of how to justify granting parents rights over children—rights which, compatibly with some of the children's interests being respected, are quite extensive, conferring on parents the authority to make many weighty decisions for their children. Providing such a justification raises a challenge for liberal egalitarians because, independently of whether they conceive of children as autonomous, liberal egalitarians recognize that children deserve equal moral consideration, so childrearing practices must be justifiable by appeal to children's interests (see Brennan and Noggle 1997; Macleod 2002; Vallentyne 2003). Moreover, since liberal egalitarians include amongst these interests the child's interest in her future autonomy, and, on some views, the child's interest in independence, any exercise of parental authority must be duly constrained, and subjected to the test of the future child's retroactive approval (Feinberg 1994; Clayton 2006).

The problem of authority, then, points to the burden of justification *to children* of their parents' having rights over them. This justification must achieve two things: first, it must show that the possession and exercise of authority over the child of the kind that characterizes parent-child relationships is legitimate; second, it must show that the exercise of authority over *particular children* by some *particular* adult(s) is legitimate. A full justification of the parent-child relationship must include both these elements: we need an account of both what may and should be done to and for children (what the caring role that some adults may and should play vis-à-vis children amounts to), and who may and should do certain things to and for children, and for which ones in particular (who should fulfill that role vis-à-vis which child). Since there is no reason to assume that the first question is normatively prior to, and sets the parameters for answering, the second, an account of the family that answered only the first of these questions would be incomplete in a troubling way.[1]

The second main challenge faced by liberal egalitarian defenses of the family, namely, that of partiality, points to the burden of justifying the family *to third parties* (other children, parents, and adults). This is the problem of partiality. Because of their egalitarian commitments, liberal egalitarians face the challenge of showing that the family is justified despite the fact that it *realizes* and *creates* inequalities that disadvantage others. The family *realizes* inequalities in the sense that the parent-child relationship that constitutes the family is itself an instantiation of unequal treatment. Adults who are parents, by parenting, favor their children over other children and adults: by raising and caring for some children rather than others, and insofar as they engage in parenting rather than in other third-parties-benefiting-activities, parents give their children valuable goods, i.e. their focused energies, affection, time, and attention, in a context in which it is highly likely, even under ideal conditions, that people's access to these goods is unequal. The family also *creates* inequalities, in that parents are disposed to promote their children's interests and to favor their children in ways other than by having a caring relationship with them (though as a result of their having that relationship), such as by investing their material resources on them. Thus the family has been seen by liberal egalitarians as a threat to equality of opportunity, and to the egalitarian commitments of liberal egalitarianism more generally, both under non-ideal and ideal conditions.[2]

---

[1] I return to this point in the next section, as this is one of the points of contention I have with both the instrumental and the relationship views of the parent-child relationship.

[2] For the classic statement of these worries, see Rawls 1971 and Fishkin 1983. For some more recent statements, see Macleod 2002, 2010; Brighouse and Swift 2009, 2014; Brake 2015. For the "distributive objection" to special obligations arising from relationships (including, but not only, family relationships), see Scheffler 2001. Very recently, Anca Gheaus and Colin Macleod have suggested, in independent work (Gheaus forthcoming; Macleod forthcoming), that framing the problem we face as constituting a challenge for the family is in fact misleading, since, they argue, there are no alternative adequate child-drearing arrangements which do not exhibit the problem of partiality to a considerable, perhaps comparable, extent. I do not treat this interesting point here.

As with the challenge of authority, a defense of the family that aims to meet the challenge of partiality must provide a justification both of what may and should be done to and for children in the name of parental partiality (whether and why some partiality towards children is justified), and of who may or should do certain things to and for particular children (who may or should be partial to which children). That is, a defense of the family must show both that the exercise of (some) parental partiality is legitimate— that children may be favored by a few adults in certain ways—and that it is justified that some particular adults (the children's parents) treat them, specifically, in ways that constitute or display partiality.

It is important to note here that the problem of partiality as I have just characterized it is different from another version of the problem of partiality that is commonly discussed in moral philosophy and with which the one under consideration is normally conflated. That problem points to the *anti-maximizing* potential of partiality, that is, the fact that partiality-inclined agents fail to maximally pursue morally mandatory aims. The fact that a parent's hefty expenditure on his child's skiing trips—or indeed, *any* expenditure on his child at all, assuming the parent could have chosen not to have the child and hence not created the need for this use of his resources—could and should be put to supposedly morally better use by being sent to Oxfam or provide food for the starving is a case in point (Brighouse and Swift 2009: 51). This objection to partiality is as much an objection to partiality towards oneself as it is an objection to partiality towards one's children.

By contrast, the problem of partiality under consideration here, as already mentioned, points to the *equality-disrupting* effects of partiality; viewing partiality as problematic for this reason is compatible with upholding a non-maximizing view of the demands of morality (and of justice), and with thinking that people enjoy an agent-centered prerogative thanks to which some self-serving behavior is perfectly admissible and consistent with morality and justice. If the worry is with the equality-disrupting effects of partiality, a parent's hefty use of his rightfully held resources on skiing trips *for himself* is unproblematic, even if this results in an identical or even greater loss to Oxfam than would have been incurred had the parent used the money for his child. By the same token, if the worry is with the equality-disrupting effects of partiality, an exercise of parental partiality that, for whatever reason, did not undermine equality is not problematic. A fanciful world in which all parents exercised partiality to the same extent and with the same impact on their children would not be unjust, on the view under consideration. The fact that this world is one in which partiality hinders the achievement of the best outcome is irrelevant. When discussing the problem of parental partiality, political philosophers often move from one to the other of these two worries (see Brighouse and Swift 2014: 144).[3] However, they are importantly different.

Noting this difference helps to make apparent that, for liberal egalitarians, the challenge presented by the problem of partiality includes the objection pithily formulated by Robert Nozick against "patterned theories" of justice. Nozick said that because they condone individuals' spending of rightfully held resources on themselves, but condemn that spending of resources on others, these views are "individualism with a vengeance!" (Nozick 1974: 167). The objection seems particularly serious for those versions of liberal egalitarianism, which I am assuming here, that view some or all inequalities that result from people's choices as compatible with justice. On these theories, justice is compatible with individuals' partiality towards themselves, as manifested in choices to avail themselves of the opportunities that are equally on offer for everyone, even if these opportunities are competitive and even if the individuals in question could make choices that display less partiality towards themselves. To take a simple example: if A and B are equally talented and, at the onset of adulthood, both have the opportunity to embark on a management course that would enable them to compete for a lucrative position, they are permitted to embark on that course in order to benefit themselves. They are permitted to do so even if this comes at a cost to the other party (because there is only one position for which they will compete), and they are permitted, by justice, to reap whatever advantage their unequal choices would lead to. These "responsibility-sensitive" versions of liberal egalitarianism take "the individualism" Nozick identifies a step further than the theories Nozick targets, in that they allow not just for self-serving spending, but also for self-serving, inequality-producing investment choices.[4]

The asymmetrical standing which liberal egalitarianism confers on partiality to self and partiality to one's children seems questionable. Some parental partiality seems to be morally commendable, and more commendable than comparable partiality towards oneself. So, in answering the challenge of partiality, it would be desirable if the justification of the family that liberal egalitarians offer could defuse the worries raised by the Nozickian objection,

---

[3] The claim that in a world like ours, much parenting is "the moral equivalent a tax shelter," which Scheffler (2001: 85) makes and Brighouse and Swift (2014: 25) endorse, is an illustration of this, since tax shelters hinder both inequality and the optimal pursuit of morally mandatory aims. Under realistic conditions, the two objections to partiality I distinguish here pull in the same direction, and this may explain why they are conflated: partiality disrupts both equality (and other distributive goals, such as priority for the worse off, or sufficiency) and the maximal pursuit of other morally mandatory goals.

[4] See Clayton 2012 for a discussion of egalitarianism and inheritance that takes Nozick's point seriously.

and capture the way in which the parent-child relationship, at least under certain conditions, is morally valuable. In what sense exactly the family is morally valuable is of course what is in contention, and the discussion that follows will attempt to tease out a plausible interpretation of that claim. Minimally, and as a starting point, we can say that recognizing the moral status of the parent-child relationship involves two things. First, it involves recognizing that some parental partiality is morally required. Second, it involves not viewing that relationship and the disposition that characterize it as an evil (not even a necessary evil). Discussion of two competing views of the family, to which I now turn, will help bring to view more aspects of the moral status of the family.

2. THE INSTRUMENTAL JUSTIFICATION OF THE PARENT-CHILD RELATIONSHIP

One possible justification of the family that tries to meet the challenges of authority and of partiality is the instrumental justification. On the instrumental view, the parent-child relationship is fully justified by the fact that it serves the realization of agent-neutral values. More specifically, this view is characterized by two central claims: that the justification of the parent-child relationship lies solely in the fact that it best serves children's interests (in some versions, also third parties', or social, interests); and that the relationship serves these interests instrumentally: it is the best available means for realizing independently defined interests, i.e., the interest of children in having their needs met, or their rights respected, where these interests make no reference to the non-instrumental interest in the parent-child relationship itself.

Two different examples of the instrumental view are Robert Goodin's and Peter Vallentyne's accounts of the parent-child relationship. On Goodin's assigned responsibility model, we must ask what distribution and configuration of parental rights and responsibilities can best ensure that the needs of vulnerable children are met as well as possible (Goodin 2005). Children's needs provide the same agent-neutral reasons for everyone, and any special responsibilities that parents have are "distributed general responsibilities," which everyone retains in residual form and which are reactivated when those with special responsibilities prove unable or unwilling to discharge those responsibilities. Any rights that parents have over and vis-à-vis their children are rights that help them discharge those distributed general responsibilities.

For a view like Goodin's, showing that the justification of the parent-child relationship can meet the challenges of authority and of partiality, in both its role definition and identification aspects, reduces to the mostly empirical task of showing that that relationship is the best means of ensuring that we attend well to children's vulnerabilities. The reason why a few adults (independently of any particular answer to the question of who these adults are, and why they are the ones entrusted with these prerogatives and obligations) may and should exercise authority over some children and display partiality towards them (independently of any answer to the question of *which* children which adults should be in charge of), in ways that justify the parent-child relationship in some form, is that so doing is the best way to ensure that their needs are met, given what we know about the nature of children's needs and adults' capacities to respond to them. Similarly, the answer to the question of why some authority should be exercised and some partiality displayed by *some particular adults over and towards some particular children* adduces empirically grounded reasons for endorsing certain criteria for the selection of parents and for matching certain parents and certain children.

Goodin suggests here that the reason why the general responsibility to meet children's vulnerability in the context of parent-child-like relationships should be distributed so that procreators may and should care for their own children is that "responsibilities for protecting the vulnerable fall, in the first instance, to those people to whose actions and choices the child's interests are particularly vulnerable." This suggestion, in my view, is problematic. The criterion Goodin deploys for answering the question at hand seems vacuous if we assume—as I take it Goodin thinks we should assume—that whether adults who procreate should have their children become vulnerable to them in the first instance is a morally open question. So, Goodin needs some other explanation of why particular adults should acquire authority and display partiality towards particular children. Various options are open to an instrumental view like his, and which of these Goodin should favor will depend on the broader political philosophy of which the instrumental view is a part. Since Goodin endorses a consequentialist view on which all adults, including procreators, have a general positive duty, and only that general duty, to respond to children's vulnerabilities, it seems that being best able to fulfill that general duty provides a sufficient as well as necessary condition for why some adults should be parents for some particular children. The nature of the reasons why some adults are best able to discharge the general duties of everyone is irrelevant. It might be that, because genetic attachment is a motivationally efficacious drive for caring for a child, biological parents should raise their genetically related children; alternatively, or additionally, it may be that willingness to adopt the parenting role, regardless of one's genetic connection to the child or the role one has played in causing that child's existence, is a good proxy of how good a parent one will be. An instrumental view like Goodin's sits well with an ecumenical answer to the identification component of a defense of the family, on which begetting, genetic connection, and intentionally taking up the parenting role can all, depending on the facts, justify identifying some adults as the ones who have authority over, and partiality prerogatives towards, some particular children.

Vallentyne's account differs from Goodin's in three main respects. First, Vallentyne adopts a different view of the claims of children. Whereas Goodin resists ascribing rights to children, and conceives of their interests in light of the noncomparative standard of needs, on Vallentyne's view children have interest-protecting rights, and the interests in question have a substantial comparative component (apart from the right to personal security, which is a right to non-interference, all children, like adults, have equality rights, i.e., "rights to have their life prospects improved by others when the demands of equality so require" (Vallentyne 2003: 992)). Second, Vallentyne explicitly views maximal promotion of the child's interests as the main but not sole criterion for justifying the family; third parties' interests are also relevant. As he notes: "The benefits to the child are the main justification for childrearing rights. They are not, however, the sole considerations. The expected effect of the childrearing rights on the child's disposition to violate the rights of others is also relevant. An individual acquires childrearing rights just in case her possession of those rights . . . ensures that the child will respect the rights of others and suitably promotes the child's interests" (Vallentyne 2003: 996).[5] Third, Vallentyne holds that although the justification of the family—of why there should be parent-child relationships, and of which adults should occupy those relationships and with which children—will be settled by considerations about what is in children's best interests (together with consideration about what is best for third parties), those considerations do *not* determine the content of parents' duties: "the claim is not that those who have childrearing rights have a duty to provide the best upbringing they can for the child" (Vallentyne 2003: 998). Parents' obligations, rather, are only to do better by the child's rights than other available parents and than childrearing arrangements other than the family. Here, as with Goodin's view, the facts that an adult is a child's biological parent, or that he was responsible for the child's existence, are only relevant, if they are relevant at all, because and insofar as they correlate with these adults' being both willing and better able than other adults to discharge the

---

[5] Vallentyne makes this claim with regard to the issue of who should exercise authority and display partiality vis-à-vis which child, but I assume he would want to invoke the same consideration when settling the question of whether there should be parent-child relationships at all.

parenting role and do better by their child than if the child were not brought up in a family.

Vallentyne's account is declaredly a "radically strong child-centered conception of childrearing rights," and meets the authority and partiality challenges to the defense of the family head on. Since, on this view, the parent-child relationship is justified if and to the extent that it is the best of the available means for protecting children's and third parties' rights, justification of that relationship is *ipso facto* an answer to those challenges. In fact, we could say that the challenges of authority and of partiality simply evaporate if we adopt the instrumental view. But on closer inspection, the way in which the instrumental view meets those challenges is unsatisfactory, in that it fails to accommodate some intuitively defensible desiderata on how those challenges should be met. To see this, recall that, as I noted in section 1, among the various possible ways of meeting the challenge of partiality only some capture the conviction that some parental partiality is morally commendable: a justification of the family that viewed parents' disposition to be partial to their children as a wrong that is nonetheless, on balance, justifiable (because, given human nature, it is the inevitable price we must pay in order to ensure that every child's needs are satisfied) would not meet this desideratum.

Instrumental views of the family do not seem to adequately capture the family's moral status. It is true that on these views, some parental partiality—that which involves fulfilling a general duty of care, or that which involves doing better by the child's rights than alternative available arrangements—is thought to be morally required. But, as others have already remarked, instrumental justifications do not seem true to our understanding of the reasons parents have to be partial to their children (Brighouse and Swift 2009; Kolodny 2010). This is so even if we focus only on the partiality that instrumental justifications would recognize to be morally required (in that it would help realize agent-neutral values such as the value of meeting needs). The reasons parents are morally obliged to duly care for their (rather than other) children are not, or not solely, that by so doing they are contributing to a scheme that ensures that all children's needs are met as well as possible (*pace* Goodin), and not even that by so doing they are doing a better job than other alternative would-be parents and childcaring institutions (*pace* Vallentyne).

Moreover, and relatedly, instrumental justifications of the family give too flimsy a protection of the parent-child relationship, and of specific parent-child relationships (Jeske 1998; Brighouse and Swift 2009; Kolodny 2010; Macleod 2015). If children's interests could be better served by a system of well-run orphanages, or by a system of periodic reallocation of children to parents, then according to the instrumental justification, parents would have no reason to favor *their* children's rather than others' children's interests, and they would have no reason for wanting it to be the case that it is *they*, the parents, who help realize their children's interests by caring for them.

These claims seem to many to be too counter-intuitive to be acceptable. We could then say the following: while the instrumental justification of the family partially satisfies a first requirement of a plausible account of the family—that of capturing the family's moral status, by accounting for the fact that some parental partiality is morally required—it does not fully meet it, because it mischaracterizes the reasons parents have to exercise authority over children and to be partial to them; moreover, it does not meet a second requirement, that of giving a *robust* defense of the family—that is, a defense of it that does not view its value as relative and contingent in the way in which instrumental justifications do.

3. THE RELATIONSHIP VIEW

Partly moved by dissatisfaction with the instrumental view, some liberal egalitarians have defended a relationship view of the family. The relationship view rejects both the distinctive claims of the instrumental view—i.e., that the justification of the parent-child relationship lies solely in the fact that it best serves children's interests; and that the relationship serves these interests instrumentally. In their place, the relationship views holds that the parents' interest in the parent-child relationship also has significance in the justification of the family; and that the relationship's contribution to parents' (on some versions of the view, as well as to children's) well-being is not merely instrumental: instead, the parent-child relationship is also a constitutively valuable component of parents' (and children's) well-being.

Two main defenses of the relationship view formulated in the context of a liberal egalitarian framework are Colin Macleod's and the account developed by Harry Brighouse and Adam Swift.[6] These views mostly focus on elaborating the second claim above and thereby, indirectly, provide support for the first. According to Macleod, the family is valuable in that it protects a number of valuable interests of its members.[7] The close parent-child

---

[6] Brighouse and Swift 2006, 2009, 2014. The dual interest view defended by Austin (2007) presents several similarities to Brighouse and Swift's account. See also Jeske (1998) for the importance of intimacy in justifying duties of partiality in the context of relationships.

[7] Macleod's attention, unlike Brighouse and Swift's, is not exclusively focused on the relationship between parents and small children—he also considers the value of the family for grown up children, for other family members, and for cultural groups. I leave these points aside here.

relationship provides the context in which children's developmental needs are met, their basic welfare is attended to, and their specific needs properly identified (Macleod 2002). These ways in which the family is valuable, it seems, identify its instrumental benefits. But the family is also non-instrumentally valuable for both parents and children in various ways: it provides them with the goods of familial intimacy (the closeness of intrinsically valuable loving relationships, in which members participate in shared activities), cherishment (the opportunity for establishing and enjoying deep emotional attachments), and expressive self-extension (the opportunity to pass on one's ideals to one's children) (Macleod 2010; see also 2002). Insofar as the family secures these fundamental goods for adults and children, liberal egalitarians have reasons to promote and protect it.

On Brighouse and Swift's view, the parent-child relationship is both instrumentally vital for the promotion of children's healthy development, and non-instrumentally valuable for adults insofar as it allows them to enjoy a particular objectively valuable good: the good of intimacy in the context of a fiduciary relationship with a child. Moreover, on this account, the instrumental and non-instrumental value of the family are closely related: the non-instrumental value of the relationship to the parent depends upon that relationship's delivering its instrumental value to the child. What is valuable for the caring adult is to be in a relationship in which she takes care of and cares for a child—a relationship which, by dint of certain characteristic features, has distinctive value, so that it is, for many people, an irreplaceable, as well as very important, source of well-being. Parents have great power to influence the child's present and future well-being, and a responsibility to exercise this power in the child's interest. By discharging their responsibilities, parents enjoy a particular type of intimate relationship with their children, one in which the children entrust and reveal themselves to their parents, with spontaneity and unconditional love, and parents, in turn, also share themselves, but also modulate display of their own love for their children so as to help them become increasingly independent. The fact that the parent-child relationship is non-instrumentally valuable for the parent, as well as instrumentally valuable for children, grounds a case for respecting and sustaining that relationship, and for helping to protect an opportunity to enjoy it for everyone.

Like the instrumental view, the relationship view can invoke the family's value for children in its response to the challenge from authority. As Brighouse and Swift emphasize, "the rights that parents have over the children they parent are...entirely a function of the interests that children have in being parented by adults with those rights" (Brighouse and Swift 2014: 74). Nonetheless, unlike the instrumental view, the interests of parents play a role here too: the relationship view holds that, provided parents are good enough, their interests in having an intimate relationship is weighty enough to count against their children's potential interests in having a better parent. It is worth noting that the fact that the account has this implication–the fact that it justifies the rights of parents who may be not be optimally good parents—does not mean that it is incapable of meeting the challenge of authority: defenders of the relationship view could point out that the view is best understood as an appeal to each single person's interests *while a child* and to his interests *while an adult.* Any potential trade-offs between parents' interest in being able to parent and children's interests' in having better parents is then an intra-personal trade-off,[8] and one where some sacrifice in one's interests as a child is justified for the sake of securing for oneself the opportunity to establish this very important relationship as an adult.

As for the challenge of partiality, the relationship view has some resources to defuse it, in that it holds that only some equality-disrupting partiality is justified, namely, that which is integral to these valuable relationships. Reading bedtime stories for one's children is Brighouse and Swift's central case of legitimate parental partiality: here is a case of partiality that is inequality-engendering but which clearly helps realize the intimacy that is distinctive of the familiar relationship goods parents (as well as children) have an interest in enjoying. By contrast, much partiality that is standardly exercised is not necessary for realizing the valuable relationships, and stands condemned by the relationship view. For example, it is not necessary, for the realization of the value of the parent-like-relationship, that the parent bestow a large inheritance on his child; nor is it necessary that the parent engage in an inequality-engendering form of intimacy-forming activity (taking worldwide sailing trips together).

The relationship view, then, can help defuse the distributive worries that liberal egalitarians have about partiality, while at the same time providing a more robust defense of the parent-child relation than the instrumental model. Nonetheless, I think the relationship view still fails to capture the whole truth about the distinctiveness and moral credentials of the parent-child relationship, and to provide a sufficiently robust defense of it. Two points, in particular, are worth noting.

Consider, first, what obligations of parents the relationship view can account for. It does account for the moral obligations parents have to act as their children's fiduciaries, *once* they have embarked on that relationship with their children. But parents do not, on this view, *have to enter* such relationships with their children. This fact is morally significant. It is one thing to say that, although *I* do not owe *you* good X (the good of being in a

---

[8] For this way of thinking of the conflicting claims of parents and children, see Clayton 2006.

Serena Olsaretti

relationship with you, which includes the good of discharging certain duties I would undertake if I entered the relationship), if I choose to provide that good for you I incur certain obligations; and another to argue that I owe you that good in the first place. The relationship view can accommodate only the first claim; yet, as I argue below, the second too seems to be true in the case of parents and children.

Secondly, and relatedly, the relationship view is silent on the question of who should parent (i.e., enter the parent-child relationship with) which child. It accounts for those obligations and prerogatives that parents acquire vis-à-vis their children once they have started parenting them, or *once* the parent-child relationship is established. It does not, however, provide any justification of why parents have a right to establish a relationship with their children before they have had an opportunity to establish it, and where no such relationship has been established.[9] What's more, the relationship view could, in fact, be deployed *in favor* of distributing children (before a relationship has been established) of parents who already have one child, to other adults who would be "willing, and adequately good, parents."[10] This is the sense in which I think the relationship view does not provide a fully robust defense of the parent-child relationship. In the next section, I sketch a view of the status of the parent-child relationship that aims to remedy these problems, but first I should consider two main replies that might be made on behalf of the relationship view.

First, defenders of the relationship view can try and argue that the relationship view does in fact have the resources to ground a duty, on the part of parents, to establish relationships. They can point to the fact that (prospective) parents have a *general* duty to ensure that children have what they need, and if what children need are relationships, then prospective parents have a duty to enter those relationships. Brighouse and Swift, like Goodin and Vallentyne, explicitly endorse this claim, holding that children have "a right to a parent" and that "adults have a duty to parent children" (Brighouse and Swift 2014: 82). In my view, this reply is unsatisfactory: that general duty

---

[9] Kolodny raises a similar criticism of Diane Jeske's friendship view of parental partiality. See Kolodny 2010: 58. I think a similar criticism can be raised against the relationship view, a version of which he too endorses.

[10] Brighouse and Swift say that because of the importance of adults' interests in having children, their view could answer affirmatively the question: "Would there be anything wrong with a system that distributed children to adults in the way that maximized the realization of chlidren's interests, even if it left out some adults who would be willing, and adequately good, parents?" (Brighouse and Swift 2014: 86). But, I am suggesting, they could not answer affirmatively the question of whether there is anything wrong with a system that distributed children to childless adults who would be willing and adequately good parents, by taking them from equally willing and adequately good parents who have brought those children into existence and already have one child.

to parent children is, as they go on to say, "best understood as the duty to play one's part in ensuring that children who need parents get them" (83), and parents (those who are morally responsible for a child's existence) do not have this duty *any more than* anyone else does. As I said earlier with regard to the instrumental view, this picture does not capture our convictions about the nature of the reasons that parents have. The reasons parents are obliged to enter a relationship with a child is not (or not solely) that by so doing they are doing their bit in a scheme that ensures that all children's rights are met. Moreover, the reply at hand would still not ground the claim that parents have the duty to enter a relationship *with any child in particular*.

Defenders of the relationship view can offer another reply which attempts to show that the relationship view has the resources to justify the assignment of some children to some parents, in particular: they can argue that an intimate parent-baby relationship can and typically does form during gestation, and that this can ground birth parents' rights to continue that relationship after the child's birth (Gheaus 2012). This argument, however, justifies only a right, and not an obligation, to establish a (post-birth) parent-child relationship, and does even that only conditionally upon an intimate bond's having been formed during gestation. Even this extended version of the relationship view, then, in my view fails to capture some important aspects of the moral nature of the parent-child relationship, which I elaborate upon in the next section.[11]

A second main reply that defenders of the relationship view can make is that the relationship view is merely incomplete. It provides an answer to the question of whether there should be parent-child relationships, and leaves open the question of who should parent which child. In response, I acknowledge that the relationship view is indeed incomplete and so the view I sketch in the next section could, in principle, be endorsed alongside a version of the relationship view. However, it is important, in my view, to note that the incompleteness of the relationship view of the parent-child relationship is not innocuous. Instead, as I anticipated in section 1, I believe that a justification of the parent-child relationship must tackle both questions mentioned

---

[11] The gestation view also faces another main objection, in my view, as an argument aimed at establishing the right to raise one's biological child that protects birth parents against reallocation of babies. This is because the argument seems able to show only that adults who have children *with the expectation of raising them* acquire the rights to raise them, since it is certainly true of these adults that they incur costs which they see as offset by the prospect of raising that child, and that they form a bond during gestation with the child they foresee being able to raise. However, if and once a system of reallocation of children is in place, presumably adults who would choose to gestate babies would be different, and form different expectations, from those who choose to gestate children with a view to raising the children they gestate.

above, and tackle them together. We need an account of both what may and should be done to and for children, and who may and should do certain things to and for children and for which ones in particular.

Defenders of the relationship view, like defenders of the instrumental view, assume that the first question is normatively prior to, can be answered independently from, and indeed sets the parameters for answering, the second.[12] But this assumption, which no one ever argues for, seems to me to be unwarranted. Our answer to *either* of these two questions can be affected by our answer to the other. Sure enough, what may and should be done to and for children can affect the answer we give to the question of who is eligible to be a parent, and in virtue of what, and for which child. But our views about who should parent which child, and why, can in turn affect our views about what the parent-child relationship may and should deliver for both adults and children. By way of illustration, consider how our views about what friends may and should do for one another would be affected if it were the case that most or all people who enter friendships are responsible for causing their prospective friends' need for a friendship. If such a fact were true, we would not think that we can settle the question of what friends owe to one another prior to, and independently from, considerations about who should be friends with whom.

4. PARENTS' OBLIGATIONS TO ENTER A PARENT-CHILD RELATIONSHIP

The two concerns about the relationship view I have just raised, I now suggest, reflect a tendency to overlook an important way in which the parent-child relationship differs from other relationships that, alongside this one, are often thought to be the site of prerogatives and/or special obligations. Unlike those other relationships (such as friendship, or the relationship between loving companions, or that between compatriots), the parent-child relationship is one that some individuals—the children's parents—have a special obligation to enter. In turn, neglect of this aspect of the parent-child relationship reflects a general tendency on the part of philosophers, rightly identified and criticized by Margaret Little, to adopt too narrow a view of the ethics of relationships. As she remarks: "In ethics, if we notice relationships at all, we tend to focus only on questions about what morally flows

---

[12] Brighouse and Swift, for example, say that their focus is on whether "there should be parents at all" and note: "It is, on our account, a separate and further question *which* adults should parent *which* children" (Brighouse and Swift 2014: 49, emphasis in the original).

from or governs relationships once they have been entered.... But there is another layer to the ethics of relationships: considerations surrounding whether one *ought* to enter—or be open to entering—a relationship, and again, whether it is permissible to exit it" (Little 1999: 307).

My central claim in this section is the following: parents—those who are morally responsible for causing someone's existence—in standard cases have a right to raise their children, grounded in an obligation to the person(s) whose existence they are morally responsible for to establish a parent-child relationship with them. Whereas the relationship view focuses on the obligations that are generated by the parent-child relationship, the duty I am drawing attention to is a duty to generate that relationship. In what follows I unfold this claim in three steps, by first explaining in what sense children need relationships, then motivating the idea that parents have an obligation to enter a relationship with their children, and finally, by clarifying the idea of what makes someone responsible for a child's existence in the relevant sense.

Before turning to that, I should clarify at the outset that my claim is that parents have this obligation *to their children*; a natural alternative candidate claim is that they have this obligation *to third parties*.[13] We might think that, unless parents provide for their children, they are imposing negative externalities on non-consenting others (both society at large for having to incur many of the costs of raising and maintaining these children, and perhaps also for those individuals who would take it upon themselves to step in and discharge the parenting role). We might think, furthermore, that, if and since parents are responsible for doing so, this would be unfair to third parties. I do not think it is true in general that if, by having and rearing children, parents create costs for others, this is necessarily unfair for these others. But what I say in what follows is compatible with either accepting or denying that parents have an obligation to a class of specified non-consenting third parties (their other family members, their fellow citizens) to provide due care to their children themselves. Let me now turn to the claims I do want to defend.

To be morally responsible for a child's existence is not only to create a vulnerable creature: it is also to create a vulnerability of a particular kind,

---

[13] John Stuart Mill, for example, thought that "to bring a child into existence without a fair prospect of being able, not only to provide food for its body, but instruction and training for its mind, is a moral crime, both against the unfortunate offspring *and against society*; and that if the parent does not fulfil this obligation, the State ought to see it fulfilled, at the charge, as far as possible, of the parent" (Mill 1978: 104; emphasis mine). For the claim that, provided that there are willing adoptive parents, those who bring children into the world but are unwilling to rear them themselves do not act impermissibly, see Archard 2010b.

due to the fact that virtually all of an infant's needs, and many of a young child's ones, both immediate and developmental, have a strong relational component. By saying that needs have a strong relational component, I mean that the adequate (and certainly the maximal) satisfaction of these needs requires that they be met in the context of a relationship, and more specifically, of an ongoing, stable relationship with one or few caring adult persons (see, for example, Gerhardt 2004). Given what we know, in order to fare well as children, and in order to become well-functioning adults who have a full opportunity to flourish, children need to be in a parent-child-like relationship: their care needs to be dispensed for them in the context of a close bond with loving adults.

So, to say that a new child has needs that must be satisfied for her to fare well, and that she is herself incapable of satisfying, as the instrumental view says, is an assertion that, while not false, under-describes the situation of a child in ways that are morally significant. To see this, consider the case of an adult person who is unable to walk or to dress herself: she has some important basic needs (to move about; to change her clothes) that she is unable to meet herself. In order to have them met, she may need another person or persons to step in to help. But these needs are not relational: they can be adequately, even maximally, satisfied by having a person or various persons one is not in a relationship with step in to discharge the specific tasks. This needy adult may be better served, in fact, by having a dependable wheelchair and, if such a device could be invented, one that changed her clothes. The neediness of children is importantly different from the neediness of adults.[14]

My second claim is that not all adults, not even all adults who would be willing and competent to enter a relationship with a child, stand equally placed, morally speaking, vis-à-vis the child's relational needs. This is not only or even primarily because, by bearing moral responsibility for the child's being needy of a relationship, they now owe it to the child to ensure that the child's need for a relationship is met so as to avoid being the cause of harm to the child, as a tort model of parental obligations would hold (more about that later). Rather, by dint of being morally responsible for a child's existence, the parents now stand in a position such that *their* entering a relationship with the child, or not entering it, expresses something different from what other adults' entering or not entering that relationship expresses.

---

[14] Is it just that they are not yet autonomous and their dependency is not an affront to their status? This is certainly part of it. But it also seems important that the child is being *trained* to become an adult and a moral agent, and that we can only develop these skills and competencies in the context of relationships.

So, even saying that the child's need is *for a relationship*, as the relationship view fully acknowledges, seems to importantly under-describe the situation in ways that are morally significant. To illustrate: if my friend is in hospital and, knowing she would be cheered up by a friend's visit, I proceed to call up another friend of hers and arrange for him to visit my hospitalized friend, although I lack a good reason for not going to hospital myself, *my* setting up this arrangement expresses something different than would be expressed by a nice nurse who performed the same action, even though we are both responding to the hospitalized friend's need for a friend's visit.[15] What an action expresses can change in line with the nature of the relationship in the context of which it takes place, as the example just mentioned illustrates. But it can also change in line with the role that the person who performs the action played in creating the need for that action: a hospital visit from the stranger who is responsible for the accident that led to my friend's hospitalization is importantly different from that of another stranger who just witnessed the accident's taking place. Similarly, I am suggesting, if someone knowingly and voluntarily causes someone to be needy of a relationship, her refusal to be a party to it can be plausibly viewed as a rejection of the needy person. Their responding to that person's relational neediness by entering the relationship themselves, or by ensuring that someone else enters the relationship, are not two morally equivalent ways of discharging the same obligation. Since for most children there are parents who are morally responsible for having brought them into existence, the parent-child relationship under conditions we are familiar with is different from other relationships, including valuable relationships in the context of which special obligations are often said to arise, such as friendship. We do not standardly have any obligation to a particular person to become their friend, even if that person is needy of a friendship, though there may well be general duties to help provide everyone with the opportunity to have valuable relationships.

So far I have talked about parents as those who are morally responsible for a child's existence, without specifying what conditions are necessary and sufficient for moral responsibility. It is important to say something about these conditions, because in my view their being what I think they are plays a role in support of the claim that parents' entering, or failing to enter, into a relationship with their children carries a special meaning. Like with ascriptions of responsibility for other actions, causal responsibility for someone's existence is a necessary but not sufficient condition for being morally responsible for it. Besides causal responsibility, it is also necessary that the

---

[15] On the expressive meaning of actions, see Sunstein 1995/6; Anderson and Pildes 1999/2000. See also Khaitan 2012.

parent *voluntarily* brings that child into existence, where voluntarily bringing into existence means that the parent knowingly brings that child into existence, and does not choose to bring the child into existence only or primarily because she has no alternative to it, or only because the alternative is unacceptable, prudentially or morally. This, in turn, means that standardly, the conditions for being morally responsible for a child's existence are that the child's existence was avoidable, i.e., it would have been possible, prudentially acceptable, and morally permissible for the parent not to bring the child into existence.[16]

Together, these conditions can be sufficient. I say that they *can* be sufficient to allow for the fact that when someone voluntarily and avoidably brings into existence a child *on someone else's behalf*, moral responsibility for that child's existence lies with the latter person. This point is important, because it shows that my view does not imply that gamete donation and surrogacy are morally impermissible: as far as moral responsibility for existence is concerned, and insofar as there are commissioning parents who are morally responsible for the existence of the children who are genetically derived from donated gametes and gestated by surrogate mothers, gamete donors and surrogates are in a position that is quite like that of an IVF doctor whose intervention is causally decisive both in starting a pregnancy and in carrying it to term. By contrast, their position is importantly unlike that of a parent who, though morally responsible for a child's existence, decides to give up his child up for adoption. The claim that gamete donors and surrogate mothers, like IVF doctors, can be seen to be acting on the commissioning parents' behalf implies that, instead of thinking of gamete donors as transferring parental responsibilities, as is often done (e.g., Benatar 1999; Bayne 2003), they should be thought of as not acquiring those responsibilities at all in the first place. This is compatible with thinking that they do have *some* responsibilities. However, in the absence of a warranted and justified intention to enable other individuals to bring a child into existence, those who voluntarily cause that child's existence are morally responsible for it, and have an obligation to enter a parent-child relation with her. (Similarly, voluntarily signing a contract binds the person who signs it, *unless* she is signing on behalf of a party who has so authorized her.)

---

[16] I say "standardly" because, on my view, what matters for voluntariness as a condition for substantive responsibility are the motivating reasons why someone chooses as she does, and it is possible that lack of an acceptable alternative does not motivate someone to choose as she does (e.g., someone could choose voluntarily to have a baby even if, if she did not have one, she would face real danger, provided that her reasons for having a baby are not only or primarily that she wants to escape danger). See Olsaretti (2016) for further elaboration and defense of this account of voluntariness.

The fact that moral responsibility for someone's existence requires more than causal responsibility helps lend some plausibility to my claim that that moral responsibility grounds an obligation to parent. This is so for two reasons. First, intuitively, mere causal responsibility on its own seems too weak to ground an obligation of the kind I am defending here, although it may ground *other* obligations (see Brake 2010. I return to this point below). If someone causes a child to exist, but was forced to do so, holding her to the obligation to raise that child, rather than to the obligation of ensuring that that child is parented by someone else, may strike us as too demanding on the procreator. This objection does not bite, however, if the procreator voluntarily brought the child into existence. Second, the fact that moral responsibility for existence requires these further conditions helps account for why parents have the obligation I ascribe to them. The fact that parents are those who voluntarily bring someone into existence—the fact, in other words, that the child's existence was up to the parents' choice in an important sense—is what makes it the case that not entering a relationship with this child would be disrespectful.

At the start of this section, I suggested that those who are morally responsible for causing someone's existence in standard cases have a right to raise their children, grounded in the obligation they owe their children. I should now unpack what I mean by "standard cases." These are the range of cases where parents are able and willing to discharge that obligation to their children sufficiently well. My claim is not that the fact of parents' obligations to enter into a relationship with their children invariably grounds a right to enter into those relationships. Whether or not it does depends on whether parents are able and willing to fulfill that obligation, that is, whether they are able and disposed to establish and maintain a caring parent-child relationship with their child, which involves meeting the child's needs in the context of that relationship.[17] If the parent is either unable or

[17] In the case in which parents voluntarily bring a child into existence with no intention to care for the child, or in which they come to lack that intention once the child exists, they are clearly in violation of the obligation and acquire no right to care for the child. But what about cases where they are unable to enter that relationship? There are relevantly different cases here, depending on whether the parents' inability preceded their choosing to create a child, whether they are responsible for it, whether or not it is remediable, and on the role that the fact of the inability plays in the parents' deliberations. Consider the case of a parent who, after conceiving a child, is struck by unforeseen misfortune which she cannot remedy, and, although she would like to raise the child herself and would be willing to take measures to remedy this if any were available, is aware that her child will suffer if she keeps him and gives him up for adoption. This parent is arguably not in violation of the obligation, as nothing in her decisions and actions evinces an attitude of disrespect for the child's value. By contrast, someone who, aware that he will not be able to care for a child, nonetheless proceeds to have one, and/or whose inability to enter that relationship is remediable but who does not take action to remedy it, does

unwilling to meet her obligation, he has of course no right to be allowed to discharge it, though the fact that he has an obligation which remains unfulfilled is important: it remains true, of this parent, that he is wronging his child.

By way of conclusion, it will be helpful to clarify how my view differs from some main alternative views of parenthood, or views of what grounds parental rights and/or obligations to which it bears some resemblance and which I have mentioned in passing: these are, first, the view that being responsible for existence amounts to imposing an unchosen risk of harm which merits compensation; second, the intentional or voluntarist account of parenthood; and third, the view that genetic ties matter.

Consider, first, the causal view that those who are causally responsible for someone's existence have duties, to that person, to eliminate or reduce the risk of harm to her that they have unilaterally imposed on her by bringing her into existence. This view, which in its most explicit statement is defended by Nelson (1991), makes two claims: that bringing into existence harms, or imposes risk of harm, on the person who comes into existence; and that those who bring into existence in the relevant sense (that is, those who are morally responsible for existence) are those who are causally responsible for it.[18] A forceful defense of the first claim is offered by Seana Shiffrin (1999), according to whom procreators engage in a "morally equivocal" activity, because no procreator can ever ensure that his child's life will not be marked by substantial suffering, and because even the most successful lives involve some such suffering. Since to procreate is to impose a risk of harm on someone, without their consent, where doing so is not necessary to save them from greater harm, and harming of this kind is wrong, procreators owe their children compensation as a result. The second claim, that those who bear causal responsibility for existence count as a child's procreator in the relevant sense (i.e., in the sense that that child's existence is justifiably attributable to them in a way that justifies considering them under the

seem to be in violation of the obligation to the child. A harder case may seem that of a parent who brings a child into the world with the intention of raising him, is capable of providing him with a decent start in life, but then decides that she should, for her child's best interests, surrender him to another family with whom, she is certain, her child will fare better. About cases like this one I would say that the parent has indeed violated an obligation she has to the child (the child would, if or when he becomes aware of this fact, still have reason to feel he was rejected), although she may be excusable if she acts in good faith. That she had an obligation (which she violated) is confirmed by the fact that we think she should make reasonable efforts to improve her own ability as a parent. We can say here some of the same things we would say about parents giving up their children once they have started caring for them, and of friends giving each other up for the sake of the friend's interest in finding a better friend.

[18] I here refer to the causal view as the conjunct of both these claims; only Nelson explicitly defends both of them, while several other people, including those I mention in what follows, defend only one of them.

obligations that procreators have), is defended, among others, by O'Neill (1979), Archard (2010b), and Porter (2012; 2014).

My view differs from the causal view just sketched in three key respects. First, on my view, as I said earlier, causal responsibility is not enough for moral responsibility for existence. Second, my view does not affirm (or deny) that parents impose risks of harm or harm on their children by bringing them into existence. Finally, while the causal view can account for the special obligations parents have towards their children, it is not clear that it can account for why parents have to discharge those obligations by caring for their children themselves.[19] Indeed, it seems that the duty to compensate a child for harming him by bringing him into existence generates a derivative duty to place that child in circumstances that minimize the risk of harms that she will be exposed to, which could mean that parents should give up their children at birth.

My view also differs from the voluntarist conception of parenthood, the accounts of parenthood on which a necessary and/or sufficient condition for acquiring the rights and obligations of parenthood is the voluntary acceptance of the parental role (O'Neill 1979; Brake 2010). Moral responsibility for existence is different from, and neither necessary nor sufficient for, the voluntary acceptance of the parental role. Moral responsibility, on my view, is enough to ground the obligation to enter the parent-child relationship, and indeed is what gives some prospective custodial parents—those who were responsible for a child's existence—reason to take up the parental role. By saying that moral responsibility for existence is sufficient to ground an obligation to enter the parent-child relationship I do not mean to deny that intentionally choosing to parent, if one is capable of doing so and if a child is "available" to be parented, can also be sufficient to ground parental rights and responsibilities. Adoptive parents meet these conditions, and a version of the intentional account, on which acceptance of the parenting role is sufficient for undertaking parental obligations, is compatible with my view. Note, moreover, that nothing I have said suggests that adoptive parenthood is in any way less valuable than non-adoptive parenthood. My claim is only that non-adoptive parents—who may include the parents who have "commissioned" a child through surrogacy—have a further responsibility

---

[19] Thanks to Andrew Williams for drawing this point to my attention with regard to Shiffrin's view. O'Neill and Archard say explicitly that they think that those who are causally responsible for existence only owe it to their children to ensure that *someone* discharges the parenting role vis-à-vis them. Porter's view, to which mine comes closest, does affirm that "makers" (on her view, those who are causally responsible for existence) have an obligation to enter a relationship with their children, but does not offer an argument as to why they have that obligation, rather than merely an obligation to ensure that their children are well cared for.

when compared with adoptive parents: they are morally responsible for the child's existence, in a way in which standardly adoptive parents are not, and they have, for the reasons I sketched earlier, an obligation to enter into a parent-child relationship with the particular child for whose existence they are morally responsible.

My view also differs, finally, from genetic accounts of what grounds parental rights and obligations (see Velleman 2005, 2008; for discussion of Velleman's view, see Haslanger 2009 and Kolodny 2010; for discussion of the biological account more generally, see Austin 2004). Genetic connectedness is neither a necessary nor a sufficient condition of being morally responsible for someone's existence. A couple who decide to have a child thanks to donated gametes and a surrogate mother, for example, are responsible for that child's existence, even though they have no genetic or gestational connection to the child. In this same case, the child's genetic and gestational parents are not those morally responsible for that child's existence. Note that to say that genetic connectedness is neither a necessary nor a sufficient condition for being morally responsible for a child's existence, and hence, for the obligation to enter a relationship with that child, is not to say that it lacks all normative significance. For example, it seems plausible to think that it is a sufficient condition for *some* obligations, such as the obligation to provide the child (and his guardians) with relevant information about his biological family history.

I cannot here engage with the merits of the genetic view, but would like to conclude with a tentative suggestion. Although genetic connectedness and moral responsibility for existence are different and can pull apart, the former has, until recently, been a practically necessary condition for the latter, and it is still the case that, typically, genetic parents are also those who are morally responsible for a child's existence. I think it is a virtue of the view of parental responsibility I have sketched that it can explain the intuitions we have in many cases in which genetic connectedness is at work, without appealing to the moral relevance of genetic ties, and where what does the requisite work in grounding someone's obligation to enter a parent-relationship is the fact that he voluntarily chose to bring that person into existence.

Acknowledgments

Previous versions of this paper were presented at the Conference on "Family Ethics: Partiality Revisited" in Bern in January 2014, at the Oxford Studies in Political Philosophy in Missouri in September 2014, and at the graduate conference in Legal and Political Philosophy at the Universitat Pompeu Fabra in September 2015. I am grateful to all members of the audiences, and Richard Arneson, Paul Bou-Habib,

Anca Gheaus, Colin Macleod, and Nina Scherrer for their comments. This project has received funding from the European Research Council (ERC) under the European Union's Horizon 2020 Research and Innovation Programme (Grant Agreement Number: 648610).

References

Anderson, E., and Pildes, R. 1999/2000. Expressive Theories of Law: A General Statement. *University of Pennsylvania Law Review* 148: 1503–75.

Archard, D. 2010a. *The Family: A Liberal Defence*. Basingstoke and New York: Palgrave McMillan.

Archard, D. 2010b. The Obligations and Responsibilities of Parenthood. In D. Archard and D. Benatar (eds.) *Parenthood and Procreation*. Oxford: Oxford University Press.

Austin, M. 2004. The Failure of Biological Accounts of Parenthood. *Journal of Value Enquiry* 38: 499–510.

Austin, M. 2007. Fundamental Interests and Parental Rights. *International Philosophical Quarterly* 47, 2: 221–36.

Bayne, T. 2003. Gamete Donation and Parental Responsibility. *Journal of Applied Philosophy* 20, 1: 77–87.

Benatar, D. 1999. The Unbearable Lightness of Bringing into Being. *Journal of Applied Philosophy* 16, 2: 173–80.

Brake, E. 2010. Willing Parents: A Voluntarist Account of Parental Role Obligations. In D. Archard and D. Benatar (eds.) *Parenthood and Procreation*. Oxford: Oxford University Press.

Brake, E. 2015. Creation Theory: Do Genetic Ties Matter? In S. Hannan, S. Brennan, and R. Vernon (eds.) *Permissible Progeny*. Oxford: Oxford University Press.

Brennan, S., and Noggle, R. 1997. The Moral Status of Children: Children's Rights, Parents' Rights, and Family Justice. *Social Theory & Practice* 23, 1: 1–26.

Brighouse, H., and Swift, A. 2006. Parents' Rights and the Value of the Family. *Ethics* 117, 1: 80–108.

Brighouse, H., and Swift, A. 2009. Legitimate Parental Partiality. *Philosophy & Public Affairs* 37, 1: 43–80.

Brighouse, H., and Swift, A. 2014. *Family Values: The Ethics of Parent-Child Relationships*. Princeton and Oxford: Princeton University Press.

Clayton, M. 2006. *Justice and Legitimacy in Upbringing*. Oxford: Oxford University Press.

Clayton, M. 2012. Equal Inheritance: An Anti-Perfectionist View. In G. Erreygers and J. Cunliffe (eds.) *Inherited Wealth, Justice and Equality*. London: Routledge.

Feinberg, J. 1994. The Child's Right to an Open Future. In J. Feinberg, *Freedom and Fulfillment*. Princeton: Princeton University Press.

Fishkin, J. 1983. *Justice, Equal Opportunity, and the Family*. New Haven: Yale University Press.

Gerhardt, S. 2004. *Why Love Matters: How Affection Shapes a Baby's Brain*. New York: Brunner-Routledge.

Gheaus, A. 2012. The Right to Parent One's Biological Baby. *The Journal of Political Philosophy* 20, 4: 432–55.

Gheaus, A. forthcoming. What Abolishing the Family Would Not Do. *Critical Review of International Political and Social Philosophy.*

Goodin, R. 2005. Responsibilities for Children's Well-Being. In M. Prior and S. Richardson (eds.) *No Time to Lose: The Wellbeing of Australia's Children.* Melbourne: Melbourne University Press.

Haslanger, S. 2009. Family, Ancestry and Self: What Is the Moral Significance of Biological Ties? *Adoption and Culture* 2, 1.

Khaitan, T. 2012. Dignity as an Expressive Norm. *Oxford Journal of Legal Studies* 32, 1: 1–19.

Kolodny, N. 2010. Which Relationships Justify Partiality? The Case of Parents and Children. *Philosophy and Public Affairs* 38, 1: 37–75.

Jeske, D. 1998. Families, Friends and Special Obligations. *Canadian Journal of Philosophy* 28, 1: 527–55.

Little, M. 1999. Abortion, Intimacy, and the Duty to Gestate. *Ethical Theory and Moral Practice* 2, 3: 295–312.

Macleod, C. 2002. Liberal Equality and the Affective Family. In D. Archard and C. Macleod (eds.) *The Moral and Political Status of Children.* Oxford: Oxford University Press.

Macleod, C. 2010. Parental Responsibilities in an Unjust World. In D. Archard and D. Benatar (eds.) *Parenthood and Procreation.* Oxford: Oxford University Press.

Macleod, C. 2015. Parental Competency and the Right to Parent. In S. Hannan, S. Brennan, and R. Vernon (eds.) *Permissible Progeny.* Oxford: Oxford University Press.

Macleod, C. forthcoming. Equality and Family Values: Conflict or Harmony? *Critical Review of International Political and Social Philosophy.*

Mill, J. S. 1978. *On Liberty.* Indianopolis: Hackett Publishing Company, Inc.

Nelson, J. L. 1991. Parental Obligations and the Ethics of Surrogacy: A Causal Perspective. *Public Affairs Quarterly* 5, 1: 49–61.

Nozick, R. 1974. *Anarchy, State and Utopia.* Oxford: Blackwell.

Olsaretti, S. 2016. Voluntariness, Coercion, Self-Ownership. In D. Schmidtz (ed.) *The Oxford Handbook of Freedom.* Oxford: Oxford University Press.

O'Neill, O. 1979. Begetting, Bearing, and Rearing. In O. O'Neill and W. Ruddick (eds.) *Having Children: Philosophical and Legal Reflections on Parenthood.* New York: Oxford University Press.

Porter, L. 2012. Adoption Is Not Abortion-Lite. *Journal of Applied Philosophy* 29, 1: 63–78.

Porter, L. 2014. Why and How to Prefer a Causal Account of Parenthood. *Journal of Social Philosophy* 45, 2: 182–202.

Rawls, J. 1971. *A Theory of Justice.* Oxford: Oxford University Press.

Scheffler, S. 2001. *Boundaries and Allegiances: Problems of Justice and Responsibility in Liberal Thought.* Oxford: Oxford University Press.

Shiffrin, S. 1999. Wrongful Life, Procreative Responsibility, and the Significance of Harm. *Legal Theory* 5: 117–48.

Sunstein, C. 1995/6. On the Expressive Function of Law. *University of Pennsylvania Law Review* 144: 2021–53.

Vallentyne, P. 2003. Rights and Duties of Childbearing. *William and Mary Bill of Rights Journal* 11, 3: 991–1009.

Velleman, D. 2005. Family History. *Philosophical Papers* 34: 357–78.

Velleman, D. 2008. Persons in Prospect. *Philosophy and Public Affairs* 36: 245–66.

4

Doing Justice to Desert

George Sher

Does justice require that goods be distributed in accordance with people's deserts? The claim that it does is appealing, but has been the target of many objections. My aims here are, first, to separate the good objections from the bad ones, and, second, to suggest a modified version of the claim which escapes even the good objections.

I

Desert and justice can both be understood in many ways. Thus, before I can ask how they are related, I must say something about what I mean by each.

Whatever else is true, any adequate account of desert is bound to imply that different people deserve different amounts of different things. Thus, any desert-based account of distributive justice is very likely to be inegalitarian. This means that building a commitment to equal distribution into our conception of justice will threaten to beg the question against a desert-based account. To avoid prejudging this issue, I will make no substantive assumptions about what justice requires. When I speak of the principles of justice, I will simply mean <u>whichever</u> principles ought to govern the distribution of goods within a just society.

By contrast, my account of desert will have a more definite shape. Following accepted usage, I will distinguish between the deserving party, the thing deserved, and the basis for the party's desert; and I will take the facts that are capable of grounding desert to consist exclusively of facts *about* the deserving party. In addition, to enforce a separation between desert and need, I will assume that these facts are always about what that person either has done or failed to do or is or is not capable of doing. Because my question is whether desert should play a role in determining which institutions are just, I will reject as irrelevant the Rawlsian idea that a person's deserts can be equated with whatever he can reasonably expect to acquire as a result of actions he has performed against a background of just institutions.[1]

Bearing these stipulations in mind, let us now consider some familiar objections to the claim that justice requires distribution in accordance with desert. I begin with three that I think can be quickly dismissed.

When philosophers deny that justice is a matter of people getting what they deserve, they often do so on the grounds that the conditions for desert are either incoherent or else incapable of satisfaction. These views generally take their inspiration from Rawls's famous claims that we have done nothing to deserve the talents upon which we draw whenever we act, and that even the efforts that a person puts forth can be traced to a character that "depends in large part upon fortunate family and social circumstances for which he can claim no credit."[2] From these claims, it is often inferred that we cannot deserve anything *for* our achievements or efforts—that the moral importance of what we do is somehow tainted by our failure to deserve the traits or abilities that make our actions possible. This inference has been disputed by many, myself included,[3] on the grounds that it rests on a premise—roughly, that we can only deserve something if we also deserve whatever grounds our desert—that is indefensibly strong. Both because I regard this premise as hopeless and because the problems with it are by now well known, I will not discuss it further here. Instead, I will confine myself to a perspective that is at least initially sympathetic to desert.

The second class of objections I want to set aside are those that appeal to the conceptual and/or normative complexities associated with desert. This line of objection can take a number of forms. In one version, it asserts that we cannot draw any concrete conclusions about how desert bears on justice until we settle the ongoing dispute about which aspects of people's actions ground their economic deserts. Should we say that a just society rewards people on the basis of their moral virtue? On the basis of their efforts?

---

[1] In my book *Desert* (Sher (1987)), I expressed my rejection of this view by saying that I took desert to be pre-institutional. However, as Samuel Scheffler (2001) has correctly pointed out, the important issue is not whether what people deserve can be understood in abstraction from the institutions under which they live, but rather whether their deserts presuppose the *justice* of those institutions. To capture this contrast, Scheffler suggests replacing "pre-institutional" with "pre-justicial."

[2] Rawls (1971), 104.

[3] See, for example, Nozick (1974), 213–27; Zaitchik (1977); and Sher (1987), ch. 2.

Of their achievements or contributions to society?[4] In another version, the problem is that even within the categories of effort and contribution, there are deep and perhaps insoluble questions about what determines a person's level or amount of the relevant quality.[5] In yet another form, the objection is that even if we can get fully clear about what different people deserve, we must acknowledge that a just society must also answer to such further values as equality, efficiency, and the satisfaction of basic needs. Because of this, we will not be able to specify the relation between desert and justice until we are able to weight the demands of desert against those of whichever other factors are also necessary for justice.[6]

Unlike the idea that we cannot deserve anything unless we also deserve whatever enables us to acquire it, these multiple unclarities in the bald claim that justice calls for distribution in accordance with desert are obviously worth taking seriously. However, instead of viewing those unclarities as objections to the desert-based approach, we can simply view them as defining the field of questions that any fully worked-out version of that approach must answer. They are, in this respect, no different from the ambiguities about value that a consequentialist must resolve in order to defend a worked-out version of the view that we are obligated to maximize it. As so understood, the unclarities are not barriers to further thought, but invitations to it. Moreover, precisely because there are so many possible ways of unpacking the connection between justice and desert, any objection that applies to only one of them—for example, that we cannot untangle the contributions of different individuals who cooperate or otherwise interact—will simply raise the stock of others.

The third objection that I want to set aside is the practical analogue of the one just mentioned. Here the issue is not that the desert-based approach is conceptually or normatively unclear, but that implementing it requires far more information and resources than any actual society can muster. If each person's deserts are grounded in specific facts about him, then giving each person what he deserves requires knowing whichever facts about each are relevant. This seems problematic because no society can be expected to monitor the shifting details of how much effort each of

---

[4] For an argument that common sense provides no way of adjudicating among these possibilities, see Sidgwick (1922), book 3, ch. 5, 282–90.

[5] For critical discussion of the idea that a person's desert depends on his contribution to society, see Hayek (2013), ch. 9. For discussion of the difficult of assessing virtue and vice, see Kant (1964), 74–5; for commentary, see Hill (1992), 176–95. For discussion of the difficulty of evaluating a person's degree of effort, see Wolff (2003), 219–32.

[6] For a defense of the view that desert is one factor among others that determine the justice of a society's arrangements, see Miller (1999).

its members has made, how much each has achieved or contributed, or how virtuous each one is.

Although Rawls did not have desert specifically in mind, he was in effect advancing a version of this objection when he wrote that

the great practical advantage of pure procedural justice is that it is no longer neces- sary in meeting the demands of justice to keep track of the endless variety of circum- stances and the changing relative positions of particular persons. One avoids the problem of defining principles to cope with the enormous complexities which would arise if such details were relevant. It is a mistake to focus attention on the varying relative positions of individuals and to require that every change, considered as a single transaction viewed in isolation, be in itself just.[7]

These remarks tell most forcefully against an entitlement theory like Nozick's, which implies that we cannot determine the legitimacy of any person's hold- ings without assessing the justice of each transaction in the multigenerational history that led to them.[8] However, even the informational demands of desert theories, which are restricted to the single generation to which the deserving parties belong, may be thought to be so extensive as to render those theories unworkable.

But is it really true that in order to avoid getting bogged down in end- less complications, we must analyze justice in terms that bear no relation to desert? Even if we follow Rawls in replacing the question of what each particular individual should have with the question of what sorts of insti- tutions should determine what different individuals have, can't we retain the connection between desert and justice by opting for institutions whose procedures are likely to yield outcomes which in turn are deserved? And, indeed, isn't this just what Rawls himself does when he allows the aim of punishing those who violate their natural duties to inform the design of our criminal justice system?[9] Because this strategy would pre- suppose an independent answer to the question of what different people should have, it would exemplify what Rawls calls imperfect rather than pure procedural justice. However, to object to the strategy on these grounds, we would need some reason to *reject* the independent desert- based answer on which it relies—a reason which, if we had it, would ren- der the current objection unnecessary.

---

[7] Rawls (1971), 87–8.

[8] As Nozick comes close to acknowledging, the likelihood that the sequence of events that led to any particular person's holdings is entirely untainted by injustice is approxi- mately zero; see Nozick (1974), 230–1. For discussion of what this implies about when we should compensate for the effects of past injustices, see Sher (1981), 3–17.

[9] Rawls (1971), 314–15.

II

Within the recent literature, most of the objections to building a theory of justice on an account of what people deserve can be assimilated to one or another of the patterns just mentioned. It seems to me, however, that there is another, deeper source of resistance—one that I have never quite seen expressed, but which I nevertheless think exerts a good deal of covert influence. Put simply and somewhat cryptically, the deeper objection is that appeals to desert simply do not mesh well with the basic question that theories of justice are designed to answer.

That question can be expressed in a variety of ways. In Rawls's famous formulation, it is the question of how to divide up the extra benefits that social cooperation makes possible.[10] Expressed in different (though not incompatible) terms, it is the question of which social arrangements are called for by the moral equality of the individuals who will have to live under them, and whose life prospects will be determined by their rules. Under both formulations (and, I think, under any other which is at all plausible), the individuals who fall within the scope of justice are held to do so simply in virtue of their status as distinct individuals with lives of their own to live. They are thus held to have this status for reasons that are independent of any of the specific actions, traits, attitudes, and histories that distinguish them from one another. A person's deserts, by contrast, are inevitably tied to some combination of his specific actions, traits, attitudes, and history; for in the absence of any such particulars, we would have no basis for saying that he deserves one thing rather than another. It is, I think, precisely this disjunction—precisely the mismatch between the shared abstract features that bring us under the umbrella of justice and the diverse and concrete features that form the basis of our deserts—that makes it implausible to take justice to be a matter of desert.

I want to emphasize that my point here is not merely that justice is forward-looking while desert is backward-looking. If that were the point, then my argument would have no force against the proposal that a set of social arrangements is just as long as everyone who lives under it will in the future get whatever he deserves for whatever actions he will at that time have performed in the past. My point, rather, is that even if we could thus integrate the relevant temporal perspectives, the specific facts about people that render them deserving of different things on different occasions would remain both distinct from and less morally fundamental than the general fact that each has a life of his own to live. That we all have futures, that we all have likes, dislikes, and plans, and that we all have points of view from which things

---

[10] Rawls (1971), 4.

matter to us: these are the sorts of facts that are standardly taken to establish that we ourselves matter, and thus to undergird whichever principles of justice govern the distribution of goods among us. Because these are facts that hold of the deserving and undeserving alike, there is no reason to expect whatever principles they undergird to make any reference to desert.

We can also arrive at this conclusion from another direction. Because what people deserve depends entirely on what they choose or do, their deserving these things cannot shed light on the justice or injustice of the circumstances under which their choices were made or their actions performed. We cannot invoke a person's desert-creating actions to find out whether the opportunities to perform such actions—opportunities to get an education, compete for desirable jobs, earn a good wage, and so on—are distributed justly within his society. There are of course cases in which a person's past actions have rendered him deserving of precisely the restricted or expansive set of opportunities that he now confronts, but even in these cases, the agent's deserts are not what determine the justice of the background against which he performed his earlier actions. To assess that background (and also to assess the claims of those who are handicapped or ill or otherwise incapable of performing desert-creating actions), we must base our account of justice on some more broadly applicable fact about persons; and that, of course, is just what we do when we invoke the fact that each has a life of his own to live.

Because this fact holds equally of everyone, any account of justice that rests on it will be egalitarian at the foundational level. Because of this, my current claim, that our views about justice must be grounded in facts of this sort, may not seem consistent with my earlier aim of not building a commitment to equality into my conception of justice. However, to block the charge of inconsistency, we need only note that a theory that is egalitarian at the foundational or justificatory level need not require the equal distribution of any substantive good. As Amartya Sen and Ronald Dworkin have both observed, the idea that each person's life is equally important, and that any adequate account of justice must take that fact as its point of departure, is compatible with a wide range of substantive distributive views.[11] Under one reading the fact leads to utilitarianism; under another, it yields the view of rights that informs Nozick's version of libertarianism; under yet others, it leads to Rawls's difference principle, to the principles of priority or sufficiency, or to some more straightforward version of distributive equality. Of all the familiar approaches to distributive justice, the only one that *cannot* be derived from this shared feature of persons (or, more cautiously, the one whose derivation would be the most difficult and would involve the greatest

---

[11] See Dworkin (1983), 24–40, and Sen (1992), ch. 1.

intellectual contortions) is the one that ties what each person should have to the specific actions that he has performed.[12]

III

But precisely because each person's life *is* equally important, any just society must allow each of its members to choose among a range of options that have significantly different projected outcomes. This is necessary because choosing among options in light of their consequences is just what living a life *is*. There is, moreover, a clear distinction between the ways in which opportunities to engage in various activities are distributed among a society's members and the consequences of engaging in each available activity. Taking my cue from this, I now want to consider the possibility that even if desert plays no role in structuring the distribution of options among persons, it may still enter by affecting the pay-offs that attach *to* the various options. Putting the same point differently, I want to consider the possibility of a layered approach under which desert plays no role in generating the fundamental distributive principles, yet does play a role in determining the rewards that attach to whichever activities the principles make available.

How, exactly, would such an approach work? How, in particular, might we introduce a system that matches rewards to deserts without thereby disrupting whichever patterns of distribution are justified by considerations independent of desert? Given the significant differences that divide the major theories of justice, I think this question has no single answer.

---

[12] It may be objected that the contrast I have been making is spurious because *every* distributive theory ties what a person should have to the specific actions he has performed. In Nozick's theory, this depends on the person's prior legitimate acts of acquisition and transfer, in Dworkin's it depends on how he has chosen to allocate his productive energies, and so on. However, in every case except that of desert, the distributive significance of the relevant acts is established by a general principle or set of principles which in turn is grounded in, or can be represented as an interpretation of, the moral equality of the parties. In the case of desert, by contrast, the linkage between the desert-basis and what is deserved is represented either as direct, as in "fittingness" accounts, or as mediated by principles which do not obviously draw their force from the parties' moral equality. So, for example, I argued in *Desert* (Sher (1987)) that desert-claims draw their normative force from a variety of sources that include the principle of veracity, the value that diligent efforts confer on their objects, and the superior moral worth of the virtuous. In his comments on this paper, Jeffrey Moriarty has suggested that the way to connect desert to the moral equality of persons is to stress the fact that "we are all agents capable of shaping our lives in different ways [and] we can become deserving of certain things (e.g. economic rewards) through this shaping." However, even if it's true both that our moral equality requires that we be free to make life-shaping choices and that life-shaping choices create desert, it does not follow that it is our moral equality that requires that we be rewarded *in accordance with* our deserts.

However, I also think that with the possible exception of utilitarianism, every major theory is structured in a way that allows us to pair it with some variant of the layered approach. To illustrate this claim, I will now defend it as it applies to (1) Nozick's theory, (2) Rawls's theory, (3) luck egalitarianism, and (4) sufficientarianism.

1. At first glance, Nozick's theory is an unlikely candidate for layering; for he explicitly denies that people's entitlements track their deserts.[13] In his view, even the most lopsided distribution of wealth can be just as long as it arises through an unbroken sequence of rights-creating actions and rights-preserving transactions. The rights in question are an amalgam of natural rights and the sorts of special rights that are created by acts of acquisition and transfer, and they are insensitive to such desert-creating factors as moral goodness, effort, and productivity. If a wicked and lazy person finds a massive gold nugget on his land or inherits a fortune, he is, by Nozick's lights, fully entitled to it; but if a virtuous, hard-working, and productive person falls ill or is laid off, he is entitled to nothing.

Taken at face value, Nozick's account leaves no room for our layered approach. However, that is not particularly damaging because Nozick gives us little reason *to* take the account at face value. As he himself acknowledges, he is more interested in showing how the justice of a set of holdings can be a function of the historical process through which it has arisen than in defending any specific account of the justice-conferring process. As a result, he simply appropriates (without mixing much of his labor with) the Lockean requirements that all transfers of rights be voluntary and that no one be rendered worse off by anyone's property rights than he would be in their absence. Within Nozick's theory, the claim that property rights are subject to these constraints is not a conclusion but an undefended starting point.

Given this paucity of argument, it is obviously fair to wonder why we should accept the constraints that Nozick takes to define property rights. However, for present purposes, the point is simply that even if we do accept Nozick's constraints, we are given no reason why they cannot be augmented by others. Whatever its exact content, any defensible set of claims about the conditions under which property rights are initially acquired, and under which they are retained, transferred, or lost, will simply be a variant of Nozick's own justice-preserving historical theory.

And this is all the opening the desert theorist needs; for to graft a reward schedule that is sensitive to desert onto Nozick's historical account of rights,

---

[13] See Nozick (1974), 155–9 and 237–8.

he need only add that the rights that arise through acts of acquisition and transfer cannot be grossly disproportional to what the parties deserve. Just as Nozick himself maintains that we cannot acquire property rights through transactions whose effect is to leave some people worse off than they would be in the state of nature—that, for example, no sequence of trades could give someone the right (as opposed to the power) to control all the world's water—the desert theorist can maintain that we cannot acquire property rights through transactions that leave some people much worse (or much better?) off than they deserve to be. This addition would leave intact the ideas that rights are created and sustained by historical processes and that the justice of someone's holdings depends on how they came about; but it would also inherit whatever independent case there is for proportioning rewards to deserts. Thus, by introducing it, we would arrive at a desert-infused variant of Nozick's historical theory.

2. The route to a desert-infused version of Rawls's theory is somewhat different; for unlike Nozick, Rawls does painstakingly defend each aspect of each of his principles of justice. Moreover, Rawls's central justificatory device, the original position, leaves little room for desert. Because the parties behind the veil of ignorance have no information about how deserving they are in the actual world, and because their sole aim is to maximize their actual share of primary goods, they have neither the knowledge nor the motivation that would make it rational for them to opt for principles that require that persons get what they deserve. And, in view of this, Rawls's defense of the difference principle may indeed appear to preclude the matching of rewards to deserts.

But, on closer examination, it does not; for even if the difference principle does not require that people be rewarded in accordance with their deserts, it is pitched at a high enough level of abstraction to be consistent with arrangements that are designed to yield precisely this result. To see why this is so, we need only remind ourselves of two broad features of the difference principle: first, that it governs the distribution of wealth and income only among groups but not among particular individuals, and, second, that it takes a society's economic justice to depend entirely on whether its *worst-off* group is as well-off as it can be. Of these features, each broadens the range of distributive schemes that are compatible with the difference principle. As long as a society's worst-off group is as well-off as possible, it does not matter how wealth is distributed within that group, and neither does it matter how wealth is distributed among the society's better-off groups (or, *a fortiori*, among *their* members).

Because the difference principle is silent about these matters, it gives Rawls ample latitude to maintain that "once a suitable minimum is provided by transfers, it may be perfectly fair that the rest of total income be settled by the price system."[14] For similar reasons, he has ample latitude to maintain that "inheritance is permissible provided that the resulting inequalities are to the advantage of the least fortunate and compatible with liberty and fair equality of opportunity."[15] But if the difference principle is consistent with the sorts of inequalities to which inheritance and economic markets give rise, then it is surely also consistent with economic arrangements that match rewards to desert. As long as a society maintains a system of transfers that is designed to keep the income of the worst-off group as high as it can be, there can be no objection to any further combination of transfers, constraints, or incentives whose collective tendency is to cause individuals to be rewarded roughly in proportion to their desert. Although Rawls himself does not endorse such a reward schedule, there is nothing in his arguments for the difference principle, and nothing in that principle itself, that rules it out. Moreover, here again, the resulting hybrid will presumably inherit whatever independent case there is for matching people's rewards with their deserts.

3. Unlike the theories advanced by Rawls and Nozick, luck egalitarianism may seem hospitable to desert from the beginning. According to the luck egalitarian, inequalities are just if and only if they can be traced to differences in the choices the parties have made under fair conditions. To the question of why choice alone can justify inequality, one tempting answer is that choice alone can give rise to desert and that desert alone can overcome the case for equality. If this answer is correct, then desert will enter the picture well before we ask which rewards should attach to which choices; and so there will be no need to adopt the layered approach.[16]

But, for reasons I have elaborated elsewhere, I think the answer is clearly *not* correct. One reason why we cannot invoke desert to justify inequalities that are due to choice is that people often do *not* deserve the predictable outcomes of their choices. Thus, to cite just one sort of counterexample, a daughter who sacrifices a promising career to care for her aging mother does not thereby come to deserve her subsequent lack of earning power. In addition, and more deeply, even when we do deserve the outcomes we bring about, the reason we deserve them is generally not *that* we have brought them about. A hard worker who deserves the success he predictably achieves would not deserve it less if he worked just as hard but did not achieve it. This does not mean that departures from equality cannot be justified by the

---

[14] Rawls (1971), 277.

[15] Rawls (1971), 278.

[16] For a view that combines a commitment to a form of equality with a willingness to allow its demands to be tempered by desert, see Arneson (2007), 262–93.

parties' choices, but it does mean that their justification is unlikely to turn on what the parties deserve.[17] Thus, if a luck egalitarian still wishes to connect justice to desert, he may indeed have to retreat to the layered approach.

That, however, is not hard for him to do; for any theory that accepts the justice of inequalities that are due to choice must be backed by some view of the pay-offs that various choices should have. Because the luck egalitarian formula can be paired with *any* schedule of rewards—because we can say that choice justifies inequality both when the gap between the pay-offs of the best and the worst available options is very large and when it is very small—the selection of an appropriate reward schedule cannot be dictated by luck egalitarianism itself. Here, therefore, is a natural point at which desert can enter. To arrive at a well-motivated schedule of rewards, the luck egalitarian can insist that the pay-offs that attach to each available type of action be roughly proportional to what an agent would deserve for performing an action of that type. Like the other variants of the layered approach, this one would presumably inherit whatever case there is for matching people's rewards with their deserts.

4. The final theory of justice I want to consider, the sufficiency view, is also the easiest to combine with the layered approach. According to the sufficientarian, a just distribution is one in which each person has enough of certain goods to bring him above some appropriate threshold(s). Although sufficientarians disagree both about which goods matter and about where the corresponding thresholds are located, their theory implies that once all relevant thresholds are reached, the demands of justice are fully met. Thus, considered by itself, the sufficiency view says nothing about how much those who surpass the thresholds should be able to gain, or should be at risk of losing, by performing any of the activities that are open to them. It seems, however, that there are legitimate questions here. If we find it hard to countenance the astronomical salaries that top entertainers, athletes, and executives can command, or if we are appalled by the huge losses that people can sustain as a result of trivial errors or omissions, we may be tempted to combine the sufficiency view with the view that the rewards and penalties that are available to individuals once they surpass the thresholds should roughly match the gains and losses of which the various acts they could perform would render them deserving. Because this combination of views would not introduce desert until after the basic requirements of justice were satisfied, it, too, would be an instance of the layered approach.[18]

---

[17] For further defense of these claims, see Sher (2014), ch. 3.

[18] As the reader may have noticed, I have not included the priority view—that is, the view that the worse off someone is, the more valuable it is to provide him with any given

IV

As I have said, I think the most serious objection to a desert-based theory of justice is that a person's deserts are determined by the specifics of what he has done or is able to do, but that his status as a subject of justice is independent of all such considerations. To blunt the force of this objection, I have argued that even if the basic principles of justice must be grounded exclusively in features that all persons share, most of the principles that might be so grounded can be realized through arrangements that tend to match the actions they make available with the rewards and penalties that people would deserve for performing such actions. By opting for arrangements of these sorts, we can simultaneously accommodate both the parties' moral equality and whatever case there is for honoring their particular deserts.[19]

Because my main emphasis has been on economic justice, the illustrations of the layered approach that spring most readily to mind are also economic. So, for example, even if very high income levels are not unjust (because, say, even the poor are sufficiently well-off or the worst-off are as well-off as they could be), a sufficientarian or a Rawslian may still favor additional redistribution on the grounds that great disparities of income are inconsistent with the parties' (comparative) deserts. Alternatively, even a luck egalitarian who views inequalities as just as long as they reflect the parties' choices may favor a safety net which prevents people's choices from having consequences that are far worse than anyone deserves. That same luck egalitarian may also favor various forms of public provision to eliminate

benefit—among the theories of justice to which we might take a layered approach. My reason for not discussing this view is that prioritarianism is not itself a theory of justice, although it becomes a part of one when it is paired with a principle that enjoins societies to maximize value (or to deal with it in some other way). In his essay (2007), Arneson defends both a principle which requires the maximization of value and an account which takes the value of a benefit to be a function both of the beneficiary's level of well-being and of his level of desert. This interesting hybrid combines elements of the layered approach, of the priority view, and of utilitarianism.

[19] Does this layered approach yield (a schema for arriving at) a desert-based account of justice? The waters here are muddied by the fact that my use of the term "justice" has narrowed over the course of my discussion. In section I, I stipulated that I would take the principles of justice to consist of whichever principles ought to govern the distribution of goods within a just society; but in section II, I restricted them to principles which are grounded exclusively in the fact that each of us is a separate person with his own life to live. Under the first, broader conception, the layered approach does provide a way of arriving at a desert-based account of justice; but under the second it doesn't because the principles of justice are established without reference to the particular facts that determine people's deserts. Still, even under the second conception, the layered approach allows us to see how a just society can *take account* of its members' deserts.

situations like those of our self-sacrificing caregiver, whose virtuous choices simultaneously render her deserving of a good outcome and cause her to endure a bad one. And although the requirements of a number of different theories of justice may be satisfied by a society in which different classes of persons are paid different wages for similar jobs, the proponents of those theories may still favor equal pay for equal (and perhaps comparable) work on the independent grounds that all who perform the same or sufficiently similar work are equally deserving of remuneration.

Of the ways of accommodating the demands of desert within a just society that I have just mentioned, each is advocated mainly by those on the (moderate) political left. However, other such accommodations are favored mainly by those on the right. It is, for example, mainly conservatives who argue for strictly merit-based hiring and college admissions (and thus against strong affirmative action) on the grounds that the best-qualified candidates for jobs and positions deserve to be selected. It is also mainly conservatives who oppose various forms of public assistance on the grounds that they do not adequately distinguish between the deserving and the undeserving poor. Although the case for such opposition is often couched in terms of justice, even someone whose conception of justice is quite abstract, and who therefore believes that his society's justice would not be materially affected by its acceptance or rejection of affirmative action or work requirements for public assistance, may nevertheless defend merit-based hiring and work requirements by appealing to the independent demands of desert.

That the proposed strategy for squaring the demands of desert and justice can be exploited by those on both the political left and the right should not come as a surprise; for the idea of desert is deeply enough engrained in our common outlook to transcend ideological boundaries. However, just because of this, no mere demonstration of its compatibility with justice can resolve any substantive question. Before we can justify any given desert-based adjustment in the rewards or penalties that define people's options, we must establish not only that that adjustment falls within the range that the applicable principles of justice allow, but also that the claims about desert upon which it rests are both defensible and weighty. That means addressing various questions that were raised but not resolved earlier: questions about which factors can ground desert, what people can deserve on the basis of these factors, and why, and in what sense, people should have what they deserve. These are just the standard hard questions about desert, and they remain the important ones. However, for present purposes, what matters is not that particular desert-based policies presuppose particular answers to them, but rather that whichever answers we give, the requirements of desert and justice will remain distinct but compatible. Although the two notions have very different normative underpinnings, there is ample room for social arrangements that answer to them both.

References

Arneson, Richard, "Desert and Equality," in Nils Holtug and Kasper Lippert-Rasmussen, eds., *Egalitarianism: New Essays on the Nature and Value of Egalitarianism* (Oxford: Oxford University Press, 2007), 262–93.

Dworkin, Ronald, "In Defense of Equality," *Social Philosophy and Policy* 1 (1983), 24–40.

Hayek, F. A., *Law, Legislation, and Liberty*, vol. 2 (London and New York: Routledge, 2013).

Hill, Thomas, "Kant's Moralistic Strain," in Thomas Hill, *Dignity and Practical Reason in Kant's Moral Theory* (Cambridge: Cambridge University Press, 1992), 176–95.

Kant, Immanuel, *Groundwork of the Metaphysics of Morals*, trans. H. J. Paton (New York: Harper and Row, 1964).

Miller, David, *Principles of Social Justice* (Cambridge, MA: Harvard University Press, 1999).

Nozick, Robert, *Anarchy, State, and Utopia* (New York: Basic Books, 1974).

Rawls, John, *A Theory of Justice* (Cambridge, MA: Harvard University Press, 1971).

Scheffler, Samuel, "Justice and Desert in Liberal Theory," in Samuel Scheffler, *Boundaries and Allegiances* (Oxford: Oxford University Press, 2001), 172–96.

Sen, Amartya, *Inequality Reexamined* (Cambridge, MA: Harvard University Press, 1992).

Sher, George, "Ancient Wrongs and Modern Rights," *Philosophy and Public Affairs* 10 (1981), 3–17.

Sher, George, *Desert* (Princeton: Princeton University Press, 1987).

Sher, George, *Equality for Inegalitarians* (Cambridge: Cambridge University Press, 2014).

Sidgwick, Henry, *Methods of Ethics*, 7th ed. (London: MacMillan and Co., 1922).

Wolff, Jonathan, "The Dilemma of Desert," in Serena Olsaretti, ed., *Justice and Desert* (Oxford: Oxford University Press, 2003), 219–32.

Zaitchik, Alan, "On Deserving to Deserve," *Philosophy and Public Affairs* 6 (1977), 370–88.

PART II
STATE LEGITIMACY

5

Counterfactual Justifications
of the State

Ralf Bader

1. NOZICK'S JUSTIFICATION OF THE STATE

In part 1 of *Anarchy, State, and Utopia* (Nozick: 1974; hereafter ASU), Nozick attempts to refute the individualist anarchist and answer what he considers to be the fundamental question of political philosophy, namely whether there should be any state at all. In particular, he tries to justify the state by means of a hypothetical invisible-hand account, specifying a complicated process by means of which a minimal state could come into existence without violating any rights.

Nozick's account begins with individuals in the state of nature who enforce their own rights. This self-enforcement brings with it various inconveniences, leading to the formation of mutual-protection associations that evolve over time into professional protection agencies. Due to the network externalities characterizing the market for the provision of protective services, a dominant protective agency establishes itself. This agency prohibits independents, i.e., people who are not clients of the agency, from enforcing their own rights, on the basis that they employ risky procedures that risk violating the rights of its clients. It thereby becomes an ultraminimal state that claims a monopoly on coercion within a certain territory. In order to be justified in prohibiting independents from engaging in risky self-enforcement, they must be compensated for the resulting disadvantage, which can be done by providing them with protective services. In this way, the rights of everyone within the territory will be protected and a minimal state will have arisen in a legitimate manner.[1]

---

[1] For a more detailed account, cf. Bader: 2010, pp. 28–35.

1.1. A Complete Non Sequitur

Nozick's justification[2] of the state is almost universally considered to be a failure. Not only do various critics find faults in assessing particular steps of his argument, for instance when it comes to Nozick's claims about procedural rights, network externalities as well as the compensation principle. In addition, it is generally held that Nozick's project is ill-conceived and that the very idea of trying to justify a state by appealing to a hypothetical invisible-hand explanation is misguided. As Simmons puts it, "given Nozick's orientation toward historical (or 'pedigree') evaluations of institutional arrangements, his justification of the state in terms of a purely hypothetical account of a minimal state's genesis might seem a complete non sequitur" (Simmons: 1999, p. 744). The thought is that, even if all the objections to the specific steps of his account could be overcome and the whole argument were to go through, Nozick would still not have managed to establish anything of significance.[3]

To begin with, it is hard to see how a hypothetical account could perform the requisite justificatory work. As Miller points out: "to say of a state that it *could* have arisen by [voluntary and permissible] means is actually to say very little" (Miller: 2002, p. 19). The fact that Nozick provides a hypothetical account is particularly puzzling, given that he develops and defends an entitlement theory of justice which is a distinctly historical theory (cf. Danley: 1978, p. 190). "The fact that a thief's victims voluntarily *could* have presented him with gifts does not entitle the thief to his ill-gotten gains" (ASU, pp. 151–2). If, as Nozick holds, the mere fact that someone could have voluntarily transferred property does not generate an entitlement, given that what matters is whether the person actually transferred the property, then how can legitimacy be conferred by the fact that an institution could have arisen without rights violations having taken place? Should it not equally be the case that what matters is whether the institutions actually did arise without violating rights? If distributions are justified in terms of the actual historical processes that generated them, then why is it not the case that political institutions are justified in a similar manner in terms of the actual historical processes that gave rise to them?

It might be suggested that all that is at issue is establishing the mere possibility of a legitimate state, i.e., showing that the state is not intrinsically immoral, in order to refute the individualist anarchist who claims that states

---

[2] 'Justification' and 'legitimacy' will be used interchangeably. For Nozick these amount to the state having the liberty right to use coercion to enforce rights, to punish wrongdoing, and to prohibit risky private enforcement (cf. ASU, pp. 133–4 and pp. 137–8).

[3] Cf. Schmidtz: 1990, Miller: 2002, amongst many others. For a more optimistic assessment cf. Gaus: 2011.

are essentially illegitimate (cf. ASU, p. 6 and p. 119) and that hypothetical arguments do suffice for establishing such a possibility claim. Whilst this conclusion can in fact be achieved by means of a hypothetical account, this can be achieved in a much less roundabout manner by pointing out the (rather remote) possibility of a state arising as a result of unanimous consent. Accordingly, no appeal to complicated invisible-hand explanations would be required.[4]

Whilst Nozick's invisible-hand justification shows that a state can legitimately arise without unanimous consent, it is unclear as to why this should be of any particular import (though cf. ASU, pp. 293–4). Moreover, it is not even clear how strong Nozick's justification is, given that the justificatory force that derives from invisible-hand processes is relatively dubious since there is no guarantee that such processes give rise to improvements. (As Nozick acknowledges, an account that would explain the state's emergence in terms of a process of deterioration would not justify the state, cf. ASU, p. 5 footnote.)

Though the actions involved in an invisible-hand process are individually rational, they can fail to be collectively rational. The possibility of this type of collective action problem is particularly relevant given the path-dependency of the process leading to the dominant protective agency that Nozick envisages. "Clearly, it does not follow from the fact that people individually have reason to choose to sign up with the largest agency in their geographic region that collectively they have reason to applaud its emergence as a dominant agency" (Miller: 2002, p. 21). By contrast, this type of collective irrationality is unlikely to be found in the case of visible-hand explanations that require that everyone approve of the collective outcome. Unlike in the case of invisible-hand explanations where the individual transactions that are voluntarily and deliberately performed do not make reference to the collective outcome that emerges from them, in the case of a social contract the collective outcome is the very thing to which everyone agrees.

Thus, it is not clear why Nozick is providing an invisible-hand explanation. What purpose does this kind of explanation serve that could not be achieved by another kind of explanation, such as a consent-based account?

In short, why should one be in any way concerned about what could have arisen by an invisible-hand process? Both the hypothetical nature of the explanation as well as Nozick's insistence on using an invisible-hand process seem to be, at best, puzzling and, at worst, deeply misguided.

---

[4] Cf. "It is curious that Nozick gives no explicit attention to a Lockean contract as an alternative, more direct, route from the state of nature to a minimal state" (Miller: 2002, p. 16).

Moreover, it is not clear in what way a hypothetical account is meant to favor the minimal state in particular. After all, one can set up a legitimate more-than-minimal state by unanimous consent.[5] Additionally, Nozick even provides an invisible-hand explanation of the more-than-minimal state in chapter 9 of *Anarchy, State, and Utopia*, which he describes as being based on a principle of demoktesis and which amounts to "ownership of the people, by the people and for the people" (ASU, p. 290). Though any state that would have arisen in such a manner would be unappealing (at least to Nozick), it would not violate any rights and would not be illegitimate. The problem is thus that it is possible both for minimal as well as more-than-minimal states to arise in a legitimate manner via both invisible-hand as well as visible-hand mechanisms, making it unclear in what way the minimal state is meant to be privileged.

We are thus faced with three questions that put into doubt the very intelligibility of Nozick's project:

1. How can a hypothetical account justify the state?
2. Why does Nozick invoke an invisible-hand explanation?
3. In what way is the argument meant to privilege the minimal state?

1.2. Rectifying Past Injustices

Prima facie, there is a stark incongruity between Nozick's attempt to justify the state on the basis of a hypothetical account and his insistence that the justification of property distributions is a historical matter. Nozick's entitlement theory of justice is concerned with how a distribution arose. In ideal circumstances,[6] every action conforms to the principles of justice in acquisition and the principles of justice in transfer. The justice of a set of holdings will then derive from the actions that brought it about, insofar as what makes a distribution just will be the fact that it resulted from actions that conformed to these principles (rather than it being just in virtue of instantiating some specified pattern). In this way, the entitlement theory is a distinctly historical theory and it would seem that hypothetical facts are of no relevance

---

[5] Simmons argues that there is a conflict between, on the one hand, the consensualist strain of Nozick's approach, which would seem to make room for justifications of both minimal and non-minimal political arrangements, and, on the other, the minimalist strain that leads him to consider only the minimal state as being justified (cf. Simmons: 2005). The interpretation put forward in this paper shows how Nozick can assign a privileged position to the minimal state, whilst recognizing that non-minimal states can be legitimate under special conditions.

[6] The contrast between ideal vs. non-ideal circumstances is to be understood in terms of full vs. partial compliance with the relevant principles of justice.

to questions of distributive justice—all that matters is the actual facts about how the distribution came about. "Justice in holdings is historical; it depends upon what actually has happened" (ASU, p. 152).

Yet, the situation is drastically different in the context of non-ideal circumstances, where there is only partial compliance with the principles of justice. While acquisition principles specify how just holdings can arise in the first place, and while transfer principles specify how justly held holdings can be transmitted in a way that preserves justice, neither of these sets of principles tells us what is to be done when injustices arise and when holdings no longer conform to these principles. In such a situation, looking at the past is no longer sufficient. Once there is deviation from what is dictated by these principles of justice, the principles of rectification come into effect and specify what needs to be done in order for the injustice that has occurred to be rectified.

Historical principles thus turn out to be only part of the full story. The entitlement theory switches in non-ideal circumstances from being a purely historical theory to a (partly) counterfactual theory. In addition to actual historical facts, one also has to appeal to counterfactual facts. "The principle of rectification presumably will make use of its best estimate of subjunctive information about what would have occurred (or a probability distribution over what might have occurred, using the expected value) if the injustice had not taken place" (ASU, pp. 152–3).[7] Justice is then no longer a matter solely of what did happen but also of what would have happened, in particular a matter of what would have happened had the principles of justice in acquisition and transfer not been violated. The fact that distributions are justified not only in terms of what did happen, but also in terms of what would have happened, implies that hypothetical facts, in particular counterfactual facts, play a crucial role in the theory of justice in contexts in which injustices were committed.

Whereas a distribution is justified in ideal circumstances if it actually arose through a process in which no property rights were violated, it is justified in non-ideal circumstances if it would have arisen had circumstances been ideal. It is accordingly possible for a distribution that has arisen through a process involving unjust steps to nonetheless coincide with what would have resulted had no property rights been violated and to be justified in virtue of coinciding with this counterfactual distribution. That is, if the actual distribution coincides with the counterfactual distribution that would have been brought about in the absence of injustice, then, despite the

---

[7] We will work with the simplifying assumption that there is a unique closest world in which the antecedent is satisfied (or that all closest worlds agree in the relevant respects), so that we always end up with would- rather than might-counterfactuals.

fact that unjust steps led to the actual distribution, this distribution will be just on the basis that these injustices will have been rectified.[8]

1.3. Counterfactual Histories

A historical theory of legitimacy that specifies which processes give rise to just political institutions will have to incorporate principles that are analogous to the principles of rectification. Such principles will specify what is to be done in non-ideal situations in which the historical principles have been violated and in which illegitimate institutions are in existence, telling us how to modify institutional structures to rectify past injustices. These principles will appeal to counterfactual facts about what institutional structures would have resulted if no rights had been violated on the part of these institutions.[9] In the same way that counterfactual considerations become relevant in justifying distributions of holdings in non-ideal circumstances, they also become relevant in justifying political institutions in such circumstances.[10] That is, in the same way that the principles of rectification require us to ask: "If no rights had been violated, what distribution of holdings would have resulted?" we can ask: "If no rights had been violated, what institutional structures would have resulted?"[11]

There is thus a general issue of how rectification is to take place in non-ideal circumstances that is equally applicable to property distributions as to political institutions. This issue is addressed by principles of rectification that are concerned with what needs to be done to right past wrongs. According to Nozick, these principles have an important counterfactual element, in that they require one to bring about that situation (conforming to the relevant

---

[8] The precise specification of the relevant counterfactual is a highly complicated matter. Identifying the correct rectification counterfactual is beyond the scope of this paper. The principle given in the main text is a rough first-pass approximation that is problematic in a number of respects but that will do for illustrative purposes (some of the relevant complications are discussed in section 2.6).

[9] The legitimizing conditions for institutional structures require only that no rights be violated by the institutions in question—rights violations on the part of individuals do not form part of these conditions. (After all, it is the rights-violating behavior of individuals that gives rise to the inconveniences of the state of nature, initiating the process that leads to the emergence of protective agencies.)

[10] Nelson has claimed that there is a disanalogy between parts 1 and 2 of *Anarchy, State, and Utopia* since the "arguments in pt. 2 of *ASU* depend on insisting that explanations (justifications) of distributions of resources *not* be process defective" (Nelson: 1986, p. 168 n. 22). However, we can see that, far from being disanalogous, the structure of justification is the same in each case. In non-ideal circumstances it is process defective, i.e., counterfactual, whereas in ideal circumstances it is non-defective, i.e., historical.

[11] As noted above, this is a simplistic first-pass approximation. A satisfactory theory of rectification will have to appeal to a much more complicated counterfactual.

principles of justification) that would have resulted had those wrongs not occurred, i.e., the situation that would have resulted under ideal conditions.[12] It is by determining what these counterfactual situations are like that potential explanations (i.e., explanations that do not fit the actual situation but would be correct explanations if things were different), in particular process-defective explanations that invoke processes that do not actually obtain but that would have obtained under suitable conditions, can justify their explananda and play a normative role (contra Wolff: 1991, p. 50 and p. 146 n. 15).

Once this parallelism is recognized, Nozick's justification of the state can be understood as a rectificationist justification of the minimal state. He is trying to provide a hypothetical account that explains what would have happened had there not been any rights violations. Part 1 of *Anarchy, State, and Utopia* constitutes a sketch of the relevant counterfactual history. The resulting political institutions are such that bringing them into existence would rectify the past injustices at the institutional level.[13] In the same way that bringing about a set of holdings that coincides with what would have resulted had there not been any rights violations ensures that a just distribution obtains, bringing about a set of political institutions that coincides with what would have resulted had there not been any rights violations ensures that just political institutions are in place. That is, a set of institutions can be justified if it would have arisen had no rights been violated, thereby making it possible for a state that results from an unjust process to be legitimate on the basis that it coincides with what would have resulted had no rights violations been perpetrated on the part of the state.

It is precisely such a coincidence of institutional structures under ideal and non-ideal circumstances that constitutes the essence of Nozick's process-defective justification of the minimal state (cf. ASU, pp. 7–8). The process described in part 1 of *Anarchy, State, and Utopia* is a process that explains and justifies the existence of a minimal state but that is defective in that this process is not actual. Yet, it is a process that could have brought about such a state and, more importantly, would have brought it about had the morally

---

[12] The transition involved in bringing actual institutions into conformity with those institutions to be found in the relevant counterfactual scenario is not allowed to violate side-constraints and might, moreover, have to satisfy certain procedural requirements.

[13] It is important to note that the sense in which a minimal state rectifies past injustices is restricted to the institutional context, i.e., it is concerned with the claims individuals have to (not) be governed by certain (types of) institutional structures. That is, the establishment of a minimal state ensures that injustices will have been rectified as far as institutional structures are concerned. The rectification of injustices as they affect the well-being of individuals and their holdings is another matter that cannot be addressed by simply putting into place certain institutional structures. (Relatedly, the notion of 'ideal circumstances' is restricted to the institutional setting.)

impermissible processes that actually occurred (or would have occurred in nearby possible worlds) not taken place. In this way, we can understand Nozick's claim that "[a] theory of a state of nature that begins with fundamental general descriptions of morally permissible and impermissible actions, and of deeply based reasons why some persons in any society would violate these moral constraints, and goes on to describe how a state would arise from that state of nature will serve our explanatory purposes, *even if no actual state ever arose that way*" (ASU, p. 7). For a state to be justified, it is not necessary that it did arise by the process that Nozick describes, since it is sufficient that it corresponds to what would have resulted under such ideal circumstances.

Accordingly, we can see why Nozick's justification of the state has to take the form of a hypothetical explanation. This is because the injustices that characterize the actual histories of political institutions make it necessary to consider counterfactual histories in which no injustices are committed, if one is to determine what needs to be done to arrive at a just set of political institutions that rectifies the past injustices. In other words, actual injustices perpetrated by states make it impossible to justify such states on the basis of historical justifications, thereby requiring a shift to counterfactual justifications.

Only counterfactual justifications can determine how the past injustices are to be rectified and hence determine what type of political institutions are justified and will have to be put in place. Given that actual circumstances are non-ideal, institutional structures need to be justified by showing that they correspond to what would have happened had circumstances been ideal. This means that, although no actually existing state can be justified in terms of its actual history, minimal states can be justified in terms of their counterfactual history, since, though such states did not actually arise in the right way, they would have arisen in the right way had circumstances been ideal.

1.4. Invisible-Hand Explanations

Moreover, we can see why Nozick's justification has to take the form of an invisible-hand account. This is because the evaluation of the counterfactual requires one to assess not just any situation in which no rights are violated, but the closest possible situation in which there are no rights violations. The invisible-hand character of the explanation precisely ensures that this closeness condition is satisfied. What makes the particular hypothetical process that Nozick envisages relevant to what institutional structures are justified in the actual world, despite the fact that the process is defective in that it does not occur in the actual world, is its closeness to the actual historical process. In particular, it is the closest process to the actual process that does not involve violations of rights and as such determines which institutional structures are justified, given that the actual as well as alternative (closer) processes are ruled out on the basis that they involve rights violations.

The closeness of the counterfactual process that legitimizes the minimal state is due to the fact that it is an invisible-hand process. Such processes appeal to filtering and equilibrium mechanisms to explain macro-level outcomes in terms of micro-level events that do not make reference to the macro-level outcomes (cf. Nozick: 1994, p. 314). The macro-level outcome will accordingly be an emergent feature of the system. The way in which the emergence of macro-level outcomes is explained by invisible-hand processes matters because the evaluation of the counterfactual that determines how past injustices are to be rectified consists in assessing the consequences of making various local adjustments that are required by the no-rights-violation condition and that amount to eradicating the particular injustices that are part of the actual process. The change from an illegitimate state in the actual world to a legitimate state in the selected counterfactual world thus consists in a series of local changes that correspond to implementing the counterfactual supposition that the relevant rights-violating actions that undermined the legitimacy of the actual state (as well as those relating to illegitimate states in closer counterfactual scenarios) had not taken place. We then evaluate the consequences of these local adjustments, thereby determining what would have happened under these idealized conditions. The macro-level outcome that results from these adjustments represents the kind of state that is justified and that needs to be brought into existence in order to rectify past injustices at the institutional level.

If Nozick is correct that a minimal state will emerge from a broad range of starting points by a process that involves no rights being violated, then making these small adjustments is very likely to take us to one of these counterfactual processes. The macro-level outcome consisting of the existence of a minimal state will result from the vast majority of close-by systems satisfying the no-rights-violation condition. This is because the process that Nozick envisages is highly stable, in that it does not rely on a particular starting point, making the macro-level outcome resilient under micro-level variations. Since a broad range of different micro-level starting points will all converge on the same macro-level outcome, it is very likely that one will end up with the same result, namely a minimal state, independently of which of the systems one should happen to be in. Accordingly, the closest world in which no rights are violated will be a particular instance of the type of process that Nozick describes, which means that the local alterations amounting to a change from non-ideal to ideal circumstances will have as their result the emergence of a minimal state.

By contrast, excepting special circumstances where a visible-hand process is already underway and only fails to be completed because of a rights violation (e.g., a situation where a state was about to be set up by unanimous consent but where this attempt was illegitimately thwarted), such a series of local adjustments will not lead to a visible-hand process, since this type of process requires a much more radical change. This is because visible-hand processes only arrive at the desired macro-level outcome from a small set of highly specific starting points. This reliance on specific starting points implies that we are not at all likely to end up at one of them by just making local adjustments that eradicate particular impermissible actions that undermine the state's legitimacy in the actual world. Instead, what needs to be done to arrive at such a starting point is to implement a global change by positing a social contract. It is this lack of stability, as well as the global and specific nature of the required starting points, that makes visible-hand processes more remote than the type of invisible-hand process envisaged by Nozick.

Accordingly, the closest process to the actual process that leads to a legitimate outcome will be an invisible-hand process rather than a visible-hand process. The reason why Nozick does not appeal to a social contract is thus not that such a contract would fail to justify the state. A state brought about by unanimous consent would be perfectly justified. The problem is rather that such a scenario is too remote and consequently not relevant for assessing the counterfactual as to what institutions would have arisen had no rights violations taken place. Even though visible-hand processes that bring about political institutions through unanimous consent legitimate the resulting institutions, they are substantially more remote from the actual world than invisible-hand processes. This ensures that it is the latter rather than the former processes that determine how the counterfactual is to be evaluated and thereby determine what is to be done to rectify past wrongs.

Moreover, not only do visible-hand processes require highly specific starting points that are far removed from the actual world if they are to yield justified institutions, the particular outcome of any such process will depend on the specific nature of the starting point. Unlike in the case of invisible-hand processes where the same macro-level outcome results from a large range of different starting points, there is no convergence in the case of visible-hand processes. For instance, in the case of consent theory, any institutional structure that people can consent to can be the justified outcome of a visible-hand process, making the outcome dependent on the specific starting point. This fine-grained dependence on the specific nature of the starting point risks leading to underdetermination, which would make it much more difficult to evaluate what institutions are justified.

1.5. Privileging the Minimal State

The proposed interpretation of Nozick's justification as consisting in determining how past injustices at the institutional level are to be rectified thus explains why the justification has to take the form of a hypothetical explanation that is based on invisible-hand processes. In addition, it can explain in what way the hypothetical invisible-hand account favors the minimal state. If Nozick is right that a minimal state would have resulted if no rights violations (on the part of the state) had taken place, then it is such a state that is to be brought about, no matter whether a more-than-minimal state could have resulted in a legitimate manner in some other context. Any explanation of legitimate more-than-minimal states will be sufficiently remote to make it irrelevant.[14]

In particular, such explanations will either rely on visible-hand processes that do not explain the emergence of the state in terms of local non-political phenomena and thus will not be fundamental explanations but will require bringing in political notions to explain the emergence of the political realm (cf. ASU, p. 6). Or these explanations will rely on the kind of complicated process characterized in the demoktesis chapter (cf. ASU, pp. 280–90), which relies on highly elaborate and specific mechanisms and is too remote to be relevant. Although the process leading to demoktesis is an invisible-hand process, in the sense that the resulting state is an emergent outcome that arises without having been intended by anyone, the process is not stable due to its high specificity and does not proceed on the basis of mundane behavior on the part of individual agents responding to ordinary incentives.

All of this ensures that, unless highly specific conditions are satisfied, one will not end up in a counterfactual scenario involving a more-than-minimal state when evaluating what would have happened had there not been any rights violations. While there are plenty of close possible worlds in which more-than-minimal states arise as a result of processes that involve rights being violated (the actual world being one of them), all those worlds in which such states come into existence without rights being violated are remote and all the close worlds satisfying this legitimizing condition are ones in which there are only minimal states. Given Nozick's moral framework, the main threat to his account does not derive from the possibility of ending up with a legitimate more-than-minimal state but instead from ending up with no state at all, and it is only by appealing to contentious

---

[14] Although more-than-minimal dominant protection agencies (which provide various services for their clients in addition to the protection of individual rights) can emerge, the provision of such additional services cannot be extended (without violating rights) to independents who did not voluntarily join the agency and subscribe to these services.

empirical claims about network externalities that Nozick can ensure that his preferred evaluation of the counterfactual comes out true.

Thus, the claim that for Nozick "[a] minimal state, and only a minimal state, could arise by an invisible hand process" (Schmidtz: 1990, p. 89) is a mischaracterization of his position. When concerned merely with what could happen, the minimal state is not privileged since more-than-minimal states can legitimately arise via invisible-hand processes (as well as by visible-hand processes). After all, this is clearly illustrated by the demoktesis chapter. Instead, as we have seen, the key issue is not what could possibly happen, what kind of state can arise, but rather what would have happened in the absence of rights violations. It is in this context that the minimal state is privileged since, on Nozick's view, the most plausible interpretation of the counterfactual specifying what kind of state would have arisen had no rights been violated will identify a world in which a minimal state arises by means of an invisible-hand mechanism.

1.6. Nozick's Project

The nature of Nozick's project can, accordingly, be explained on the basis that the non-ideal circumstances in which we find ourselves require us to assess what happens in the closest possible world in which circumstances are ideal, making it necessary that the account takes the form of a hypothetical explanation based on an invisible-hand mechanism. This means that the suggestion that "Nozick could have presented his solution—less stylishly—without mentioning invisible hands, potential explanations, or hypothetical processes" (Wolff: 1991, p. 52) turns out to be mistaken. Rather than being inessential features of the solution, these elements are indispensable to a rectificationist justification. Moreover, we can see that there is no incongruity between parts 1 and 2 of *Anarchy, State, and Utopia*, but that they cohere nicely and constitute a unified and systematic project.

This account has the further advantage that it also explains why the transition from an ultraminimal state to a minimal state is unproblematic, despite the fact that this transition differs in nature from the other steps of the process, given that it requires that a compensation scheme be put in place, the setting up of which requires that the agents of the ultraminimal state are morally motivated.[15] What is doing the work in this step of the

---

[15] Moreover, the aims and intentions of these agents might seem too close to the explanandum, namely the existence of a state, for this step to be straightforwardly classified as resulting from an invisible-hand mechanism (cf. Gaus: 2011, p. 122). Nozick addresses this concern by noting that the explanation "does not specify people's objective as that of establishing a state. Instead, persons view themselves as providing particular other persons with compensation for particular prohibitions they have imposed upon

argument is not an appeal to economic incentives and empirical claims about how people behave, but instead a claim about what is morally required. As Nozick notes, "the transition from an ultraminimal state to a minimal state morally must occur.... The operators of the ultraminimal state are morally obligated to produce the minimal state" (ASU, p. 52). This turns out to be unproblematic on the grounds that a failure to compensate would result in the violation of individual rights and would, accordingly, contradict the counterfactual supposition that no rights violations (on the part of the institutions) take place.

Nozick's justification in this way relies on the interaction between two features, namely (i) moral constraints and (ii) empirical mechanisms, that jointly determine how the counterfactual is to be evaluated, i.e., what the worlds that are closest to the actual world that do not involve any rights violations are like. These two features are responsible for the two stages in the emergence of the minimal state. Empirical mechanisms underlying the invisible-hand process lead to the prohibition of independents and thereby to an ultraminimal state. The moral constraints in the form of the no-rights-violation condition, in turn, lead to the compensation of independents and thereby to a minimal state.

In addition, it becomes clear that the condition of there not being any rights violations should be understood as there not being any uncompensated rights violations. Accordingly, it turns out that the fact that prohibiting independents requires compensating them for the resulting disadvantage is unproblematic. In this way, we can see that the objection that Nozick's favored invisible-hand process itself involves rights violations and as such cannot generate a legitimate state does not succeed.

This objection takes the form of a dilemma insofar as it is held that either (i) the prohibition of independents is legitimate in which case no compensation is required, or that (ii) this kind of prohibition is illegitimate in which case compensation is due (cf. Holmes: 1981, p. 61; also cf. Wolff: 1991, p. 72).[16] In the former case, we do not end up with a minimal state but are instead stuck with the ultraminimal state. In the latter case, we do get to the minimal state yet only via a process that involves rights violations, which ensures that the resulting minimal state is illegitimate.

In response, we can note that the second horn of the dilemma turns out to be unproblematic once it is recognized that a state is legitimate if there

---

them. The explanation remains an invisible-hand one" (ASU, p. 119). In other words, the transition is the result of a series of local adjustments, each of which can be understood in non-political terms.

[16] According to Nozick, this is a false dilemma, cf. ASU, pp. 83–4. This type of objection has also recently been criticized by Hyams: 2004.

are no unrectified injustices. For a state to be justified, it does not need to have an unblemished history but only needs to be such that all its blemishes have been removed, insofar as injustices have been rectified and compensation has been provided to those who have been prohibited from engaging in risky activities. Accordingly, Nozick can either hold that this dilemma is a false dilemma, insofar as compensation can justify boundary crossings, making it the case that there is no injustice even though compensation is required since the provision of compensation is precisely what makes it the case that the boundary crossing is justified, or he can accept that the boundary crossing is not justified and accept that there is an injustice but then hold that this injustice is addressed if the independents are compensated for the resulting disadvantage, since compensation ensures that the resulting situation is legitimate despite having a blemished history.

The three questions we started out with can thus all be answered by the counterfactual interpretation that understands Nozick as being concerned not with a mere possibility claim about what could have happened but a counterfactual claim about what would have happened, in particular with what type of institutional structures would have arisen if no rights violations had been perpetrated on the part of these institutions:

1. How can a hypothetical account justify anything (given Nozick's emphasis on historical processes in establishing legitimacy in general)?

A hypothetical account can justify insofar as it is a counterfactual account concerned with what would have happened had there been no rights violations, thereby specifying what kind of situation would amount to a rectification of the past injustices that have actually occurred.

2. Why does Nozick provide an invisible-hand explanation (rather than, for instance, a consent-based explanation)?

Invisible-hand explanations ensure closeness to the actual world, thereby making them process-defective explanations that determine how the relevant counterfactuals are to be evaluated, whereas consent-based explanations only characterize remote possibilities.

3. In what way is the minimal state privileged (when other states could also have come about in a legitimate manner)?

The minimal state is privileged in terms of its closeness to the actual world, since any scenario that satisfies the condition that no rights violations occur and that involves a redistributionist state (whether one resulting from a social contract or a demoktesis-style process) will be much more remote than one involving a minimal state.

It is worth noting that this does not mean that Nozick's justification is a success. After all, there are numerous problems relating to particular steps in the invisible-hand account. These problems are both normative in nature, in particular when it comes to his appeal to procedural rights and the application of the compensation principle in relation to the prohibition of risky activities, as well as empirical in nature, in particular his invocation of network externalities in explaining why a dominant protective agency would arise.[17] In addition, the notion of rectification is riddled with problems and difficulties (cf. ASU, p. 152, and Davis: 1981). Nozick's brief remarks concerning rectification are completely underdeveloped and there are many difficult questions that need to be addressed if a rectificationist justification of the state is to stand on a firm footing. Yet, what has been shown is that the project that Nozick is engaged in is intelligible and that it in fact constitutes an interesting alternative to the well-known traditional methods of justifying political institutions, such as hypothetical consent accounts. Nozick is offering neither a purely historical nor a teleological justification but instead a counterfactual or rectificationist justification.

2. THE GENERAL FRAMEWORK

We have identified an account according to which a state can be justified in non-ideal circumstances on the basis of counterfactual facts. It is possible for such facts to play a justificatory role because it is not the state's actual history that matters in non-ideal circumstances. What matters instead is the counterfactual history that would have unfolded and the kind of state that would have emerged had circumstances been ideal. Rectificationist principles allow us to deal with non-ideal circumstances and in this way supplement historical principles of justification that only apply in ideal circumstances.

2.1. Supplementing Historical Accounts

A complete (non-teleological) theory of justification needs to do two things:

1. It needs to provide an account as to how institutions are justified in ideal circumstances.

This function is performed by historical principles of justification.[18]

---

[17] Some problems, such as the regressive character of procedural rights (cf. Paul: 1981, p. 73), threaten to undermine Nozick's account altogether, whereas others merely restrict the range of cases in which the account is applicable and in which (minimal) states can accordingly be justified, for instance the problem that it is not possible to compensate a thoroughly committed anarchist for being prohibited from enforcing his own rights.

[18] These principles are the analogues of the principles of acquisition and transfer. For Nozick they are concerned with (1) consent, and (2) the prerogative to enforce compliance

2. It needs to provide an account as to how institutions are justified in non-ideal circumstances.

This function is performed by rectificationist principles of justification.

A complete theory consists of both historical and counterfactual principles, covering ideal and non-ideal circumstances respectively. This implies that the characterization of legitimacy will be disjunctive: institutional structures are justified iff they either (i) did arise in a certain way, or (ii) would have arisen had conditions been suitably ideal.

These two types of principles are not on an equal footing. In particular, counterfactual principles are dependent on historical principles and are unable to generate content by themselves. This is because what should happen in non-ideal circumstances is understood in terms of what would have happened in ideal circumstances. The counterfactual justification of a set of institutions is based on these institutions coinciding with those that would result from a historical process under ideal circumstances, which implies that the rectificationist project of explaining legitimacy in non-ideal circumstances in terms of legitimacy in ideal circumstances presupposes an account of the latter. Counterfactual principles, accordingly, are not independent but instead implicate historical principles.

This means that counterfactual principles do not constitute a complete theory by themselves. Rather than replacing historical principles, they supplement them. They do this by showing how we are to make sense of justification in non-ideal circumstances in which states have blemished histories in terms of institutions coinciding with those to be found in counterfactual scenarios in which the historical principles are satisfied. They are thus not a substitute but a supplement that needs to be included in a complete theory.

2.2. Incomplete Theories

Historical theories of justification will be incomplete without principles of rectification. A purely historical account that only specifies the mechanisms by means of which a legitimate state can come into existence, such as consent theory, tells us which institutional structures are justified (namely those that have received the appropriate form of consent) and which ones fail to

---

with certain rules and to prevent people from engaging in certain types of risky behavior (given that they are compensated for the resulting disadvantage). That is, one can be forced to comply with rules and give up self-enforcement either if (1) one has consented to being forced (i.e., one is a member of a protective association), or if (2) one's non-compliance would constitute a certain type of risky behavior that can be prohibited, given that one is compensated for resulting disadvantages (i.e., one is an independent employing risky procedures).

be justified (namely those not resting on consent). Yet, by itself, it is an incomplete theory (in the same way that an entitlement theory consisting only of principles of acquisition and transfer is an incomplete theory) that docs not provide adequate guidance in non-ideal circumstances where the historical principles have not been complied with. It only determines that there is injustice but does not tell us how it is to be addressed, in particular how the past wrongs are to be rectified. It thereby ignores that there are injustices that call for rectification, i.e., that there are particular steps that are required to address the particular injustices that obtain.

Non-ideal circumstances do not give rise to a blanket prescription to replace extant unjust institutions by institutions that conform to the historical principles. Simply instituting a political system that is considered to be justified according to the historical principles is not the appropriate response, since this does not address the past injustices that are in need of rectification. Insisting in the context of non-ideal circumstances that justification can only be based on actual consent amounts to ignoring the need for rectification. It is like insisting that all transfers of holdings have to be voluntary even when some holdings are illegitimate. What is required when a thief has illegitimately acquired certain goods is that the stolen goods be returned to their rightful owners. This transfer obviously does not have to be voluntary and the thief can instead be forced to return the goods. Voluntary transfers preserve justice and ensure that no new injustices are introduced. Yet, voluntary transfers are no longer what is called for when faced with unjust holdings. Similarly, while consent justifies political institutions in ideal circumstances, actual consent is not what is needed when institutions are unjust. Instead, what is required in each case is that the extant injustices be rectified.

Rectifying past injustices might even be required for the historical mechanisms of justification to be applicable. This is because a tainted past can undermine the normative force of consent. In particular, consent is only binding and only gives rise to justified institutions if the choice-situation is suitably untainted. This means that it can be necessary in non-ideal circumstances to address past injustices first before a consent-based justification can become applicable.

This problem can be illustrated by a situation in which an unjust state is in existence, but in which the citizens are given the opportunity to form a new state by means of a social contract based on unanimous consent. For instance, a dictator could allow the people to create a new state, where failure to reach agreement will mean reverting to the status quo, i.e., to the dictatorship. Since the status quo point of the bargaining problem is the unjust state, the incentives for reaching agreement are substantially different from those that would be faced if agreement were sought in the context of a justified status quo point. The problematic nature of this bargaining situation impugns the resulting social contract. As a result, it is far from clear whether unanimous consent in such a situation would (fully) justify the resulting set of institutions.

Not only is it unlikely that there will ever be unanimous consent, it is also not clear that such consent would classify as genuine consent, given that past injustices taint the choice situation. Consent theory thus only constitutes a self-standing theory in ideal circumstances. A complete theory, however, must also tell us how one is to deal with non-ideal circumstances, how past injustices are to be rectified, and how one is to get to a situation in which the historical principles are applicable.

Dealing with non-ideal circumstances is precisely what is achieved by rectificationist principles. They determine what is to be done in non-ideal circumstances, i.e., how one is to deal with the injustices that are to be found at the level of institutions. They do this by showing which institutional structures are such that bringing them into existence would amount to a rectification of past wrongs. In this way, they show how institutions can be legitimate, despite failing to conform to the historical principles, insofar as they stand in the relevant correspondence to the institutions that would have emerged in ideal circumstances. Accordingly, one needs to supplement historical principles by principles of rectification to arrive at a complete theory that is applicable in both ideal and non-ideal circumstances.

2.3. Degrees of Justification

When it comes to providing guidance as to how to get from institutions that lack justification to ones that are justified, it is important to have a comparative notion of justification that admits of degrees.[19] Recognizing degrees of justification enables a theory to provide guidance as to how a non-ideal situation is to be improved bit by bit, allowing one to approximate a state of affairs in which institutions are fully justified. This is particularly relevant when it comes to making improvements where the ideal cannot be reached (either in principle or in practice) but can only be approximated.

The rectificationist account naturally generates a comparative notion of justification, insofar as rectifying particular injustices amounts to partial rectification which corresponds to the institutions in question being partially justified, whereas rectifying all injustices amounts to the institutions being fully justified. In non-ideal circumstances, justification is understood in terms of a coincidence of actual institutions with those in the relevant

---

[19] Certain understandings of justification will require one to think in terms of degrees of illegitimacy since only illegitimacy will admit of a scalar construal.

counterfactual scenario. Whilst coincidence with a scenario in which no rights violations occur and in which the historical principles are perfectly complied with amounts to full justification, coincidence with a scenario in which only certain rights violations fail to occur and in which the historical principles are only imperfectly complied with can be construed as partial justification. In this way, comparative facts regarding the extent to which the counterfactual scenario is idealized generate an ordering of institutional structures. Institutional structures can accordingly be more or less justified, depending on the extent of unrectified rights violations that they involve.

In determining the extent of rights violations, one can distinguish different ways in which rights can be violated and attach different weights to different violations (for instance, one might like to discount or set aside what Thomson calls mere infringements of rights (cf. Thomson: 1990, p. 122)), such that the extent becomes a weighted function of certain types of violations. Weightings allow us to construct not just a quantitative measure of the deviation from the ideal case that is based merely on the number of rights violations, but also a qualitative measure that considers the significance of the deviations.[20]

The degree of rectification is then determined by the proportion of (weighted) injustices that are rectified. A certain set of injustices are rectified if the actual institutions coincide with those in the closest counterfactual scenario that is based on the local adjustments amounting to eradicating these injustices (without introducing any new ones). We can thus order counterfactual scenarios in terms of the range of local adjustments that generate them. With which counterfactual scenario the actual institutions coincide determines comparative facts about the extent to which injustices are rectified. Past injustices are fully rectified if the actual institutions correspond to those in the counterfactual scenario in which no rights violations occur. By contrast, if no counterfactual scenario based on supposing that certain rights violations had not occurred contains the institutions to be found in the actual world, then no injustices are rectified, i.e., the only institutionally coinciding counterfactual scenario is that in which none of the actual injustices failed to occur, i.e., the actual world.

How many (weighted) rights violations are to be found in the actual history determines the degree of injustice.[21] Together, the degree of rectification

---

[20] Since the requirement not to violate rights is distinct from the duty to rectify past rights violations, one does not end up with a utilitarianism of rights, i.e., what is at issue is not bringing about fewer violations of side-constraints but rectifying past injustices to a greater extent. Moreover, weightings can be applied even if one considers rights to be side-constraints, given that the importance or urgency of rectification need not derive from the status of the right that has been violated.

[21] Comparisons across different states require the scales to be normalized.

and the degree of injustice determine the degree of justification. This corresponds to the degree of injustice of the relevant institutionally coinciding counterfactual scenario. We can thus order institutional structures to be found in various counterfactual scenarios based on the extent to which these scenarios deviate from ideal circumstances. The closer they are to the ideal case, the smaller the (weighted) number of unrectified rights violations and hence the more justified the institutions are. Institutional structures are maximally justified if they correspond to those found in the counterfactual scenario that involves the minimal violation of rights. That is, they are fully justified if the institutional structures to be found in the actual world completely coincide with those of the ideal counterfactual scenario, which can happen either if there are no past injustices and hence no need for rectification, i.e., in ideal circumstances this counterfactual scenario is the actual scenario, or if there are injustices but they are fully rectified.

2.4. Moral Principles and Empirical Mechanisms

Which institutions are justified on the basis of counterfactual facts in a particular non-ideal context depends on two factors:

1. The moral framework specifying the historical principles of justification as well as the principles of rectification.
2. The descriptive account of the empirical mechanisms that explain how the behavior and interactions of individuals lead to the formation of institutional structures.

A rectificationist justification is concerned with evaluating what structures would be generated by these mechanisms in the context of the counterfactual scenario in which the past injustices that occurred in the actual world and that need to be rectified do not take place but where instead institutions arise in conformity with the historical principles of justification. Since the resulting structures would arise in compliance with the constraints and requirements specified by the normative framework, they would be justified in those counterfactual situations and accordingly constitute the ideal case to which the non-ideal actual institutions need to be made to conform. Moral principles and empirical mechanisms jointly determine what the relevant ideal counterfactual scenario looks like and how the non-ideal actual scenario is to be made to coincide with it.

Rights, compensation principles, and rectification principles constitute the moral framework.[22] This determines, on the one hand, which actions,

---

[22] The compensation principle is to be distinguished from the principle of rectification. (Davis: 1977, p. 220, for instance, conflates these principles.) The former is concerned

if any, leading to the situation in question generate (uncompensated) injustices that need to be rectified. On the other, it determines the constraints that institutional structures need to satisfy in order for them to be justified in virtue of their historical genesis, and thereby fixes the conditions that counterfactual processes must satisfy in order to generate legitimate outcomes that can be candidates for determining what needs to be done in order for past injustices to be rectified.

In addition to depending on one's understanding of morality, this type of justification also involves a dependence on the empirical mechanisms that generate the relevant institutions. These mechanisms determine how the counterfactual is to be evaluated. In particular, they determine the closeness facts and thereby determine which of the counterfactual processes satisfying the moral conditions are the ones the outcomes of which are to be brought about. Whilst all counterfactual processes satisfying the moral conditions are on a par as far as the normative framework is concerned, the descriptive part of the theory differentiates amongst these candidates in terms of their closeness to the actual world.

As a result, one ends up with an interesting dependence on positive social science, insofar as one needs to appeal to empirical mechanisms to determine which set of institutions would have arisen within the moral constraints. Since it is necessary to specify both moral constraints and empirical mechanisms in order to evaluate this counterfactual, the normative project of justifying the state becomes intertwined with the empirical project of explaining the state. This is because justification becomes a function of explanation in ideal circumstances. The rectificationist principles connect the explanation as to how institutions arise in ideal circumstances with the account as to which institutions are justified in the actual world.

This implies that one's views about issues such as network externalities and public goods will have a direct impact on the nature of the institutions that will be justified. For instance, different sets of institutions will be justified, whilst holding Nozick's moral framework fixed, depending on whether one accepts the empirical claim that a dominant agency would arise, which is based on Nozick's understanding of the network externalities involved in the provision of protection services. If the claim about network externalities is accepted, then the counterfactual will take us to a situation in which a

---

with a special range of cases in which a boundary crossing can be justified by compensating the person for the disadvantages that result from prohibiting him or her from performing certain risky activities, whereas the latter is concerned with what needs to be done to right past wrongs, whereby this rectification in no way makes it the case that the boundary crossings are justified. The compensation principle plays a role within the ideal counterfactual history, whereas the principles of rectification connect the counterfactual history to the actual history.

minimal state arises. Yet, if this claim is rejected, then the counterfactual will take us to an anarchic situation in which a plurality of different protective agencies compete, without any of them being dominant and without any of them having a (de facto) monopoly. This means that Nozick's commitment to individual rights could equally lead one to anarchism as to the minimal state, if one were to adopt a different view about the empirical question as to how protective agencies operate and interact.

In the same way that one can vary the account of the empirical mechanisms to end up with different institutional structures being justified, one can also vary the account of morality. This method of justification can, accordingly, be generalized beyond Nozick's framework by modifying the background understanding of rights. A modification of the understanding of rights that is operative will affect the nature of the political institutions that can be justified in this manner, given that the counterfactual scenario picked out by the rectificationist principle is dependent on what moral constraints are in place.

For instance, if an alternative moral framework that includes positive rights were to be adopted, then this could necessitate a transition from a minimal state to a more-than-minimal state, in the same way that the transition from an ultraminimal state to a minimal state is required due to the compensation principle within the context of Nozick's theory. In particular, if a minimal state were to violate the positive rights of its citizens—for instance if it should fail to provide them with the level of welfare/resources to which they have a rightful claim—then this would constitute a wrong that would have to be rectified. The way in which it would have to be rectified (at the institutional level) would involve bringing into existence the institutions that are to be found in ideal circumstances in which no rights are being violated by the state. Since these counterfactual circumstances involve more-than-minimal states that ensure that the positive rights of their subjects are fulfilled, it would follow that the rights-violating minimal state would have to be transformed into this type of more-than-minimal state in order for the injustice resulting from the violation of positive rights to be rectified.[23]

The fact that the rectificationist account generates a comparative notion of justification enables it to deal with cases in which rights fail to be compossible, as happens in the case of positive rights that are not co-satisfiable.[24]

---

[23] In the case of positive rights, the distinction between rectification at the level of institutional structures and the level of property distributions that was drawn above is particularly clear, and it would seem that, in addition to transforming the state into a more-than-minimal state, a rectification of property holdings would have to take place, which presumably would require the state to make up for arrears.

[24] Some consider compossibility to be a necessary requirement on a system of rights, especially those defending a choice theory of rights (cf. Steiner: 1977). An interest

There is a concern that if the compossibility condition is not satisfied, then one ends up with all no-rights-violations counterfactuals being vacuously true. If rights are not compossible, then rights violations are unavoidable, which means that there is no ideal scenario in which the moral constraints are fully complied with. Accordingly, the no-rights-violations antecedent will be impossible, thereby ensuring that any counterfactual with this antecedent will be vacuously true and that any set of institutions is, accordingly, trivially justified.[25]

In order to avoid this problem, one has to require the non-vacuous truth of the relevant counterfactual. Since there will be no non-vacuously true no-rights-violations counterfactual, no institutional structures will be fully justified. But this does not imply that all institutions will be equally unjustified. Instead, one can make various comparative claims. In particular, one can evaluate what institutions would have arisen in the situation in which the extent of rights violations is minimized. Rather than evaluating what would have happened had no rights been violated, one evaluates what would have happened had rights been violated to the minimal extent possible. This counterfactual then determines which institutional structures are maximally justified and hence what needs to be done to rectify all rectifiable injustices.[26]

2.5. Hypothetical Justifications

Rectification principles involve counterfactuals. This means that hypothetical facts have to be brought in to justify political institutions (except in ideal circumstances in which there are no injustices that need to be rectified and in which the justification is purely historical). Whilst being hypothetical

---

theory of rights, by contrast, is likely to lead to non-compossibility (cf. Waldron: 1989, p. 503).

[25] The requirement that the no-rights-violation condition of the counterfactual be satisfied not by supposing that the relevant rights had simply been alienated, waived, or forfeited is particularly important in this context, since this condition could otherwise be satisfied even when dealing with non-compossible rights. That is, a rights violation can be avoided in two ways: (1) by means of the perpetrator acting differently, or (2) by means of the victim having different rights. The counterfactual relevant for rectification identifies scenarios in which the rights-violating action is not performed or does not succeed, i.e., the rights are held fixed in evaluating the counterfactual, rather than a scenario in which the action is performed but does not classify as a rights violation. In short, the condition of there not being rights violations is to be satisfied by getting rid of violations rather than by getting rid of rights.

[26] Additionally, any plausible theory that allows for there to be conflicts of rights should identify a procedure or mechanism for resolving such conflicts. Accordingly, one should not assess the situation in which no rights are violated, but rather the situation in which there are no unresolved rights violations.

in nature, these principles differ radically from traditional hypothetical accounts for justifying the state. In particular, traditional accounts are not understood as supplementing historical principles in order to address non-ideal circumstances, but are instead taken to constitute complete theories that are meant to replace historical accounts. Such hypothetical principles are thus construed as independent principles that apply unrestrictedly, and not as restricted principles that are parasitic on certain logically prior principles that they are meant to supplement.

2.5.1. Justificatory Force

The rectificationist type of justification is partly hypothetical in nature. However, it is not vulnerable to the objections that are usually raised against hypothetical justifications. Any historical justification, such as a consent-based justification, needs to be actual—"hypothetical contracts do not supply an independent argument for the fairness of enforcing their terms. A hypothetical contract is not simply a pale form of an actual contract; it is no contract at all" (Dworkin: 1976, pp. 17–18). The fact that hypothetical contracts lack normative force in the actual world implies that traditional hypothetical consent models are at risk of collapsing into teleological models. Since hypothetical contracts are not actually binding, they can, at best, indicate that a certain state of affairs is rational or desirable.[27] Hypothetical explanations will then lack justificatory force in their own right and will only be able to play a role insofar as they point to teleological justifications (cf. Schmidtz: 1990). In this way, hypothetical accounts that, on the face of it, seemed to be forms of what Simmons calls transactional justifications collapse into generic justifications (cf. Simmons: 1999, p. 764). The appeal to hypothetical scenarios then becomes merely a heuristic device. Since idealized agents would consent to those principles or institutions that are independently justified, entertaining hypothetical situations can help us to identify what reasons there are and what institutions are justified, without providing any independent support.[28]

Unlike traditional hypothetical accounts, the appeal to hypothetical scenarios that forms part of a rectificationist justification is not a mere

---

[27] Cf. "What we 'could agree to' has prescriptive force for the Hobbesians, not because make-believe promises in hypothetical worlds have any binding force but because this sort of agreement is a device that (merely) reveals the way in which the agreed-upon outcome is rational for all of us" (Hampton: 2007, p. 482; also cf. p. 486).

[28] Given that it would seem that in order to determine whether idealized agents would consent to certain principles one would already have to know whether these principles are justified, hypothetical accounts would appear to presuppose the very thing that they are meant to establish.

heuristic device that helps us to identify which institutions have the relevant features that are required for them to be teleologically justified. Instead, the principles of justification themselves are specified counterfactually, i.e., these principles have counterfactual content. In order to determine what they require, one needs to determine what happens, in particular what institutional structures emerge, in the hypothetical circumstances in which agents do not violate the moral requirements specified by the historical principles. What type of institutional structure needs to be brought about is thus a function of counterfactual facts. In this way, counterfactual facts have justificatory force. They determine which institutions are justified and what is required if actual injustices are to be rectified.

2.5.2. Idealization

Relatedly, the notion of 'ideal' circumstances differs from that which features in standard hypothetical accounts. Since the rectificationist account is not concerned with considering what idealized agents would choose or consent to in order to identify a privileged set of institutions, the idealization does not pertain to the nature of the agents and the conditions in which they choose principles or create institutions. There is no need to idealize away their biases and imperfect information, nor to suppose that they are fully rational or 'reasonable'. Instead, what is being idealized is the history that generates certain institutions, given that one is concerned with what would have happened had there not been any injustice. The idealization, in this way, concerns the behavior of the agents (in particular, the behavior of those acting on the part of the institutions, i.e., agents of the state). Their behavior is idealized insofar as one supposes that they do not violate the normative requirements that bind them.[29]

Given that rectification principles supplement rather than replace historical principles, idealization is only required if the actual history diverges from the historical principles. By contrast, facts about the actual history drop out entirely in the case of hypothetical consent accounts. Such accounts do not assign any significance to historical principles—the fact that people actually consented or failed to consent is of no significance. What matters is not actual consent but idealized consent, such that if

---

[29] To idealize the behavior of the agents need not imply supposing that they are virtuous. All that is required of the relevant ideal scenario is that no rights violations occur, which need not imply that no rights violations are attempted. What exactly is required to implement the counterfactual supposition that no rights violations occur depends on how rights violations are construed, in particular on how much of the causal chain they implicate, i.e., on whether the rights violation is only constituted by the harmful effect, or also by the action that produced it, or even by the agent's intention.

idealized agents would not consent to a certain institutional set-up, then those institutions will not be justified even if they have been generated on the basis of actual consent. Only if people actually happen to be ideal in the relevant way will their consent suffice for justification, and even in that case what is doing the work is not the fact that they consented but the fact that they are ideal.

2.5.3. History-Dependence

The fact that the rectificationist account is not a traditional hypothetical account concerned with what suitably idealized actors would choose or agree to implies that what is justified is not a fixed set of institutional structures that are meant to be applicable across the board. Rather than being concerned with the intrinsic suitability of certain institutions, what is at issue is the question as to which institutions are justified in a particular context. Evaluating the counterfactual requires one to take into consideration the closeness of various hypothetical scenarios to the actual world. The relevant ideal counterfactual scenario is thus a function of the particular historical circumstances. If the actual histories differ, then the ideal counterfactual histories can diverge, which, in turn, makes it possible for different institutions to be justified. What classifies as ideal is, accordingly, not constant and fixed. Which institutional structures are justified can thus vary from context to context (though, if Nozick is right, there will not be much variation in practice, since the relevant hypothetical histories will in most cases converge on the minimal state). It is worth noting that this context variation is not to be explained in terms of the differential suitability of various institutions to present circumstances, but in terms of different societies having different histories.

The kind of reasoning that is traditionally invoked in hypothetical consent arguments does not, however, have to be discarded altogether. Instead, it can play a role in determining what reasonably rational people would have consented to, and hence can help us to determine what would have been likely to emerge in sufficiently ideal circumstances. In other words, this kind of reasoning can inform our understanding of the ways in which the empirical mechanisms would operate in the ideal counterfactual scenario. The advantage of the rectificationist approach is that it does not require excessive idealization of the agents. Nor is there a need to apply a veil of ignorance, which would bring with it the risk of making the deliberative position too attenuated to generate any substantive content. Instead, one only needs to make the empirical claim that people on the whole respond in reasonable ways to the incentives that they face (whereby these incentives, as well as what classifies as reasonable, can be culturally determined and can vary from context to context).

2.6. Evaluating Counterfactuals

In order to determine which institutional structures are justified in a certain context, one needs to evaluate a complicated counterfactual about what would have happened had the relevant historical principles of justification not been violated. Evaluating this kind of counterfactual brings with it a number of difficulties that might be thought to cast doubt on the adequacy of rectificationist justifications.

The first concern is that a rectificationist account is hopeless due to epistemic problems, insofar as the evaluation of such counterfactuals cannot be settled with any degree of determinacy. If it cannot be determined what the rectificationist principle requires in a given situation, then any such account would fail to be applicable and would not yield substantive insights.

In response we can note that, even though problems arise when it comes to evaluating the counterfactuals relevant for rectification, these difficulties are not especially significant in the case of institutional structures (in fact, they are notably less prominent than in the case of property distributions). In particular, the invisible-hand explanation ensures that the resulting outcome is stable, in that it will arise from a large range of initial starting points. Accordingly, a significant amount of convergence can be expected when concerned with the nature of the institutional structures that will arise in close-by worlds in which there are no (uncompensated) rights violations perpetrated on the part of these institutions, thereby making the evaluation of the relevant counterfactuals relatively straightforward. By contrast, no such convergence can be expected in the case of property distributions, which means that the rectification of violations of property rights faces more serious epistemic obstacles.[30,31]

---

[30] Property distributions also result from invisible-hand mechanisms, yet the type of stable features that they involve and in terms of which there is convergence are macro-features, such as those studied by economists, e.g., efficiency. The particular micro-realizations, i.e., who gets what, are not stable, however. Additionally, the rectification of violations of property rights is rendered especially problematic by the fact that property can be transformed, destroyed, improved, and damaged, which makes room for situations in which it is very difficult or even outright impossible to return holdings in the relevant condition to their rightful owners.

[31] The sharp separation of rectification regarding property and rectification regarding institutional structures is an oversimplification due to the fact that the territoriality of states implies an inseparable connection with property. As a result, even though there is convergence in terms of institutional structures, there need not be any convergence when it comes to the territories that are governed by the institutional structures in question. There are, however, two mitigating considerations. First, there is likely to be more convergence in the case of territory than in the case of movable material goods, due to the limited transferability of territory as well as due to the existence of various geographical focal points that naturally tend to become territorial boundaries. Second, the widespread convergence at the institutional level ensures that how geographical space is carved up

Moreover, the comparative conception that recognizes degrees of rectification helps us to address epistemic concerns. For practical purposes we do not need a precise evaluation of the counterfactual. All that is required is identifying the rough shape of justified institutions. This limited knowledge allows us to move in the right direction. Even if we do not have a fully determinate characterization of which institutions are (fully) justified, we can know that certain institutional structures are not justified and that changing them in various ways will lead to a more justified set of institutions. Accordingly, despite only having imperfect information that prevents us from perfectly realizing justified institutions, we can nonetheless improve things by approximating the fully justified state of affairs. The applicability of the rectificationist account thus does not impose excessively onerous epistemic requirements.

For instance, in Nozick's theory, any reduction in the size of more-than-minimal states will amount to a greater rectification of past injustices and hence lead to a situation that enjoys a higher degree of justification. By getting closer to a minimal state, one will get closer to the institutions to be found in the relevant ideal counterfactual scenario. This holds true even if there is some uncertainty as to whether the relevant ideal scenario might contain not a minimal state but rather no state at all or only an ultraminimal state. Settling this issue is required only when it comes to completely rectifying past injustices, not when approximating the institutions that are fully justified.

A second concern is that the counterfactual that tries to identify the institutional structures in the closest world in which no rights violations take place runs into difficulties due to non-identity problems. This is because the identity of the people who actually exist may be dependent on the rights violations that took place, such that different people would have existed had these rights violations not occurred. Insofar as the ideal situation contains different people from the non-ideal actual situation, it would not seem to be possible to make sense of the idea that existing people have claims to rectification that can be addressed by bringing the latter situation into conformity with the former.

In order to address non-identity problems, one needs to complicate the antecedent of the counterfactual in such a way that identities are held fixed. This follows from the general principle that one needs to distinguish rights violations from the side-effects to which they give rise, i.e., distinguish facts that involve rights violations from facts that merely depend on rights

into different territories is not of all that much significance, at least when we are concerned with the claims that individuals have to (not) be governed by certain types of institutional structures.

violations. Since rectification only requires one to address the former, the relevant counterfactual will hold fixed mere side-effects. Although it is often said that rectification amounts to undoing the effects of injustice, this characterization is too broad since there is no need to undo side-effects of injustice that do not involve rights violations but are only contingently causally connected to rights violations. Applied to the case at hand, this means that, rather than considering the closest scenario in which no rights violations take place, one has to evaluate the closest possible world in which the same people exist and in which there are no rights violations. Put differently, one has to require that rectification proceeds on the basis of an identity-preserving counterfactual.[32]

For instance, if x violates y's rights, whereby one of the side-effects of this rights violation is that z_1 rather than z_2 exists, then the counterfactual that simply assesses what would have happened had no rights been violated will select a world in which z_2 exists. By contrast, the ideal same-people counterfactual will select a world in which there is no rights violation and the 'side-effect' that z_1 rather than z_2 exists is brought about in some other way (which does not involve any rights violations). As long as the identity of z (i.e., whether z_1 or z_2 exists) is not essentially implicated in the wrongdoing but is only contingently causally connected to the rights violation, one can separate out the injustice from the effects that the injustice has on z's identity. If the injustice that needs to be rectified can be separated out from contingently causally connected processes that have an effect on identities, then one can rectify the injustice whilst holding the latter processes fixed. In this way, we can 'localize' the effect of the rectification of the injustice and then determine the overall effect that results from this rectification together with identity-affecting facts that are being held fixed. For instance, if the rights violation occurs at t_1, and if the identity-affecting action occurs at t_3, then one can evaluate would have happened at t_2 had no rights been violated as well as what would have happened at t_4 given the ideal situation at t_2 together with the identity-affecting action at t_3. The combined effect of the localized rectification together with the identity-affecting process determines the relevant ideal counterfactual situation with which the actual world is to be made to coincide.

There might be some injustices that are not rectifiable due to non-identity problems, i.e., cases where the identity-affecting fact is not merely a side-effect but involves a rights violation. The antecedent of the ideal same-people

---

[32] Since what matters is that the claims of those who do exist are met, i.e., that they are not suffering any disadvantages as a result of past injustices, all that is required strictly speaking is that the people who actually exist constitute a subset of the people in the counterfactual scenario.

counterfactual will then not be satisfiable, thereby making it the case that any such counterfactual will be vacuously true. Yet, even if there should be such cases, one can still use the proposed account to determine what is to be done in order to rectify those injustices that are rectifiable, i.e., those injustices that have corresponding non-vacuously true rectification counterfactuals. This means that one should restrict the antecedent of the counterfactual to those particular injustices that are rectifiable. Rather than assessing what would have happened had no rights violations occurred, one assesses what would have happened had no rectifiable rights violations occurred.

3. CONCLUSION

A counterfactual or rectificationist justification of political institutions thus constitutes an interesting (though as yet underdeveloped) alternative to traditional methods of justifying the state that treats the justification of institutional structures as being analogous to that of property distributions, subsuming these domains under a unified theory of justification.[33] This kind of justification is applicable in the non-ideal circumstances in which we find ourselves where the actual processes that led to existing political structures are far removed from what would be required for a purely historical justification to be applicable and where the prospects for genuine unanimous consent are beyond being slim.[34]

References

Bader, R. M. *Robert Nozick*. Continuum, 2010.
Danley, J. R. 'An examination of the fundamental assumption of hypothetical process arguments'. *Philosophical Studies* 34 (1978), 187–95.
Davis, L. 'Nozick's entitlement theory'. In *Reading Nozick: Essays on Anarchy, State, and Utopia*, ed. J. Paul. Rowman & Littlefield Publishers, 1981, pp. 344–54.
Davis, M. 'Necessity and Nozick's theory of entitlement'. *Political Theory* 5, 2 (1977), 219–32.

---

[33] Whether the proposed account is ultimately viable depends on whether this parallelism can be substantiated. This paper has focused on exploring this approach, identifying the kind of theory that can be constructed and the desirable features that it has, rather than on providing a foundational theory that undergirds this parallelism.

[34] For helpful comments, I would like to thank Bas van der Vossen, Joseph Carlsmith, Peter Jaworski, Fabian Wendt, as well as audiences at Oxford and at the OSPP conference in Syracuse. I am grateful to Jerry Gaus and an anonymous referee for very detailed and helpful referee reports.

Dworkin, R. 'The original position'. In *Reading Rawls*, ed. N. Daniels. Basic Books, 1976, pp. 16–52.

Gaus, G. 'Explanation, justification, and emergent properties: an essay on Nozickian metatheory'. In *The Cambridge Companion to Nozick's 'Anarchy, State, and Utopia'*, ed. R. M. Bader and J. Meadowcroft. Cambridge University Press, 2011, pp. 116–42.

Hampton, J. 'Contract and consent'. In *A Companion to Contemporary Political Philosophy*, ed. R. Goodin, P. Pettit, and T. Pogge, 2nd ed., vol. 2. Blackwell Publishers, 2007, pp. 478–92.

Holmes, R. 'Nozick on anarchism'. In *Reading Nozick: Essays on Anarchy, State, and Utopia*, ed. J. Paul. Rowman & Littlefield Publishers, 1981, pp. 57–67.

Hyams, K. 'Nozick's real argument for the minimal state'. *The Journal of Political Philosophy* 12, 3 (2004), 353–64.

Miller, D. 'The justification of political authority'. In *Robert Nozick*, ed. D. Schmidtz. Cambridge University Press, 2002, pp. 10–33.

Nelson, A. 'Explanation and justification in political philosophy'. *Ethics* 97, 1 (1986), 154–76.

Nozick, R. *Anarchy, State, and Utopia*. Basic Books, 1974.

Nozick, R. 'Invisible-hand explanations'. *The American Economic Review* 84, 2 (1994), 314–18.

Paul, J. 'The withering of Nozick's minimal state'. In *Reading Nozick: Essays on Anarchy, State, and Utopia*, ed. J. Paul. Rowman & Littlefield Publishers, 1981, pp. 68–76.

Schmidtz, D. 'Justifying the state'. *Ethics* 101, 1 (1990), 89–102.

Simmons, A. J. 'Justification and legitimacy'. *Ethics* 109, 4 (1999), 739–71.

Simmons, A. J. 'Consent theory for libertarians'. In *Natural Rights Liberalism from Locke to Nozick*, ed. E. Frankel Paul, F. D. Miller, Jr., and J. Paul. Cambridge University Press, 2005, pp. 330–56.

Steiner, H. 'The structure of a set of compossible rights'. *The Journal of Philosophy* 74, 12 (1977), 767–75.

Thomson, J. J. *The Realm of Rights*. Harvard University Press, 1990.

Waldron, J. 'Rights in conflict'. *Ethics* 99, 3 (1989), 503–19.

Wolff, J. *Robert Nozick: Property, Justice and the Minimal State*. Stanford University Press, 1991.

6

Political Philosophy and Epistemology

The Case of Public Reason

David Enoch

1. INTRODUCTION: THE SEEMINGLY EPISTEMOLOGICAL COMMITMENTS OF PUBLIC REASON

Public reason theorists routinely make seemingly epistemological claims. They talk about justifying principles to others (Rawls 1999, 508–9), about the uncertainty with which we should hold our evaluative commitments (Barry 1995), about reasonable persons and comprehensive doctrines,[1] about a morally-politically motivated higher epistemic standard (Nagel 1987), about intellectual modesty (Leland and van Wietmarschen 2012), and, of course, about the burdens of judgment: that is, Rawls's suggested explanations for the widespread moral and political disagreement we see, even among the reasonable (Rawls 1993, 56–7).

It certainly *seems* like epistemological claims are being made here.[2] What exactly are they, then? How are they related to contemporary discussions in epistemology proper, so to speak? Most importantly, can the epistemological commitments of the public reason tradition in political philosophy—whatever exactly they are—withstand criticism?

Unfortunately, and for reasons that are not entirely clear to me, public reason theorists do very little to explain—let alone defend—their

---

[1] *Everyone* in that tradition talks about those. For references to the many different categories of things to which Rawls applies the term "reasonable," see Wenar (1995, 34).

[2] Others in the public reason tradition reject reliance on epistemological considerations of the kind I mention here. See Larmore (1990, e.g. 342) and Nussbaum (2011, e.g. 20; though, see p. 29 for a role Nussbaum still allows the burdens of judgment to play). I reject such theories too, but for reasons that are independent of the discussion in this paper.

epistemological commitments.[3] In this paper I do some of this work for them, though with a critical twist. I try to understand what the epistemological commitments of public reason theorists need to be, and I eventually conclude that they are by and large indefensible. But I hope that the discussion is of value even regardless of its negative conclusions: For public reason theorists really do owe us much more by way of details regarding their epistemological commitments, and they really do have to engage the relevant current epistemological literature. If nothing else, I hope this paper will encourage them to do that.

The kind of views I will be discussing—and which for current purposes can be grouped together and called "public reason accounts" or sometimes "political liberalism"—all share a commitment to public justification, in something like the following sense: For political action to be legitimate, it must be based on public, shareable reasons; it must not be justified only in some general, impersonal sense, but must also be justifiable *to* all members of the relevant constituency. Thus, political justification must in some important, non-trivial[4] sense be *accessible* to all who are subject to the relevant political institutions (or to an important subset thereof, namely, the reasonable).[5] According to such views, then, even though you can hold on to your religious beliefs, your evaluative beliefs, your commitments with regard to what makes your life worth living, which relationships are of value and why, and so on—still, when it comes to political discussion and action, you should bracket these deep commitments (to comprehensive doctrines, perhaps), and restrict your reasons to only those that are accessible to all, only those that it is in some sense reasonable to expect that others too will accept. Different public reason accounts fill in the details here differently, offering different ways of understanding the accessibility requirement[6] (and other relevant details), and some of these varying details will emerge as relevant in the discussion below. But they all (or almost all) seem to have

---

[3] Leland and van Wietmarschen (2012) are a welcome exception. They also note with similar disappointment the gap here in the literature in political philosophy (722–3). Note also that they are not officially public reason theorists—they offer their discussion not as a defense of public reason, but rather as a way of checking its implications and furthering the debate (723).

[4] This qualification is important. It may be argued (it *has* been, by Raz 1998) that *all* justification is by its nature accessible to all. If so, the accessibility requirement is always trivially satisfied. Public reason accounts are characterized by a *non-trivial* accessibility requirement.

[5] For characterizations of the public reason tradition, see Quong (2013), Vallier and D'agostino (2013). See also my "Against Public Reason" (2015, section 2).

[6] For a critical survey of different ways of fleshing out this guiding idea within the public reason tradition, see Vallier (2011). Vallier rejects the accessibility requirement as he characterizes it, but endorses a closely related alternative.

epistemological commitments, and it is those commitments that I will be discussing in what follows.

One more preliminary: As already hinted, public reason accounts restrict the relevant constituency of the accessibility requirement. Typically, they don't require, as a necessary condition for the legitimacy of a political action based on some principle, that the principle be justified to *all* (or even all citizens), but to all *the reasonable*. It is not clear that such restriction can be motivated and defended from the perspective of a public reason account and its underlying motivations.[7] For the most part, though, I will be putting such worries to one side, simply because I want to focus in this paper on other issues. And so, I will restrict my entire discussion to just the reasonable. Of course, it's not immediately clear how to understand this notion, and—especially relevant in our context—whether the appropriate conception of the reasonable includes *epistemic* content. I return to this below. But throughout, I will be assuming that all believers and agents I'm talking about are reasonable. (This holds even when, for ease of exposition, I will not repeat the word "reasonable" every single time.)

The discussion proceeds as follows. In section 2, I try to understand better what it is that, according to public reason theories, a reasonable person believes. In particular, how is she supposed to combine commitment to her own (private) comprehensive doctrine with thinking that others adhering to competing comprehensive doctrines are reasonable, with an understanding of the burdens of judgment, and so on? I argue that on some possible suggestions incoherence follows, and on other, coherent understandings, the use that public reason theorists try to make of the reasonable person's beliefs is undermined. The burdens of judgment are also relevant here, but because I am not interested in Rawlsian exegesis, I quickly discuss them in an appendix. In sections 3 and 4, I address two possible readings of Nagel's (1987) thoughts. In section 3, I discuss the thought that some epistemic facts are directly morally relevant—perhaps, for instance, it is morally impermissible to coerce someone based on a principle one doesn't *know* the truth of—voicing doubts about the plausibility of any such epistemically sensitive moral-political standard. Then, in section 4, I address the thought that there are moral considerations making different, higher epistemological standards appropriate in the political context. I highlight some problems with this suggestion, and I tie the discussion to the current epistemological discussion of pragmatic encroachment. In section 5, I return to the central public reason notion of accessible justification, or

---

[7] In fact, I think that it cannot. For my reasons, and for many references to others developing different versions of this familiar point, see my "Against Public Reason" (2015, section 3.3).

justification-to, asking again how this accessibility should be understood, and in particular whether it can be understood epistemically. In the concluding section, I voice my suspicion that public reason theorists should not have been making epistemic claims in the first place. The underlying motivations, I argue, are neither epistemological nor epistemologically sensitive. If so, then—especially given the negative conclusions of previous sections—public reason theorists should find non-epistemic ways of making and motivating their main theses.

2. WHAT DOES A REASONABLE PERSON BELIEVE?

While the reasonable, according to the public reason tradition, acknowledge that their private commitments are private (that is, roughly, are not ones that can be expected to be accepted by all the reasonable), still, they remain (privately) committed to their comprehensive doctrines. Though different public reason theorists endorse different understandings of the reasonable, *this much* seems common to all. So the reasonable can be, for instance, Catholics, or Millian comprehensive liberals, fully committed to these (or other) comprehensive doctrines. Yet they are also committed—as reasonable—to not relying on these comprehensive doctrines in the public, political sphere. The reason for this is, as reasonable people appreciate, that some reasonable people will reject their comprehensive doctrines, perhaps because of the influence of the burdens of judgment.

This point—that the reasonable too can remain fully committed to their comprehensive doctrines—is not a Rawlsian anecdote. It is of central importance to this entire tradition (as Rawls himself explains (1993, 62–3, 150–4)). The hope of presenting a political conception of liberalism that is to a large extent free-standing, that doesn't rely on controversial so-called metaphysical assumptions, that is neutral as between different metaphysical commitments—this hope depends on the reasonable being able to remain committed to their (reasonable) comprehensive doctrines. After all, if this were not so, political liberalism would depend on rejecting all comprehensive doctrines—presumably, a serious metaphysical commitment, and one that Rawls is (with good reason) eager to avoid. It would also mean that hardly anyone in the real world is reasonable, as almost everyone is committed (if only implicitly and not always coherently) to some comprehensive doctrine.[8]

---

[8] It is unclear to what extent such a result—that hardly anyone in the real world is reasonable—is bad news for the public reason theorist. Estlund's (2008) and Quong's (2011) being entirely satisfied to do ideal theory seems to suggest that they don't find such a result problematic (and both have confirmed this in conversation). For statements

What, then, on such theories, do reasonable people believe? Take the reasonable Catholic. Presumably, she believes in Catholicism. Perhaps she also believes that other religions have many advantages to them, or that atheists too can be good people, and that she should interact with all these others as free and equal, and so on. But she also believes, I take it, that Catholicism is the one true religion. If no reasonable person can consistently believe *that*, then no reasonable person can remain committed to Catholicism, as this is presumably a part of the very content of Catholicism; if it isn't, feel free to pick an example of a reasonable comprehensive doctrine of which the analogous claim is a part.[9] What, then, does this reasonable Catholic believe? What does she believe, in particular, about (reasonable) non-Catholics?

Given the centrality of the construct of the reasonable person to political liberalism, this question is of central importance. If there is no way of answering it satisfactorily—if, in other words, there is no way of filling in the details here so that the reasonable turns out to be coherent, and to be plausibly owed accessible justification, the theory collapses. What, then, on this picture, do reasonable people believe about other reasonable people who reject their comprehensive doctrines?[10]

2.1. Nihilism, Skepticism, Relativism

Can the reasonable Catholic also be a nihilist about comprehensive doctrines (believing that no comprehensive doctrine is true, or nothing is of genuine value), or a skeptic about them (believing that we cannot know which comprehensive doctrine is true, or what is of value), or a relativist of sorts about them (believing that, roughly, Catholicism is "true for her" but not necessarily "true for others," or some such)?

We can afford to be quick here. Nihilism is strictly inconsistent with Catholicism (or any other comprehensive doctrine or value judgment). The nihilist Catholic—if he can exist—is incoherent. Skepticism about comprehensive doctrines is not strictly speaking inconsistent with comprehensive

---

in the other direction—also attributing such a view to Rawls—see Wenar (1995, 45) and Leland and van Wietmarschen (2012, 739, 743). For discussion, see my "Against Public Reason" (2015, 124–6).

[9] Or perhaps no *reasonable* doctrine includes such exclusivity claims as their content? I return to quick discussions of relativism below.

[10] A related question is What does *the political philosopher* believe? (See, for instance, Raz (1990, 76).) This question raises further complications that I cannot discuss here. In the text I discuss the commitments and beliefs of the reasonable citizen (rather than the political philosopher) because it's the reasonable citizen, not the political philosopher, who is a central construct of political liberalism.

Alexander (1993) seems to focus on the political philosopher—hence his emphasis on the claim that liberalism is inconsistent with many religions.

doctrines, but it gets very close: "P, and no one can know whether P" is not a contradiction, but is at the very least an instance of Moore's Paradox (of which much more in section 2.2). And assuming—as seems plausible about Catholicism, for instance—that a commitment to some reasonable comprehensive doctrines includes a commitment to knowledge of their truth (or of the truth of parts of the relevant doctrine), then Skepticism *is* strictly inconsistent with these comprehensive doctrines.[11] Relativism is a harder case, partly because it is not always clear how exactly to make sense of "true-for-me" locutions.[12] But the point just made vis-à-vis skepticism seems to hold: The commitment to at least some reasonable comprehensive doctrines seem inconsistent with such a relativist understanding. A reasonable person adhering to one of them, then, cannot be a relativist (Alexander 1993, 788).

And with regard to all three of these options (and possibly to other, related ones) it can again be noted that it would be highly surprising if political liberalism had to presuppose a commitment to such highly controversial, clearly metaphysical (in Rawls's sense) theses like nihilism, skepticism, or relativism. It is no wonder, then, that Rawls and his followers go to great lengths to deny such commitments.[13]

So the reasonable person cannot, on public reason accounts, coherently mitigate her commitment to her comprehensive doctrine in one of these ways. When she retains her commitment to Catholicism being the one true religion, she must also think that atheists, Orthodox Jews, Buddhists, Shiite Muslims, and many others adhere to false comprehensive doctrines. All of these, she must conclude, have false beliefs about such central things as what is of value, what is important in life, what makes life worth living, and so on. What, then, *does* her thinking of them as reasonable amount to?

2.2. Catholicism, but the Evidence Doesn't (Exclusively) Support Catholicism

One natural way of understanding what political liberals sometimes say is that the reasonable Catholic at least acknowledges—while remaining

---

[11] As far as I can see, the points in the text here suffice in order to undermine Brian Barry's (1995) defense of something like a public reason account, grounded in skepticism (or at least uncertainty) about comprehensive doctrines. For detailed discussion, see Clarke (1999, 634–7).

[12] But for a more precise version of relativism (sometimes called "new-age relativism"), see MacFarlane (2012), and the references there.

[13] Again, see Rawls *Political Liberalism* (1993, 62–3, 150–4). Also, endorsing any of these views will get the public reason theorist deeply into the so-called asymmetry problem (to which I return later in the text)—he would have to show why nihilism, or skepticism, or relativism is the way to go regarding comprehensive doctrines, but not regarding political liberalism itself. It's hard to see how this could be done.

committed to Catholicism—the relative paucity of the evidence for Catholicism. She should acknowledge, that is, that the atheist may be responding to the available evidence just as well as she is.

But it's not clear how the details should go here. If the thought is "Catholicism; but the available evidence[14] does not support Catholicism," then we are clearly in Moore's Paradox territory.[15] The original Moore's Paradox was about the absurdity of asserting a proposition while denying that one believes it;[16] but many related versions have been discussed since, including the assertions, or even just the belief, for some proposition p, "p, but I don't know that p" and "p, but my belief that p is not justified" (Williams 2015b, 33ff.). True, none of these contain a contradiction, exactly: Presumably, when I say "p, but I don't know that p" what I say has the same content as when you say "p, but David doesn't know that p," and so, seeing that what *you* say is not contradictory, neither is what *I* say. But still, in a perfectly straightforward way, denying that I know that p is not coherent with asserting, or even believing, p. And because a belief being justified is a necessary condition for it being known, if "Catholicism is true, but I don't know that Catholicism is true" is Mooreanly incoherent, "Catholicism is true, but the evidence doesn't support Catholicism" is even more clearly Mooreanly incoherent. Similarly, it seems, for "Catholicism is true, but it's just as likely to be false as it is to be true," and therefore, for "Catholicism is true, but my non-Catholic friend is just as likely to be right about this as I am"[17] or "Catholicism is true, but my atheist friend is just as likely as I am to be right about this."[18] This conclusion is also corroborated by direct intuitions about such assertions and beliefs: It does sound absurd, in precisely this Moorean way, for someone to assert—or even just to believe—such things as "Abortion is wrong, but my belief that abortion is wrong is not justified," and "Abortion is wrong, but my pro-choice friend is responding just as well to the evidence as I am on this."[19] This, then, is not

[14] By "evidence" I mean here something like "anything that can epistemically justify belief." If things other than evidence (more narrowly understood) can do that, I mean to include them here.

[15] For related points, see Raz (1989, 107) and Clarke (1999, 632).

[16] For very helpful surveys, see Williams (2015a, 2015b).

[17] See Raz (1989, 107) for related points.

[18] Without referring to Moorean incoherence, Alexander (1993, 780) notes how thoughts about sensitivity to evidence raise problems here.

[19] As noted, to me this sounds absurd. But suppose that it does not. Then one *can* believe these things. Still *should* one? Arguably, a belief—certainly, a justified one—that one's first-order belief is not justified can defeat whatever justification one had for the first-order belief. (I thank Ofer Malcai for this point.) Attributing to the reasonable person irrationality does not seem much more attractive, from a public reason perspective, than attributing to her incoherence.

a good reading of the reasonable person's beliefs: it renders her Mooreanly incoherent.[20]

But there are other possibilities in the vicinity here. I want to discuss three.

2.2.1. Not All the Evidence is Shared

Perhaps the thought is that the reasonable Catholic thinks of the reasonable atheist as reasonable in the way he's responding to evidence, but as not privy to the same body of evidence. Perhaps there's some evidence that is available to the Catholic but not to the atheist. Or perhaps there's some *misleading* evidence that the atheist is under the influence of but the Catholic is not.

Certainly, exposure to different bodies of evidence can explain disagreement even among equally competent, reasonable people. But how does this help the cause of political liberalism? Problems arise. First, it is not entirely clear how to understand the unavailability of evidence to the atheist. After all, testimony is one important way of rendering evidence (indirectly) available. What prevents, then, the atheist from being exposed to all the evidence the Catholic is exposed to, if need be, by way of the testimony of the Catholic? More importantly, though, why be neutral— even just in the political arena—between the commitments of those who are and those who are not exposed to all the relevant evidence?[21] We often take such asymmetry in exposure to evidence to be extremely important, even politically—think, for instance, about Mill's famous discussion of the bridge example, where the asymmetry in exposure to evidence about the bridge's condition justifies a rare (if temporary) exception to the no-paternalism rule (Mill 1869, ch. 5). Lastly, public reason theorists do not seem to think of the Catholic who thinks to herself "Ah, all these non-Catholics, if only they had been exposed to this evidence [*what* evidence?] they too would have seen the truth!" as reasonable.[22] To be reasonable, it seems, she has to acknowledge that some non-Catholics share all her evidence, and still—mistakenly, but reasonably—reject Catholicism.[23]

---

[20] Nagel's (1987, 230) talk of the need to view one's view as justified only from the inside, while from the outside to consider it to be merely one's view, is not clear enough to determine whether this too is subject to Moorean incoherence. See Clarke (1999, 632).

There are in the literature some doubts about the incoherence of such Mooreanly incoherent statements. See, for instance, Frances (2016). But as far as I can see these local doubts (about some specific cases) don't challenge what I say in the text.

[21] Quong (2011, 246) notices that sometimes the disagreement is due to difference in exposure to evidence. But he doesn't note the problem in the text.

[22] Notice that I nowhere rely on intuitions about reasonableness—a term that in public reason theories has a technical meaning, not its natural language one. I rely on what public reason theorist seem to say (and to have to say) about reasonableness.

[23] This is clearest in Leland and van Wietmarschen (2012).

So on somewhat ad hominem grounds as well it seems inadvisable to think of the reasonable Catholic as thinking of (all) non-Catholics as being merely deprived of access to some evidence she has.

2.2.2. Epistemic Permissiveness

In order to avoid Moorean incoherence, our Catholic cannot think that her belief in Catholicism is not (epistemically) justified, or that it is not supported by the evidence. But perhaps she can still think that it is not *exclusively* supported by the evidence. Perhaps, that is, she can believe that while her belief in Catholicism is, given the evidence, epistemically permissible, so is her Jewish friend's belief in Judaism, or her atheist's friend's rejection of both.

In the epistemological literature, there is now some discussion of epistemic permissiveness: the thought, perhaps roughly, that in a given state of evidence with regard to p, there is more than one credence that it is maximally rational to have regarding p (White 2005), or perhaps that regardless of *maximal* rationality, there is more than one credence that it is *acceptable* to have.[24] And admitting epistemic permissiveness need not involve one in Moorean incoherence, or so at least I am happy to assume for the sake of argument: Certainly, "I am very confident that p, but it's also okay, given the evidence, to be somewhat less confident that p" doesn't sound *as* problematic as the Moorean sentences above. So perhaps this is what the reasonable Catholic should think of non-Catholics—that while they are wrong, their false beliefs are epistemically permissible (just like her own).

But this too won't do. The first thing to note here, of course, is that whether epistemic permissiveness is even real—whether there is ever a case where two different credences in a proposition are both maximally rational, or even both epistemically acceptable—is a hotly debated issue.[25] The jury is still out, so to speak, on epistemic permissiveness. So if this is the best the public reason theorist can do in fleshing out the beliefs of the reasonable, stakes have been raised—he is now tying the acceptability of his theory to that of epistemic permissiveness; he is gambling, so to speak, on the future of epistemology.

Second, even if epistemic permissiveness in general makes sense, it is very hard to believe it could help *here*. For notice that what is needed in our context is not just permissiveness as applied to credences—our Catholic is not merely supposed to think it acceptable to be somewhat less confident in Catholicism than she is. What is needed is permissiveness as applied to

---

[24] In "Not Just a Truthometer" (Enoch 2011, 957, n. 9) I argue that this understanding better captures the suggested analogy between epistemic and moral permissiveness.

[25] See, for instance, White (2005); Brueckner and Bundy (2012); Weintraub (2013).

outright belief:[26] She is supposed to believe that it's permissible to *believe* Catholicism, but also permissible to *believe* its denial (presumably implied by atheism, for instance). But it is no accident that when epistemic permissiveness is discussed, epistemologists typically talk of credences, not of beliefs. Perhaps there is plausibility to the thought that, given a body of evidence, there's more than one level of confidence that it's okay to have in the relevant proposition. But the thought that given the evidence it's okay to believe p, and it's also okay to believe not-p, is much, much less plausible. And so, even if the supporters of permissiveness win the epistemological day, it still seems that this won't help the public reason theorist.[27]

Third, wouldn't it be surprising if the fate of a major general view in political philosophy turned on such intricate epistemological discussions? Partly, I take this rhetorical question to support the suspicion (to which I return in the final section) that epistemology is not really what's at issue here. But in the context of this section, there's more. For there is something *especially* problematic about the fate of *this* view in political philosophy depending on the plausibility of epistemic permissiveness. This is so because presumably, whether epistemic permissiveness is real is something reasonable people differ on. If so, there's a case to be made that the public reason theorist cannot consistently rely on epistemic permissiveness even if it is true, nor can he restrict the scope of the relevant constituency (justifiability to whom is a necessary condition of legitimacy) to just those who accept epistemic permissiveness. I offer this point (which will return from time to time below) in a somewhat tentative way—perhaps the public reason theorist can insist that the accessibility requirement does not apply to itself and to the theory in political philosophy of which it is a part.[28] At the very least, though, there's a complication here in need of attention from the public reason theorist, if she wants to rest her theory on such highly controversially epistemological theories.

---

[26] Weintraub (2013, 744) calls this "extreme permissivism."

[27] In another way, though, the kind of permissiveness needed here may be more plausible than others—for it seems like the public reason theorist at most needs *inter-personal* permissiveness. She need not accept also *intra-personal* permissiveness. (Weintraub (2013) is especially clear about this distinction.) Perhaps, for instance, the Catholic may think that while rejecting Catholicism is not permissible *for her*, it *is* permissible for others, perhaps those starting with very different prior probabilities regarding the relevant propositions (I thank Levi Spectre for relevant discussion here). Indeed, perhaps for *them*, Catholicism is not even epistemically permissible! I don't think that this way of thinking—while interesting—is one that public reason theorists should find appealing, for the reasons in the text.

[28] Similar points come up in the discussion of the self-defeat objection to public reason. See my "The Disorder of Public Reason" (2013, 170ff.), and the references there.

2.2.3. *Not a Belief at All*

Perhaps the public reason theorist can argue, though, that much of the discussion so far has been rooted in the mistake of thinking about the commitment of the reasonable to her comprehensive doctrine as a *belief.* Perhaps the nature of our Catholic's commitment to her Catholicism is not cognitive. If so, Moorean incoherence doesn't apply, and perhaps there is even room for greater permissiveness. Perhaps then she can see her fellow citizens who reject Catholicism not as having false beliefs (not even as merely lacking some true ones), but as differently committed in some other, non-cognitive way. And perhaps this is a possible way of allowing her to retain her commitment to Catholicism while also seeing them as reasonably rejecting it?

I agree that a commitment to a comprehensive doctrine often involves more than just cognitive states. Perhaps, in the case of Catholicism, it also involves a resolution to live one's life in a certain way. So there's some plausibility to the thought that commitment to a comprehensive doctrine is not merely a cognitive affair. Still, this too won't do.

For note, first, that even if *more* than beliefs are involved in a commitment to a comprehensive doctrine, beliefs too are often involved. It is at the very least natural to think that a commitment to Catholicism—even if it involves practical resolutions, or some such—*also* involves some beliefs. And while with regard to any specific religion, it is, I guess, possible to differ on this, the thought that there is *no* (reasonable) comprehensive doctrine a commitment to which involves beliefs seems very hard to accept.

Second, the non-cognitivist tradition in metaethics—according to which value judgments, for instance, are not the expressions of beliefs, but rather of a conative, more desire-like state—has been evolving, and most contemporary followers of the non-cognitivist tradition will now resist the temptation to put things in this way. Rather, they insist that they can fully accommodate moral beliefs, and moral propositions, and moral properties, and moral facts, and moral knowledge (Blackburn 1993; Gibbard 2003). And they have their reasons for going down that road—the difficulties facing more traditionally and straightforwardly noncognitivist views seem insurmountable. If the public reason theorist has to rely on the claim that the reasonable person's commitment to his or her comprehensive doctrine and value judgments does not include a belief, then, he has to rely on an especially implausible (and, for what it's worth, unpopular in the current metaethical literature) version of non-cognitivism.

Finally, a point from the previous subsection again applies. A commitment to such controversial metaethical theses—presumably, controversial even among the reasonable—is precisely what the political liberal was hoping to avoid.

So much, then, for attempts—on behalf of the public reason theorist—to allow the reasonable Catholic to see the beliefs of the reasonable (e.g.) atheist as justified, in a way that is both epistemically respectable and that is consistent with the political implications the public reason theorist is after. Perhaps, though, the public reason theorist can get what he needs even if the reasonable Catholic has to think of reasonable citizens adhering to other comprehensive doctrines as *un*justified?

2.3. They Are as Competent as I Am, but Subject to a Performance Error

Here is another—natural, but altogether different—suggestion as to the beliefs of the reasonable Catholic. Being committed to Catholicism, she has to think that those rejecting Catholicism are wrong, and have false beliefs. But she can still think of them as epistemically competent, indeed as just as epistemically competent as she is.

This suggestion has recently been developed in great detail by Leland and Van Wietmarschen (2012). They argue that the requirement of restraint—not to rely in the public sphere on one's conceptions of the good, or other private judgments—has to be justified; and that in the range of relevant views it is justified by appeal to *reciprocity in justification:* "When deliberating about fundamental political issues, each citizen must only appeal to those considerations she can reasonably expect all other reasonable people to accept" (724). As to what it is reasonable to expect people to accept, they suggest a condition of intellectual modesty: the reasonable person must accept "Universal Disagreement" (731): "For each of his nonpublic convictions and political conclusions, he believes that reasonable people at all levels of competence endorse views that conflict with his own." Because this holds for any level of competence, it is not reasonable to expect one's fellow reasonable citizens to agree on one's non-public convictions.

Importantly, Leland and Van Wietmarschen include in their conception of competence also exposure to all the relevant evidence (2012, 726). So we are not back in the scenario discussed in section 2.2.1. Rather, on this picture, the reasonable person acknowledges that for each of her private commitments, it would remain controversial even when we idealize the evidence and the epistemic competence in responding to them all the way up to what is currently humanly possible.

Notice that the reasonable person who is intellectually modest in this way need not be Mooreanly incoherent. It is certainly possible for you to believe a proposition p, while also believing that someone who is as competent in such matters as you are, and who is exposed to the same evidence, believes not-p. It is no less possible than believing that the reading of one thermometer is accurate and the other isn't, even though they are equally reliable in the relevant set of cases—presumably one of them is guilty of a performance error. No big mystery there. Similarly, thinking that people at all competence levels differ on the truth of Catholicism does not preclude one from thinking that Catholicism is true. In this—quite important!— way, Leland and Van Wietmarschen's suggestion is significantly better than several of the other suggestions already considered. But this way too will not save the political liberal, for the following three reasons.

First, while it is *possible* to believe p while also believing that an equally competent believer believes that not-p, whether this is ever *rational* is a deeply controversial matter. Recent discussions of peer disagreement[29] debate precisely this point. According to some of the central views in this debate—the Equal Weight View, or perhaps conciliatory views more generally—the rational thing to do in the face of such disagreement is to "split the difference" between the two views, and in the case of an outright belief that p and an outright belief that not-p, to suspend judgment. According to such views, the situation is similar to that of the two thermometers: if two thermometers are equally reliable, and they issue different readings in a specific case, then though it is *possible* to believe all that and also that the reading of one of them is accurate, the only *epistemically justified* thing to do (in the absence of further evidence) would be to suspend judgment between the two readings (or to go for some other *symmetrical* solution). It should be obvious, then, that if such views of peer disagreement in general are true, then what follows from Leland and Van Wietmarschen's Universal Disagreement is that we should suspend judgment on all comprehensive doctrines, and on all value judgments that are controversial among the reasonable. This would take us back to skepticism, and so to section 2.1, and would spell doom for public reason accounts.[30] Of course, it's not as if the Equal Weight View is the obvious way to go on peer disagreement.[31] But we again come up against the points made above in different contexts: It seems highly unlikely that whether we should accept a public reason account in political philosophy depends on who wins the day in the epistemological discussion of peer disagreement, and anyway, the thought that a Rawlsian would have to rely on a highly controversial epistemological thesis (like the

[29] See, for instance, Kelly (2005, 2009), Elga (2007), and the papers collected in Christensen and Lackey (2013); see also my (2011) and the references there.

[30] Leland and van Wietmarschen note all this (2012, 745), and say that the challenge of avoiding this result may be the most serious one their understanding of intellectual modesty raises for public reason accounts (746).

[31] I offer reasons for rejecting it in my "Not Just a Truthometer" (2011). Quong (2011, 252–3) seems to take for granted that nothing like the Equal Weight View is true.

rejection of the Equal Weight View and related views) in her attempt to establish a free-standing political liberalism seems implausible.[32]

Assume away the first problem—the relevance of the discussion of peer disagreement. Another problem arises here, one that is perhaps of more interest in the specific context of discussing Leland and Van Wietmarschen. In the relevant high level of idealized competence that they are happy to consider, what can explain the remaining disagreement about conceptions of the good and comprehensive doctrines? The burdens of judgment, for instance, seem like a particularly bad option here, because (as I show in the appendix) they involve failures of sufficient idealization. (Perhaps this is why Leland and Van Wietmarschen nowhere rely on them.) It seems that given sufficient high competence and sufficiently good evidence, disagreement can only be explained by something worth calling a performance error on at least one side. It cannot be something more systematic, after all, because had it been, competence would have been compromised.[33] Assume, then, that our reasonable Catholic accepts Universal Disagreement, and so also thinks that all non-Catholics (among the suitably idealized, competent thinkers) are guilty of a performance error: While they are in general as good as she is (or as good as the idealized thinker who does endorse Catholicism is) in responding to evidence, still on this occasion they haven't responded to evidence as well as she does. This, to repeat, is a perfectly coherent thought. No Moorean incoherence is involved. But other problems arise: First, it is not entirely clear whether thinking that what explains the (idealized) reasonable non-Catholic's rejection of Catholicism is a performance error—an epistemic glitch, as it were—is consistent with treating her with the kind of respect that public reason theorists tend to emphasize. (I put things tentatively—it's not clear to me whether this is consistent with the relevant kind of respect, because it's not clear to me what the relevant kind of respect is.) Second, recall that the thoughts of the reasonable Catholic regarding the reasonable non-Catholics are supposed to shape expectations of acceptance. That is, the reasonable Catholic can only refer—in public, political discourse—to considerations that she expects others to accept, and what she can expect others to accept is, on Leland and Van

---

[32] For a recent example of what looks like a confusion about peer disagreement expressed in the context of defending a public reason account, see Gaus (2015, 1085).

[33] In correspondence, Leland and van Wietmarschen resisted the point in the text, suggesting that there's *a* sense of systemic failure (on just one side) that is consistent with equal competence. But it's not clear to me how this can be so. They suggested that this can be so if the disagreeing parties have widely diverging epistemic standards. But even assuming that this is so, and that what it is epistemically permissible for one to believe strongly depends on one's epistemic standards (rather than on the *right* epistemic standards), this will render this suggestion a particular instance of the epistemic permissiveness line, already discussed above.

Wietmarschen's view, what would be a matter of consensus among the suitably idealized agents. Matters that are not the subject of such a consensus are barred from political discourse. But now we know that the disagreement among the most competent, idealized thinkers is a matter of a performance error, a glitch by the erring party. So it makes sense to ask—why exclude from political debate considerations that are only controversial because of such glitches? This doesn't seem to rationalize excluding these considerations. Much less does it make sense to issue a demand addressed at the reasonable Catholic that she avoid relying on Catholicism-based considerations in the public sphere, merely because the competent atheist is subject to a performance error of this kind.

Third—and this point applies much more widely than Leland and Van Wietmarschen's suggestion—we should be suspicious of public reason accounts that demand too much by way of philosophical reflection and sophistication as a necessary condition for reasonableness. This is important—sometimes, public reason theorists write as if in order to count as reasonable, you must have read Rawls. This can't be right. Similarly, though, it can't plausibly be considered a necessary condition of reasonableness that the reasonable believe, say, that even the most competent thinkers, suitably idealized, with access to suitably idealized evidence, will disagree about the truth of Catholicism. After all, most people—even most reasonable people, presumably—are not epistemologists. Not only don't they believe such things, they typically don't even entertain such thoughts. It is therefore highly implausible to understand the reasonable Catholic's beliefs about her fellow citizens as incorporating really complicated, abstract, theoretical epistemic concepts.[34]

Putting the reasonable Catholic's beliefs about her fellow citizens in terms of intellectual modesty—understood, as in Leland and Van Wietmarschen, in terms of competence—does not help, then, in drawing a picture of the reasonable that is both coherent and plausible, and that can ground the arguments public reason theorists want it to ground.

2.4. They Responded Well Enough; or Perhaps: They Are Epistemically Excused

Let me make another suggestion, then, for a plausible way of understanding the reasonable Catholic's beliefs about the reasonable non-Catholics—one that is not, as far as I know, anywhere explicitly stated or developed by public reason theorists, but that is nevertheless worth thinking about.

---

[34] This line of thought also applies to the general attempt to make sense of the intuitive thought that "reasonable people may differ," which I return to in section 2.5.

According to this suggestion, the Catholic does not think there's any significant symmetry between her and non-Catholics: after all, she believes the truth, and they don't; she's responded well to the evidence, and they have not. Still, there is an important distinction that the reasonable Catholic can make between the mistakes of her reasonable fellow citizens and other mistakes. I have in mind two related ways of drawing such a distinction.

One would be that though her reasonable fellow citizens make a mistake, it's not too bad a mistake—perhaps, in some intuitive sense, though their beliefs are false, they are *almost* true; or perhaps, though they have failed to respond in the appropriate way to the available evidence, still their miss was a *near* miss—they haven't responded well, but perhaps they've responded *well enough*. This way of thinking about the mistakes of the non-Catholics seems in line with the thought that a reasonable person respects, in some sense, her fellow citizens—they are not, on this picture, very bad reasoners. They're just not maximally good.

It is not clear to me whether there's a way of filling in the details here that will make this way of proceeding succeed. In order to pursue this line, the following things have to be shown: First, the idea of a *near miss* must be made more precise. Furthermore, it must be made more precise in a way that makes it plausible to think that all reasonable comprehensive doctrines allow for some misses to be thought of as near, and furthermore, count all other reasonable comprehensive doctrines as near misses. If, for instance, we want (some versions of) Catholicism to count as reasonable, and (some versions of) atheist comprehensive liberalism to count as reasonable, and if no version of Catholicism views any version of atheism as a near miss, then public reason theorists cannot understand the reasonable person's beliefs in terms of such near misses. Even if the needed idea of a near miss can be developed in a way that satisfies this first condition, though, a second also needs to be satisfied: it must be plausible to think of the distinction between near misses and other misses as one that grounds the relevant kind of accessibility requirement. That is, it must be plausible to argue that we should exclude from political discourse all and only those ideas and judgments that are a matter of controversy among those whose misses are (always? typically?) near misses.

I can't think of a conclusive argument showing that these conditions cannot be satisfied. But I think enough has been said to raise suspicions here (especially about the first). If a public reason theorist wants to pursue this line of thought and step up to the challenge set by these two conditions, let him or her fill in the details, so that we can then check them for plausibility.

The second—related, but distinct—way of distinguishing here between the mistakes of the reasonable non-Catholics and other mistakes is by utilizing the idea of an *excuse*. In the philosophy of the criminal law, and also in normative ethics, we sometimes distinguish between *justifying* and *excusing* defenses (for instance, Greenawalt 1984). Justifying defenses show that a token of an act type that is usually unlawful or wrong (say, the intentional killing of another) is not in this case (say, a case of self-defense) wrong at all. Excusing defenses are different: Rather than challenging the wrongness of the specific act, they concede it, and deny (at least some of) the culpability of the relevant agent. You may think, for instance, that the fact that the agent was drunk when he spoke in a way that hurt your feelings doesn't make speaking in this way morally alright, but takes away (some of) his culpability for doing so.

A similar distinction may apply in epistemology. Perhaps there are some considerations that do not *justify* a belief, but that nevertheless negate the believer's responsibility or culpability or blameworthiness for believing unjustifiably. Perhaps, for instance, the fact that a proof that p is sufficiently hard to follow—while falling short of justifying my belief in not-p—still excuses this belief of mine. Or perhaps, when the psychological or social costs of believing in accordance with the evidence is too high, believing otherwise—though still unjustified—is excused.[35]

The reasonable Catholic cannot—as was argued above—think of her non-Catholic fellow citizens as *justified* in their rejection of Catholicism. But she can still think that these non-Catholics are epistemically excused.[36] Perhaps because it's so hard to shape one's beliefs and one's way of life in ways that are in such tension with that of one's immediate environment, they are not epistemically to blame for not seeing the truth of Catholicism. And notice that so thinking of non-Catholics seems both coherent and—to an extent, at least—respectful.

But we are again up against the other horn of the dilemma: If this is what the reasonable Catholic thinks of non-Catholics, can this rationalize the requirement not to rely in the public sphere on Catholicism-based considerations? Excuses, recall, do not undermine the wrongness of the relevant action or the unjustifiability of the relevant belief. They merely speak to (in this case, epistemic) culpability. But why should the epistemic non-culpability of non-Catholics make a difference here? In order to argue that it does, the public reason theorist would have to defend a version of the accessibility requirement according to which, roughly, it is wrong to politically rely on

---

[35] Obviously, the topic of epistemic excuses raises a whole host of issues that I cannot discuss here. For some initial discussion and references, see Boyd (2015); Littlejohn (forthcoming); and Williamson (forthcoming). I hope to discuss epistemic excuses in detail in future work.

[36] I don't know of anyone developing this line in detail. But some comments made in this context can be understood as flirting with this line of thought. See, for instance, Raz (1989, 105) on the difficulty of responding appropriately to complex evidence.

all and only those considerations that are only *culpably* rejected. And it is hard to believe that anything like this accessibility requirement can be made to work: Excuses can apply very, very widely. In fact, it is very hard to imagine any belief at all—however epistemically ludicrous or indeed morally repugnant—that cannot be non-culpably held. By raising the psychological costs of acknowledging the relevant truth, and by making appreciating the evidence harder, we can always give examples where pretty much any belief is held blamelessly, where an epistemic excuse applies. So if the version of the accessibility requirement that the public reason theorist defends excludes only those beliefs that are culpably held (or even more clearly, those that *can* only be held culpably), it dangerously flirts with anarchism. It may exclude everything.

2.5. Disjunctions; or: "Reasonable People May Differ"

Perhaps the public reason theorist can avoid some of the problems above by going disjunctive. Perhaps, that is, all he has to insist on is that while for every reasonable Catholic (etc.) there must be some epistemic story of the kind searched for throughout this section, it need not be the same epistemic story that is true of all. What is common to all reasonable people who are committed to a comprehensive doctrine is the disjunction—they have to think of the reasonable who reject their comprehensive doctrines either as guilty of a performance error, or as lacking some evidence, or . . . This is not a line that is pursued in any public reason text I am aware of, but perhaps it is implicitly assumed (perhaps this is why public reason theorists are so epistemically nonchalant). And anyway, it seems a line worth pursuing.[37]

Perhaps the plausibility of this point can be bolstered by the thought that sometimes, with regard to some things, reasonable people may differ. This thought—that reasonable people may differ—seems intuitively very plausible, and so is worth accounting for quite independently of the commitments of public reason theory. Perhaps, then, the public reason theorist can insist that all reasonable people accept that with regard to their comprehensive doctrines, reasonable people may differ—this is what's common to all the reasonable—and then allow different reasonable people to be committed to different underlying stories of the reasonable-people-may-differ phenomenon.

In response, let me make the following three points.

First, we mustn't make the mistake of thinking that by "reasonable" public reason theorists mean *reasonable*. In the context of public reason theory,

---

[37] For making me see this, I thank Teresa Bruno Nino, Jon Quong, Stefan Sciaraffa, and Steven Wall.

"reasonable" is a technical term, with a stipulated meaning (or meanings) (Enoch 2015, 121, and the references there). So from the plausible thought that reasonable people may differ it just doesn't follow that reasonable people *as this term is understood in public reason accounts* may differ. Perhaps this is also true, but this has to be shown, not assumed or "inferred" by equivocation. And there's reason for concern that this isn't true—the natural, intuitive thought that reasonable people may differ seems to apply to many issues—like public reason theory itself—about which public reason theorists insist that reasonable people (in the stipulated sense) do not differ.

Second, a disjunction is only helpful if it's not the case that all the disjuncts fail. With regard to some of the suggestions above, if my arguments succeed, this unfortunate situation is precisely the case. It must be admitted, though, that at some points I emphasized problems in generalizing—insisting that even if a solution applies to some comprehensive doctrines or to some reasonable people holding them, it doesn't apply to others. Such objections from generalization failures are indeed threatened by the disjunctive move. Luckily, nowhere did I rely, in rejecting a suggestion, *only* on generalization failure.

But you may still be worried, because of the plausibility of the thought that reasonable people may differ. That thought remains plausible, and so if the discussion above precludes making sense of it you may take that as reason to doubt that discussion rather than to reject that natural thought. So the following, third, point is especially important: Some ways of making sense of the thought that reasonable people may differ will not help the public reason theorist. Think, for instance, about unshared evidence. There, I argued not that there's an epistemic problem with the reasonable Catholic thinking that non-Catholics lack evidence, but that from the point of view of the public reason theorist there's a *political* problem with it. Wherever this is the kind of difficulty I highlighted, I can accommodate natural ways of thinking that reasonable people may differ, while resisting the public reason theorist's suggested political implications.

Going disjunctive too, then, won't help the public reason theorist explaining the beliefs of the reasonable Catholic. The challenge stands.

3. EPISTEMICALLY SENSITIVE MORAL STANDARDS

The discussion in this and the following section follows Nagel (1987), offering two possible ways of understanding his main points there.[38] On both

---

[38] With Nagel as with Rawls, I am not primarily interested in exegesis. Let me just note that at the end of the day, it's not clear to me what his position is. In *Equality and*

these readings, epistemology is relevant, but in a different way from that discussed in the previous section. Here, we will no longer ask about the beliefs of the reasonable person, but will ask directly about the moral constraints applying to state action. And Nagel seems to think that in asking about these, epistemology is relevant.

Nagel starts from the emphasis on state action being *coercive*. Though I think the emphasis on coercion is exaggerated, I will not question this starting point here. Now, there are moral constraints that apply to coercion. And perhaps some of them have epistemic content. In other words, perhaps one can't justifiably coerce based on some principle, unless one stands in a privileged epistemic status regarding it. Here's an instance of the argument schema I have in mind:[39]

(i)   It is morally impermissible to coerce a policy on someone, based on a principle (that they do not accept), unless the principle has epistemic status P.

(ii) When it comes to comprehensive doctrines, nothing has epistemic status P.

(iii) Therefore, it is morally impermissible to coerce a policy on someone, based on a comprehensive doctrine (that they do not accept).[40]

Notice that in this argument schema disagreement plays somewhat minor or secondary roles. Disagreement may be relevant in the explicit way that I highlighted in the bracketed parts of (i) and (iii). Perhaps more importantly, disagreement may be relevant—depending on the details—to premise (ii). Perhaps, that is, disagreement (or disagreement of a special kind) about comprehensive doctrines makes it the case that they do not enjoy the privileged epistemic status needed for justifiable coercion.

The argument schema is not implausible, it seems to me. And it is valid. But we need, of course, details about epistemic status P. And what is needed for the argument to go through is for there to be some epistemic status P that renders both (i) and (ii) true, or at least plausible: In other words, we need to find some epistemic status such that it's wrong to coerce based on a principle that doesn't enjoy it, *and* that no comprehensive doctrine (or some

---

Partiality (1991, 163, n. 49), Nagel takes back the earlier arguments, which he characterizes as epistemological. Two pages earlier (161), though, he seems to endorse something like epistemic permissiveness (perhaps restricted to the domain of the political), and to ground his theory in it. So it's not clear to me whether at the end of the day Nagel thinks that epistemology is relevant to political philosophy in these ways.

[39] This argument is inspired also by ones given by Sturgeon in a different context (1986).

[40] See Hampton (1993, 296), who reads a similar suggestion into Rawls, substituting *provability* for P.

such) enjoys. And we need to do all of this without deteriorating into skepticism. As if all of this is not hard enough, there's more: For an argument of this schema to justify something like a public reason account, the relevant epistemic status must be such that it avoids the asymmetry problem[41]—it must be such that while comprehensive doctrines lack it, the principles of political justice itself possess it.[42] Otherwise, what will follow from (i) is anarchism—the denial of *any* acceptable ground for state action. (This may be seen as an instance of the requirement to find a privileged epistemic status that renders (i) plausible; an epistemic status that makes (i) entail anarchism presumably does not render (i) plausible.)

Can all of this be done? *Is there* an epistemic status that satisfies all these desiderata?

Provability won't do, it seems to me, because however exactly understood, it renders (i) highly implausible. (For one thing, I take it that even devoted Rawlsians don't think that his principles of justice are *provable*.) When it comes to political philosophy, proofs are few and far between. We often base—justifiably, it seems—coercive action on grounds that are reliable, justifiable, supportable, plausible, intellectually respectable, even without being provable. Provability won't do, then.

Nor will *knowledge*: If the epistemic status P is that of knowledge, then (ii) leads to skepticism about comprehensive doctrines. And this means that (ii) is then both independently implausible and, more clearly, in tension with the underlying motivations of public reason accounts, accounts that are supposed to be consistent with full commitment to comprehensive doctrines.

Let me mention two more epistemic statuses that may be relevant here: One is hinted by Nagel (1987, 232): it has to do with the *kind* of evidence with which the relevant belief is supported. For a belief to have the needed privileged epistemic status, it has to be *based on public, shareable evidence*. Now, it is not entirely clear what it is for a piece of evidence to be (or to fail to be) shareable. But paradigmatic examples can help: The paradigm of beliefs based on public, shareable evidence are scientifically based beliefs. Perhaps not all scientific evidence is actually shared, but it is all in principle shareable and available to all. The paradigm of beliefs based on private, non-shareable evidence is religious beliefs based on divine revelation. If I was not lucky enough to experience divine revelation, and you were, the thought seems to be, you have available to you evidence regarding the one true religion that I do not have, and furthermore that you cannot share with me.

---

[41] See, for instance, Leland and Wietmarschen (2012, 738ff.).
[42] This point is central to Clarke (1999).

There is considerable plausibility to the idea expressed in (i), with this understanding of the relevant epistemic status. The thought seems to be that if you treat someone—certainly, if you coerce them—based on considerations that they cannot come to appreciate (because the evidence for them is in no way available to them), then you fail to engage their rational faculties in the appropriate way, you somehow offend against their nature as rational, self-directing beings, in a way that you do not if you treat them— even coerce them—based on considerations the evidence for which is in principle available to them too. This is all very sketchy, and it is anything but obvious that this line of thought can be made suitably precise and then defended. But it has to be said that it is not without initial plausibility.

How about (ii), though? How plausible is the thought that comprehensive doctrines cannot (and furthermore, that political principles can) be supported by public, shareable evidence? One problem relevant here has already been mentioned: epistemically speaking, one central way of rendering evidence (indirectly) available is by testimony. Indeed, most scientific evidence—presumably, the paradigm of public evidence—is only available to most of us via testimony. So even in the divine revelation case, it is not clear why the evidence supplied by divine revelation is not shareable in the relevant sense (Raz 1990, 91; Clarke 1999, 633). A related problem is that even if beliefs based on divine revelation are not shareable, it is not at all clear that this extends beyond this one, central example. Even within religions this is not clear—even according to the official doctrine of many religions, most believers only have testimonial evidence regarding the revelations experienced by the few, and yet this is considered evidence enough for the many as well. More generally, though, think of comprehensive *secular* doctrines, doctrines that public reason theorists are just as eager to exclude from political discourse. What, in Mill's arguments for his comprehensive, "metaphysical" liberalism, constitutes private, non-shareable evidence? Nagel suggests an answer, I think. He suggests (1987, 233) that relying on *moral intuitions* is, in the relevant respects, just as private as is relying on divine revelation. But this is highly implausible: when I rely on moral intuitions, I rely on a special (perhaps intellectual) kind of a seeming. True, I am the only person who *has* that seeming (token). In *that* sense, my evidence is private. But in *that* sense, any perceptual evidence is just as private. And I doubt that Nagel wants to (or consistently can) exclude any perception-based beliefs from the legitimate grounds for political action.[43] I don't see in what *other* sense—not shared by perception—moral intuition

---

[43] The nature and status of moral intuitions is, of course, a matter of considerable philosophical discussion. But what I say about it in the text is rather minimal, it seems to me, and should not be too controversial.

can be thought of as private evidence.[44] Furthermore, if all normative intuitions are excluded in this way (because they are private, non-shareable), it is very hard to see how any political principles can be based on public, shareable evidence. The asymmetry problem raises its head again.

It won't do, then, to substitute "based on shareable evidence" for P in the above schema. Another, related, alternative I want to consider is that of "based on arguments from neutral grounds."[45] Here the thought seems to be that so long as I coerce you based on arguments the premises of which you accept, even if you don't accept the conclusion, I am not in violation of the requirement to treat you as free and equal. If, though, I base political actions on arguments even the *premises* of which you reject, this is not so.[46]

On this reading, (ii) is rather plausible—it does seem plausible that no comprehensive doctrine can be established based on arguments the premises of which everyone (or even just the reasonable) accepts. On this reading, though, (i) is highly implausible. Hardly anything satisfies this standard. Not even the law of non-contradiction, as David Lewis (1982, 101) notes:

> No truth does have, and no truth could have, a true negation. . . . That may seem dogmatic. And it is: I am affirming the very thesis that Routley and Priest have called into question, and—contrary to the rules of debate—I decline to defend it. Further, I concede that it is indefensible against their challenge. They have called so much into question, that I have no foothold on undisputed ground. So much the worse for the demand that philosophers always must be ready to defend their theses under the rules of debate.

The public reason theorist may only, it seems to me, get out of this trouble by including in his conception of reasonableness a commitment to the very premises needed in order to get him the conclusion that he wants. Only this way will he get the result of being able to justify to all the reasonable—from neutral grounds—whatever he thinks is politically justified. This, it seems to me, would be clearly ad hoc. But because I have pursued a similar line in detail elsewhere (Enoch 2015), let me not spend time on it here.

---

[44] Raz does not discuss moral intuitions, but he does highlight the perception case. See Raz (1990, 40).

[45] Though Quong (2011, 141–2) sets things up differently, I think he can be understood as going along these lines: indeed, inspired by Rawls (1999, 508–9). He certainly takes very seriously the thought of justifying from neutral grounds. So does Larmore (e.g., 1990, 347), but in a somewhat different way.

[46] If we understand shareability as "based on premises one accepts," the two epistemic statuses discussed in this subsection collapse into one.

Instead, let me note two other problems with the suggestion that the relevant epistemic status is that of justifiability on neutral grounds.[47] First, as again can be seen from the Lewis quote and the example to which it relates, there is arguably *no* interesting epistemic status that depends on the possibility of justification from neutral grounds. This serves to reinforce the suspicion that the underlying concern here is not epistemic at all, that things are, as it were, practical all the way down. Second, this suggestion—the needed status is that of justification from neutral grounds—relies on *actual* consent (of the reasonable, regarding the premises). Doesn't it matter, though—at least epistemically—when someone rejects the relevant premises, whether they do so *justifiably*? Or perhaps whether they *could* reject them justifiably? The thought that for some relevant purposes it's important to use only premises someone else *actually accepts* seems implausible (and also, not very public-reason-ish); the thought that it's important to use only premises they *epistemically should* accept seems more plausible, but doesn't help the public reason theorist (for perhaps what they should accept, what is best supported by evidence, is my comprehensive doctrine).

Talk of justification from neutral grounds, then, also fails as a way of substituting for P in the argument schema that started this section, as do thoughts about provability, knowledge, epistemic justification, and justification based on only shareable evidence. All of this falls short, of course, of a conclusive case for there being *no* way of substituting for P, that there is no privileged epistemic status such that no comprehensive doctrine has it, and such that it is plausibly required for legitimate coercion. Perhaps some other privileged epistemic status—one that I haven't considered here, and that perhaps hasn't yet been suggested by public reason theorists—can do the work.[48] But at this point a serious suspicion is called for, that perhaps something more deeply wrong is going on. Perhaps the mistake was to think that

---

[47] One may also be worried about the strong distinction such a suggestion introduces between the status of premises and that of conclusions, and about the question whether "neutral grounds" include also a requirement of agreement regarding rules of inference, and not just premises. I won't pursue these points here.

[48] Mike Ridge suggests an interesting one, which connects the discussion here with the discussion of permissibility from section 2. Perhaps the reasonable Catholic believes that though it's epistemically impermissible to reject Catholicism, it *is* permissible to not believe Catholicism. And so, perhaps we can substitute *permissibly-unbelieved* for P in Nagel's schema. This is an interesting suggestion, but I don't see that it renders (i) sufficiently plausible.

Another suggestion (from Rowan Cruft) is that perhaps what matters is not whether *I* stand in some privileged epistemic relation to the relevant doctrine, but whether *we* do. In other words, Cruft suggests that perhaps public reason is tied not to the epistemic norms governing the beliefs of individuals, but those of collective agents. Though it's not clear to me how to fill in the details here, this sounds to me like a line worth pursuing.

the kind of status that can do the work needed for P is *epistemic*. I return to this suspicion in the final section.

4. MORAL ENCROACHMENT

Rather than putting forward a moral requirement that is partly in epistemic terms—such as not to coerce based on a principle unless the principle enjoys some specified epistemic status—Nagel can be understood as claiming that whether a principle enjoys some privileged epistemic status depends on some morally relevant considerations. And here, the relevant privileged epistemic status *can* be knowledge. The thought seems to be, then, that what is at stake makes a difference as to whether someone knows something. Perhaps, for instance, in a private context, our reasonable Catholic does know that Catholicism is the one true religion. At least, the public reason theorist is not willing to base his theory on rejecting such a knowledge claim, and certainly not on inviting the Catholic to reject it (with the penalty, if she does not, of being pronounced unreasonable). It's just that in the political context—when the stakes have to do with coercion, perhaps—the Catholic no longer knows the truth of Catholicism (even if it is true). Though shifting from the private to the public sphere need not change the evidence that is available to the Catholic, it may still make a difference as to whether she knows—this may be so if the conditions needed for knowledge are partly determined by what is at stake.

This way of understanding Nagel is modeled after subject-sensitive or interest-sensitive invariantist views in epistemology. Such views accept pragmatic encroachment—they think that pragmatic considerations, such as what is at stake, can (constitutively, directly, not causally) make a difference to whether someone knows something. Such views are often motivated by examples in which we are comfortable with knowledge attributions when the pragmatic stakes are low, but not so when the stakes have been raised, and this even though evidence has been held fixed throughout (Hawthorne 2003; Stanley 2005; Ichikawa and Steup 2012, section 11, and the references there). One common example is that of so-called "bank cases," where based on the same evidence (remembering going to the bank and making a deposit on a Saturday, a couple of weeks ago) one is said to know that the bank will be open tomorrow, on Saturday, when the stakes are low; but once the stakes are high (if a deposit is not made by tomorrow, we will lose our house), we tend to retract the knowledge attribution.

The analogous thought in our context seems to be similar to pragmatic encroachment, except with a moral twist—the stakes that are relevant to whether a knowledge attribution is appropriate (or even true) are moral, not merely (other) pragmatic considerations. We can call this, then, *moral* encroachment.[49] And interestingly, the relevance of stakes according to moral encroachment is not just in terms of *how high* they are, but has to do with their *nature*. Thus, it may be quite alright for our Catholic to rely on Catholicism in making private decisions even when the stakes are quite high; and she may, in that context, know the truth of Catholicism. Still, in a political context—even when the stakes are quite low—such a knowledge attribution may be false, because something in the nature of coercion, or of the political context more generally, makes other, stricter epistemic standards the standards that are required for knowledge.[50]

Can moral encroachment, then, give the public reason theorist what she needs? Here are some reasons to think that we should again answer in the negative.[51]

First, everything depends here on the plausibility of pragmatic, and in particular moral, encroachment. Of course, I cannot discuss here in detail the arguments for and against pragmatic encroachment. But it should come as no surprise that whether pragmatic encroachment is real is a hotly debated issue in contemporary epistemology (indeed, pragmatic encroachment was introduced into epistemology as a somewhat revolutionary view). Naturally, then, if pragmatic encroachment in general fails, this line won't help the political liberal. Even if pragmatic encroachment in general can be defended, it remains to be shown that *moral* encroachment in particular can also be defended. And let me again stress two points made above in several other contexts: It would be highly surprising if the success of the public reason tradition in political philosophy were to depend on the success of something like the pragmatic encroachment project in epistemology; and relying on such highly controversial views in epistemology seems to fly in the face of political liberalism's hope of remaining independent of such "metaphysical" theses.

---

[49] The epistemological literature on pragmatic encroachment has for the most part not, as far as I know, discussed the specific case of moral encroachment. But for the term, and for some relevant discussion, see Pace (2011) and Haydon (2011). See also my (2016).

[50] This may be related to some pragmatic encroachment theorists tying knowledge very closely to reasons for *action* (so that to know that p is very close to being entitled to rely on p in action). It may be the case that we should distinguish here between different *kinds* of action—perhaps the Catholic is not entitled to act *politically* on Catholic doctrines, and so doesn't know, in the political context, that Catholicism is true; but perhaps she is entitled to *privately* act on Catholicism, and so in a private context does know the truth of Catholicism (assuming, at least, that it is true).

[51] Alexander's (1993) emphasis on questions about epistemic unity or continuity can be seen as very close to talk of moral encroachment, I think. Some of his reasons for rejecting, then, the kind of epistemic disunity he takes political liberalism to be committed to are very relevant here.

Second, it is not clear that moral encroachment allows the public reason theorist to avoid attributing Moorean incoherence to the reasonable person who remains committed to her comprehensive doctrine, for instance, our reasonable Catholic. True, on this theory the reasonable Catholic can claim knowledge of Catholicism (and certainly doesn't have to deny such knowledge) in private contexts. In the political context, though, she *is* required to deny such knowledge. Her situation, on this theory, is similar to that of the person in the bank scenario who learns about the high stakes. At this point, she too has to retract her (self-) knowledge attribution. Similarly, then, once in the public arena, the Catholic is required, on the suggestion at hand, to acknowledge that she doesn't know the truth of Catholicism. This seems like a highly problematic result—it seems Mooreanly incoherent. Perhaps this is not necessarily so with regard to *all* comprehensive doctrines, perhaps, in other words, whether this is so depends to an extent on their content. But it seems obvious that some reasonable comprehensive doctrines are not going to be consistent (or won't Mooreanly cohere) with a denial of knowledge in the public sphere.

Third, and putting to one side the previous two points, even with the moral encroachment line in place, it must still be shown that whether our Catholic *knows* the truth of Catholicism is morally and politically important. In other words, we would still need something like premise (i) of the argument schema in the previous section.[52] And we've already seen that showing this is not an easy task.

Moral encroachment is an interesting (purported) phenomenon, and it deserves more attention than it has been getting, from epistemologists and moral philosophers alike. But it is hard to see how it can help the cause of the public reason theorist.

5. SO: NOT EPISTEMOLOGY AFTER ALL?

As the previous sections show, then, it is very hard to make coherent sense of the epistemic-sounding commitments of public reason theorists, from

---

[52] According to the moral encroachment suggestion, one epistemic status—knowledge—is needed for justified action, in private as well as public contexts; but the standards that need to be satisfied for a belief to amount to knowledge differ between the two contexts. An alternative suggestion would be that there are two epistemic statuses involved—say, knowledge$_{private}$ and knowledge$_{public}$—one needed for private action, the other for public action. It is hard to see what significance, in the political context, there is to the difference between these two epistemically different ways of viewing things. I take this to strengthen the suspicion that in the political context we don't really care whether a belief amounts to knowledge. I return to this suspicion in the following section.

Rawls and on. When they do—or seem to do—epistemology, public reason theorists seem to be in especially serious trouble. Perhaps there is some pressure, then, to read them as not really doing epistemology at all?

The point is not just one of charitable interpretation. Arguably, the most pre-theoretically powerful ways of putting the motivations underlying such accounts have nothing to do with epistemology. Think here, for instance, of Estlund's (2008, 5) Pope example, where it is stipulated that Catholicism is true, and that the Pope is infallible. Still, Estlund insists with pretty much everyone else,[53] it would be objectionable for the state to subject me—non-Catholic as I am—to the Pope's directives. This intuition—central, it seems to me, to the attraction of public reason accounts—is epistemology-free. Even if the Pope is infallible, even if the non-Catholic citizen is actually epistemically at fault for not accepting Catholicism, even if the evidence for Catholicism is shareable and indeed shared—add whatever epistemological story you like—the objectionability of imposing the Pope's directives on non-Catholics survives.

Here's another way of strengthening the suspicion that nothing here should be about epistemology at all. Think of standards of proof in the law. Presumably, there are practical—moral, political—reasons to go for a stricter standard of proof in criminal cases compared to other cases. Perhaps influenced by Nagel or by discussions of pragmatic encroachment, you may find it tempting to put the point by saying that a different epistemic standard is rendered appropriate in such different contexts, because of moral considerations. You may even want to say that in the civil lawsuit against O. J. Simpson we all knew that he did it, but not so in the criminal case. Within certain bounds, there's no harm putting things in this way. But we shouldn't let that confuse us—the epistemic language drops out of the justificatory story altogether. The reason it was morally and legally acceptable to find O. J. Simpson not guilty in the criminal case and liable in the civil one (if indeed it was) "runs through" the talk of epistemic standards, and directly relies on the practical reasons there are for having different standards of legal proof in these different contexts. Whether it's also true to say that in one of them we know and the other we do not is—for moral and legal purposes—beside the point.[54] Something similar is going on in the case of public reason accounts. We can put things epistemically, but that would not be perspicuous. What does the work—what makes it objectionable

---

[53] Including me, though I argue that accommodating this important intuition doesn't require going for a public reason account. See the final section of my *Against Public Reason*.

[54] In Enoch, Spectre, and Fisher (2012) my co-authors and I suggest that the law in general should not care about epistemology.

(if indeed it is) to impose on people directives based on comprehensive doctrines they do not share—are the moral and political reasons themselves that presumably make a different epistemic standard appropriate. The epistemic stuff itself just drops out of the picture.

I tentatively conclude, then, that public reason theorists are better off not relying on epistemology at all. This is good news for them, it seems to me, because—as I argued throughout—the amateurish epistemology they do gets them in trouble, and because it seems to me that what they really care about can be stated without any epistemology at all. But this suggestion is not without cost.

A public reason theorist accepting this result must put forward non-epistemic accounts of central concepts and ideas in the theory that are usually understood epistemically. The two central ones I have in mind here are *reasonableness* and *accessibility*. Thus, in order to avoid the problems in section 2, and to remain loyal to the underlying intuitions (as exemplified in the Pope example), the public reason theorist must clean the notion of the reasonable person from any epistemic luggage. Reasonableness can still be understood in terms of substantive moral commitments (to the values of freedom and equality, perhaps), or motivationally (so that the reasonable is most strongly motivated to interact with others as free and equal), but not epistemically (say, in terms of acknowledging the burdens of judgments and their effects). And the accessibility requirement—restricting public reasons to just those we can expect others to accept—must be given a non-epistemic reading (perhaps, say, in terms of the psychological and other costs of acceptance). And once the non-epistemic conceptions of reasonableness and accessibility are developed, central public reason arguments and theses have to be re-evaluated, to see whether they work with these non-epistemic conceptions.

I am not optimistic about such a project (then again, I was not a fan of public reason accounts going in). Let me end with just the following obvious worry. Once it's clear that epistemology is out, how are public reason theorists to support the accessibility requirement? How can they justify requiring that citizens bracket, in the public sphere, their deepest comprehensive commitments? It seems to me that the most natural way to do so would be to rely on substantive moral values, perhaps primarily the value of personal autonomy. It is (pro tanto) wrong to impose directives based on a comprehensive doctrine on people who don't share it not because of some epistemic consideration, but because that would offend against their autonomy. The problem for public reason theorists of going down that line, of course, is that this would abandon the hope of a free-standing conception of political justice, as it relies on the value of autonomy, and indeed, on a fairly thick, substantive understanding thereof; the liberalism that will emerge will thus be metaphysical in Rawls's sense; and this would support only a *defeasible* version of an accessibility requirement—for other autonomy considerations, and indeed other values altogether, may override the value of autonomy as giving rise to the accessibility requirement (Enoch 2015, section 6). This will lead, I think, to a more plausible position, but arguably not one worth calling a public reason account at all.

Appendix: The Burdens of Judgment

Throughout this paper—and mostly, in section 2—I've been highlighting the following dilemma: the public reason theorist must fill in the details of the reasonable person—in particular, her beliefs about other reasonable people, who don't share her comprehensive doctrine—in a way that, first, renders her coherent (and plausibly reasonable), and second, that can justify the requirement not to rely in the political sphere on considerations that are controversial (in the relevant way) among the reasonable. And the results have been rather pessimistic: It's relatively easy to satisfy any one of these two conditions, but we have yet to see a plausible way of satisfying both.

I have barely mentioned the burdens of judgment, but—as you may have noticed—much of what was said is directly relevant to their critical assessment. In this appendix I explicitly discuss them, showing how points made above are relevant to them, and how their understanding too is vulnerable to a similar dilemma. I will not here question, though, their explanatory force—that is, I will concede, for the sake of argument, that the burdens of judgment do explain, to an extent at least, the disagreement we see about conceptions of the good (and perhaps other things as well). Conceding this, I will argue that they cannot be made epistemological sense of in a way that allows them to justify the requirement not to politically rely on matters that are controversial among the reasonable.

The first burden is Complex Evidence: The relevant evidence, Rawls argues plausibly, is often hard to assess. That is certainly true. But remember that on pain of Moorean incoherence, the reasonable Catholic must think of herself as having overcome the complexity, and responded well to the evidence (at least, she cannot think of herself as having failed to respond well to the evidence). She must also think of non-Catholics as having succumbed to these difficulties. How, then, does the complexity of the evidence matter? How can it justify excluding Catholicism-based considerations from the public sphere? Perhaps Rawls is here alluding to something like an epistemic excuse: Given the complexity of the evidence, perhaps the mistaken non-Catholics can't be blamed for their mistake. But then the discussion in section 2.4 applies, as does its pessimistic conclusion.

The same point applies, it seems to me, to Rawls's second burden of judgment, Weight—even agreeing on the relevant considerations, people may disagree on their relative weight. This may certainly explain disagreement, but not in a way that can help political liberalism, it seems to me. Perhaps Rawls thinks that according different weights to the relevant considerations is epistemically permissible. If so, the discussion of epistemic permissiveness in section 2.2.2 applies. Or perhaps the thought is that according weights that differ from the maximally rational way can amount to responding to the evidence well enough, or in a non-culpable way. Then the discussion in section 2.4 applies. Given the negative conclusions of those discussions, it is hard to see how the second burden of judgment helps. The same applies, mutatis mutandis, to Rawls's fifth burden of judgment, Comparability: the fact that often there are different kinds of normative considerations of different force on both sides of an issue and it is difficult to make an overall assessment.

The third burden of judgment is about vagueness and indeterminacy, which make relying on judgment and interpretation indispensable. But this too won't help. A part of the problem is that it's not at all clear that in the face of vagueness and indeterminacy disagreement is reasonable—it is *definitely* not clear whether in such cases the disagreeing parties can be epistemically justified in their conflicting beliefs. Perhaps, if I am a borderline case of being tall, the thing to believe about me is precisely that, namely, that I am borderline tall. It is not clear that it is also justified (or permissible? or non-culpable?) to believe that I'm tall, and that I'm not tall. But whether this is so depends on intricate issues regarding vagueness that I cannot address here (and that it would be weird if political liberalism needed to take a stand on). More importantly, there is clearly something at least Mooreanly incoherent about "Catholicism is true; but it's indeterminate whether Catholicism is true." So reading this burden of judgment into the beliefs of the reasonable Catholic seems to render her incoherent. Furthermore, and now regardless of incoherence: it just doesn't seem to be a loyal reading of the commitments of many of those committed to comprehensive doctrines. Surely, the political liberal wants reasonableness to be consistent with the kind of commitment to a comprehensive doctrine that takes it to be *determinately* true and *determinately* supported by the evidence.

The fourth burden of judgment, Total Experience, draws attention to the fact that our beliefs are shaped by our total experience, and so are likely to diverge. This too seems true, but unhelpful. It's not clear that it would cohere well with the spirit of political liberalism if the reasonable Catholic thought that all non-Catholics would see the truth, if only they were not subject to their distorting total experience. Furthermore, how is the causal influence of past experiences supposed to be relevant? It seems to me that it can speak either to justification or to excuse. If the latter, the discussion in section 2.3 applies. If it's relevant to justification, this means that the reasonable Catholic must think of non-Catholics as exposed to a different body of evidence, and then the discussion in section 2.2.1 applies; or else, must think of them as exposed to the same body of evidence but still being justified in rejecting Catholicism, in which case either the discussion of Moorean incoherence in section 2.2 or the discussion of permissiveness in section 2.2.2 apply. Either way, no progress has been made.

Based on the discussion of previous sections, then, I conclude that there is no way of understanding the burdens of judgment that satisfies the two relevant desiderata: rendering the beliefs of the reasonable person who is nevertheless committed to a comprehensive doctrine coherent, and justifying excluding from politics ideas that are controversial among the reasonable.[55]

Acknowledgments

I presented earlier versions of this paper in Joseph Raz's seminar at the Columbia Law School, in philosophy department colloquia in Madison and in Edinburgh, at the law and philosophy workshop at the Hebrew University, and at the third Oxford Studies in Political Philosophy workshop in Syracuse. I thank the participants for the helpful discussions—especially Sahar Akhter, who was my commentator in Syracuse, and Re'em Segev, who was my commentator in Jerusalem. For comments on earlier versions and for relevant conversations, I thank Larry Alexander, Kenneth Boyd, Teresa Bruno Nino, Tom Hurka, R. J. Leland, Ofer Malcai, Jon Quong, Joseph Raz, Seana Shiffrin, Levi Spectre, Kevin Vallier, Chad Van Schoelandt, Han van Wietmarschen, and a reader for Oxford University Press.

References

Larry Alexander (1993) "Liberalism, Religion, and the Unity of Epistemology", *San Diego Law Review* 30, 763–97.

Brian Barry (1995) *Justice as Impartiality* (Oxford: Oxford University Press).

Simon Blackburn (1993) *Essays in Quasi-Realism* (Oxford: Oxford University Press).

Kenneth Boyd (2015) "Assertion, Practical Reasoning, and Epistemic Separabilism", *Philosophical Studies* 172, 1907–27.

Anthony Brueckner and Alex Bundy (2012) "On 'Epistemic Permissiveness'", *Synthese* 188, 165–77.

David Christensen and Jennifer Lackey (eds.) (2013) *The Epistemology of Disagreement: New Essays* (Oxford: Oxford University Press).

Simon Clarke (1999) "Contractarianism, Liberal Neutrality, and Epistemology", *Political Studies* 47, 627–42.

---

[55] There is also this: Sometimes—under pressure of some objections, perhaps (see discussion in my (2015, 124–6))—public reason theorists emphasize that theirs is an *ideal* theory. This is why, for instance, it is okay to restrict the constituency of public justification to just the reasonable. But then, it seems natural to idealize the reasonable also epistemically. And then we can reread the burdens of judgment, to see whether they are consistent with such idealization. Seeing that at least some of the burdens of judgment seem to highlight what are still epistemic *flaws* (pace Quong (2011, 36), who seems to think the burdens of judgment show that remaining disagreements are not irrational), it is not clear how relying on them is consistent with doing ideal theory. At least, if the public reason theorist wants to idealize some features but not others, she needs to offer a rationale for this discrimination.

Adam Elga (2007) "Reflection and Disagreement", *Noûs* 41, 478–502.

David Enoch (2011) "Not Just a Truthometer: Taking Oneself Seriously (But Not Too Seriously) in Cases of Peer Disagreement", *Mind* 119, 953–97.

David Enoch (2013) "The Disorder of Public Reason: A Critical Study of Gerlad Gaus's *The Order of Public Reason*", *Ethics* 124, 1–36.

David Enoch (2015) "Against Public Reason", *Oxford Studies in Political Philosophy* 1, 112–42.

David Enoch (2016) "What's Wrong with Paternalism: Autonomy, Belief and Action", *Proceedings of the Aristotelian Society* 116, 21–48.

David Enoch, Levi Spectre, and Talia Fisher (2012) "Statistical Evidence, Sensitivity, and the Legal Value of Knowledge", *Philosophy and Public Affairs* 40, 197–224.

David M. Estlund (2008) *Democratic Authority: A Philosophical Framework* (Princeton: Princeton University Press).

Bryan Frances (2016) "Rationally held 'P, but I fully believe ~P, and I am not equivocating", *Philosophical Studies* 173, 309–13.

Gerald Gaus (2015) "On Dissing Public Reason: A Reply to Enoch", *Ethics* 125, 1078–95.

Allan Gibbard (2003) *Thinking How to Live* (Cambridge, MA: Harvard University Press).

Kent Greenawalt (1984) "The Perplexing Borders of Justification and Excuse", *Columbia Law Review* 84, 1897–927.

Jean Hampton (1993) "The Moral Commitments of Liberalism", in David Copp and Jean Hampton (eds.), *The Idea of Democracy* (Cambridge: Cambridge University Press), 292–314.

John Hawthorne (2003) *Knowledge and Lotteries* (New York: Oxford University Press).

Nathan Haydon (2011) "Moral Encroachment", MA thesis, University of Waterloo, available here: https://uwspace.uwaterloo.ca/bitstream/handle/10012/6379/Haydon_Nathan.pdf?sequence=1.

Jonathan Jenkins Ichikawa and Matthias Steup (2012) "The Analysis of Knowledge", *Stanford Encyclopedia of Philosophy*, available here: http://plato.stanford.edu/entries/knowledge-analysis/.

Thomas Kelly (2005) "The Epistemic Significance of Disagreement", in John Hawthorne and Tamar Gendler-Szabo (eds.), *Oxford Studies in Epistemology*, Volume I (Oxford: Oxford University Press), 167–96.

Thomas Kelly (2009) "Peer Disagreement and Higher Order Evidence", in Richard Feldman and Ted Warfield (eds.), *Disagreement* (Oxford: Oxford University Press), 111–74.

Charles Larmore (1990) "Political Liberalism", *Political Theory* 18, 339–60.

R. J. Leland and Han van Wietmarschen (2012) "Reasonableness, Intellectual Modesty, and Reciprocity in Political Justification", *Ethics* 122, 721–47.

David Lewis (1982) "Logic for Equivocators", *Noûs* 16, 431–41; reprinted in his *Papers in Philosophical Logic* (Cambridge: Cambridge University Press, 1998), 97–110.

Clayton Littlejohn (forthcoming) "A Plea for Epistemic Excuses", forthcoming in F. Dorsch and J. Dutant (eds.), *The New Evil Demon* (Oxford: Oxford University Press).

John MacFarlane (2012) "Relativism", in Delia Graff Fara and Gillian Russell (eds.), *The Routledge Companion to the Philosophy of Language* (New York: Routledge), 132–42.

John Stuart Mill (1869) *On Liberty* (London: Longman, Roberts & Grec; Bartleby. com, 1999, www.bartleby.com/130/).

Thomas Nagel (1987) "Moral Conflict and Political Legitimacy", *Philosophy and Public Affairs* 26, 215–40.

Thomas Nagel (1991) *Equality and Partiality* (Oxford: Oxford University Press).

Martha Nussbaum (2011) "Perfectionist Liberalism and Political Liberalism", *Philosophy and Public Affairs* 39, 3–45.

Michael Pace (2011) "The Epistemic Value of Moral Considerations: Justification, Moral Encroachment, and James' 'Will To Believe'", *Noûs* 45, 239–68.

Jonathan Quong (2011) *Liberalism without Perfectionism* (Oxford: Oxford University Press).

Jonathan Quong (2013) "Public Reason", *Stanford Encyclopedia Online*, available here: http://plato.stanford.edu/entries/public-reason/.

John Rawls (1993) *Political Liberalism* (New York: Columbia University Press).

John Rawls (1999) *A Theory of Justice: A Revised Edition* (Oxford: Oxford University Press).

Joseph Raz (1989) "Liberalism, Scepticism, and Democracy", *The Iowa Law Review* 74, reprinted in *Ethics in the Public Domain* (Oxford: Oxford University Press), 97–124.

Joseph Raz (1990) "Facing Diversity: The Case of Epistemic Abstinence", *Philosophy and Public Affairs* 19, 3–46, reprinted in *Ethics in the Public Domain* (Oxford: Oxford University Press), 60–96.

Joseph Raz (1998) "Disagreement in Politics", *American Journal of Jurisprudence* 43, 25–52.

Jason Stanley (2005) *Knowledge and Practical Interests* (New York: Oxford University Press).

Nicholas S. Sturgeon (1986) "What Difference Does It Make Whether Moral Realism Is True?", *The Southern Journal of Philosophy* 24 (Supp.), 115–41.

Kevin Vallier (2011) "Against Public Reason Liberalism's Accessibility Requirement", *Journal of Moral Philosophy* 8(3), 366–89.

Kevin Vallier and Fred D'Agostino (2013) "Public justification", *Stanford Encyclopedia Online*, available here: http://plato.stanford.edu/entries/justification-public/.

Ruth Weintraub (2013) "Can Steadfast Peer Disagreement Be Rational?", *The Philosophical Quarterly* 63, 740–59.

Leif Wenar (1995) "Political Liberalism: An Internal Critique", *Ethics* 106, 32–62.

Roger White (2005) "Epistemic Permissiveness", *Philosophical Perspectives* 19, 445–59.

John N. Williams (2015a) "Moore's Paradox in Speech: A Critical Survey", *Philosophy Compass* 10, 10–23.

John N. Williams (2015b) 'Moore's Paradox in Thought: A Critical Survey", *Philosophy Compass* 10, 24–37.

Timothy Williamson (forthcoming) "Justifications, Excuses, and Sceptical Scenarios", in Julien Dutant and Fabian Dorsch (eds.), *The New Evil Demon* (Oxford: Oxford University Press).

7

Proxy Battles in Just War Theory

Jus in Bello, the Site of Justice, and Feasibility Constraints

Seth Lazar and Laura Valentini

1. INTRODUCTION

Interest in just war theory has boomed in recent years, as a revisionist school of thought has challenged the orthodoxy of international law, most famously defended by Michael Walzer [1977]. These revisionist critics have targeted the two central principles governing the conduct of war (*jus in bello*): combatant equality and noncombatant immunity.[1] The first states that combatants face the same permissions and constraints whether their cause is just or unjust. The second protects noncombatants from intentional attack. In response to these critics, some philosophers have defended aspects of the old orthodoxy on novel grounds.[2] Revisionists counter. As things stand, the prospects for progress are remote.

In this paper, we offer a way forward. We argue that exclusive focus on first-order moral principles, such as combatant equality and noncombatant immunity, has led revisionist and orthodox just war theorists to engage in "proxy battles." Their first-order moral disagreements are at least partly traceable to second-order disagreements about the nature and purpose of political theory. These deeper disputes have been central to the broader

---

[1] For example, McMahan [1994]; Rodin [2002]; McPherson [2004]; McMahan [2009]; Fabre [2012]; Frowe [2014].

[2] Appealing to a broadly rule consequentialist framework: Buchanan [2006]; Shue [2010]; Waldron [2010]. Appealing to a contractarian framework: Benbaji [2008]; Statman [2014]. Appealing to a deontological framework that methodologically has much in common with the revisionist approach: Emerton and Handfield [2009]; Lazar [2015].

discipline of political theory for several years; we hope that bringing them to bear on the ethics of war will help us move beyond the present impasse.

In particular, we focus on two second-order questions:

- *The site question*: Should fundamental principles of *jus in bello* concern institutional design or individual conduct?
- *The feasibility question*: What real-world facts, if any, should constrain the demands of *jus in bello*?

In each case, our analysis comes in two parts. We first summarize the relevant debate in political theory, and illustrate how it underpins the controversy between revisionist and orthodox just war theorists. We then show how this novel framing advances first-order disputes about war. Although we do not advocate a particular first-order view about *jus in bello*, our analysis points towards a fruitful middle ground between revisionists' moral rigorism and orthodox theorists' fidelity to the laws of war.

Before we start, two caveats. While our approach should illuminate all areas of just war theory, we focus only on *jus in bello*. Furthermore, by saying that orthodox and revisionist theorists have engaged in "proxy battles" we do not mean that a given approach to the site of justice or to feasibility constraints *automatically* induces a first-order view about war. We only suggest that different second-order stances about the site of justice and feasibility help us both to explain the substantive disagreements between orthodox and revisionist just war theorists and to move beyond them.

2. THE SITE OF JUSTICE AND JUST WAR THEORY

In this section, we first outline the political theory debate on the site of justice, and then draw parallels with recent disputes between orthodox and revisionist just war theorists. This novel framing will allow us, in section 3, to point to a number of important implications for *jus in bello*.

2.1. The Site of Justice: Political vs. Non-Political Approaches

Much contemporary political theory expounds principles of *socio-economic* justice. These set out individuals' entitlements to particular bundles of socio-economic opportunities and resources within a social system. Unsurprisingly, scholars disagree about the content of these principles. For instance, some defend distributive equality, others distributive sufficiency, others still support whichever distribution maximally benefits the most deprived (e.g., Frankfurt [1997]; Parfit [2000]). Although much ink has been spilled on the first-order moral question of what justice demands, theorists of justice have also been sensitive to the equally important second-order question of the "site of justice": the particular *subject* to which principles of justice apply.

Two competing approaches have emerged, which we call "political" and "non-political."[3] Political approaches hold that, at the fundamental level, principles of justice apply to the most important legal, political, and economic institutions within any given social system, and only derivatively to individuals. Non-political approaches, by contrast, hold that fundamental principles of justice apply directly to the conduct of individual human beings.

John Rawls is the most prominent proponent of the political approach (Rawls [1999]; see also Scheffler [2006]; Young [2006]). On his view, justice is the "first virtue of social institutions," and his principles of socio-economic justice—fair equality of opportunity and the difference principle[4]—are meant to guide us in selecting between different possible configurations of the "basic structure of society," namely society's main institutions. As A. J. Julius puts it, for Rawlsians,

> to conclude that a society is just or unjust, I don't have to know what everyone in the society is doing. It's enough that I know how the society's institutions are arranged, or that I understand the basic framework that shapes its members' interaction over time or the basic mechanisms that distribute them over a range of prospects for living better and worse lives.   (Julius [2003: 321])

Justice, on this view, is a property of institutional systems, and its bearing on individuals' conduct is indirect. The demands of justice binding individuals derive from principles for institutional design. In particular, when institutions are fully just, individuals' duties of justice are exhausted by the demands institutions place on them (i.e., by the law); when institutions are unjust, individuals have duties of justice to reform them.

To be sure, on the political approach, individuals in a complex social system do face other moral demands besides institutionally mediated ones. That is, they not only face moral demands of justice "as citizens"—i.e., as participants in legal, political, and economic institutions—but also as friends, parents, workers, and so forth (Rawls [1996: 262]). But, at least under ideal circumstances where a just background is in place, these further demands do not conflict with those of justice; instead, justice sets the boundaries within which we may legitimately honor our other moral obligations.[5]

---

[3] Cf. the distinction between dualistic and monistic approaches to justice in Murphy [1998].

[4] We are setting aside the equal liberty principle since this does not concern socio-economic justice.

[5] The specification "under ideal circumstances" is necessary for the following reason. In cases of justice deficits, it may well be that one's special responsibilities conflict with justice. For instance, against an unjust social background, a father's duty to give special

Philosophers like G. A. Cohen [1997] and Liam Murphy [1998] reject the political approach, arguing that, at the fundamental level, justice applies to individuals' actions and behavior.[6] Institutions are, in turn, means to achieving ends the worth of which is to be judged by appeal to principles for individual conduct. In Murphy's words:

> any plausible overall political/moral view must, at the fundamental level, evaluate the justice of institutions with normative principles that apply also to people's choices. We should not think of legal, political, and other social institutions as together constituting a separate normative realm, requiring separate normative first principles, but rather primarily as the means that people employ the better to achieve their collective political/moral goals.   (Murphy [1998: 253])

On this view, the particular "oughts" (e.g., laws) embedded in a given institutional scheme derive from moral principles that apply directly to individuals. Non-political theorists are not always fully transparent about how to effect this derivation. Two options are available. The first is to require the demands embedded in institutions to *mirror* the principles of justice that apply to individual conduct.[7] An obvious difficulty with this option is that so arranging one's institutions might be counter-productive. For example, if fundamental moral principles are epistemically and/or substantively too demanding, their direct embodiment in institutional rules may result in widespread, perhaps catastrophic non-compliance.

This concern motivates the second option, which consists in developing *principles for institutional regulation*, which are geared towards the realization of the values underlying fundamental moral principles. As G. A. Cohen understands them, principles of institutional regulation do not reflect the moral truth. Instead, they are means to achieving certain results, which should be adopted "in light of an evaluation [of their] likely effects, and, therefore, in light of an understanding of the facts" (Cohen [2008: 265]).[8]

To illustrate, we may think that the following "luck-egalitarian" principle is a true demand of justice: individuals ought to act so as to eliminate the effects of brute luck on each others' lives. However, we also recognize that

---

care to his child may conflict with egalitarian justice, resulting in the child's having an *unfair* advantage later on in life, compared to underprivileged children. But if the underlying social background is just, within the limits imposed by the law, one may attend to one's special responsibilities knowing that this will not be at odds with what justice requires.

[6] For discussion, see Pogge [2000]; Ronzoni [2007].

[7] See what Buchanan [2013: 14ff.] calls the "mirroring view" in the philosophy of human rights. Murphy [1998: 254] explicitly rejects this option.

[8] Note that, for Cohen, principles of regulation may also apply to individuals' conduct directly. Here, we specifically focus on principles of regulation in the context of institutional selection. Thanks to Miriam Ronzoni and Mike Otsuka for discussion.

designing institutions in light of this principle would be a bad idea. First, determining what equalizing the effects of brute luck on people's lives requires is extremely epistemically burdensome. Second, even if the demands of this principle were institutionalized, due to selfish motives, individuals would refuse to act on them. This renders our principle a poor candidate for institutional regulation. A better alternative could be the Rawlsian principle that one ought to maximize the position of the socio-economically worst off, since this would incentivize the talented to be maximally productive. Arguably, selecting institutions—e.g., a tax scheme—on the basis of this principle would *better serve* the mitigation of the effects of brute luck on people's lives than selecting them directly on the basis of the "true" demands of justice (Cohen [2008: 286]).[9]

So far, we have outlined two contrasting approaches to the site of principles of justice: political and non-political. To sum up, these approaches crucially differ in how they characterize the relationship between:

a) moral demands that apply to individuals;
b) principles on the basis of which to select institutional configurations;
c) institutional demands that apply to individuals.

On the political approach, fundamental principles of justice are of type (b), and the demands of justice that apply to individuals are exhausted by institutional ones (c). On this approach, demands of type (a) are an empty set in the realm of justice. The most fundamental layer of justice-morality is (b). On the non-political approach, by contrast, fundamental demands of justice are of type (a), and the institutional demands that apply to individuals (c) either mirror moral ones, or are derived from principles for institutional regulation (b) that "serve" the values underlying the moral demands at level (a).

What does the distinction between these two approaches have to offer to debates about *jus in bello*?

2.2. *Jus in Bello* and the Site of Justice

When it comes to *jus in bello*, we care about all normative principles that govern the conduct of war, rather than norms of justice strictly conceived. Still, the "site question" arises all the same and underpins some of the main first-order disagreements between orthodox and revisionist just war theorists. Bringing the distinction between political and non-political

---

[9] For Cohen, principles of regulation should be responsive to concerns beyond justice, also including, e.g., stability, efficiency and publicity. For simplicity's sake, here we do not discuss this further feature of Cohen's view, but only focus on its general structure.

approaches to bear on these disagreements can thus help us better frame and understand them.

Political approaches to the just conduct of war hold that, at the fundamental level, principles of *jus in bello* apply to the institutions that govern armed conflict: they allow us to select the "morally correct" laws of war. In turn, whatever set of laws is recommended by these principles exhausts the just-war-related permissions and prohibitions applying to combatants. This fully mirrors the structure of the political approach in relation to socio-economic justice.

Many orthodox just war theorists—who defend combatant equality and non-combatant immunity, in line with the existing laws of war—appear to endorse the political approach. There are two broad camps, each defending a distinctive substantive principle for institutional design. The first justifies the institutions governing armed conflict on rule consequentialist grounds, by appeal to a general principle mandating the minimization of harm. Henry Shue [2008] prominently advocates this position.[10] The second strand holds that justified laws of war result from a fair and mutually advantageous hypothetical contract. As it happens, the object of the contract corresponds to the existing laws of war, whereby combatants waive their rights against one another to grant each other the license to obey the military orders of their state. This view is most associated with Yitzhak Benbaji [2008] and Daniel Statman [2014].[11] Independently of these differences, however, these two groups of theorists hold that fundamental principles of *jus in bello* concern the selection of morally justified laws of war.

Non-political approaches to the just conduct of war, by contrast, hold that, at the fundamental level, *jus in bello* specifies moral principles that apply directly to individual combatants, and to their military and political leaders. A war is fought justly only if these individuals adhere to the dictates of the moral principles that apply to them. Like their counterparts in the socio-economic justice debate, non-political just war theorists think that we should derive—in more or less direct ways—the institutional rules governing armed conflict from these fundamental moral principles.

At a first pass, the non-political approach seems to underpin the revisionist critique of orthodox just war theory. Many revisionist arguments challenge traditional principles of *jus in bello* by appealing to the demands of interpersonal morality. As revisionists have argued in detail, according to ordinary interpersonal morality it is very hard to see how combatants advancing an unjust cause could be morally permitted to intentionally kill just combatants,

---

[10] See also Brandt [1972]; Mavrodes [1975]; Buchanan and Keohane [2004]; Buchanan [2006]; Shaw [2011]; Dill and Shue [2012]; Shue [2013]; Jenkins [2014].

[11] Estlund [2007] has developed a further version of the political approach, grounded in democratic authority.

or to kill noncombatants as unintended side-effects of pursuing their unjust goals.[12] Combatant equality, as it is conceived in the laws of war, cannot track combatants' interpersonal moral duties. There is more dispute over noncombatant immunity, but most revisionists think that it, too, lacks foundations in interpersonal morality, since noncombatants can be responsible for contributing to unjustified threats, and this responsibility grounds liability to be killed.[13]

Although revisionists discuss the institutional implications of their views only cursorily, they hold that the laws of war should derive, in more or less complex ways, from interpersonal moral demands. In particular, some think the laws of war should *mirror* interpersonal morality. For example, David Rodin [2011] has argued that his rights-based account of permissible killing should be directly implemented in the laws of war: killing is permissible if and only if either the target has lost the protection of his right to life, or killing him is a (rare) justified lesser evil. Helen Frowe [2011: 45] has tentatively endorsed this thesis, arguing against licensing wrongful harm in order to minimize it.

A second set of revisionist theorists hold that the laws of war should be selected on the basis of principles for institutional regulation that take account of the values embedded in interpersonal morality, but also consider "the consequences of the adoption and enforcement of [given] laws or conventions" (McMahan [2004: 730]).[14] Acknowledging that straightforward legal implementation of combatants' interpersonal moral duties and permissions would have bad consequences, Jeff McMahan [2008] concludes that the laws of war should be based on the principle that one ought to minimize *wrongful* harm (note the subtle contrast with Shue and Dill, whose aim is to minimize all harm).[15] Cécile Fabre [2009: 39] also expresses sympathy for this view, on grounds similar to McMahan's.

2.3. Concluding Remarks

As our discussion has shown, second-order disagreements about the site of fundamental principles of *jus in bello* underpin first-order disputes over the

---

[12] E.g., McMahan [1994]; Rodin [2002]; Coady [2008].

[13] McMahan [1994]; Fabre [2012]; Frowe [2012]. For dissent, see Rodin [2008].

[14] Cohen [2008: 265 n.58] himself explicitly links his distinction between fundamental principles of justice and rules of social regulation to McMahan's distinction between deep morality and the laws of war. Thanks to Mike Otsuka for the pointer.

[15] Although McMahan clearly thinks that this principle (minimize wrongful harm) would generate the same laws of war as Shue and Dill's principle (minimize harm), that is presumably an open question. Shue and Dill settle on their version because they think that almost all suffering in war—including that of unjust combatants—exceeds what the sufferers deserve to bear.

moral equality of combatants and noncombatant immunity. The first-order dispute is, at least in part, a proxy battle, fought by theorists whose disagreements run much deeper. Orthodox just war theorists tend to endorse a political approach. Revisionist just war theorists lean towards versions of the non-political approach. For this debate to make progress, we must settle the underlying second-order question. Otherwise just war theorists will talk past each other: political just war theorists might develop the most plausible account of the institutional norms governing war; non-political just war theorists might develop the most plausible account of our interpersonal moral duties; but their proposals would not strictly compete, because each presupposes an approach to the site of normative theorizing about war that the others reject. Indeed, quite strikingly, once we hold a given site constant, orthodox and revisionist just war theorists appear to largely agree at the level of substance. Table 7.1 summarizes the findings of this section.

Table 7.1 Political and non-political approaches to socio-economic justice and *jus in bello*

	Moral demands for individuals	Principles for institutional selection	Institutional demands for individuals
Political approach to justice (cf. Rawls)		Fundamental principles of justice	Demands of justice for individuals (just laws)
Non-political approach to justice (cf. Murphy/Cohen)	Fundamental principles of justice	Principles of institutional regulation	Institutional demands for individuals (optimal laws)
Political approach to *jus in bello* (Orthodox theorists)		Fundamental principles of *jus in bello* E.g., Minimize harm	Institutional demands for individuals (laws of war) Non-combatant immunity/combatant equality
Non-political approach to *jus in bello* (Revisionist theorists)	Fundamental principles of *jus in bello*	Principles of institutional regulation of *jus in bello* E.g., Minimize wrongful harm	Institutional demands for individuals (laws of war) Non-combatant immunity/combatant equality

3. THE SITE OF JUSTICE AND JUST WAR THEORY: IMPLICATIONS

So far, we have observed that orthodox and revisionist just war theorists' disagreement about first-order questions is partly accounted for by their disagreement about what the site of fundamental principles of *jus in bello* should be. In this section, we outline the implications of this observation. We highlight that both political and non-political approaches to *jus in bello* face important challenges, and gesture at possible responses to them. These in turn cast doubt on the plausibility of orthodox and revisionist stances on *jus in bello*, pointing instead to a "middle ground" between them.

3.1. Challenges to the Political Approach

The political approach underpins orthodox just war theory and, in its purest form, states that one's obligations and permissions in war are exhausted by those set out by the morally justified laws of war, in particular the principles of combatant equality and noncombatant immunity.

The central challenge for the political approach underpinning orthodox *jus in bello* is to explain what happens to basic interpersonal moral demands—such as the prohibition on intentionally killing the innocent— in the context of war. This challenge does not arise for political approaches to justice. There, the typical approach is to use institutions to set a context within which we are permitted to act on our interpersonal moral reasons. Once a just background is in place, there is no further scope for a clash between institutional and interpersonal demands. For example, parents may show special concern towards their children, without worrying about their children being unfairly advantaged as a result. Just background institutions would in fact prevent such unfair advantage from arising. In the context of war, however, this is not the case. Clashes between institutional and interpersonal demands are endemic.

The challenge is relatively easily met for noncombatant immunity. After all, even the most ardent revisionists are uneasy about their views' radical implications for the permissibility of intentionally killing noncombatants. Everyone recognizes the intuitive pull of noncombatant immunity. So if the political account vindicates that intuitive pull, then that is all to the good.

Combatant equality poses a more serious difficulty. Nobody can plausibly deny that profound moral reasons weigh against intentionally killing people who are justifiably defending their lives and homes, and against collaterally killing wholly uninvolved people in the pursuit of an unjust objective. We ordinarily consider these the weightiest moral reasons that there are. Why should the presence of an institutional scheme that licenses such killings make any difference to their permissibility?

To answer this question in a manner that vindicates existing norms, political just war theorists must account for the authority of current international law (Christiano [2010]).[16] In other words, they must explain why the mere fact that some act is prohibited (or permitted, required, etc.) by morally justified laws of war gives the addressees of these laws a moral reason not to do it, even if it would be permissible at the bar of interpersonal morality. What is more, the substantive tenets of *in bello* orthodoxy could be justified only if the moral reason in question was not merely *pro tanto* but *decisive*, in a large enough set of cases. Vindicating such a strong conception of the authority of international law is a daunting task. Many political philosophers recognize that, even in the best states, accounting for a weaker *pro tanto* obligation to obey domestic law is hard (Simmons [1979]). And international society is a far cry from the ideal liberal state. Yet, short of a convincing account of the conditions under which international law has authority in the strong sense, and an argument showing that the existing laws of war satisfy those conditions, the normative priority that the political approach assigns to institutional demands remains unvindicated.

That said, if political just war theorists fall short of defending the authority of international law, they might still salvage their approach by lowering its ambitions. On this interpretation, the morally justified laws governing the conduct of war apply to individuals only given that they have taken up their role as combatants and state leaders. These institutional demands are silent on whether the roles they attach to may be taken up in the first place. Considerations external to the morality of the practice of war—e.g., fundamental interpersonal moral demands—determine whether that is the case. On this view, it remains true that combatants who fight unjust wars ought not to fight all things considered. The laws of *jus in bello* only set out necessary, but not sufficient, conditions for the moral permissibility of one's actions in war. For just combatants, there is no conflict between interpersonal moral duties and the permissions and prohibitions attached to their institutional roles. For unjust combatants, such a conflict exists: the laws of war apply to them conditional on the breach of an interpersonal moral prohibition. Interpersonal morality prohibits combatants on the unjust side from participating in the practice of war. Yet, once they take up their role as combatants,

---

[16] An alternative approach is to argue not that *international law* has authority, but that the commands of a "morally acceptable" state do, so that unjust combatants' reasons to obey orders can override their reasons not to kill the innocent. See, for example, Estlund [2007]; Renzo [2015].

they at least ought to obey the *jus in bello* (for a similar idea, see Dill and Shue [2012]; Shue [2013]).

This reinterpretation of the political approach would make it more defensible, but would also render it less amenable to orthodox substantive conclusions. Indeed, so reinterpreted, the approach leads to first-order views not too far from those of revisionists. Some structural and substantive differences, though, would still remain. Structurally, political just war theorists' conclusions would still be reached via a distinctive line of argument, according to which principles for the conduct of war are "internal" to a given practice, and do not adjudicate the question of whether one may participate in the practice in the first place. Substantively, proponents of the political approach might still be able to vindicate the moral significance of the laws of war for unjust combatants, even if abiding by them would not suffice to render their actions morally permissible. For instance, they could point out that, when soldiers from different sides are symmetrically positioned with respect to the laws of war—in that they all endorse and follow them—their moral standing vis-à-vis each other changes. Suppose the soldiers of state A commit some interpersonal wrong—for example, fighting in an unjust war—that is allowed by international law, and that the same international law is also upheld by state B and its soldiers. If so, it would seem that by following the common legal system that binds both A and B, B and its soldiers lack standing to condemn the morally wrongful actions of the A-soldiers, given that they themselves abide by the rules licensing those kinds of actions.

To conclude, our discussion reveals that, unless a compelling defense of the strong authority of international law becomes available, a political approach may fail to offer a plausible basis for vindicating orthodox substantive conclusions. Arguably, the most promising version of the political approach involves making some concessions to revisionists.

3.2. Challenges to the Non-Political Approach

The non-political approach, recall, holds that the principles governing the design of the laws of war are derived from the principles governing the conduct of individual soldiers. On the simplest, purist version of this approach, the laws of war should mirror interpersonal morality (Rodin [2011]). We think that this view about institutional design should be rejected in general, and find it particularly problematic when adopted in conjunction with revisionists' account of interpersonal morality.[17] On this point, we agree with orthodox theorists like Shue, and revisionists like McMahan.

---

[17] Cf. Buchanan's rejection of the "mirroring view" in relation to human rights specifically, in Buchanan [2013: ch. 2].

The rejection of this view stems from the simple observation that the answers to the questions "What are the true moral principles and values?" and "What institutional rules should be adopted to best realize them?" need not always coincide (compare Cohen [2008: 266]). It is an open question whether directly reproducing fundamental moral principles in the law will best instantiate the values underlying those principles in the relevant circumstances. This depends on both the content of the principles and the nature of the circumstances.

For example, having the laws of war entirely mirror the morality underlying revisionist *jus in bello* is potentially problematic. If, as is often the case, combatants on both sides believe themselves to be justified, they will hold themselves to the revisionist standards applying to just combatants, with the associated reduced immunity for civilians. This will predictably lead to the death of many more innocent individuals than under a different institutional scheme. Mirroring the revisionist morality of war in the laws of war is thus likely to be counterproductive, especially to the extent that the value of innocent lives is central to that very morality (McMahan [2008]; Shue [2008]).

Reproducing interpersonal moral demands in the laws of war would arguably be less problematic under a *more orthodox-friendly account* of what those demands are. Seth Lazar and Adil Haque have defended an account of this kind, according to which interpersonal moral demands are quite close to those embedded in the laws of war: combatant equality and noncombatant immunity (Lazar [2015]; Haque [Forthcoming]). Regarding the former, Lazar and Haque observe that, on the one hand, the moral protections that just combatants enjoy are somewhat *less robust* than those enjoyed by justified self-defenders in ordinary interpersonal conflicts. Unlike justified self-defenders, just combatants have voluntarily exposed themselves to the risk of harm, and as between those who have and have not chosen to put themselves in harm's way, it is morally preferable to harm the former. This judgment derives from a general principle that, when a cost is unavoidable, it is other things equal *pro tanto* better that it be borne by the individuals who had most opportunity to avoid its coming about. Moreover, most combatants go to war recklessly, without examining the justice of their cause. If they happen to respect their adversaries' rights, they do so only through good fortune. The protections enjoyed by unjust combatants, on the other hand, are somewhat *more robust* than those of unjustified attackers in interpersonal conflicts. Unjust combatants are typically in the same epistemic position as their just counterparts, and they often act out of reasonable partiality for their compatriots. Moreover, on each side of a war, many individual combatants fight permissibly, and many fight impermissibly—all wars involve just and unjust aims and, more narrowly, just and unjust operations. These facts together suggest that, although just and unjust combatants are not always morally on a par, they often are, so combatant equality might be a sensible approximation of the moral truth, given the difficulty of calibrating obligations and permissions to the precise normative standing of each combatant.

Similarly, manifold arguments show that killing noncombatants in war is more seriously wrongful than killing combatants, which, combined with further premises, helps ground noncombatant immunity and other legal doctrines, like proportionality and necessity. In particular, noncombatants are more vulnerable than combatants, killing them involves running a greater risk of killing innocent victims than does killing combatants, and killing noncombatants typically involves an egregiously wrongful mode of agency, in which they are used as a mere means (these arguments are developed and defended in detail in Lazar [2015]).

Embedding this orthodox-friendly understanding of interpersonal moral demands in the laws of war would probably have less deleterious consequences than embedding revisionist moral principles. Indeed, the resulting laws of war would not be too different from those that currently exist, which already approximate—without yet perfectly tracking—what interpersonal morality requires on this account.

Acknowledging this fact, however, does not suffice to address our general concern about the "mirroring" approach.[18] Whether institutional rules should mirror interpersonal morality should be treated as an open question, to be answered *a posteriori*. Depending on the circumstances, in some cases the answer will be affirmative, and in other cases negative. What we object to is what one might call the "*a priori* mirroring" approach; and nothing in the discussion so far addresses our objection. In light of this, let us turn to the second type of derivation of institutional demands from individual moral ones, namely that mediated by principles of institutional regulation.

Like us, adherents of this approach are concerned that any attempt to mirror interpersonal morality in the laws of war might be counter-productive. On their view, we should develop principles to design the laws of war that are quite distinct from those of interpersonal morality, while still being sensitive to the values underlying it. Taking this kind of view, McMahan [2008] argues that the laws of war presuppose consequentialist foundations—they aim to minimize wrongful harm—while the morality of war is avowedly nonconsequentialist in structure. Yet, at the heart of both is a fundamental concern with the value of the lives of innocent individuals.

This view could potentially let us have our demanding principles of interpersonal morality, without accepting their radical and likely problematic

---

[18] Compare Buchanan [2013].

implications if implemented in international law. But of course this view must now explain what soldiers should do when moral and institutional demands for individuals conflict with one another. McMahan briefly argues that, when morality requires what the law permits or prohibits, and when morality prohibits what the law permits, soldiers should obey their moral duties. But when the law prohibits what morality permits, combatants should adhere to the law (McMahan [2008: 37–8]). Problematically, this discussion is neither exhaustive (it is silent on legal requirements, such as the requirement of due care, and obligations to obey lawful orders), nor does it have deep theoretical foundations. McMahan [2008] never explains why legal demands can override moral ones, except by appealing to consequentialist considerations that clash with the deontological approach to interpersonal morality he otherwise endorses (Lazar [2012]).

Like advocates of the political approach, those who invoke principles of institutional regulation must explain *under what circumstances/in what domain* the international law of armed conflict has the kind of authority that can override combatants' interpersonal moral demands. Yet, for the reasons we mentioned in connection with our discussion of the political approach, establishing the authority of international law is a difficult task to accomplish.

However, one avenue for doing so unavailable to political just war theorists might be open to their non-political counterparts. This consists in appealing to a broadly Razian justification for the authority of international law (Raz [1985]). Following the Razian approach, the authority of international law depends on whether treating its demands as authoritatively binding makes combatants and political leaders more likely to act on the (moral) reasons that independently apply to them. Since, on the non-political approach, institutions are selected on the basis of considerations that ultimately trace back to moral reasons that apply to individuals, this Razian line of analysis is open to its proponents. On this view, the authority of the law of war depends on its subjects more closely following the requirements of morality when they obey the law than they would if they followed their own judgment.

The difficulty for non-political revisionist theorists is that it is not clear when, if ever, the laws of war meet the aforementioned condition. If the moral reasons individuals ought to act on include a near-absolute prohibition on intentionally killing the innocent, then when they are not sure about the justice of their cause soldiers should simply refuse to fight. This is clearly a more accurate guide to abiding by interpersonal moral reasons than following laws of war that may quite clearly diverge from interpersonal morality. Although, structurally, revisionist adherents to the non-political approach could in principle invoke Raz's justificatory strategy, doing so would probably still not allow them to vindicate the authority of international law.

This strategy can be more fruitfully invoked by theorists who, like Lazar and Haque, defend an orthodox-friendly picture of the interpersonal moral demands applying to combatants in war. For these theorists, it will be true that following the law (as opposed to interpersonal morality directly) will often better allow combatants to comply with their moral duties. In those cases, the laws of war will have authority. By contrast, in cases where it is obvious that combatants may better comply with independent moral demands just by following their own judgment, international law will have no authority.[19] Still, this view would fall short of vindicating *jus in bello* orthodoxy, since it allows for circumstances in which soldiers and leaders ought to act contrary to what international law requires.

Once again, then, our discussion reveals that—in the absence of an adequate defense of the authority of international law—what looks like the most promising version of the non-political approach fails to vindicate just war revisionism, and involves making some concessions to orthodox views.

3.3. Concluding Remarks

Much of the dispute between orthodox and revisionist just war theorists depends on what the correct account of the relationship between moral and institutional demands applying to individuals is. If orthodox theorists wish to vindicate combatant equality and noncombatant immunity as exhaustive of the permissibility of combatants' conduct in war, they must argue that the existing laws of war have legitimate authority. As we have suggested, this is a hard task to accomplish.

If revisionists wish to uphold the interpersonal moral prohibition on killing the innocent, while not subscribing to the problematic "*a priori* mirroring

---

[19] It might be objected that, if the most effective way for us to comply with interpersonal morality in the context of war is to follow the laws of war, then, by hypothesis, the latter *always* have authority. This does not seem right. While it may well be true that, *in the main*, following justified laws of war is most conducive to compliance with interpersonal moral demands, this need not always be the case. Consider the following analogy. (For discussion of a similar case, see Smith [1973: 971].) Obeying traffic rules is generally most efficient and safe. But there are exceptions. If I am at a pedestrian crossing at 4 a.m. in a deserted village with no person or vehicle in sight, and the traffic light goes red, it is plainly false that not crossing—i.e., obeying traffic rules—would be most conducive to safety and efficiency. In that case, following my own judgment and crossing would be most responsive to considerations of safety and efficiency. Similar situations might occur, *mutatis mutandis*, in the context of war, and when they do, deviation from the relevant laws in direct compliance with morality is required. Cf. the discussions in Raz [1986: 73–5]; Soper [1989: 227–8]. Thanks to Massimo Renzo for raising this point.

approach," they must explain why and when obedience to the laws of war affects one's moral standing. This again requires either developing a theory of the authority of international law or, more modestly, of the normative significance of international law, short of authority.

Without any ambition of solving these disputes, our discussion has suggested that the most plausible versions of political and non-political approaches to the just war vindicate positions that depart somewhat from just war orthodoxy and revisionism, occupying the middle ground between the two.

We do, however, hope that our discussion has shown how progress in the first-order dispute between revisionist and orthodox just war theorists can be aided by considering the second-order question of how the moral and institutional demands applying to individuals relate to each other.

4. FEASIBILITY CONSTRAINTS AND JUST WAR THEORY

In this section, we first sketch the political theory discussion on feasibility constraints and the design of normative principles, then draw parallels with the contemporary just war theory debate. Once again, this new framing will help us illuminate that debate and make some substantive advances within it.

4.1. Feasibility Constraints in Theorizing about Justice

When attempting to act on our most cherished moral ideals, we often find that facts about human character and behavior, our empirical circumstances, and the perverse incentives that we face make those ideals hard to implement successfully. We call these facts feasibility constraints.[20] Political theorists have, in recent years, expended much effort identifying which feasibility constraints should set the parameters for principles of justice that aim to deliver action-guiding prescriptions.[21] Their views can be represented on a spectrum, from what might be called "utopian" theorists at one end, to "realists" at the other (Carens [1996]; Valentini [2012]).[22]

---

[20] For discussion, see Raikka [1998]; Gilabert [2011]; Gilabert and Lawford-Smith [2012]; Gheaus [2013]; Lawford-Smith [2013].

[21] For simplicity's sake, once again we focus on the notion of justice. Discussions of feasibility, however, are equally applicable to other ideals, such as democracy.

[22] Here by "realists" we do not mean "political realists" such as Bernard Williams or William Galston. We use the label "realism" to denote a particular view about feasibility constraints; not about what counts as politics, and what implications this has for political theorizing. See Rossi and Sleat [2014].

Utopian theorists think that justice is unconstrained by the demands of feasibility (e.g., arguably, Cohen [2003]); realists think that all facts that render a principle even minimally unlikely to be successfully realized should be taken as parametric—that is, they should limit the scope of that principle's application. Between these unpopular extremes, many believe that normative theorizing should make *some* concessions to feasibility constraints, but they differ over the extent of those concessions. Inspired by vocabulary introduced by David Estlund [2008: ch. 14], we distinguish between weakly and strongly concessive approaches.

Weakly concessive approaches consider only a thin set of feasibility constraints relevant to theorizing about justice. Provided some action enjoined by a principle of justice is physically and psychologically possible for the agent, it can be required of him.[23] Facts about physical and psychological possibility will depend on (i) the agents in question and (ii) the environment around them. Ascertaining what (i) and (ii) involve may seem relatively straightforward. For example, it may sometimes be physically impossible for a deaf person to act on the obligation "you ought to reply when your name is called out." Similarly, it may be physically impossible for a well-meaning but desperately poor state to provide subsistence for all of its citizens.

Other cases are less clear-cut. Imagine John is standing on the shore of a lake, and sees a small child drowning, not far from him (Singer [1972]). John knows how to swim, and can pull the child out without risking drowning; however, he is paralyzed by what he recognizes as an irrational fear of entering the lake. He developed this fear as a child, after his father died in a boating accident. Is it psychologically impossible for John to walk in and pull the child out? It is hard to say, but weakly concessive theories must explain when psychological debilities count as genuine feasibility constraints.

Strongly concessive approaches emphasize not only facts about physical and psychological possibility, but also facts about what agents are likely to do given their preferences and dispositions (for a critique of these approaches, see Estlund [2011]). To appreciate the difference, consider this prescription: "Every person ought to donate 50 percent of their income to the global poor, provided this is compatible with each still satisfying their basic needs." Weakly concessive approaches could not object to this: though this prescription asks a lot, it is clearly physically and psychologically possible to donate half one's income to others (barring exceptional circumstances or unusual pathologies). By contrast, on the strongly concessive approach, this

---

[23] Estlund [2011] appears to be concerned with physical possibility alone, hence he arguably belongs somewhere in between utopian and weakly concessive approaches.

prescription is indeed invalid, because it is so unlikely that people will comply with it. Given predictable selfishness and partiality, very few will be disposed to donate so much of their earnings, which is enough to undermine the prescription.[24]

4.2. Feasibility Constraints in Just War Theory

The divide between weakly and strongly concessive approaches is again reproduced in the split between orthodox and revisionist just war theorists, and in a rather stark way. The former are strongly concessive, the latter are weakly concessive.

Orthodox theorists defend combatant equality and noncombatant immunity on strongly concessive grounds. The institutions governing armed conflict should not make demands that their addressees will predictably ignore. More specifically, as was briefly mentioned in the previous section, some facts about warfare, human nature, and our predictable moral failings make revisionist laws of war highly unlikely to be observed.[25]

First, the circumstances of warfare mean that combatants are rarely able to find out, given the time and resources available, whether their cause is just, or whether their targets are liable to be killed. Moreover, there may be reasonable disagreement about what makes a war just, so different combatants' judgments will presuppose different standards. Rawls's reflections on the "burdens of judgment" apply here as elsewhere (Rawls [1996: Lecture II, sec. 2.]). And even if—counterfactually—most combatants could converge on the same standard of justice, find out whether the war they are fighting is just, and distinguish the liable from the nonliable, they would not be able to confine their attacks to the liable, given how the two groups are intermingled, and given how relatively indiscriminate military technology still is.

Second, human nature is such that, arguably, the extreme exigencies of warfare, especially *in bello*, make adhering to strict moral norms psychologically impossible, or at any rate excessively onerous, for many combatants. Their own lives and the lives of their friends are immediately in danger; death and pain surround them; psychological trauma is, for many combatants, inevitable. This extreme stress reduces their ability to deliberate about the right course of action; it also almost certainly inclines them to reason more partially.

---

[24] Some forms of so-called "realism in political theory" may be seen as leaning towards this position. For discussion, see Galston [2010]. But see note 22 for clarification.
[25] Buchanan and Keohane [2004]; Buchanan [2006]; McMahan [2008]; Roberts [2008]; Shue [2010]; Waldron [2010]; Shue [2013].

Third, and perhaps most importantly, combatants will often convince themselves that they are fighting for a just cause, no matter how much of a cognitive leap that requires. Their leaders will aid this self-deception through propaganda, deceit, and misinformation.

Together, these facts mean that if the laws of armed conflict rejected combatant equality and noncombatant immunity, then those laws would be, respectively, disregarded and brutally abused. If the law prohibits unjust combatants from fighting, they will fight nonetheless, whether because of the difficulty of knowing that their cause is unjust; or because, once their lives are at stake, they will predictably fight regardless of the justice of their cause; or because they convince themselves that their cause is just despite evidence to the contrary. Similarly, if the laws were to permit just combatants to intentionally kill liable noncombatants, they would predictably be abused. Many unjust combatants would arrogate to themselves the extra permissions reserved for just combatants (believing themselves justified), and many just combatants would take advantage of the additional permissions without adequate justification for doing so—in part, no doubt, because of the psychological exigencies of combat.

If a critical mass of combatants disobey the laws of armed conflict, then those laws cannot minimize the (wrongful) harms involved in war. Laws cannot achieve their goals if they are ignored. So the laws should not make demands of people that they will, predictably, not fulfill. Facts about likely compliance constrain which institutions can justifiably govern armed conflict. Orthodox theorists are strongly concessive.

Revisionists, as already noted, focus primarily on interpersonal moral demands, and, unlike orthodox theorists, they are weakly concessive, as well as highly optimistic about what is psychologically possible for combatants at war. For revisionists, the pervasive uncertainty of war, psychological trauma, and predictable self-deception are at most problems of application. Normative principles are derived from sanitized hypothetical cases with none of these characteristics.

Faced with the objection that their normative theorizing makes epistemic and psychological demands that normal combatants cannot meet, revisionists have a ready response: their demands govern whom combatants may kill, if they kill anyone. They can be satisfied either by killing only those who may permissibly be killed, or by not killing anyone at all. Although, for at least some combatants, it might be impossible to discriminate between the liable and the nonliable in war, it is certainly possible to adhere to the principle "kill only the liable": simply kill no one. This would mean failing to fulfill any duties to defend the innocent. But provided one accepts a substantial asymmetry between doing and allowing harm, as most revisionists do, perhaps this is a tolerable result.

Moreover, although stress and trauma might undermine some people's agency in war, many combatants overcome their circumstances and oppose unjust actions in war, so why should we assume that all humans are incapable of opposing wars that are unjust simpliciter? Revisionists believe that many human beings can resist the corrupting effects of violence and war, and that, despite their survival instinct, they can adhere to norms that demand sacrificing their own lives, rather than take another person's life to protect themselves. Since resisting one's survival instinct is undeniably hard, norms in opposition to that instinct are unlikely to be universally complied with. But for revisionists, predictable wrongdoing is no ground for removing interpersonal moral obligations we would otherwise have.

5. FEASIBILITY CONSTRAINTS AND JUST WAR THEORY: IMPLICATIONS

As with the dispute over political and non-political approaches to the site of *jus in bello*, we again see that the controversy between orthodox and revisionist just war theorists derives, at least in part, from a deeper disagreement about feasibility constraints in normative theorizing. It is another proxy battle, which cannot be resolved without settling the second-order dispute. However, we think that this task is easier for the feasibility question than for the site question, because revisionist and orthodox approaches can be reconciled. Not only are they fighting proxy battles; they are engaged in a phony war. Why? Because there is no uniquely correct set of feasibility constraints.

Which constraints we should recognize depends on the site for which we are issuing prescriptions. Orthodox and revisionist just war theorists—for all their disagreement—actually endorse compatible approaches, and each is broadly right about the role of feasibility for the site that they consider. Orthodox theorists are right that, when designing institutions, we should be strongly concessive. But revisionists are also right that, at the level of interpersonal morality, we should be only weakly concessive.

The key point is simple. When deciding what I, as an individual, ought to do, I cannot use my moral weakness as an excuse, because—setting genuine pathologies aside—I have sufficient control of whether or not I am morally weak, and of how I behave more generally. By contrast, we cannot reasonably expect the same level of control on the part of an institutional system, no matter how effectively enforced its rules are. It is not in the law's power to secure compliance with its content, independently of what that content is. How likely individuals are to obey given rules therefore makes a difference to what a system of rules *can* achieve in any given circumstance (Weinberg [Unpublished]; Valentini [Forthcoming]). For this reason, institutional—as opposed to purely moral—rules for individual conduct ought, in the main, to take into account individuals' likely non-compliance.

While the strongly vs. weakly concessive attitudes of orthodox and revisionist just war theorists at the institutional and the interpersonal level are laudable, some objections to both views still arise from thinking about feasibility constraints. In what follows, we set them out in turn.

5.1. Challenges to Orthodox Theorists' Treatment of Feasibility Constraints

Orthodox theorists are arguably *too* concessive in their understanding of which institutional norms might win assent. For example, one might have thought, during the Second World War, that any legal convention prohibiting intentional attacks on noncombatants would be infeasible to implement, and yet over the twentieth century attacks on noncombatants became taboo, at least among liberal democracies (Kahl [2007]). In the same spirit, we should not be too pessimistic about the prospects for further reform of the laws of war. We should endorse and pursue concrete institutional proposals that might materially improve the likelihood of unjust combatants both finding out about the impermissibility of their wars and acting on that knowledge.

For example, whatever the shortcomings of McMahan's proposal for an international court of *jus ad bellum*, using advances in technology and the increasing reach of international organizations to provide more public information about the proximate causes of war (along the lines already attempted by the OSCE, for example in South Ossetia in 2008) increases combatants' prospects of discovering whether their causes are just (McMahan [2014]). Making greater provision within national armies for selective conscientious refusal could also materially diminish predictable voluntary wrongdoing (McMahan [2013]). New technologies, such as unmanned aerial vehicles equipped with high-powered cameras, promise to make both distinguishing and discriminating between the liable and nonliable more tractable, as well as mitigating at least the antecedent psychological stress that makes conscientious action by soldiers in conventional wars so difficult (Strawser [2010]). Though international law advances glacially, it does advance, and orthodox just war theorists should ensure they guide, rather than hinder, that progress.

5.2. Challenges to Revisionist Theorists' Treatment of Feasibility Constraints

Revisionist just war theorists are too inattentive to real-world constraints characterizing the human condition in war, and to uncertainty and psychological stress in particular. We can indeed always abide by the duty not to kill nonliable people, by simply refusing to fight, but this is like saying that a blind person can adhere to the prohibition "you must not cross roads when the red man is lit" by never crossing roads. If they give us no more guidance than this as to what to do given the uncertainty and stress characterizing war, then our only option is to endorse pacifism.[26]

Let us begin by considering uncertainty. Combatants at war are typically unable to reliably distinguish between liable and nonliable combatants and noncombatants; even if they could do so, they could not discriminate between them; that is, confine their attacks only to the liable (Lazar [2010]; Dill and Shue [2012]). Invariably, they are also uncertain whether their cause is just, and whether it will be proportionate and necessary. If they are told that they may intentionally kill only the liable, when doing so is necessary and proportionate to the service of a just cause, then their only way to avoid risking breaching a near-absolute prohibition on intentionally killing the innocent is to refuse to fight. Although pacifism should remain a live option, most just war theorists want to offer a middle ground between realism and pacifism, to explain why common sense is right, and some wars can permissibly be fought, despite their costs. This means explaining how to apply revisionist just war theory in the context of uncertainty.[27]

Without aiming to be comprehensive, we can illustrate two approaches available to revisionists who wish to extend their theories in these ways. One involves first identifying all of the objective moral reasons, and then choosing a decision rule that allows us to optimize compliance with our objective moral reasons, given our uncertainty (Lazar [2016]). Paradigmatically, this means applying decision theory to our moral reasons. For any given decision

[26] As Ralf Bader and Peter Vallentyne have pointed out in discussion, *any* moral theory should give an account of how its principles are to be applied under conditions of uncertainty. We agree, but we also think that the topic is particularly germane to "feasibility constraints," as understood in this paper: i.e., real-world facts that make it hard for us to act on, or realize, important moral ideals. Specifically, the "fog of war" means that combatants will predictably fail to do what they objectively ought to do, so revisionists owe us an account of what they ought to do given their uncertainty. This will take one of the two forms outlined in the text.

[27] McMahan has some rough advice that combatants are permitted to kill people when it is reasonable for them to presume that their targets are liable to be killed, and Cécile Fabre has alluded to a precautionary principle, which enjoins refraining from the use of lethal force when there is doubt as to the targets' liability.

problem, we first identify the options available to the agent, then the possible states that the world might be in, and the outcomes of those options dependent on those states. We assign probabilities to the states given that one acts, and moral worth (e.g., "utilities") to the outcomes, sum the products of those two values for all possible outcomes from the option, and choose the option that maximizes expected moral worth.

On most accounts this is our best tool for decision-making under uncertainty, but it poses distinctive problems for just war theory, given its apparently consequentialist cast, and the avowedly nonconsequentialist approach to ethics of most just war theorists—certainly of those in the revisionist camp. It also raises its own problems—after all, we aimed to provide useful advice in the circumstances of war, but doing expected "moral worth" (e.g., utility) calculations is often no easier than working out the objectively right thing to do. Identifying salient outcomes and states, assigning moral worth to the outcomes and probabilities to the states will often be an inordinately complex task. Some might even question whether we can assign probabilities in an endeavor as unpredictable and complex as warfare.

The second approach is to argue that first-order moral reasons govern what is permissible given our uncertainty, and reject the idea that we need a decision rule to apply our theory of objective morality. On this view, we would need to work out, for example, a theory of recklessness and of negligence, and we might argue that acts with uncertain consequences are permissible just in case they are neither reckless nor negligent. We might also develop an evidence- or belief-relative theory of rights, according to which my claims against others are in part a function of the evidence available to them, or what they believe to be the case (Ferzan [2005]; Zimmerman [2008]; Frowe [2010]). Or we could perhaps adopt Aboodi, Boorer, and Enoch's suggestion that whether a harm counts as intentional can depend on the agent's beliefs about whether the target was liable to that harm (Aboodi et al. [2008]; see also McMahan [2011]). The challenge for those who favor this approach is to give a detailed account of those reasons, and to explain both why they cannot be simply integrated into the first approach, and what we should do when our first-order reasons governing action under uncertainty must be combined with, or conflict with, our reasons to optimize compliance with objective norms.

Lastly, and as anticipated, revisionist just war theorists should re-examine their views on whether psychological stress and trauma can defeat obligations that we might otherwise have. The standing assumption is that the unique exigencies of war do not diminish the constraints that govern belligerent practice. But in other contexts, we often think of pathological psychological debilities as being, as Estlund puts it, "requirement-blocking" (Estlund [2011]). Of course, this is easier to explain when the requirements are, as in the drowning case presented earlier, positive requirements to aid others. In war, our central focus is on the ethics of killing, and it is hard to come up with cases outside of war in which a putative duty not to kill is blocked by the psychological stress faced by the duty-bearer.

But the revisionists tell combatants fighting for an unjust cause that they are morally required to lay down their weapons, even if that means sacrificing their lives. Consider a terrified soldier, worn down by weeks or months of near misses, seeing his friends and enemies arbitrarily cut down one after the other, who now faces attack. It seems relatively easy to think of cases in which it is psychologically impossible for such an individual to lay down his arms and let himself be killed. And we can perhaps go further. Is it psychologically possible, in such a case, to do nothing to defend yourself? Grant the revisionists that mere fear for one's life cannot block the requirement not to kill an innocent person. But could it perhaps block the requirement not to subject an innocent person to a certain level of risk? Perhaps the psychological impossibility of doing nothing might license this combatant to spray suppressive fire in the direction of his adversaries, in the hopes of pinning them down and preventing them from dealing the decisive blow. We do not mean to present a decisive case for this solution here. But we do believe that revisionist just war theorists should think more carefully about cases like these, which illustrate how the psychological impossibility of adhering to some constraints might block their application in war.

6. CONCLUSION

In this paper, we have argued that revisionist and orthodox just war theorists have fought proxy battles: their first-order disagreements over substantive questions in just war theory—in particular combatant equality and non-combatant immunity—derive, at least partly, from second-order disputes over the nature and purpose of just war theory. Bringing these debates to the surface shows both how these different camps have been talking past each other, and how we can make advances in the debate and, perhaps, reconcile their views.

In particular, we have argued that normative theorizing about war should concern itself both with the grounds on which the institutions governing armed conflict are morally justified, and with the moral demands that apply to individual actors in war. The interesting question is how the two relate to each other, and we have mapped out the relevant possibilities, and their virtues and vices. We have also argued that implicit disputes over feasibility constraints underpin orthodox theorists' concessive attitude to unjust combatants who fight despite their interpersonal moral requirements not to, as well as revisionists' moral rigorism. In this dispute, we think a happy accommodation between revisionists and orthodox theorists should be possible: when designing institutions to govern war, we should consider all kinds of predictable non-compliance; in the principles governing individual actors, only physical and psychological impossibility should be parametric. Revisionists have not adequately adapted their theories to accommodate these considerations, but there is nothing to prevent them from doing so. And once they do, the gulf between their prescriptions and those issued by orthodox theorists may shrink, pointing towards a "middle ground" between the two.

Acknowledgments

We are grateful to the participants in the workshop on just war and feasibility (ANU, July 2014), to the audience at the Nathanson Centre (York University), and at the 3rd Oxford Studies in Political Philosophy Conference (Syracuse University) for their questions, and particularly to Jessica Flanigan, Pablo Gilabert, Jeff McMahan, Mike Otsuka, Massimo Renzo, and Miriam Ronzoni for their written comments. We also thanks the editors and two reviewers for their feedback on the paper.

References

Aboodi, R., A. Borer, and D. Enoch 2008. "Deontology, Individualism, and Uncertainty," *Journal of Philosophy* 105/5: 259–72.

Benbaji, Y. 2008. "A Defense of the Traditional War Convention," *Ethics* 118/3: 464–95.

Brandt, R. B. 1972. "Utilitarianism and the Rules of War," *Philosophy & Public Affairs* 1/2: 145–65.

Buchanan, A. 2006. "Institutionalizing the Just War," *Philosophy & Public Affairs* 34/1: 2–38.

Buchanan, A. E. 2013. *The Heart of Human Rights*, Oxford: Oxford University Press.

Buchanan, A. and R. O. Keohane 2004. "The Preventive Use of Force: A Cosmopolitan Institutional Proposal," *Ethics & International Affairs* 18/1: 1–22.

Carens, J. H. 1996. "Realistic and Idealistic Approaches to the Ethics of Immigration," *International Migration Review* 30/2: 156–70.

Christiano, T. 2010. "Democratic Legitimacy and International Institutions," in *The Philosophy of International Law*, ed. Samantha Besson and John Tasioulas, Oxford: Oxford University Press, 119–38.

Coady, T. 2008. *Morality and Political Violence*, Cambridge: Cambridge University Press.

Cohen, G. A. 1997. "Where the Action Is: On the Site of Distributive Justice," *Philosophy & Public Affairs* 26/1: 3–30.

Cohen, G. A. 2003. "Facts and Principles," *Philosophy & Public Affairs* 31/3: 211–45.

Cohen, G. A. 2008. *Rescuing Justice and Equality*, London: Harvard University Press.

Dill, J. and H. Shue 2012. "Limiting the Killing in War: Military Necessity and the St. Petersburg Assumption," *Ethics & International Affairs* 26/03: 311–33.

Emerton, P. and T. Handfield 2009. "Order and Affray: Defensive Privileges in Warfare," *Philosophy & Public Affairs* 37/4: 382–414.

Estlund, D. 2007. "On Following Orders in an Unjust War," *Journal of Political Philosophy* 15/2: 213–34.

Estlund, D. 2008. *Democratic Authority: A Philosophical Framework*, Princeton: Princeton University Press.

Estlund, D. 2011. "Human Nature and the Limits (If Any) of Political Philosophy," *Philosophy & Public Affairs* 39/3: 207–37.

Fabre, C. 2009. "Guns, Food, and Liability to Attack in War," *Ethics* 120/1: 36–63.

Fabre, C. 2012. *Cosmopolitan War*, Oxford: Oxford University Press.

Ferzan, K. 2005. "Justifying Self-Defense," *Law and Philosophy* 24/6: 711–49.

Frankfurt, H. G. 1997. "Equality and Respect," *Social Research* 64/1: 3–13.

Frowe, H. 2010. "A Practical Account of Self-Defence," *Law and Philosophy* 29: 245–72.

Frowe, H. 2011. *The Ethics of War and Peace: An Introduction*, London: Routledge.

Frowe, H. 2012. "Self-Defence and the Principle of Non-Combatant Immunity," *Journal of Moral Philosophy* 8/4: 530–46.

Frowe, H. 2014. *Defensive Killing*, Oxford: Oxford University Press.

Galston, W. 2010. "Realism in Political Theory," *European Journal of Political Theory* 9/4: 385–411.

Gheaus, A. 2013. "The Feasibility Constraint on the Concept of Justice," *Philosophical Quarterly* 63/252: 445–64.

Gilabert, P. 2011. "Feasibility and Socialism," *Journal of Political Philosophy* 19/1: 52–63.

Gilabert, P. and H. Lawford-Smith 2012. "Political Feasibility: A Conceptual Exploration," *Political Studies* 60/4: 809–25.

Haque, A. A. Forthcoming. *Law and Morality at War*, Oxford: Oxford University Press.

Jenkins, R. 2014. "An in-Bello Rule Consequentialist Code of Morality," unpublished MS.

Julius, A. J. 2003. "Basic Structure and the Value of Equality," *Philosophy & Public Affairs* 31/4: 321–55.

Kahl, C. H. 2007. "In the Crossfire or the Crosshairs? Norms, Civilian Casualties, and U.S. Conduct in Iraq," *International Security* 32/1: 7–46.

Lawford-Smith, H. 2013. "Understanding Political Feasibility," *Journal of Political Philosophy* 21/3: 243–59.

Lazar, S. 2010. "The Responsibility Dilemma for *Killing in War*: A Review Essay," *Philosophy & Public Affairs* 38/2: 180–213.

Lazar, S. 2012. "Morality & Law of War," in *Companion to Philosophy of Law*, ed. Andrei Marmor, New York: Routledge: 364–79.

Lazar, S. 2015. *Sparing Civilians*, Oxford: Oxford University Press.

Lazar, S. 2016. "In Dubious Battle: Uncertainty and the Ethics of Killing," MS.

Mavrodes, G. I. 1975. "Conventions and the Morality of War," *Philosophy & Public Affairs* 4/2: 117–31.

McMahan, J. 1994. "Innocence, Self-Defense and Killing in War," *Journal of Political Philosophy* 2/3: 193–221.

McMahan, J. 2004. "The Ethics of Killing in War," *Ethics* 114/1: 693–732.

McMahan, J. 2008. "The Morality of War and the Law of War," in *Just and Unjust Warriors: The Moral and Legal Status of Soldiers*, ed. David Rodin and Henry Shue, Oxford: Oxford University Press: 19–43.

McMahan, J. 2009. *Killing in War*, Oxford: Oxford University Press.

McMahan, J. 2011. "Who Is Morally Liable to Be Killed in War?," *Analysis* 71/3: 544–59.

McMahan, J. 2013. "The Moral Responsibility of Volunteer Soldiers," *Boston Review* November 6.

McMahan, J. 2014. "The Prevention of Unjust Wars," in *Reading Walzer*, ed. Yitzhak Benbaji and Naomi Sussman, New York: Routledge: 233–56.

McPherson, L. 2004. "Innocence and Responsibility in War," *Canadian Journal of Philosophy* 34/4: 485–506.

Murphy, L. 1998. "Institutions and the Demands of Justice," *Philosophy & Public Affairs* 27/4: 251–91.

Parfit, D. 2000. "Equality or Priority," in *The Ideal of Equality*, ed. Matthew Clayton and Andrew Williams, Basingstoke: Palgrave: 81–125.

Pogge, T. 2000. "On the Site of Distributive Justice: Reflections on Cohen and Murphy," *Philosophy & Public Affairs* 29/2: 137–69.

Raikka, J. 1998. "The Feasibility Condition in Political Theory," *Journal of Political Philosophy* 6/1: 27–40.

Rawls, J. 1996. *Political Liberalism*, Chichester: Columbia University Press.

Rawls, J. 1999. *A Theory of Justice*, Oxford: Oxford University Press.

Raz, J. 1985. "Authority and Justification," *Philosophy & Public Affairs* 14/1: 3–29.

Raz, J. 1986. *The Morality of Freedom*, Oxford: Clarendon Press.

Renzo, M. 2015. "Duties of Citizenship and Just War," unpublished MS.

Roberts, A. 2008. "The Principle of Equal Application of the Laws of War," in *Just and Unjust Warriors: The Moral and Legal Status of Soldiers*, ed. David Rodin and Henry Shue, Oxford: Oxford University Press: 226–54.

Rodin, D. 2002. *War and Self-Defense*, Oxford: Clarendon Press.

Rodin, D. 2008. "The Moral Inequality of Soldiers: Why Jus in Bello Asymmetry Is Half Right," in *Just and Unjust Warriors: The Moral and Legal Status of Soldiers*, ed. David Rodin and Henry Shue, Oxford: Oxford University Press: 44–68.

Rodin, D. 2011. "Morality and Law in War," in *The Changing Character of War*, ed. Sibylle Scheipers and Hew Strachan, Oxford: Oxford University Press: 446–63.

Ronzoni, M. 2007. "Two Concepts of the Basic Structure, and Their Relevance to Global Justice," *Global Justice: Theory, Practice, Rhetoric* 1: 68–85.

Rossi, E. and M. Sleat 2014. "Realism in Normative Political Theory," *Philosophy Compass* 9/10: 689–701.

Scheffler, S. 2006. "Is the Basic Structure Basic?," in *The Egalitarian Conscience*, ed. Christine Sypnowich, Oxford: Oxford University Press: 102–29.

Shaw, W. H. 2011. "Utilitarianism and Recourse to War," *Utilitas* 23/04: 380–401.

Shue, H. 2008. "Do We Need a Morality of War?," in *Just and Unjust Warriors: The Moral and Legal Status of Soldiers*, ed. David Rodin and Henry Shue, Oxford: Oxford University Press: 87–111.

Shue, H. 2010. "Laws of War," in *The Philosophy of International Law*, ed. Samantha Besson, New York: Oxford University Press: 511–30.

Shue, H. 2013. "Laws of War, Morality, and International Politics: Compliance, Stringency, and Limits," *Leiden Journal of International Law* 26/02: 271–92.

Simmons, A. J. 1979. *Moral Principles and Political Obligations*, Princeton: Princeton University Press.

Singer, P. 1972. "Famine, Affluence, and Morality," *Philosophy & Public Affairs* 1/3: 229–43.

Smith, M. B. E. 1973. "Is There a Prima Facie Obligation to Obey the Law?," *The Yale Law Journal* 82/5: 950–76.

Soper, P. 1989. "Legal Theory and the Claim of Authority," *Philosophy & Public Affairs* 18/3: 209–37.

Statman, D. 2014. "Fabre's Crusade for Justice: Why We Should Not Join," *Law and Philosophy* 33/3: 337–60.

Strawser, B. J. 2010. "Moral Predators: The Duty to Employ Uninhabited Aerial Vehicles," *Journal of Military Ethics* 9/4: 342–68.

Valentini, L. 2012. "Ideal vs. Non-Ideal Theory: A Conceptual Map," *Philosophy Compass* 7/9: 654–64.

Valentini, L. Forthcoming. "On the Messy Utopophobia vs Factophobia Controversy: A Systematization and Assessment," in *Political Utopias: Contemporary Debates*, ed. Kevin Vallier and Michael Weber, New York: Oxford University Press.

Waldron, J. 2010. *Torture, Terror, and Trade-Offs: Philosophy for the White House*, Oxford: Oxford University Press.

Walzer, M. 1977. *Just and Unjust Wars: A Moral Argument with Historical Illustrations*, New York: Basic Books.

Weinberg, J. "The Agency of Justice and the Limits (If Any) of Political Philosophy," unpublished MS.

Young, I. M. 2006. "Taking the Basic Structure Seriously," *Perspectives on Politics* 4/1: 91–7.

Zimmerman, M. J. 2008. *Living with Uncertainty: The Moral Significance of Ignorance*, Cambridge: Cambridge University Press.

PART III
FURTHER TOPICS

8

The Moral Neglect of Negligence

Seana Valentine Shiffrin

The moral significance of negligence is regularly downplayed in the legal and philosophical literature.[1] Some question whether negligence is a coherent wrong at all, while others locate it on a fairly low rung of a moral hierarchy of wrongfulness. Whatever the flaws of the culpably negligent person or the culpably negligent act, they are thought to pale in comparison with the malicious person or act.

Even those philosophers who are not skeptical about negligence have too quickly accepted the idea that negligence is a rather slight wrong. They tend to accept two tenets about negligence that diminish its importance: first, that culpable negligence is substantially less significant than malice (as well as other intentionally inflicted wrongs) and second, that even when culpable, negligence is a rather petty moral wrong. The attitude conveyed is that, considered apart from its consequences, the wrong of negligence is real, but paltry.[2]

By contrast, I regard culpable negligence as a more significant moral wrong, even when considered separately from its consequences. Concomitantly, I take non-negligence to be a significant, but often overlooked, moral virtue. Here, I defend their importance and attempt to sketch distinct moral and political conceptions of negligence as distinguished from the legal conception, one that reflects institutional and remedial concerns that may be inapplicable in the non-legal moral domain. I do not seek to

---

[1] Joseph Raz's recent work marks a happy exception. *See* Joseph Raz, *Responsibility and the Negligence Standard*, 30 Oxford J. of Legal Stud. 1 (2010); Joseph Raz, *Being in the World*, 23 Ratio 433 (2010).

[2] Sometimes, however, this point arises in the different context of wondering whether it is fair that a negligent person bear heavy burdens of liability, whether civil or criminal, for major consequences. *See, e.g.*, Jeremy Waldron, *Moments of Carelessness and Massive Loss*, in David G. Owen, Philosophical Foundations of Tort Law 387 (1995). I do not aim to vindicate such liability, but to explore the moral evaluation of negligence considered apart from any remedial ramifications.

upend the hierarchy and argue that, all things considered and *mutatis mutandis*, negligence is worse than malice. My aim is to explain why negligence can be a serious moral and political wrong, to contend that we go astray in diminishing its significance, and to disrupt the rigidity and severity of the standard moral hierarchy.

To get a sense of what is on my mind, consider the example of Anthony Elonis, the subject of a recent Supreme Court case.[3] Mr. Elonis, angry and estranged from his spouse and children, posted on Facebook a series of "self-styled rap lyrics containing graphically violent language and imagery concerning his wife, co-workers, a kindergarten class," and the police.[4] His posts "frequently included crude, degrading and violent material about his wife."[5] One lengthy discussion concerned whether it was illegal for him to say he wanted to kill his wife.[6] It included details and diagrams of how to fire a mortar launcher at her home and escape with impunity.[7] His posts, many in lyric or poetic form, bragged that he had "sinister plans for all my friends," that he planned "to initiate the most heinous school shooting ever imagined," and that he would detonate a suicide bomb were the FBI to arrest him.[8] Accompanying some posts were references to free speech and disclaimers that the lyrics were fictional and therapeutic.[9] These references did not diminish the heightened concern of the police and the terror of his wife, who understandably felt threatened.[10]

Mr. Elonis was convicted of threatening to harm others. Part of his successful challenge to his conviction complained that the jury was instructed only to find that he intentionally communicated what a reasonable person would regard as a threat, but Mr. Elonis contended that proof of negligent threatening should not suffice to convict him. The relevant statute should be interpreted to demand proof that either he intended to threaten his wife and others or he knew his posts would threaten them.[11] Putting aside the legal issues about the statute's proper interpretation, I'm more interested in the moral interpretation of Mr. Elonis's conduct. To focus only on the

---

[3] *Elonis v. U.S.*, 135 S. Ct. 2001 (2015).

[4] Id. at 2002.

[5] Id. at 2005.

[6] Id.

[7] Id. at 2005–6.

[8] Id.

[9] Id.

[10] Id. at 2006.

[11] Id. Mr. Elonis also complained if the statute did not require proof of intent to threaten, it would violate the First Amendment. The Court did not reach the free speech issue.

morality of his threatening behavior as such,[12] assume that Mr. Elonis would not have realized his fantasies. In one version of the events, his victims' terror mattered enough to him to try to elicit it. In another version, his victims meant so little to him that they did not penetrate his self-absorbed bubble of rage; he either didn't register their predictable terror or didn't register it as providing subjectively decisive reason to alter his conduct. Both versions of his behavior involve subordinating the vulnerabilities and interests of others to his perceived interest in voicing his self-indulgent and horrific fantasies, and both versions would show a culpable imperviousness to the evidently more important needs of others. I am hard pressed to say one version of the story is morally worse than another. Both pathways to others' terror, one malicious and one negligent, are morally awful in different ways.

To pursue the more general point about the moral significance of negligence that this example illustrates, I first advocate for a moral conception of negligence (and non-negligence) and provide illustrations of it and its political counterpart, focusing on some examples that a legal lens might filter out. Second, I contend that culpable negligence, morally, is more important than our denigrating hierarchy often suggests.

While I have alluded to the negligence skeptics,[13] I will not directly address their worries. I will start by presupposing that negligence exists, that there are reasonable standards of due care that may be transgressed negligently or maliciously, and that such negligence (when unexcused) can be the basis of moral responsibility. Assuming that one may be morally responsible and morally culpable for at least some negligent acts, my aim is to explore the moral significance of such culpable negligence. Fleshing out an account of the moral seriousness of negligence may help to make the stakes of skepticism clearer and to survey some of the resources for answering it.

---

[12] I work with an objective understanding of what it is to threaten such that Mr. Elonis threatened his wife by intentionally communicating content that: (a) would raise apprehension of harm in reasonable recipients; (b) when his wife would foreseeably be a recipient of that content; and (c) she experienced the content as threatening. The question then is whether it makes a significant moral difference whether Mr. Elonis *intentionally* or *negligently* threatened her.

[13] There are many. *See, e.g.,* Larry Alexander & Kimberly Kessler Ferzan, *Confused Culpability, Contrived Causation, and the Collapse of Tort Theory,* in John Oberdiek, ed., Philosophical Foundations of the Law of Torts 406 (2014); Claire Finkelstein, *Responsibility for Unintended Consequences,* 2 Ohio St. J. Crim. L. 579 (2005); Matt King, *The Problem with Negligence,* 35 Soc. Theory & Practice 577 (2009); Michael S. Moore & Heidi M. Hurd, *Punishing the Awkward, the Stupid, the Weak and the Selfish: The Culpability of Negligence,* 5 Crim. L. & Philos. 147 (2011). One classic defense of negligence against some forms of skepticism appears in H. L. A. Hart, *Negligence, Mens Rea, and Criminal Responsibility,* in his Punishment and Responsibility: Essays in the Philosophy of Law (1968).

MORAL NEGLIGENCE

I begin with an effort to characterize the moral phenomena of interest by attempting to distinguish negligence from malice not by reference to the agent's external behavior, but with respect to the agent's motive. I start by drawing a contrast between negligence and malice and then later turn to some finer grained distinctions between causing harm purposefully, knowledgeably, recklessly, and negligently. For now, I will work with the blunter tools of malice versus negligence, in part because this contrast plays a role in our discourse that bears examination and in part because two moving parts are simpler to follow than four. Later consideration of the further compartments and moving parts will refine but not change my basic point.

By emphasizing motive and starting with only malice and negligence, I should acknowledge that what I emphasize as important about moral negligence differs from common legal uses of 'negligence.'[14] I believe my conception has purchase and familiarity within our moral discourse.[15] Indeed, part of my mission is to wrest the topic of negligence away from the monopolistic grip of legal commentators and to enliven a discussion about it within moral and political philosophy, one that might pay more attention to the motives that characterize moral negligence. Legal accountability for negligence has, in some respects, drawn salutary attention to our responsibilities to exert due care, but in other respects, its efforts to promulgate objective standards of appropriate behavior have

[14] In particular, I do not track the meaning of negligence and other categories of culpability as they are captured in the Model Penal Code. *See* MPC §2.02. One important difference is that the Model Penal Code distinguishes knowledge from negligence more sharply than I believe the moral conception does. Suppose, for instance, Mr. Elonis was focused on chronicling his rage for therapeutic purposes but was dimly aware that his posts would be taken as threats, and kept pushing that concern from his mind. The Model Penal Code might classify him as knowingly threatening his wife and not as negligently threatening his wife. Whereas, if he did not purposely threaten his wife as a means or as an end, morally, this may be a case of both knowingly and negligently threatening. Another difference: the Model Penal Code classifies recklessness as acting with conscious disregard of a substantial and unjustifiable risk. MPC §2.02 (2)(c). While I agree that actions so described may be reckless, I think the moral conception of recklessness is not limited to cases of conscious disregard, but may include, as I later discuss, cases where an agent's culpable indifference, conscious or not, to compliance with the standard of due care has few limits.

[15] Those inclined to think the moral conception of negligence closely tracks legal conceptions, whether from criminal law or tort, will inevitably classify some cases differently than I do. Even after some such translations, my argument suggests that at least some cases of negligence, legally construed, may be as worthy of moral concern as some cases of purposive harm and that a strict hierarchy of culpability may be worth reconsideration.

had the side effect of diverting our moral attention from the motives of the negligent agent.[16]

Morally speaking, as a first pass, we might characterize negligence as a failure to take due care (or to perform due diligence) not to cause or allow harm for a particular set of motives, ones that distinguish the negligent agent from the malicious agent. In particular, the negligent agent's failure does not involve a deliberate attempt to impose or allow harm as an end-in-itself or as a means to an end-in-itself. Often, that characterization will do, but one may be negligent with respect to other moral ends than just harm avoidance. One may be negligent with respect to fulfilling a promissory obligation or a duty to report. A more accurate, if unwieldy, characterization would represent negligence as: a failure to take due care (or to perform due diligence) with respect to an applicable moral end, restraint, or duty, where the relevant failure does not involve a deliberate attempt to bring about the specific consequences occasioned or risked by the lapse in due care, whether as an end-in-itself or as a means.

Many, if not most, discussions of negligence attempt to give a formula-, principle-, or factor-based account to identify exactly what efforts due care requires or, at least, how large the circumference of due care is. I leave that task to others. My topic is not what efforts due care requires in any particular context. But, I note there may be no unified theory of due care or any simple algorithm that applies across a variety of moral contexts. I think it likely that which actions or omissions due care requires may depend largely on the nature of the particular moral values, ends, and duties appropriate to the relevant context in a way that frustrates efforts to specify broad principles of due care from which specific results for concrete contexts may be derived. 'Due care' does not signal a foundational value or first moral principle; it points toward actions and omissions necessary to show adequate respect and appreciation for distinct moral constraints, ends, and values.[17]

For this paper, to focus on the moral significance of negligent failures of due care, I will simply presuppose there is a plausible account of what

---

[16] The emphasis on objective standards of behavior for purposes of legal accountability has also coincided with the overweening influence of economic analysis of torts and its general inattention to motives. Driven by a concern with outcomes and how to elicit them, economists largely reduce negligence law, conceptually, to the law of (preventable) accidents. In response, non-skeptical, non-economic, non-consequentialist theorists struggle to re-distinguish accidental damage from negligently inflicted damage and to remind the culture (and many skeptical philosophers) that negligence exists and that it is a wrong. Fighting this rearguard battle has deprived us of the opportunity to consider the rich expanse of moral territory in front of us.

[17] Barbara Herman discusses the relationship between due care and other moral principles, ends, duties, and values in her "Thinking about Imperfect Duties," MS.

actions or omissions due care requires in various contexts given the moral values and duties governing those contexts.[18]

So, I assume that there is a non-negligible domain of deliberative behaviors, attitudes, and actions that constitute due care and, likewise, there is a non-negligible domain of examples of negligent activity where that care is not taken in ways that constitute culpable negligence. In discussing the negligent agent, I will assume the agent has transgressed against an actual, valid moral standard of due care in a negligent manner for which she is morally responsible. My interest is in discussing the *significance* of this negligence— that is, the moral significance of violating the standard of due care under conditions that constitute negligence, as opposed to malice, on the one hand, or non-culpable accident or mistake on the other.

Rather than offer a provisional account of how to identify what due care requires, I'll offer some examples of what I take to constitute negligence, just to establish potential common ground. Non-skeptical readers need not agree with these examples, but may substitute other examples of conduct they agree constitute moral negligence.

1. For speed and convenience, a worker discards shingles off a roof without checking to ensure that anyone is below.
2. A worker discards shingles off a roof, checking first to make sure no one is directly below, but, for convenience, decides not to cordon off the area, arrogantly believing his aim with shingles is unerringly true.
3. To create a comfortable surplus, a factory manager decides not to replace a small cadre of retiring workers, making it likely that the remaining employees will be more burdened and will make more mistakes on the production line.
4. A professor makes an appointment to meet a student but does not write it down because she is in a hurry. She tells herself she'll remember, although she sometimes forgets appointments or cross-schedules.
5. She remembers while driving home but worries it will slip her mind later, so she quickly texts herself while driving.
6. Your teenage child seems distracted and troubled, but when you ask, he snaps at you and it's a struggle to converse. You decide to give him some space in the moment, but the moments stretch on into days without

---

[18] I deliberately sidestep whether the standard of due care is objective, calibrated to the reasonable person's understanding and behavior in the circumstances, or subjective, calibrated to what the *particular* moral agent was capable of doing and knowing in the circumstances. The use of objective standards when paired with particular remedial responses may be an important source of resistance to negligence liability. *See also* note 3. One interesting issue is whether the true object of some of the hostility to objective standards is not the objective standards themselves but the coupling of particular remedial responses with liability based on objective standards.

your mustering your resolve to break through his defenses and find out what is going on.

7. A job candidate wows the head of a search committee who decides, in the glow of the person's brilliance, that taking the trouble to check references and degree reports is unnecessary.

8. A speaker agrees to give a talk across town at 4 p.m. If he leaves at 2:30, he will definitely be on time and probably early. If he leaves at 3 p.m., there's a 50 percent chance there will be traffic that will make him late but it is certainly possible that he will be on time. He leaves at 3 p.m. in order to take more time to review his notes.

A few things are worth noting about my characterization of negligence and these illustrative examples. First, moral negligence does not necessarily involve a bad outcome. Agents may be culpably morally negligent, yet lucky when they inflict no damage. The texting driver is negligent whether her car crashes or not. The crucial element of negligence is the agent's failure to take appropriate actions or precautions, thereby leaving the correct outcome more of a hostage to fortune than is warranted. So, the misfortune that leads to a bad outcome is not a necessary component of negligence, but when such an outcome ensues, it need not be a surprise; the same may be said of malicious action when an attempted battery succeeds in breaking a nose.

Second, negligence is distinctively characterized by the agent's motive—how her reasoning motivates her action (and what her reasoning omits). The sort of moral negligence I am interested in may be advertent, in the sense that the negligent agent may be aware of her action and its possible consequences; she may even be aware that she is violating a rule. Not all negligence involves unknowing failure, forgetfulness, clumsiness, or mere risk. The chair who fails to call references may be perfectly aware that she is skirting the rules; the same may be said of the texter and the roofer. Further, negligence does not always involve running a risk.[19] One may be negligent when it is definite that *some* harm will result. Think of the parent who neglects, for a period, to attend to her child's emotional needs. Consciously permitting a definite harm of small proportions may constitute a form of negligence. Hence the distinction between malice and negligence is not the distinction between

---

[19] Here, I depart from such thinkers as Kenneth W. Simons, *Negligence*, 16 Soc. Phil. & Pol., 52, 54 (1999), who understands negligence to involve running a risk short of the definite imposition of harm. The idea that negligence involves running a risk may reflect some people's instinct that negligence involves some form of unawareness—here, the lack of knowledge of whether the risk will mature.

advertence and inadvertence, awareness and unawareness, or even certainty versus running a risk.[20]

Rather, the distinction of interest to me hinges on *why* the agent fails to take due care. The malicious agent values what is risked (or chosen) as a means or an end. The negligent agent often fails to take due care because another end (or means) displaces the appropriate end in perceived importance or salience; what is risked (or permitted) is not valued for itself or as a means, but is an insufficiently disvalued side effect of the agent's primary agenda in action. The negligent agent implicitly or explicitly demotes the practical significance of her actions regarding matters that do not occupy her primary focus of concern.

In other cases, the negligent agent may correctly understand the moral relation between her private ends and morally compulsory means and ends, but she may improperly appreciate the range of her agency. Often, she may overestimate her abilities or underestimate her vulnerabilities and flaws. An inflated sense of self may propel the conviction in action that, on this occasion, her aim is sufficiently true to render safety precautions merely advisory for her or a practical sense that her focus while driving is expansive enough to permit texting. Both sorts of cases seem to involve an elevation of one's self, propelled by self-exempting rationalizations (whether through a subjective misvaluation of the importance or relevance of one's private ends or of one's abilities). Importantly, the misestimation of agency may involve a failure to perceive the need for (and entitlement to) cooperation with others. That is, not infrequently, negligence emanates from hubris or from other pathologies of independence that shade into isolation, obstructing a person from asking and arranging for supplements to her individual agency, otherwise known as help. (The skeptic often suffers from a similar flaw in her third-personal judgments, classifying a person's inability to perform a task on her own at a specific time as a hard inability full stop, rather than taking the broader view and assessing a person's abilities in terms of what she could achieve over time, in conjunction with the enlisted assistance of others.)[21]

---

[20] I contend this as against, e.g., Henry W. Edgerton, *Negligence, Inadvertence, and Indifference; the Relation of Mental States to Negligence*, 39 HARV. L. REV. 849 (1924); Joel Feinberg, *Sua Culpa*, from his DOING AND DESERVING 187, 193 (1970). Others acknowledge the possibility of advertent negligence, but regard unawareness as the central case. *See, e.g.*, Stephen Sverdlik, *Pure Negligence*, in Am. Phil. Q. 137–8 (1993). *But see* Holly Smith, *Negligence*, in Hugh LaFollette ed., THE INTERNATIONAL ENCYCLOPEDIA OF ETHICS (2013) (describing a negligent technician who works quickly and "consciously fail[s]" to scrub every surface).

[21] Likewise, the ought-implies-can literature also oversubscribes to an overly narrow individualism in its stock examples and assumptions about the range of what a person 'can' do.

There is a wide variation here in the forms of negligence and their causes, but what unites them is that the negligent agent shows a culpable indifference to a moral failure. For the merely negligent agent, this is an indifference with limits. A close call may snap her back to attention. Whereas, with the reckless agent those limits are much further out or hard to discern at all. (Depending on the details, Mr. Elonis might be considered simply negligent if he would have stopped once he became aware that his subjects were scared; given the facts reported in the opinion, including his continued posting after an FBI visit, it seems a toss-up whether he was maliciously aiming to instill fear or whether he was extremely reckless.)[22] The merely negligent agent may tolerate knowledge that a small portion of her duty will go unsatisfied, whereas the reckless agent may tolerate knowledge that the bulk or the whole of her duty will go by the wayside. The reckless agent, then, represents the extreme or limit case of negligence.[23]

Another way to put the point is by reference to the doctrine of double effect. Although the principle has many formulations, roughly, it says: an agent may perform an action with both good and significant harmful effects (or their potential) only if the agent merely foresees but does not intend the harm for itself or as a means to the good effects *and*, in some relevant sense, the potentially good effects significantly outweigh, compensate for, or otherwise justify the potentially harmful effects. The second clause places some limits on how substantial or disproportionate the harmful effects of an action may permissibly be, independent of the content of one's intention.

One may conceive of the malicious agent as one who directly violates the prohibition on intending harm (or other illicit ends) as a means or an end. Whereas, the negligent agent fails to comply in a deliberate fashion with the second limit of the doctrine of double effect—by not paying due attention to the significance of the potential collateral casualties of her behavior and whether they are disproportionately high. Her direct intentions may be innocuous but she fails to ensure that the collateral casualties of her actions fall within acceptable limits. The failure properly to attend to the *significance* of such casualties does not equate to ignorance that they may occur; for this reason, I reiterate that moral negligence need not involve inadvertence. The negligent agent does not intend the harm she causes, but culpably permits her possibly innocuous primary intention to do all her moral work. Our discussions of the doctrine of double effect usually center on the

---

[22] After he received a restraining order, his posted lyrics referred to the order, intimating it would be ineffective because he possessed sufficient explosives to "take care of the State Police and the Sheriff's Department." *Elonis*, 135 S. Ct. at 2006.

[23] This represents a different way of understanding the distinction between recklessness and negligence than the legal conception of that distinction. The law may have its own institutional purposes for drawing the distinction differently, which I do not examine here.

fact that it (controversially) permits some sorts of unintended collateral damage that could not be directly intended. But, even if that controversy is resolved in favor of the doctrine, it is worth remembering that the doctrine of double effect does not permit innocuous intentions to sanitize all side effects. It allows only specific, qualified forms of collateral damage. One might think of the negligent agent as a person who mistakenly acts as though the exceptional permissions granted by the doctrine of double effect for *some* unintended collateral damage extend much further than in fact they do, thereby rationalizing poor behavior on the grounds that it isn't intended as such. One hypothesis is that those who make light of negligence have partly but unwittingly bought into this rationalization as containing some sliver of truth.

A final point: negligence may involve culpable indifference to more than just the risk of harm but also to other mandatory ends and the objects of other duties, as the examples involving negligence toward promissory performance (the appointment, the talk) illustrate. To be non-negligent is to be both attentive and responsive in thought and agency to *how* the pursuit of one's (permissible) aims and the state of one's agency affect one's ability to satisfy one's other duties and responsibilities. Non-negligence may involve not only direct efforts to fulfill one's duties on the date due, but also prior thoughtfulness about what obstacles may arise, how one's different aims interact, and what efforts should be taken to ensure effective agency, including advance preparations, maintenance of apt conditions for performance, avoiding tempting circumstances of violation or slack, and enlisting help.

POLITICAL NEGLIGENCE

So far, I have concentrated upon the interpersonal dimension of moral non-negligence. To illustrate these points from another angle, I consider the political side and the obligations of non-negligence for citizens, partly because the territory is less familiar, hence less saturated with legal intuitions. I am eager to avoid those legal intuitions because another limitation of many legal approaches is to view duties and wrongs primarily through the lens of remedies. On the one hand, where remedies are limited, their contours may exert a distorting influence on what can be recognized as negligence. On the other, where remedies are overwhelmingly large or harsh, concerns about disproportionality and unfair burdens may infect and depress one's assessment of the moral significance of negligence. To recalibrate one's moral intuitions, it may be worth taking a detour onto terrain that is, for other reasons, less hospitable to a litigation-oriented focus.

Moral negligence, like political negligence, is often a product of a sort of personal overestimation through the prioritization of one's personal projects to the exclusion of one's public obligations. But, many contemporary manifestations of political negligence also seem to emanate from another sort of misevaluation—an implicit or explicit *under* estimation of one's abilities and the importance of one's own vigilance and public participation. This underestimation may complement an overestimation of the abilities, efforts, or importance of others, yielding a different path to rationalizing permissions to make an exception for oneself. The underestimation of the importance of one's political participation may lie behind the complacency that atrophies democratic institutions. This breed of political negligence, in social situations, can harbor disastrous potential when the hubris of some couples with the self-underestimation of others.

Some substantive aspects of political non-negligence are fairly obvious. For individual citizens, in ideal theory, there is the obligation to support just institutions through a strong default practice of legal compliance, a duty to engage in political participation including electoral participation, and a duty to keep oneself and others sufficiently informed and educated to play a responsible role in self-government. More interesting questions emerge in the harder realm of non-ideal theory. In particular, what does non-negligence require when fulfillment of one's duty to stay informed and the duty to support just institutions generate a conflict with the default practice of legal compliance? In what follows, I discuss a corner of this problem, highlighting a part of the civil disobedience tradition that recently seems to have been forgotten or, to use a cognate, *neglected.*

I will focus on the example of Edward Snowden.[24] The debate about whether Snowden is a hero or traitor seems mostly about *what* he disclosed and *whether* he should have disclosed it. I think much of what he disclosed either should not have been secret or involved government activities that should never have happened. He was right that the government was engaged in illegitimate activity, of a highly serious nature, meriting exposure. We may be unaware of damage caused by the revelations, but, given the current state of information, I concur with those who think the consequences were mainly salutary in light of our deepest commitments to freedom of speech, legitimate privacy expectations, and governmental transparency and veracity. So, this case well illustrates that one may be negligent without bringing about a bad consequence.

For, I regard Snowden as negligent, not for *what* he revealed but for *how* he conducted his revelation campaign. I will offer a description of Snowden's actions and why they trouble me to illustrate why I think his behavior

---

[24] Some like points might be made about Chelsea Manning and Julian Assange.

amounts to a variety of political negligence. Snowden was no mere individual observer reporting from the outside on others' politically relevant behavior. His revelations were not simple political commentary but were political speech acts. Moreover, he did not simply behave as a passive resister, by refusing to cooperate or by quitting his job.[25] Rather, he behaved as a political actor, making major political decisions. He took it upon himself to change jobs with the sole purpose of collecting classified information with the ultimate aim of unilateral revelation;[26] he revealed a massive amount of classified information to the global community at a time of his choosing and relocated a substantial cache of classified information to Hong Kong, without giving advance notice to various affected agencies and persons to prepare responses, apologies, explanations, and other gestures of mitigation and repair.[27] In other words, he reversed a major set of public policies in one fell swoop at the time, manner, and location of his choosing—implementing massive reforms. His actions were not just political in effect but in intent. By his own descriptions, he engaged in these policy reversals in virtue of his status as a US citizen, "doing this to serve my country...working for the government," by forcing the government to comply with its deepest ideals.[28]

What troubles me is that Snowden's legitimate objections were made as a citizen, yet his response, procedurally, was as an individual. He mistakenly inferred from the premise that government acts illegitimately to the practical conclusion that because he was well situated, he, virtually alone, could act non-institutionally to remedy the defect. In responding to a rather substantial defect in our political institutions, he not only abandoned allegiance to our particular government but he abandoned allegiance to political institutions altogether, whether governmental or non-governmental. Yet, normatively, the sort of decisions he made *have* to be made politically, in a deliberative setting involving multiple perspectives, checks and balances, and a commitment to the rule of law and other public values. Adhering to political procedures may still matter even if we affirm, with Snowden, that

[25] Snowden aimed to transform, directly, the government's methods of information gathering. He was not merely aiming to prevent an imminent episode of injustice, by contrast with the iconic protestor of Tiananmen Square (whose name remains unknown) who seemed to intervene to induce deliberation by the individual tank drivers to prevent imminent intimidation and, possibly, to prevent imminent murders by the military.

[26] Glenn Greenwald, No Place to Hide, 42–49 (2014).

[27] Id.

[28] *See, e.g.*, Snowden's interview with Brian Williams, May 28, 2014 (available at http://www.nbcnews.com/feature/edward-snowden-interview/edward-snowdens-motive-revealed-he-can-sleep-night-n116851).

the situation merited departure from the rule of law as interpreted and administered by our government.

The obvious analog, Daniel Ellsberg and the Pentagon Papers, provides an instructive contrast. Ellsberg's decision to copy the Pentagon Papers was made after discussing the matter with another expert at RAND. Thereafter, Ellsberg consulted with a diversity of knowledgeable people, including US senators, his spouse, and members of the Institute of Policy Studies, a think tank involved in analysis of policy in Southeast Asia. He consulted experts in the area, enmeshed within organizations that themselves debated the relevant issues on a regular basis and considered different perspectives in a somewhat systematic way. He tried to have the papers read publicly into the Congressional Record and only thereafter did he approach the *New York Times*. The *Times* then engaged in a thorough internal process to reason through the risks of the disclosures and the public's vital interest in the information, consulting only minimally with Ellsberg.[29] All told, Ellsberg's process involved consultation and deliberation with a range of other knowledgeable, disinterested people and institutions over more than a year.[30]

Snowden, by contrast, unilaterally embarked on a mission to collect information for exposure. Thereafter, he consulted only two freelance journalists, Glenn Greenwald and Laura Poitras, who themselves understandably maintained a strong degree of distance from and contempt for political and institutional structure.[31] I do not doubt their sincere commitment to transparent government, but they also had strong personal-professional stakes in these revelations. Snowden approached the *Washington Post* only because he believed his efforts to bypass traditional journalism were failing, but quickly became irritated at the *Post*'s efforts to engage in independent assessments of the merits of publication. Snowden's timeline for revelation seemed largely driven by impatience. The materials were released within a whirlwind of days from the moment of his first successful contact with Glenn Greenwald.[32] In the end, the Snowden revelations were largely the

---

[29] INSIDE THE PENTAGON PAPERS 54–55 (John Prados & Margaret Pratt Porter, eds., 2004).

[30] That may have been too long and I am not celebrating delay as such. Still, there is an important but overlooked contrast between the cases. For his account, see Daniel Ellsberg, SECRETS: A MEMOIR OF VIETNAM AND THE PENTAGON PAPERS (2002).

[31] Poitras was repeatedly detained and questioned at airports for a six-year period following the release of her documentary in 2006 about the US occupation of Iraq. *See* Glenn Greenwald, *U.S. filmmaker repeatedly detained at border,* Salon.com (April 8, 2012) (available at http://www.salon.com/2012/04/08/u_s_filmmaker_repeatedly_detained_at_border/); Complaint for Injunctive Relief, *Laura Poitras v. Dept. of Homeland Security et al.* (D.D.C.) (2015) (1:15-cv-01091).

[32] Glenn Greenwald, NO PLACE TO HIDE (2014).

product of three politically isolated people (Snowden, Greenwald, and Poitras), acting alone together, with haste. The revelations were not the product of any procedure that aimed responsibly and thoroughly to consider the legitimacy, timing, whereabouts, and impact of his massive copying and revelations.

My objection is that Snowden acted outside of politics to engage in political forms of resistance. Snowden did not object, nor would he have reason to object, to the idea that decisions about national security should be made in political bodies that incorporate structures of deliberation that encourage the airing of multiple viewpoints, that attempt to weave in checks and balances to rein in personalities or mistaken lines of thought from gaining too much sway, and that try to counteract inevitable forms of human fallibility and limited knowledge. However bankrupt the NSA and the Obama administration were on these issues, it is a non sequitur to think that national security issues of this magnitude should be decided by a tiny handful of people without comprehensive expertise, a deliberate set of commitments to public values, and a procedure to debate the merits and risks for the public that introduces a wider range of perspectives than merely Mr. Snowden's. Properly political activities cannot be done alone but require collective deliberation and organization.

The responsible, non-negligent civil disobedient does not strike out on her own against the current political structure, but relocates herself in another (possibly non-governmental) political structure to deliberate about the most responsible and effective forms of resistance.[33] This may seem like a demanding, perhaps impossible requirement. Non-negligent civil disobedience cannot require the establishment of a full shadow government, complete with an ersatz bicameral legislature and an executive to debate and craft an appropriate mechanism for dismantling these totalitarian policies.

Still, there are a great many options between rogue individualism and erecting a full-fledged government in exile. One might have expected Snowden to work with independent organizations of experts in the area who were not captured by the corrupt military-industrial complex and who could think their way around the issues' complexities, collecting insights that a single mind or two might miss. The experienced attorneys at the ACLU come to mind. They have devoted their careers to thinking about the proper scope of liberty and how to calibrate resistance to government excesses in a manner that does not amount to anarchism. So does the organized fourth estate with which Snowden could have cooperated, rather than

---

[33] *See also* HANNAH ARENDT, *Civil Disobedience*, in her CRISES OF THE REPUBLIC 49 (1972).

merely used and resisted when it attempted to exercise independent deliberation of its own.[34]

The fault does not lie exclusively with Snowden. Although he could have worked with extant independent organizations, the level of informal, extra-governmental organization by liberals and the left has certainly fallen into decline. While the right is extremely well organized, the left has, largely, become populated by a different set of left libertarians than those imagined in the distributive justice literature.

Consider the intentional disorganization of the Occupy movement,[35] the most important domestic, non-electoral, progressive, alternative political activity in recent memory. Although its lack of structure signaled an admirable openness to input, it also disabled itself from accomplishing much beyond the important tasks of criticism and the disruption of social complacency. The contrast with other major resistance movements of the twentieth century pulls one up short. Even as late in the century as the AIDS crisis, major resistance movements were committee-laden *movements*—not topic-specific coups by outraged individuals or loud discussion groups in the park. In its heyday (and still), ACT-UP had committees and structures, debates lasting long into the night, and its members considered the ramifications of their actions both for their interest groups and others.[36] So too for EARTH First![37] Such groups are not full-fledged political entities: they tend not to be maximally inclusive, even if they are internally radically democratic, and they often pursue narrow, issue-specific agendas that privilege their base. Nevertheless, what they had that Snowden lacked was the idea that responsible political resistance requires a deliberative structure open to

---

[34] I take there to be a difference between the *New York Times*, the *Washington Post*, and the two freelance journalists he collaborated with to publicize the revelations. These three together do not a political body make. Greenwald and Snowden were impatient and contemptuous of delays occasioned by oversight by editors. Part of their objection was to what they regarded as co-optation by the *Washington Post* and an excessively deferential relationship to the government. But, here, they seemed to throw out the baby with the bathwater. With respect to the *Guardian*, they also pushed to circumvent the sort of questioning and oversight process aimed to stimulate deliberative decisions about how responsibly to undermine illegitimate policy. See, e.g., Glenn Greenwald, No Place To Hide 68–69 (2014).

[35] *Statement of Autonomy*, #OccupyWallStreet, NYC General Assembly (November 11, 2011), accessed on October 24, 2015, at http://www.nycga.net/group-documents/statement-of-autonomy-as-passed-by-the-general-assembly/.

[36] Committees and structures need not mean hierarchy. ACT UP had a democratic structure that stressed consensus as the linchpin of decision-making. *See, e.g.*, Nathan H. Madson, *The Legacy of ACT UP's Policies and Actions from 1987–1994*, 69 NAT'L LAW GUILD REV. 45 (2012); Deborah Gould, MOVING POLITICS: EMOTION AND ACT UP's FIGHT AGAINST AIDS 188–192 (2009).

[37] *See* Martha F. Lee, EARTH FIRST!: ENVIRONMENTAL APOCALYPSE 35–37, 48–49, 58–91 (1995).

a plurality of inputs and potential plurality of viewpoints. That openness corresponds to patience toward some conflict and delay. In other words, I am contending that the impulse to immediate political gratification that Snowden indulged is not merely jejune; it is close to oxymoronic. Politics is essentially a joint, consultative activity. Even where resistance is not only appropriate but a duty, no single person can coherently and responsibly make massive decisions with wide-ranging political ramifications on his own and avoid those who might question those decisions. It is probably fair to say that liberals and the left have been negligent toward sustaining a full-bodied political culture, one that supplies responsible outlets for both supporting government and supporting thoughtful *political* resistance. The Snowden affair may represent, then, an example of a mass(ive) practical underestimation of the significance of active political agency by individual citizens meeting personal overestimation in the guise of Snowden—one form of negligence enabling another.

You may worry that I underappreciate the personal risks Snowden faced. I am sympathetic that wider consultation would have been frightening and would have required extraordinary care, although Snowden seemed equipped to take such care; I acknowledge Snowden's fear might excuse, if not justify, his fairly solitary approach.[38] Perhaps I am overly optimistic about how a more politically deliberate revelation could have gone down had Snowden been less impatient. These issues, however, are not about whether the process of revelation was or was not negligent, but rather where the negligence is predominantly situated—whether in Snowden alone, in the trio of Snowden, Greenwald, and Poitras, or in the public for failing to ensure the existence of enough safe, extra-governmental watchdog networks in which politically structured checks on governmental abuse could operate.

To take stock, the Snowden example illustrates a few points about negligence. In his pursuit of a reasonable end, Snowden's single-mindedness neglected a fully democratic approach to law and its violation, running roughshod over *political* obligations. He was right that intelligence methods should be a public, jointly decided matter, but, for many of the same reasons, so should the dismantling and rethinking of an extant apparatus. Snowden allowed his devotion to the former aim to eclipse the fact that he was privately making an extraordinary number of decisions about the

---

[38] His fear was partly for others whom he did not want to place under suspicion. George Packer, *The Holder of Secrets*, THE NEW YORKER, 50, 52 (October 20, 2014). Some combination of concern for others and self-aggrandizement seemed to drive his conviction that he should monopolize both decision-making and responsibility, adopting the stance of a martyr.

latter, rather than facilitating alternative political decisions.[39] In doing so, he was negligent with respect to the possible harm he might cause to people and institutions; further, he was negligent, perhaps even reckless, with respect to a wider range of democratic values than the particular ones he aimed to vindicate.

The Snowden example underscores that negligence, whether moral or political, involves a procedural defect first and foremost in the deliberations that give rise to action. Negligence is a serious wrong because it either involves a failure to notice one's impact on others' relevant rights and interests or a failure to keep that impact appropriately salient in one's agential decision-making. It involves a sort of blindness to others which violates the central tenet of morality that everyone matters and everyone, in some sense, matters equally. To fail to take others into account is to fail to treat them as equals by failing to recognize them fully (in the relevant context).

THE SIGNIFICANCE OF NEGLIGENCE

With these characterizations and examples in mind, I turn to the issue of the relative significance of negligence and to the standard hierarchy classifying malicious wrongs as worse or morally more serious than negligent wrongs, all else equal. I do not argue for the inverse—that negligence is, all things considered, worse than malicious action. Rather, I aim to orient our attention to the distinctiveness and the seriousness of the wrong of negligence. Negligence is not just a paler or more dilute version of malicious action, a minor variation on a major theme. It should be recognized as a distinct, serious wrong. Moreover, we should evince greater moral appreciation for the moral importance of non-negligence and the sustained and steady moral efforts it requires.

The blunt way to put the primary point is this. Negligence, whether in its inadvertent or advertent form, involves a failure to take and exercise appropriate responsibility for one's agency; and, when that failure involves other people, negligence involves a failure properly to recognize and acknowledge their moral significance. Such failures may have dire consequences. As Hannah Arendt pointed out fifty years ago, such failures that take the form of political negligence may be crucial collaborative elements of the success

---

[39] This specific case captures a point about the broader category of active civil disobedience. Efforts to transform illegitimate political practice through illegal means implicate duties of political consultation more clearly than passive refusals to comply with injustice.

of evil enterprises.[40] When, unlike Snowden, political negligence takes the form of apathy or operates through forms of unthinking obedience, the negligent actor may become a tool of those with nefarious aims and thereby may expand the scope of agency of the malicious. One could worry that negligence may be an efficacious and more likely method of producing disasters than the rarer collaborations between the actively malicious. These are non-accidental byproducts of a more basic defect of the negligent agent, which involves the basic failure to treat her own agency as her responsibility, a responsibility to be exercised with sensitivity to the reality and equal importance of others. Moral norms and reasons presuppose they have an audience; they are directed toward agents for consideration, incorporation, and implementation into motives and action. The negligent agent is, with respect to some portion of morality, unavailable and impervious to its content—not because she is mistaken or in the grip of a mistaken ideology, but because she has opted out, as though she wore earplugs during part of the relevant briefing.

So framed, there is a contrast with the malicious agent, but it is hard to form a clear hierarchy with respect to the two. The malicious agent is not apathetic or unthinking; she takes in the reality of others and responds to reasons with respect to them. Her defect is that she gets them (very) wrong, whether by actively seeking their harm or by unacceptably prioritizing her welfare over others. In some cases, the negligent agent may have the right intellectual conception, but the connection of this insight to her agency is only haphazard—like a button barely clinging by a thread to one's coat rather than being closely secured. Often one gets by for the day, but the coverage is precarious and more happenstance than deliberate. In other cases, the negligent agent fails to form a complete conception; the elements that are present are not defective, but she's drawn practical conclusions before surveying the entire terrain, betraying an implicit arrogance, laziness, or, in some cases, a faulty underestimation of her capabilities. Whereas, the malicious agent's intellectual conception has positive defective components.

A loose metaphor: while the malicious agent points the lens in the wrong direction, the negligent agent fails to focus. Both will fail to get the shot. Whether the negligent agent's failure is cognitive or agential in some other sense, both agents suffer from a significant defect that prevents them from acting in a way that reflects the appropriate value of others. In different ways, the negligent agent, like the malicious agent, fails to take the needs of others to exert appropriate weight in her thought and agency. It is unclear why we should affirm the broad generality that one defect is more serious or

---

[40] *See* Hannah Arendt, EICHMANN IN JERUSALEM: A REPORT ON THE BANALITY OF EVIL (1963).

morally significant than the other. (Or to put the point another way, why think one sort of violation of the doctrine of double effect is more significant than another?)

DOES THE ACT/OMISSION DISTINCTION EXPLAIN THE TRADITIONAL HIERARCHY?

I have been discussing the comparative flaws of the malicious and negligent agents, but perhaps the traditional hierarchy emanates from a difference in their actions. It might be suggested that the malice/negligence hierarchy flows from the legitimate distinction between acts and omissions. One may think that the malicious violation is purposive, whereas the negligent violation consists of a mere failure to take due care, an omission to satisfy an underlying duty.

This defense seems misguided because it is not clear that the act/omission distinction clearly maps onto the distinction between malice and negligence. Omissions may be purposive and malicious. Further, as I argued earlier, negligence may involve purposive, positive actions, such as throwing tiles to the ground, laying off workers, or speeding. Often negligence involves an omission—a failure to check one's brakes, to plug a crack, or to clean a line—but, notably, negligence can involve the *failure* to omit and err through action. One may negligently defame another, negligently deceive, or negligently violate someone's privacy by speaking carelessly in a way that allows a listener to draw an invasive inference. These involve actions and the flaw may be described in either of two ways: one could have avoided the wrong via omission—by remaining quiet—or, by more and better action—checking one's facts, clarifying one's meaning, or speaking more precisely. Similar points may be made in the classic omission cases: one could have avoided the wrong by further omissions—by not driving or closing the shop—or by engaging in corrective action—checking the brakes or cementing the crack. Given these cases, it is hard to stuff negligence completely into the omission category. Negligence may involve a failure to take due care, where due care requires an omission or an action, and the failure may itself involve an omission or an action.

Still, there is the more specific worry that negligent behavior is often the product of a particular sort of *mental* omission. Negligence often stems from a failure to recognize that or how one's duty of care applies in the situation, e.g., that someone is at risk from one's behavior or that one's actions happen not to conform to the required boundaries. Some skeptics regard moral liability as inappropriate because we should not hold people responsible for thoughts they did not have, since one cannot control one's thoughts.

Negligence need not always involve a failure to notice. One may be aware that one's brake check is overdue and that running an errand nevertheless runs a small risk of harm. Given the slight nature of the risk, one may only be morally negligent in the resultant accident for failure to maintain one's brakes but the liability does not issue from any mental omission (other than the failure to form the intention to repair one's brakes). It issues from the failure to *act* on one's belief that one needs to maintain one's brakes.

But, even when negligence does stem from a failure to notice, this argument is puzzling. We commonly hold people accountable for failing to have certain thoughts. Standard examinations reward students for having and expressing particular thoughts and penalize them for failing to know or remember certain facts or to 'see' or draw certain inferences. (Indeed, sometimes we give partial credit for the *action* of trying and getting the wrong answer, giving more credit for the wrong answer than for the complete omission.) One may not be able to will that one recollect the right answer, remember one's duty, or observe the relevant risk in the moment. But one can, in advance, enact internal and external mechanisms of learning, reminders, and aid to ensure that one does remember, that one avoid situations in which such recollection is requisite, or that safeguards prevent one's failure from having an adverse effect. When such measures are not taken or are inadequate to the task, finding moral liability seems unexceptional.

Negligence may seem *de minimis* when one considers it in snapshot terms. In one instant, one failed to look or to remember and something unfortunate ensued. Where negligence is culpable, a longer look would often show a failure to engage in a pattern of non-negligent activities, over time, which would build habits, fixes, and stopgaps to protect against occasional lapses and to prevent them from manifesting in failures of deliberation or agency. To engage in non-negligent activity and to erect this infrastructure is a decision, as is the decision not to bother and to rely on one's present resources in the moment whenever it strikes. A slower shutter speed, so to speak, seems more appropriate if we gauge moral wrongs by reference to the agent's character and motives as they are expressed in action. We could, instead of adopting the snapshot perspective, understand the significance of culpable negligence in terms of these prior decisions not to practice non-negligence and the ongoing indulgence in rationalizations that render this inactivity a live option. Keeping the lens open longer, it's hard to see these decisions as mere omissions or their products as mere accidents. They are, instead, the unsurprising products of ongoing patterns and continually made and reaffirmed decisions. In this respect, they may not differ importantly from malicious actions, at least those that are in character.

Keeping one's focus on the agent's character and motives as expressed in action may enable the separation of issues about the relative danger malicious agents pose compared to negligent agents. When considering a specific scenario, one may be tempted to think that the malicious agent is the more dangerous agent because if the harm she aims at does not occur, she will try again. So, goes the thought, malicious agents are more likely to cause harm than negligent agents who will not double back if harm is avoided. But, this only holds true of the determined malicious agent and not the one who suffers a flash of temper that quickly subsides. It is difficult to generalize, and so the implicit frame in this contrast seems to be a flawed way of investigating the comparative question. The negligent agent who subjects others to her negligence may cause harm only 0.1 percent of the time when driving; most agents who act maliciously manage to control their defective temperaments most of the time and may only unleash their malicious motives and implement them a very minor portion of the time—suppose it were 0.1 percent of occasions in which they could do others harm. They are equally dangerous individuals, assessed in terms of outcomes over time. Over time, the consistently negligent person may be far more dangerous to others than the agent whose malicious act is quite out of character; the rarely negligent person who lives in pedestrian circumstances will pose a slight risk to others while a dedicated mass murderer will be supremely dangerous. I find it difficult to draw clear conclusions about the relative danger of the malicious and the negligent. The question I pursue instead is whether, holding things like risk and outcome equal, the different content of their motives represents itself a qualitative moral difference that supports a judgment that one sort of act or character is worse than another.

MIGHT THE DOCTRINE OF DOUBLE EFFECT ITSELF UNDERLIE THE HIERARCHY?

Could the hierarchy be justified by the doctrine of double effect? Earlier, I suggested a connection between negligence and the doctrine of double effect, something to the effect that negligence involves a perversion or abuse of the permissions of what the doctrine allows. But, one might advert to a different connection to justify the traditional hierarchy. That is, the doctrine of double effect may be thought to codify the moral view that it is worse to bring about harm, say, as an end or as a means rather than to bring it about as a side effect. One may think that whatever justifies the doctrine of double effect may explain the related view that impermissible forms of intentional infliction of harm are worse than negligence, the impermissible bringing about of harmful side effects.

I do not find this move persuasive, but not because I reject the doctrine of double effect—as is probably evident from my invocation of it. Notably, the hierarchy does not directly follow from the doctrine, at least those versions couched in terms of permissibility and impermissibility. The doctrine itself declares that there are *some* harms whose production as a collateral effect may not be impermissible. It draws a distinction between a permissible and an impermissible pathway by which *certain* harms may be produced. It does not follow that there is a moral difference between two distinct *impermissible* pathways of producing other harms (or other magnitudes of harm).

More important, the doctrine's justification does not lend much support to the hierarchy. For the purposes of the objection, the justification cannot just be that intentionally harming is worse than negligently harming; that would amount to a mere repetition of the very thesis in question. For the same reason, the comparative formulations of the doctrine cannot be appealed to as a reason to affirm the comparative judgment under challenge.[41] On the justification that I think is promising, the traditional hierarchy does not glean support from the doctrine of double effect. Roughly speaking, the doctrine may be justified in terms of what sort of demands may be made on an agent's attention and direct efforts. Take the imposition of harm on innocents. Where harm's imposition has no positive justification (i.e., it isn't merited by the recipient's past behavior or rehabilitative/educational needs), then, given the very nature of harm, a moral agent cannot rationally endorse its imposition as an end in itself. But, given the innumerable pathways of causation emanating from one's activity, the behavior of others, our myriad forms of interconnection, and the limited attention and agential capacities of human agents, moral agents cannot be expected to avoid (and prevent) *all* causation of predictable harm.[42] That would be an unreasonable demand, one that would interfere with the pursuit of reasonable projects and the goods associated with directed and focused forms of attention. Still, given the badness of harm, our interconnection, and our interests in each other's welfare, we may expect agents, consistent with an appreciation of their limited agency and the goods of devoted attention, to make (strong) efforts (i.e., to take due care), to avoid some levels of harm and some pathways of harm.

---

[41] That is, some versions of the doctrine of double effect do not draw a line between permissible and impermissible action but instead posit a comparative difference—that intending harm is *per se* worse (whether or not it is impermissible) than foreseeing harm without intending it.

[42] Usually, the prohibition on harming innocents as a means would often escape this concern because the endeavor of conceiving harm as a means already implicates an agent's attention. Possibly one may negligently harm an innocent as a means where one is negligently unaware that those treated as means are innocents. I put this complication to the side.

That agency-oriented justification does not give us reason to think that an abdication of the limited forms of responsibility for indirect harm we do have is less important or less wrong. It does suggest that the underlying account of why malicious harm is wrong differs from the underlying account of why negligent harm is wrong. Malicious harm involves acting on a contradiction, a direct affirmation of the false, or the direct embrace of evil; one affirms the bad as the good, whether as an end or as an instrument. Negligent harm involves at least a partial abdication of responsibility. The malicious agent, through action, denies that a person's harm is a bad worth forswearing; the negligent agent's action does not express *that* but instead expresses the denial that she bears responsibility for the harms her actions or omissions produce.[43] The negligent agent's implicit denial goes to her own agency and relationship to the victim, whereas the malicious agent's denial more directly concerns the victim's status as such. So, my questioning of the traditional hierarchy does not involve an equation of malicious and negligent harm. I agree they involve distinctive wrongs with distinctive qualities that give rise to distinctive complaints from their victims. I am less certain that one form generally is more problematic than the other, whether one considers the acts (all other things equal) or the characters that produce them.

WORKING WITH A FINER GRAIN

One may object that not all cases are on a par and that we should work with a finer grain than we have so far. I do not disagree in principle. Part of what troubles me about the traditional hierarchy is the terrific generality with which it classifies, other things equal, the malicious wrong as worse than the negligent wrong. Although I generally agree with the methodological point, I remain unconvinced that a finer grain vindicates the hierarchy.

It may help to consider some dimensions where we might make finer-grained distinctions. One might think that malicious actions and negligent actions are likely on a par when the negligent actions involve patterned behavior, knowledge, or advertence, or at least when one's duty could easily be apprehended, but that the hierarchy is more plausible when these factors are missing. Let's examine those three factors more closely: patterned vs.

---

[43] Here, I assume one's action may reflect a stance that yet may not figure in one's conscious, contemporaneous mental contents. The negligent agent may not actively deny, verbally or mentally, her responsibility, but still her action may express the defects of her internal moral architecture. Jeff Helmreich illuminatingly discusses the idea that actions may express stances rather than one's momentary mental contents in Jeffrey S. Helmreich, *The Apologetic Stance*, 43 Phil. & Pub. Aff. 75 (2015).

atypical behavior; knowledge vs. ignorance; and readily available vs. difficult inferences, observations, or moral insights. For convenience, I'll work with cases involving harm and risk, although, as I've argued earlier, harm and risk are not essential features of all cases involving negligence.

One may think my case is strongest where the negligence that gives rise to the harm reflects a *pattern* of unconcern, blinkered, or unreasonably deferred concern, or the agency counterparts of such defective concern, and the harm is a predictable outcome of such a pattern. Where it is clear that the agent fails to meet a duty of care because of a well-established character defect or omission that she was obliged to alter, to avoid situations that would trigger it, or to seek help to supplement the gaps in her agency,[44] the fact that the harm was negligently caused on the occasion does not seem to reduce the severity of the wrong or render it evidently less substantial than wrongful harming as a means or an end.[45] But, the traditional hierarchy may seem more intuitive in those cases where, objectively, a person should have acted otherwise and fell short of the duty of care but the shortfall was out of character. Such cases may seem to pale in comparison to the consciously elected wrong. I see the point, but I doubt that it is one that turns on the contrast between the malicious and the negligent. Where the shortfall was out of character, some may think that reduces the severity of the wrongness or, depending on the explanation, may serve as a partial excuse that reduces culpability. But, that would also be true in the case of malicious behavior, some of which may be consistent with one's character or

[44] A reviewer's note raises two questions worth further thought: First, if others take the initiative to establish a back-up system to shield potential victims from one's patterned unconcern, does this negate an assessment of negligence? I tentatively suggest 'no'; it's important that the flawed agent herself has a role in recognizing the need for assistance and obtaining it and that it isn't all arranged for her behind the scenes. Whether others pick up her slack successfully but she is oblivious to their help, it seems like a case of negligence without harm. Second, if the flawed agent takes that initiative but the back-up system fails, is the agent responsible for the negligence that ensues, is the back-up system responsible for failing to fill the gaps of another person's shortcomings, or do they share moral liability?

[45] As I discuss in the next section, different remedies may be appropriate for comparable wrongs associated with different motivations. For this reason, although I am unsure that the distinctions drawn by the Model Penal Code reliably track a hierarchy of moral wrongfulness, my target here is not the Model Penal Code or similar distinctions that define criminal offenses. Although the criminal law separates the conviction from the sentencing stage, our conception of what constitutes a criminal offense may be influenced by the overall purposes and activities of the criminal system. The divisions made in the Model Penal Code, and analogous divisions in the criminal law, might be justified not by the differential wrongness of the behaviors, but may reflect a preliminary judgment about the range of appropriate remedies associated with those classes of behaviors. Without examining such arguments in detail, it would be hasty to criticize the MPC's distinctions from a legal perspective.

past actions, and some of which may be aberrational. We may have reasons to distinguish between actions that are out of character and those that are consistent with character, but that distinction does not line up squarely with the distinction made by the traditional hierarchy.

Might one object that the examples that are the most compelling for my case are those in which there is some admixture of advertence with mere negligence—as where the department chair elects not to check references knowing that she runs a small risk of missing a red flag? Whereas, when the agent acts negligently but without awareness of the risk she runs, it may seem that the wrong is of a different kind of severity when contrasted to the case where the agent acts with full awareness of the risk she runs but proceeds nonetheless. I am unconvinced. Again, I assume we are discussing cases in which there is a wrong for which the agent is morally responsible. So, I am assuming, against the skeptics, that an agent may be morally culpable for some derelictions of duty even where he is unaware he is running a risk or inflicting harm. He may be culpable because he may have been responsible both to operate whatever discovery mechanisms would have revealed the risk and then to avoid running it. Assuming the agent may be culpable for his inadvertence, I am not convinced that the hierarchy only falls under attack where we have a case combining advertence and negligence. Returning to the example of Mr. Elonis, I resist the idea that it would have been morally worse if Mr. Elonis intended to threaten his wife than if he intended to vent his all-consuming anger publicly but, paying no attention to who would read his online posts, he was unaware that his online rantings ran a substantial risk of threatening his wife. These are different, but both scary, forms of moral monstrosity.

At this point, one might object that knowledge or awareness is not always the crucial factor, but that it does matter whether awareness of the risk or of the possible violation of duty was close to hand or difficult to achieve. That is, the traditional hierarchy may seem more intuitive in cases where knowledge of the risk or harm was not just absent from operative awareness but would have required unusual effort or imaginativeness to come by, such as where the hazard is unusual and was understandably far from the mind of the agent. Negligence under such situations may be culpable but less serious than deliberate infliction of harm. It may be wrong to have ignored the hazard, but given the difficulty of correct attention to it, the moral failure seems of a different magnitude of intellectual difficulty than recognizing that one should not deliberately inflict harm.

Perhaps these points about difficult insights are true, but I'm not sure where they get us with respect to vindicating the traditional hierarchy. First, although some sorts of purposeful infliction of harm are obviously wrong, people are capable of great rationalizations for deliberate, wrongful inflictions of harm, especially when under strain. Those rationalizations may also be intellectually and emotionally difficult to suppress or resist. We do not seem to be in a well-informed position to speculate about which cases are more common or typical in a way that would suggest negligence more often involves a failure to do something difficult.

Further, I suspect that unusual difficulties of compliance speak more to a partial excuse of the agent than they do to judging the action less wrong. Concerns about the difficulty of compliance or the elusiveness of an agent's having a mental grasp of the salient features of a situation may not support the traditional hierarchy as much as they reveal discomfort about the demandingness of some objective standards of due care and the distance between those standards' demands and the individual circumstances of some agents. Such discomfort may suggest reconsideration of whether a particular standard of care really is required (or whether standards of care should be more closely tailored to the circumstances of particular agents). But, I have been working with the assumptions that the agent has transgressed against an actual, valid standard of care and that she is responsible for that transgression. Where those assumptions hold true, I do not see why the moral seriousness of the transgression varies dramatically depending on whether the specific outcome is intended, clearly in view but subjectively and wrongfully dismissed as insufficiently relevant, or distant from the agent's active range of concerns for culpable reasons.

Although I challenge the rote adherence to any general hierarchy elevating the malicious as always worse than the negligent, I do not deny that some wrongs may be worse than others and, indeed, some acts of malice may be worse than some acts of negligence. My skepticism about the traditional hierarchy is compatible with the idea that things may not be equal, even when outcomes remain equal. Some wrongs may be worse than others and some characters may be worse than others. Intentional, unjustified killing that is carefully planned for pleasure may well be worse than intentional, unjustified killing occurring (more) spontaneously in the heat of passion, though still in character. We could fashion parallel cases involving negligence.[46] The character of the reckless agent in my sense (one who has few or no limits to her indifference to moral limits) may be worse than the character of the merely negligent agent (whose indifference to moral limits and the duty of care has limits—just the wrong ones); the actions that are the product of such characters may likewise vary in their moral severity.

---

[46] Notably, though, planning and spontaneity are not reliable drivers of greater and lesser moral severity respectively. A carefully and compassionately planned, yet wrongful act of euthanasia may be a less severe wrong than a spontaneous murder in the heat of passion. I'm grateful to Mark Greenberg for the example.

Such distinctions are compatible with thinking that the passionate killer's episodic lapse of restraint and the negligent killer's episodic lapse of diligence, both lapses attributable to engrained defects in character, are not so different in moral significance. So, I do not dispute that certain finer-grained distinctions may reveal different degrees of moral significance. That concession, however, does not support a general distinction between malice and negligence, nor does it suggest that forging a general set of distinctions turning on the more differentiated categories of purpose, knowledge, or awareness of the specific risk supports a more sophisticated but still reliable version of the traditional hierarchy.

REASONING FROM THE REMEDY

Another reason the moral significance of negligence may be downgraded is that we tend to punish it less severely than malicious action and this differential treatment resonates with us as appropriate. We also tend, concomitantly, to have more moderate reactive attitudes toward negligence than toward malicious action. The latter may often provoke greater anger and resentment than the former and these reactions resonate with us as appropriate.

One response to these phenomena is to regard this resonance as the product of the moral hierarchy I am challenging and of our relative over-casualness about negligence. This resonance may trace more to rationalizations associated with our greater personal familiarity with negligence than to wisdom encoded in intuition. We may fail to react to negligence with sufficient strength, whether in our reactive attitudes or in our punishment practices. My thesis, however, may be defended with a more moderate observation. My point does not depend on or imply that we should react more harshly to negligence than we do or that negligence should be punished as or more harshly than malicious action. For, we may overreact to malicious action. Further, with respect to punishment, our remedial decisions may reflect considerations other than just our assessment of the degree of wrongfulness.

Indeed, I think it is a methodological mistake to take too many cues from our remedial practices, however justified. Our punishment practices do not merely express our degree of moral disapproval. If practices of remediation also play an educative or rehabilitative function, as I think they should, then the form they take may depend upon the nature of the underlying problem and what it takes to address it. Combating malice may involve delivering a greater shock to the system than correcting tendencies of oversight, which may require working on patterns and habits, even if the two are not so distant in terms of moral severity as the common picture allows.

But, it might be objected, punishments are supposed to be proportionate to the underlying wrong, so a harsher punishment must respond to a more significant wrong. I submit that the proportionality principle should not be interpreted in this ordinal way. I understand it as demanding that a punishment not amount to an overreaction to a wrong and, further, that the punishment be somehow fitting as a response to the wrong. What fittingness and appropriateness amount to, however, are not determined only by the nature of the wrong but also by the purposes of punishment. These purposes, I submit, are only partly expressive but also educative and rehabilitative in nature. Proportionality demands that, *inter alia*, we must not use the occasion of a wrongdoing and the liability of the wrongdoer to punishment as an occasion to accomplish any old ends we please; wrongdoing may involve some waivers of some rights, but it does not involve a wholesale waiver of all rights. This interpretation of 'proportionality' does not, however, entail that 'morally worse' wrongdoings receive harsher punishments or that justified harsher punishments signal a worse wrongdoing. Horizontal equity is not sufficiently judged simply by looking at sentencing outcomes. In the sense that she might have no complaint of unfairness, a wrongdoer may 'deserve' harsher punishment than serves any purpose. Because it serves no purpose, we should not administer it, but no injustice is thereby done to another wrongdoer who 'deserves' an equally harsh punishment and receives it where that punishment would serve a distinctive rehabilitative or educative function.

Rather than reading off the harshness of punishment and our retrospective reactions to moral failure, we could gauge the significance of a wrong by considering the magnitude of our *ex ante* investment in preventing that failure. Such consideration requires greater attention to the tremendous efforts involved in cultivating the non-negligent agent. To have the ability to act non-negligently involves the development of a sufficiently comprehensive moral understanding so that one's aims do not inappropriately overshadow other mandatory ends, the honing of one's agency to ensure one's understanding is reflected in one's action, and sufficient self-knowledge to gauge when one's individual agency requires supplementation. That's a rather heady agenda. (The earlier discussion of political non-negligence suggests parallel points about the efforts required to build and learn to participate in a democratic, consultative culture.) The cultivation of this base of knowledge and skill comprises much of our moral education and is a more nuanced, time-consuming task than conveying the basic prohibitions and the forms of self-control necessary to avoid malicious behavior. Although the greater simplicity of avoiding malicious wrongs may make the assignment of blame for transgressions easier from an *epistemic* perspective, it does not show the relevant transgressions are more severe in moral kind. It seems telling that despite the difficulty and practical effort, we do invest in the arduous effort to train agents to be capable of non-negligence.

While telling, our behavior is not so mysterious. We are interested in the achievement of our ends, the appropriate practical appreciation of their relation to other people and other ends, and avoiding calamity. The coupling of opportunities with temptations to engage in malicious behavior that threaten these interests is rare. Resisting such temptations is not normally taxing. Perhaps that is why such violations are so fascinating. Still, daily maintenance and execution of the myriad quotidian obligations is where the action is in building and maintaining moral relationships and community. Preparing the mortar and bricks and protecting them from rain, subtle shifts in ground, weather changes, and material deterioration are the first priorities of the mason, important as it may also be to prepare for the emergency of the battering ram or the calamitous earthquake.

This last point about daily maintenance motivates my conviction that non-negligence is a natural (but overlooked) topic for philosophical and legal feminists who, in other domains of inquiry, have done a great deal to unearth and celebrate the everyday work women are often tasked with, work that builds and continually replenishes the infrastructure of life.[47] Creating and living as a non-negligent agent involves similar reinforcing attentions and behaviors, administered on a regular basis. Historically and still to a troubling degree, many of these behaviors happen to be performed by women, often for men, none of which may on their own stand out as heroic moments, worthy of an epic poem. In the same vein, negligence should strike feminists as a significant wrong because it often involves a failure to take the other seriously while one goes about one's business. There's a failure fully to take in the other as equally important to oneself and then to observe and react to how one's behavior affects her. When enacted repeatedly in patterned behavior, these uncorrected oversights of attention, appreciation, and appropriate response work as major mechanisms of ongoing gender oppression. Among other things, they reify an operational blindness to the structures of inequality left in place from centuries of intentional discrimination. Like points may be made about racial discrimination and the role of negligence in the persistence of racial inequality.

---

[47] Sophia Moreau has also drawn connections between discrimination and negligence in her very interesting *Discrimination as Negligence*, 36 CAN. J. PHIL. 123 (2010). Moreau starts from a very different, motive-insensitive view of negligence—focusing solely on the objective standard and the duty of care, not on the motives of negligent agents and their defects.

CONCLUSION

I have discussed why some of the arguments for the hierarchy of malice over negligence and why some of the resistance to strong moral liability to negligence seem unpersuasive. The law, in one sense, is an inspiration to this enterprise because, strangely, the framing of negligence as a wrong is more salient in legal circles than in our everyday moral talk. Yet, I have gone to some pains to explore some aspects of the significance of moral and political negligence that are submerged or absent from its legal treatment. Perhaps this absence is explained by the dominance of economic and remedy-forward approaches in law, or perhaps it is because of the special purposes the law pursues; for the latter reason, objective, legal standards of due care, vectors of criminal liability and punishment, and moral culpability may not fully overlap. My main interest has been to articulate an understanding of the moral wrong of negligence as a corrective to a sort of cultural permissiveness about negligence and to celebrate the sustained efforts and attention required for that non-negligent activity that in turn are essential components of full moral compliance. More attention and celebration may improve our moral understanding, our methods of moral education, and the quality of our efforts to achieve egalitarian relations.

Although my focus is on the moral, I do not mean to forswear all possible legal implications of these ideas. Whether we are thinking about criminal law or tort law, the general legal lesson may be that when justifying significant legal hierarchies and other legal conclusions (and vice versa), we should be dissatisfied by blunt appeals to an assumed significant moral hierarchy. We should probe deeper to ask how the distinction between malice and negligence (or finer-grained distinctions) bears upon the specific legal purposes we are pursuing or whether we are really tracking a different distinction.

More speculatively, in light of the moral seriousness of negligence, it may well be that, legally, we should take negligence more seriously than we do.[48]

---

[48] For instance, we might question the grounds for the presumption against interpreting a statute to encompass negligence liability in cases like *Elonis v. U.S.*, 135 S. Ct. 2001 (2015). Justice Alito's concurring opinion muses that "[w]hether negligence is morally culpable is an interesting philosophical question, but the answer is at least sufficient debatable" to ground a presumption against interpreting a statute implicitly to authorize criminal negligence liability (Alito, J., concurring in part, dissenting in part, at 2014). The Court's opinion hints that its decision may rest on the idea that negligence involves a lesser form of culpability. If that is another way of saying the behavior is less morally wrong, then we might reconsider the presumption. 135 S. Ct. at 2011. It is unclear whether the Court's concern with a negligence standard centers on the hypothetical worry that Mr. Elonis failed to recognize, as the reasonable person would, that his posts were threats, or on the hypothetical worry that Mr. Elonis, or other defendants like him,

Perhaps, for example, we should acknowledge civil causes of action for those bouts of negligence that, fortunately, do not result in harm when, nonetheless, they culpably put others at risk. Others may take my argument to suggest greater penalties for negligent behavior, whether in tort or criminal law. I am less sure. As discussed earlier, different remedial responses may fit morally comparable, but differently motivated, flaws. My thoughts turn less toward enhancing penalties for negligence than toward asking whether we might reconsider the severity of our current carceral reactions to many intentional wrongs.

One reason to re-examine negligence and the standard hierarchy is that we may be more prone to negligence and it represents a more familiar sort of moral failure. Perhaps our mutual susceptibility to negligence lures us to devalue its significance, instead of combining a serious critical stance with a generous posture of mutual forgiveness and renewed resolve. I worry that its familiarity may fuel the misconception that the moral gap between negligence and malice is more significant than it is. This misconception may, in turn, rationalize more punitive reactions to the less commonplace forms of intentional wrongs. We once made this mistake about diseases—fearing leprosy more than cancer. We're now less prone to that mistake with diseases and have internalized that commonplace diseases like diabetes and heart disease are killers, even if often treatable, that rarer diseases are not necessarily more serious, and that taking these commonplace diseases seriously involves routine vigilance, exercise, and dietary moderation. My suggestion is that we take our everyday moral activities as seriously as we have come, at least intellectually, to take our diet.

Acknowledgments

Much of this paper was developed with Barbara Herman in a joint seminar we taught in Fall 2013. Although we may not converge on every point, it's happily difficult to disentangle who first thought what. For critical and constructive reactions to this material, I'm grateful to Elizabeth Anderson, David Brink, Joshua Cohen, Mark Greenberg, Barbara Herman, Tom Hurka, Mark Kelman, Mark Migotti, Sophia Moreau, Liam Murphy, Dana Nelkin, Michael Otsuka, Arthur Ripstein, Samuel Scheffler, Howard Shatz, Steven Shiffrin, Zachary Taylor, Andrew Williams, two anonymous referees, members of the University of Calgary Philosophy

may have lacked the capacity to recognize, as the reasonable person would, that his posts were threats. I strain to have sympathy with the former because it is a version of the moral hierarchy I mean to challenge. The latter, if valid, seems less a concern with criminal liability for negligence than with using a particular objective standard of negligence in criminal contexts.

Department, members of the NYU Colloquium on Legal, Political, and Social Philosophy, members of the UCSD Philosophy Department, members of the Yale Center for Law and Philosophy, members of the University of Pennsylvania Philosophy Department where this paper was originally one of two Seybert lectures, members of the Stanford Political Theory Colloquium, members of the University of Toronto Law and Philosophy Reading Group, members of the University of California, Berkeley Law, Philosophy, and Political Theory workshop, and attendees of the Oxford Studies in Political Philosophy Workshop at Syracuse University.

9

How to Guard against the Risk of Living Too Long

The Case for Collective Pensions

Michael Otsuka

I shall defend the realization here and now of a type of occupational pension that is collective rather than individualistic in nature, as it involves the pooling, both pre- and post-retirement, of the individual defined contribution (IDC) pension pots that characterize retirement plans in the US and the UK.* This type of pension, known as "collective defined contribution" (CDC), is based on a simple idea: namely, that it is possible to limit the employer's liability to nothing more than a set contribution (a "defined contribution") while retaining many of the benefits of the collectivization (pooling) of risks of a traditional defined benefit (DB) pension, which are absent in an IDC. Such a collective pension can be defended against a freedom-based objection from the right via an appeal to the following Hobbesian voluntarist justification: CDC constitutes a "Leviathan of Leviathans" into which it is rational for workers to choose to associate in order to tame longevity and investment risks. CDC pensions that arise from and mirror existing income inequalities can also be defended against an egalitarian objection from the left, by demonstration that they can be grounded in Rawlsian principles of reciprocity and property-owning democracy.

* I have presented earlier versions of this chapter at the Institute for Future Studies and the Universities of Syracuse, York, and Zurich and thank the members of the audiences for their comments. I also thank Nicholas Barr, Joseph Heath, Con Keating, Mark van Roojen, Juri Viehoff, Alex Voorhoeve, and two anonymous readers for their comments.

1. THE RISKS OF INDIVIDUAL DEFINED
CONTRIBUTION PENSION POTS

The familiar and increasingly common individual defined contribution (IDC) retirement savings plan works roughly as follows.[1] A worker, and typically also one's employer, make monthly contributions into one's "pension pot" during one's working years. The worker decides how to invest that pot. When one retires, one is able to transform these investments into retirement income by exchanging one's pot for an annuity, which provides a specified guaranteed income until death. Alternatively, one can provide oneself with income in retirement by drawing down one's funds, via withdrawals from a continually invested pot until it is depleted.

An IDC gives rise to significant exposure to investment risk. One must choose among multiple opportunities for investment (which therefore carry opportunity costs), ranging from bonds with relatively low variance and low expected monetary value to stocks and other equity with higher variance and higher expected monetary value. Seemingly safe low-variance options typically carry the risk of erosion by inflation, against which it is costly to purchase protection. In order to protect against investment risk, workers are often advised to engage in "life cycle" (aka "lifestyle") de-risking of their pension pots by shifting from equity such as stocks to less volatile assets such as bonds as one nears retirement. The rationale that is offered is that one should protect against a great fall in the value of one's assets, from which it will be difficult to recover, close to the point at which one will need to transform these assets into retirement income.[2] One is advised to do so even though this involves a shift into investments with lower expected monetary value. Historically, however, such de-risking would have been a typically costly and ineffective form of protection against downturns in the stock market for US and UK workers. In the vast majority of years from 1948 to 2007, even those preceded by fairly sharp downturns in the stock market, this sort of de-risking would have made such workers poorer in retirement than a high wire strategy of remaining invested purely in equity throughout one's career. Alternative strategies of investing purely in bonds, or else 50% in equity and 50% in bonds, throughout one's career, fare even worse at the median for US and UK workers than life-cycle de-risking. All of these investment strategies involve a flattening of the market volatility

---

[1] In the US, the most common of these is known as a "401(k)," named after a subsection of the Internal Revenue Code that provides tax relief for such plans.

[2] This rationale is more applicable to those who plan to convert their entire pension pot into an annuity at retirement than to those who plan to remain continually invested in retirement for income drawdown.

of equity only at the cost of a substantial amount of leveling down into lower-return assets.[3]

An IDC pension pot also exposes an individual to longevity risk. If one knew exactly how long one would live in retirement, one could budget to cover precisely that number of years. But one typically doesn't know the date of one's death. So, with IDC, one must either take out insurance against living a long time, via the purchase of the guaranteed income of an annuity, or else draw down one's pot in retirement. An annuity carries significant upfront costs, which vary unpredictably depending on the moment at which one purchases it.[4] With income drawdown, one runs the risk of one's money running out before one dies. Drawdown is deemed one of the more difficult options for an individual to navigate, since, not only does one not know how long one will live, but one doesn't know how much the investments in one's pot will grow or shrink during retirement.[5]

2. THE LEVIATHAN AS THE SOLUTION TO LONGEVITY AND INVESTMENT RISKS

By joining together as a collective in the manner famously depicted on the frontispiece of Hobbes's *Leviathan*, it is possible to tame the longevity and investment risks we face as individuals each with our own private IDC pot.

First let us consider longevity risk. By the law of large numbers, each generation (cohort) of the same age that retires at the same time has a predictable, "statistically stable" (low variance) post-retirement average longevity, which is typically somewhat higher than twenty years. This knowledge facilitates precise budgeting. Our prediction of the average longevity of the cohort might end up missing the mark, but not by much. We can contrast this with the much wider range of live possibilities for which we need to plan and budget in the case of any given individual, who might live anywhere from one to forty years beyond retirement. Though each individual's longevity varies unpredictably, we can solve this problem by risk pooling into a large collective whose average longevity is predictable within a small margin of error. This involves mutual covenants to transfer contributions from those with below average longevity to those with above average longevity.

---

[3] See Cannon and Tonks (2013). They also found that the median lifestyle or life-cycle de-risked pension pot across sixteen different OECD countries would have been only 73.4% as large at retirement as the median pot that had been invested in equities throughout.

[4] On the volatility of annuity rates, see Merton (2014).

[5] See Brown and McInnes (2014, 18).

We draw down our collectivized pension pot on these terms to ensure that nobody's payments run out before he dies. Each member of the collective is treated as an individual. There is no involuntary sacrifice of anyone's expected interests for the sake of the greater good.

Investment risk remains. This risk is tamed by our Leviathan entering into covenants with younger Leviathans (cohorts). The different cohorts are bound together into a multigenerational corporate body. The cohorts whose invested contributions exceed the expected growth rate agree to transfer to cohorts whose investments fall short, thereby smoothing over investment risk and allowing constant investment in high-yield, high-risk assets.

A collective pension can therefore be justified as a "Leviathan of Leviathans." Each first-order Leviathan is created by a set of covenants that unites the members of a cohort who will retire at the same time. Such covenants are to the mutual benefit of each, as they pool and tame the longevity risk that each faces as an individual. The different cohorts in turn will find it rational to enter into covenants with one another in order to pool and smooth over the investment risk that remains.

In comparison with such a collective pension scheme, an IDC is a pension scheme consisting of a single member. Within at most a few decades, his working life and his life itself will come to an end. This is for the simple reason that the "days of our years *are* threescore years and ten; and if by reason of strength *they be* fourscore years, yet *is* their strength labour and sorrow; for it is soon cut off, and we fly away" (Psalms 90:10). When he retires, an individual's one-person pension fund will stop receiving further contributions into it. If he would like a guaranteed pension income for life, he will need to arrange for the assets of his pension scheme to be "bought out" by an insurance company that provides an annuity in exchange. As noted above, such an individual will feel pressure to de-risk his pension fund from stocks to bonds, in order to provide protection against the risk of a great fall in the value of his assets just before the point of exchange for an annuity.

Things are very different in the case of a collective pension scheme, especially a large multi-employer one that pools the pensions contributions of workers across an entire sector and keeps these assets pooled during the retirements as well as the working lives of each individual. The multigenerational corporate body that arises via a collective pension scheme is "an ongoing entity with a long-time horizon," which can, given realistic assumptions, remain continually invested in higher-risk, higher-expected yield assets, in order to provide each of the individuals that constitute this collective a better pension than she could hope to generate through her own personal IDC pension pot: "In a pooled-asset . . . plan, . . . while the individual worker ages one year per year, the collective group of workers does not age as rapidly as any individual, so that the portfolio can remain invested longer in higher return assets such as equities, infrastructure and private equity" (Brown and McInnes 2014, 23, 17).[6]

Before drawing this section to a close, I would like to propose that we rename this "Leviathan of Leviathans" a "social union of social unions." This more collegial and less forbidding latter phrase from Rawls (1971, §79) is also more accurate than the Hobbesian notion, since we don't need an authoritarian sovereign to secure the collective benefit. We have Rawlsian cooperation rather than mere coordination.[7] Although here he is discussing the complementary nature of different people's realized talents rather than their longevity and investment risk pooling, the following passage from Rawls nevertheless serves as a fairly accurate description of the nature of the intra- and inter-generational unions that constitute a collective pension:

[I]t is through social union founded upon the needs and potentialities of its members that each person can participate in the total sum of the realized natural assets of the others. . . . This community may also be imagined to extend over time, and therefore in the history of a society the joint contributions of successive generations can be similarly conceived.   (1971, 523)

In other words, which modify Burke's famous description of "society" as "a contract," a collective pension constitutes "a partnership not only between those who are living [working], but between those who are living [working], those who are dead [retired], and those who are to be born [employed]" (Burke 1835, 498).

3. FROM DEFINED BENEFIT (DB) TO COLLECTIVE DEFINED CONTRIBUTION (CDC)

Traditional defined benefit (DB) pensions are collective in nature. They deliver their benefits via the investment and longevity risk pooling described

---

[6] The regulation and management of collective occupational schemes in the UK in recent years has involved a failure to recognize the ongoing, corporate, multi-generational existence of multi-employer pension schemes such as the Universities Superannuation Scheme (USS). Funding requirements and practices in the UK are based on the premise that one must have enough assets on hand so that one can wind up one's pension scheme in the relatively near future.

[7] Rawls writes: "Cooperation is distinct from merely socially coordinated activity, for example, from activity coordinated by orders issued by some central authority. Cooperation is guided by publicly recognized rules and procedures that those cooperating accept and regard as properly regulating their conduct" (1993, 16).

in the previous section. On account of such risk pooling, they are more efficient than IDC pots at generating pensions income.[8]

In spite of this advantage, DB pensions are an endangered species. They are derided as obsolete, collectivist relics. Public sector and state DB pensions that are "pay as you go" rather than funded are regularly branded Ponzi schemes. Especially in the US and the UK, there has also been a seemingly inexorable decline in funded DB pensions in the private sector. Private sector employers are abandoning DB mainly on account of the risks to them of having to make up for shortfalls in the funding requirements that are imposed by government regulations and the high and volatile liabilities such pensions place on a firm's balance sheets under current international accounting standards.

I shall not argue here for the revival of occupational DB pension schemes in the private sector. Rather, I shall draw attention to and defend a type of pension known as collective defined contribution (CDC). Because, like DB, it is a form of collective pension provision, CDC shares many of the benefits of DB over IDC. CDC is, however, a more viable form of collective pension than DB under current circumstances, since it addresses the aforementioned employers' objections to the latter. CDC would not add any debt to employer balance sheets, since the benefits to workers do not constitute a promise. Rather than making any promises that the employer might have to make good through an increase in their contribution rates, CDC relies on targets. If the targets turn out over time to have been too optimistic, workers make good the shortfalls via a reduction in their future or current pensions income, which might later be restored if the financial situation improves. CDC should also be attractive to employers because it would make it possible for them to provide better pensions in comparison with IDC without contributing a penny more in contributions.

Strictly speaking, CDC is a type of DC pension. Like the more familiar IDC version of DC, and unlike DB, risks are placed on workers rather than employers. But, with CDC, risks are borne by workers collectively rather than individually, in a manner reminiscent of the insurance schemes of friendly and mutual societies tracing back to the eighteenth century.[9] Longevity risk is pooled and investment risk is smoothed via the methods of a collective pension described in my earlier discussion of the "Leviathan." Under CDC, workers who happen to retire when the stock market is at a peak typically end up doing less well than they would have done under IDC. But workers who retire when the stock market is lower end up doing

---

[8] It has been estimated that these two factors provide DB with at least a 20% advantage over IDC. See Brown and McInnes (2014, 23–4).

[9] See Heath (2006, 333–4).

better. As I shall explain below, the collective investment of pensions contributions post-retirement as well as pre-retirement provides further advantages, the upshot of which is that the median return is higher under CDC than under IDC.[10]

Versions of CDC have been extensively pioneered in the Netherlands and Denmark in recent years.[11] Those in the Netherlands are constructed to deliver pensions that approximate the DB pensions they have replaced. Pension income is typically set as a percentage of career average salary multiplied by the number of years worked. This percentage might be determined as that which could be delivered given the best estimate of the average rate of return on pension fund investments. Unlike a DB pension, this formula for pension income constitutes a target rather than a promise. One's pension might be reduced in the light of lower than predicted investment returns and other uncertainties.[12]

There are also versions of CDC that retain many aspects of a DC pension. It would not be difficult to transform IDC pensions into such CDC pensions, thereby providing a pathway to CDC in those countries in which IDC dominates. A simple and elegant form of CDC called "SAFE" mimics individual DC pension pots with notional pots. One's notional pot consists of the actual value of one's employer and employee contributions, plus the investment growth of an actual fund into which all employer and employee contributions are collectively invested.[13] This collective fund remains constantly invested mainly in return seeking assets such as equity. To guard against investment risk, the growth of one's notional pot is smoothed by a "collar": all investment growth over 8% goes, not into one's pot, but rather into a reserve fund that is used to support a 0% floor, so that one's pot remains unchanged in cash terms in years in which the fund's performance is negative. If, as is predicted will happen over time, the money in the reserve fund exceeds the money needed to support the floor, then people are paid bonuses into their notional pots. Upon retirement, these pots are converted

---

[10] Although risks to workers are mitigated in comparison with IDC because pooled, CDC does not protect workers as fully against longevity and investment risks as DB does, given that the latter entirely shifts most of these risks onto employers.

[11] "[I]n the case of both Denmark and the Netherlands, CDC arrangements are an integral part of pension systems that are recognised world-wide as being high quality. According to the 2012 Melbourne Mercer Global Pension Index, the Danish pension system was ranked number 1 on a list of 18 countries that fully reflect the significant range of different pension systems around the world. The Netherlands was ranked second on this list, which takes into account the adequacy, sustainability and integrity of a pension system" (UK Department of Works and Pensions, 2013, 47).

[12] See Bovenberg et al. (2016).

[13] Insofar as these notional pots are convertible into actual pots for those who leave the scheme, portability to other schemes would be a straightforward matter.

into targeted pensions via a commutation factor of 20: $20 from one's pot for every $1 of annual pension income. This commutation factor remains relatively constant over time, even as the market price of annuities goes up and down. This is a further respect, beyond the collar, in which there is smoothing in order to pool investment risk among workers.[14]

The pooling of risks via CDC renders pension income in retirement both less unpredictable and higher at the median, relative to IDC. Figure 9.1 captures Aon Hewitt's modeling of the pension that would have been generated at retirement via CDC (green line) as compared with various IDC pots. On their modeling, IDC "lifestyle" de-risking (red line) provides a superior pension, in comparison with 100% IDC investment in equity (black line), in only a small minority of the years modeled; moreover, it does so at the cost of a significant lowering of the median performance. By contrast, CDC provides a superior pension to IDC equity across a greater number of years. Furthermore, the median performance of CDC is slightly higher than that of IDC equity. CDC efficiently fills in the valleys of a high-risk, high-return investment in equity via transfers of benefits from the peaks. By comparison, both IDC alternatives to equity—low-risk UK government bonds in the form of "gilt" (gold line) as well as "lifestyle"

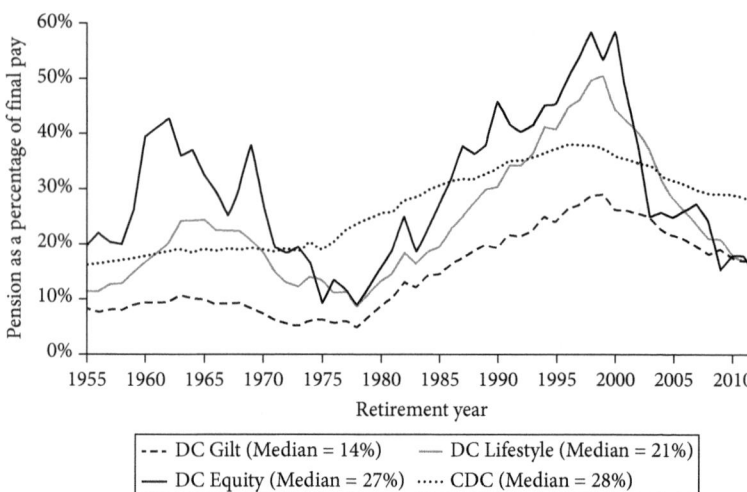

Fig. 9.1 Historic CDC versus IDC performance (source: Wesbroom et al., 2013, 40)

---

[14] See Davis and Madland (2013, 14–17) for further details regarding the mechanics of SAFE.

de-risking—inefficiently reduce high variance by leveling pensions down below the valleys as well as the peaks of equity throughout most of the modeled time period.[15]

It is significant that, under CDC, unlike IDC, and like DB, one's pensions contributions remain collectively invested in the pension fund during one's retirement as well as one's working career. Such collective investment eliminates the pressure that individuals with IDC pots face to de-risk from stocks to bonds as they near retirement and the cost of purchasing an annuity to secure a reliable lifetime pension from retirement until death.[16] As Wesbroom et al. explain, this contrast provides a primary reason for the superior performance of CDC over IDC in providing pension income:

> The fact that pensions are paid from the plan rather than being purchased by way of annuities in the open market means that greater amounts can be held in return seeking assets, thereby leading to superior expected outcomes. Annuities backed by bonds represent poor investment decisions, if expected pension lifetimes are 25 or 30 years or even more. In addition, avoiding an annuity purchase means that the profit margin and cost of capital for an insurer are avoided, and more of the assets are applied to improving members' benefits. (Wesbroom et al. 2013, 5)

4. THE HOBBESIAN VOLUNTARIST CASE FOR THE FREEDOM TO BE BOUND BY A CDC

In a document entitled "Freedom and Choice in Pensions," the recent Chancellor of the UK Exchequer voices the following appeal to "pension freedoms" that resonates with many on the right:

> This government believes in the principle of freedom. Individuals who have worked hard and saved responsibly throughout their adult life should be trusted to make their own decisions with their pension savings.... [Therefore], individuals from the age of 55 with a defined contribution pension will be able to access their entire pension flexibly if they wish. Annuities will remain the right product for some,

---

[15] See Wesbroom et al. (2013, 40). The UK Department of Works and Pensions (DWP) commissioned the Pensions Policy Institute (PPI) "to seek to independently replicate the approach taken by Aon." The PPI's modeling yielded "a similar [income] replacement rate [in retirement] to Aon Hewitt when similar assumptions are used." The PPI found, however, that "CDC outperforms DC to a lesser extent compared to Aon Hewitt's reported results." For example, "If we compare our CDC result against Aon's reported median DC lifestyle outcome (20%), CDC produces results approximately 48% higher than DC. Aon found this result to be 66%." See Popat et al. (2015, slides 9, 50–1).

[16] Recall the explanation for this in section 2.

but I believe that people should be free to make their own choice about how to use their savings. . . . I want as many people as possible to be able to access their pension flexibly.   (Osborne 2014, 3)

Is there a good case, based on the values of freedom and flexibility of choice, for employers to provide their employees with options beyond enrolment in a CDC (or otherwise collective) pension scheme? In particular, should they provide workers with the options to invest in an IDC instead of, or as well as, a CDC pension pot, along with all of the former chancellor's pension freedoms to convert or cash in one's pension pot? The answer is "no" if these options encompass an inalienable and unconditional liberty to withdraw from the CDC collective by, for example, cashing in and withdrawing the monetary value of one's notional pension pot at point of retirement. Such an inalienable right is really a *restriction* on the freedom of workers to bind themselves on terms of their own choosing that will make them better off collectively. It is, in fact, contrary to the free market values that champions of pension freedoms profess, as it prevent workers from making primarily self-regarding choices more effectively. CDC pensions are not collectivist rather than individualistic. They're both: a mutual society into which each individual voluntarily associates and thereby binds himself.

There are at least two reasons why the gains of CDC risk pooling would be threatened by what economists call "adverse selection" if people were allowed to withdraw their pension pots from the collective fund at retirement.[17] First, the effectiveness of CDC in pooling longevity risk would be undermined. By the time they retire, people will have a better idea of their life expectancy than they did when they entered the pension scheme as young adults, since they will know how healthy they have managed to remain over the past several decades of their working life. Those who know at that point that they are likely to live longer than average will have more of an incentive to receive a CDC pension than those who know that they are likely to live shorter on average, the latter of whom will have more reason to draw down their pension pot individually, if they are able to do so. The long-lived might not, however, have enough to generate sufficient pension income if they pool only among themselves. A second reason why an inalienable right to withdraw and cash in one's DC pot at retirement would undermine a CDC scheme is that it would render it less effective in pooling investment risk. People who reach the age at which they would like to retire when the stock market is high or when annuities on the insurance market are a good deal will have an incentive to withdraw their pension pots from the CDC scheme at that point. That will make it more difficult to smooth investment risk between lucky and unlucky cohorts.

---

[17] A classic text on adverse selection is Arrow (1963).

Without undermining risk pooling, employers could provide workers with pension freedoms on the following terms. They could provide each with the choice of entering into the CDC risk pooling option when and only when they *join* the pension scheme, typically at the outset of their career in the case of a sector-wide multi-employer occupational scheme. Having signed up, they would need to remain collectively invested from that point onward, or else pay a heavy penalty for withdrawing.[18] At the outset, but *only* at the outset, they would also have the choice to invest in traditional IDC, which provides them with complete freedom to cash in, or draw down, etc., when they retire. All this would be consistent with pension freedoms, assuming, as one should, that freedom encompasses the right to bind oneself. In the case of Ulysses, such binding was necessary to protect himself against the indulgence of his imprudent impulses. Here, the binding would not be for the purpose of protecting individuals against such weakness of will. Rather, its point would be to prevent rational defections from a pension scheme that would destroy the cooperative benefit of risk pooling for the reasons sketched in the preceding paragraph.[19]

For the following reason, provision of such a limited choice to opt out of CDC and go it alone would not threaten the viability of the collective scheme. At typical point of entry at the beginning of one's career in a given occupation, each will be choosing under a fairly thick natural veil of ignorance regarding his or her own prospects for a long life and for a retirement when the stock market is bullish rather than bearish. Although people's known longevity risks differ at point of retirement, at this much earlier point each person's known longevity as well as investment risks will be roughly the same as any other person's of a comparable age. This will be generally true so long as we restrict ourselves to the sort of pension scheme that is occupation-specific, the upshot of which is that the physical demands of work and the socio-economic circumstances of the different members of the scheme will not vary significantly. In large part because of the fact that known longevity and investment risks are both significant and roughly equal at early point of entry into the scheme, most will have compelling reasons of self-interest to damp down these risks, via their collective pooling into the CDC scheme at this point, rather than going it alone via IDC. Risk pooling can be effective even if we partition people into different occupational sectors whose members have different known life expectancies and average retirement

---

[18] Members could, however, be provided with the option of moving from one to another collective fund, within the CDC pension scheme, where these different collective funds would involve different ethical investment values. I mention the possibility of ethical investment in section 6 on property-owning democracy.

[19] This is not, however, a classic many-person prisoners' dilemma, since it would not be rational for every single person to defect.

ages, so long as there remains a sufficient number of individuals within each sector to benefit from the law of large numbers.[20] Those who have lower retirement ages and life expectancies because their jobs are physically demanding or less well paid would not want to collectively annuitize, in undifferentiated fashion, with others who are longer lived and able to retire later. But in an occupation-specific pension scheme, they would be able to reap the advantages of pooling just among themselves.[21]

Recall that entry into an occupation will be the only point at which a person will be able to choose to join with others in pooling risks. If a person instead opts, at point of entry, to go it alone via investment in his own IDC pot, he will not have any future opportunity to collectivize his risks in this scheme. Most will therefore find it rational to enter into CDC at the outset, even though the cost of exit is high. This will be in their ex ante rational self-interest. Hence, there will be a sufficient number of people enrolled in the CDC scheme to facilitate effective risk pooling and to sustain it over time.

It will be useful to draw some parallels here with health insurance.

The requirement that one can enter CDC only at the outset, conjoined with a high exit penalty, is in order to prevent behavior along the lines of refraining from purchasing medical insurance while one is young and healthy and purchasing it only when one is older and in less good health. The Obamacare mandate to purchase insurance when young and healthy is justified as a means of making possible a ban on excluding, or charging higher premiums to, those with pre-existing medical conditions. If there were not something along the lines of such a mandate, such a ban would give rise to a serious problem of adverse selection, whereby people purchase insurance only after they discover that they have an illness or disability that requires expensive medical care. Were that to happen, risks would not be spread sufficiently thinly across a large enough pool, and premiums would skyrocket, thereby defeating the purpose of purchasing insurance.

Unlike the Obamacare insurance mandate, workers are not required to enroll in CDC on my proposal. They have the alternative of IDC from the outset. Obamacare could be transformed in this direction, so that there is no longer a requirement to purchase medical insurance when young and healthy. Dropping this requirement would silence the objection against the insurance mandate that it is an unjustifiable restriction on freedom.

---

[20] See Heath (2014b).

[21] Even if we limit ourselves to occupation-specific schemes, the natural veil will not be complete, as one will be able to infer statistical differences in longevity on the basis of gender and race. But partitioned risk pooling would be problematic if it involved segregation by gender or race.

Nevertheless, the purchase of insurance from the beginning of, and throughout, one's adult life could be made a necessary condition of protection from exclusion or higher premium on the basis of pre-existing condition.[22] There would be no liberty-based argument for barring insurance companies from charging actuarial premiums in the case of those who have chosen not to take out health insurance at the beginning of their adult lives. The risk of not being able to take out affordable insurance later would provide each with a rational incentive to purchase health insurance from the outset.

In this section, I have shown how a case for CDC can be made that overcomes a freedom-based objection shared by many on the right. In the next section, I shall turn to a demonstration of how the realization of CDC even in existing conditions of inequality can be defended against objection from the egalitarian left.

5. CDC AS RAWLSIAN FAIR TERMS OF SOCIAL COOPERATION FOR MUTUAL ADVANTAGE

In the actual world of unequal income, CDC pensions proportionate to earned income would be an improvement over a status quo characterized by IDC pensions proportionate to similarly unequal incomes. On account of the benefits of risk pooling and the transfer from those who would otherwise be richer to those who would otherwise be poorer that this involves, CDC pensions would often be more egalitarian in comparison with the pensions that IDC would yield under the same employer and employee contributions.[23] CDC would tend to be worse than IDC for some of the unlucky who will die prematurely. They would lose out on the opportunity to bequeath their pension pot that IDC allows. But egalitarianism speaks against bequests. CDC would also tend to be worse than IDC for those whose investments would fare best under the latter, since their high returns would be transferred to the less fortunate under CDC smoothing. But egalitarians should welcome such transfers. The move from IDC to CDC would also promote equality via a modest increase in the ratio of the income of the "bottom 99 percent" to that of the "top 1 percent." This is because the average level of those in the bottom 99 percent, whose income is mainly earned, would rise under CDC via an improvement in the delivery of their

---

[22] As in the case of Obamacare, this could be accompanied by state subsidies for those who could not otherwise afford insurance.

[23] Given the declining marginal utility of money, the egalitarian effects of these transfers would be more pronounced when measured in terms of welfare rather than money.

pensions, but better pensions would make less of a proportional difference to the more largely unearned incomes of the top 1 percent.

Though it would generally constitute an improvement over IDC in the dimension of equality, the introduction of CDC pensions proportionate to income here and now would nevertheless fall short of the realization of egalitarian justice. In particular, it would fail to realize a "luck egalitarian" principle of pensions proportionate to incomes that are unequal if and only if these inequalities are traceable to people's responsible choices rather than circumstances beyond their control. On this principle, differences in people's income should, in Ronald Dworkin's terminology, be ambition-sensitive but endowment-insensitive.[24] Actually existing inequalities in incomes satisfy neither criterion to a substantial degree. Insofar, therefore, as pensions are proportionate to existing earnings, their efficient delivery via the risk pooling advantages of CDC over IDC would at least mirror, even if not magnify, any injustices in the actual distribution of earned income.

In contrast to a typical occupational pension, some basic state pensions are largely sensitive to number of years worked rather than the amount of money earned. A pension whose levels were sensitive to nothing other than number of years worked would perfectly capture the luck egalitarian principle of endowment insensitivity under the idealized assumptions that the number of years one works is completely under one's control and the utility of labor per unit of time is the same across different people. These assumptions do not hold in the real world: some people lack a choice regarding years worked on account of involuntary unemployment or disability, and the disutility of low-paid jobs tends to be greater than that of high-paid jobs. A pension whose level is based only on years worked would, however, capture the ambition sensitivity and endowment insensitivity of luck egalitarianism better than occupational pensions such as CDC that are highly proportionate to earnings.

Insofar, therefore, as the imperative of equality is concerned, it will be difficult to make the case for CDC proportionate to existing income as opposed to occupational pensions that are sensitive only to numbers of years worked. Alternatively, CDC pensions proportionate to income might be defensible only after one has realized policies that redistribute the underlying

---

[24] See Dworkin (2000, ch. 2). Dworkin (2002, 107) disowns the name "luck egalitarianism," since he notes that his version of egalitarianism "does not aim to eliminate gambles...from people's lives." Alive to this defect with the term "luck egalitarianism," Peter Vallentyne (2002) calls the view "brute luck egalitarianism," where "brute luck" is Dworkin's term for unchosen bad luck. "Option luck" is Dworkin's contrasting term for bad luck that traces to choice under known risk or uncertainty (e.g., gambles in a casino). I shall employ the term "luck egalitarianism" as an abbreviation of the more accurate and informative term "brute luck egalitarianism."

income itself, perhaps via a complex system of progressive taxation, so that this income is ambition- but not endowment-sensitive.

In this section, I shall argue that an important element of justice is nevertheless captured by CDC pensions proportionate to income, even when the distribution of income itself is not in accord with egalitarian principles. There is a justice-based case for collective pensions, because justice should be conceived of, not as entirely a matter of the elimination of the unfairness of unchosen, brute bad luck, but rather as also involving Rawlsian fair terms of social cooperation for mutual advantage in the division of the fruits of the labor of workers.[25]

At its most fundamental level, the principle that constitutes Rawlsian justice is one of reciprocity. In particular, we do things to reciprocal advantage, on fair terms, where such terms are egalitarian. Rawls writes that

the idea of reciprocity lies between the idea of impartiality, which is altruistic (being moved by the general good), and the idea of mutual advantage understood as everyone's being advantaged with respect to each person's present or expected future situation as things are. As understood in justice as fairness, reciprocity is a relation between citizens expressed by principles of justice that regulate social world in which everyone benefits judged with respect to an appropriate benchmark of equality... (1993, 16–17)

In rejecting the "idea of mutual advantage," Rawls maintains that justice might call for the transformation of a present-day "society in which property, in good part as a result of fortune and luck, is very unequal into a well-ordered society regulated by [his] two principles of justice." Justice might call for such a transformation even if, as is likely, not all will gain from it, relative to the inegalitarian status quo. Those, for example, "owning large properties" may lose "greatly" (Rawls 1993, 17).

We can agree with Rawls that it is not a necessary condition of justice that all must benefit, relative to an unequal status quo. But this does not rule out the possibility of mutually beneficial moves from an unjustly unequal status quo that promote justice.

In the quoted passage, Rawls analyzes reciprocity as fair terms of social cooperation for mutual advantage, as measured against a benchmark of

---

[25] Elsewhere, I have proposed that

justice is by no means exhausted by the call to minimize unfairness. The promotion of the general welfare is also an element of justice, one which might come into conflict with and outweigh the minimization of unfairness. The sacrifice of the general welfare in the...leveling-down case is sufficiently great that it outweighs the call to minimize unfairness. On this approach, justice broadly conceived consists of the proper balancing of a plurality of distinct and potentially conflicting values or principles such as distributive equality, utility, liberty, and the right not to be sacrificed for the greater good.

(Otsuka 2002, 47–8)

equality. Both mutual advantage and equality figure in Rawls's idea of reciprocity. Each element has a role.

The very fact that Rawls describes equality in the distribution of goods as a benchmark implies that such equality does not exhaust justice. If, for example, there were no cooperation in a world where, as nature would have it, there were no unchosen inequalities among different individuals, we would have perfect luck-egalitarian justice. But an element of Rawlsian justice would be missing: fair terms of cooperation that make all parties better off, when measured against a benchmark of equality. There would also be no social justice in such luck-egalitarian circumstances. Only natural justice would obtain.

Cohen's (2008, 315–23) luck-egalitarian case against the justice of strong Pareto improvements that do not promote equality might plausibly apply to benefits to all that are the result of brute natural forces—e.g., manna that falls from heaven. But when the question is one of how to distribute the fruits of the labor of socially cooperating individuals, considerations of justice might apply, which are absent in the natural case. A principle of "to each according to his contribution," where what a worker receives is proportionate to the value of his labor contribution, has plausibility when applied to the distribution of the fruits of social cooperation from an equal baseline. Such a principle isn't, however, applicable, at least not in any obvious way, to the distribution of manna from heaven.

In addition to mutual advantage that arises from an equal baseline, there is another way in which equality might combine with mutual advantage to constitute fair terms of cooperation: mutual advantage might be realized among parties who regard one another as equals. Rawls refers to the benchmark of an equal division in the passage I have quoted. But elsewhere he often speaks of "fair terms of social cooperation between citizens *regarded as free and equal*" (2001, 79 [emphasis added]). These two conceptions of equality can come apart, in ways that bring out the importance of the latter, as I shall now illustrate.

It is plausible to maintain that a benchmark of equality should be choice sensitive—one involving equality of opportunity for goods rather than equality of outcome when the two come apart. Rawls (1993, 181–2 n. 9) himself is sympathetic to the idea that a Malibu surfer who has chosen not to work has received all the primary goods to which he is entitled in the form of leisure, even though he lacks enough material resources to sustain himself. From a baseline of equality of opportunity, such a surfer might seek earnings from employment when his hunger becomes too great. It would, however, be unjust because exploitative for a capitalist to take advantage of the surfer's vulnerability by offering him sweatshop terms even if the transaction is mutually advantageous. The capitalist would not be showing regard for the surfer as an equal, but rather regarding him as someone to be taken advantage of, even though the exploitative transaction arises from a justly equal baseline.

I have just argued that mutual advantage from the surfer-capitalist baseline of equal opportunity for goods needn't be just because it might involve failure to treat people as equals. I shall now argue that mutual advantage from an *unequal* baseline needn't be *unjust* because it might involve a regard of one another as equals in a manner that vindicates the transaction.

Among mutually advantageous moves from an unjustly unequal baseline, we should distinguish the following types of case:

1. The mutually advantageous move is *coerced via violation of negative rights*, as in the case of a gunman's money or life threat.
2. The mutually advantageous move involves an *exploitative offer that takes advantage of the vulnerability of the weaker party*. An exploitative sweatshop work contract in which the vulnerability of the worker is not chosen in Malibu-surfer fashion is one such example. Wage bargaining by the talented, of the sort that Cohen (2008, ch. 1) condemns in his discussion of the incentives argument for inequality, would also qualify.
3. The mutually advantageous move involves neither of the above defects. It is *voluntary rather than coerced*, and *the stronger party does not take advantage of the weaker party*.

The move from IDC to CDC is of this third type. It therefore counts as a case of genuine reciprocity even though it falls short of an ideal case of justice because it arises from an unjustly unequal baseline. Under CDC, each party voluntarily brings his pension contributions to the collective, risk pools these resources with the resources of others, and then gets back in proportion to what he puts in. How much one is able to put in might be a reflection of an unjustly unequal baseline distribution of income. But the unjustly rich do not take advantage of, or otherwise benefit from, the fact that others are poor. Rather, insofar as their agreement is concerned, the positions of the different parties are symmetrical.[26]

---

[26] Rawls speaks of "fair terms of social cooperation between citizens regarded as free and equal, and as fully cooperating members of society over a complete life, *from one generation to the next*" (1993, 3 [emphasis added]). CDC's investment risk pooling is sometimes characterized as designed to subsidize older pensioners by younger workers. That is a mischaracterization. Rather, CDC is designed so that those who enjoy more favorable returns on the stock market during their lifetimes subsidize those who enjoy less favorable returns. The smoothing favors the unlucky over the lucky, irrespective of their age or the generation to which they belong. Such a bias is fair both to different generations and to the young versus the old.

Consider an analogous case in which a wealthy carpenter has constructed a sailboat without a sail and a poor weaver has weaved sails. They would each like to sell what they have produced. Suppose that the value of each sold separately does not add up to the value of the two together, given the synergy of their combination. If the poor weaver were desperate for the extra proceeds from the synergistic sale, perhaps the wealthy carpenter could drive a hard bargain for a disproportionately great share of these proceeds. That would be to take advantage of unequal bargaining power. By contrast, an agreement analogous to CDC is one in which they voluntarily split the extra proceeds in a manner that is proportional to the market value of each when sold separately. As in the sailboat case, the baseline in CDC is the value of what each owns when it is not joined together with what another owns—i.e., the market value of the assets in one's non-risk-pooled IDC pension pot.[27]

Here I am endorsing a principle which calls for each to receive according to his labor contribution. Marx famously rejected such a principle according to which "the individual producer receives back from society…exactly what he gives to it [and the] right of the producers is *proportional* to the labour they supply." He dismissed this as a bourgeois notion that would be superseded: "In a higher phase of communist society,…after…all the springs of co-operative wealth flow more abundantly—only then can the narrow horizon of bourgeois right be crossed in its entirety and society inscribe on its banners: From each according to his ability, to each according to his needs!" (Marx 1970, 17–19). Leaving aside surfers and others who are in need by purely voluntary choice, we might acknowledge duties on the part of the better off to transfer resources to those in need, even when such transfers are not mutually advantageous. But when everyone has

---

[27] Joseph Heath suggests a different interpretation of Rawls as judging occupational pension schemes just simply insofar as they have been voluntarily entered into in accordance with the law, on grounds that such schemes are not part of the basic structure. Heath notes that Rawls claims that his principles of social justice do not apply to voluntary associations such as universities and business firms, which lie outside of the basic structure. (See Heath 2014a, 160–3.) But the questions of whether CDC should be permitted by the state rather than regulated out of existence, and, if permitted, whether tax relief should be extended to CDC pensions contributions, seem clearly to be questions regarding the basic structure. Moreover, for reasons G. A. Cohen has offered, I would maintain that Rawlsian principles of justice ought to apply, far more extensively than Rawls thought they should, to the private choices of employers and employees. (See Cohen 2008, esp. ch. 3.) Discussions among USS members regarding recent pension reforms reflect the conviction that considerations of equality, fairness (equity), and progressivity of effect are highly relevant to the justification of reforms to the pension scheme. Typically, however, the scope of these concerns is limited to the membership and doesn't extend to those outside the scheme who are worse off. Perhaps this reflects the belief that there is a special requirement for terms of cooperation to be fair.

enough so that nobody is in need, the demands of equality needn't always trump the strong Pareto improvements of mutual advantage when the two come into conflict. In these circumstances beyond the realm of needs, these two elements of justice—equality and mutual advantage—stand in a more equal relation to one another. A state pension should be sufficient to meet our basic needs for income in retirement. Above that floor, there is a sound case for the mutually beneficial risk pooling of CDC even if it arises from a baseline of unequal income.[28]

6. PROPERTY-OWNING DEMOCRACY

Unfunded "pay-as-you-go" DB pensions conform to the model of a redistributive welfare state that is characterized by transfers of income from one group of people in society to another—in this case, from those who are working to those who are retired. A funded pension scheme such as CDC, by contrast, fits the model of a "property-owning democracy," which Rawls endorses in preference to "welfare state capitalism."[29] Rawls maintains that

the background institutions of property-owning democracy work to disperse the ownership of wealth and capital . . . not by the redistribution of income to those with less at the end of each period, so to speak, but rather by ensuring the widespread ownership of productive assets and human capital (that is, education and trained skills) at the beginning of each period. . . . The intent is not simply to assist those who lose out through accident and misfortune . . . but rather to put all citizens in a position to manage their own affairs on a footing of a suitable degree of social and economic equality.   (2001, 139)

Rawls expresses the hope that, in a property-owning democracy, "most things can be left to citizens and associations themselves, provided they are put in a position to take charge of their own affairs and are able to make fair agreements with one another under social conditions ensuring a suitable degree of equality" (2001, 159).

---

[28] There is also the following pragmatic argument that we should not hold the aspect of justice involving mutual advantage hostage to the egalitarian aspect: the latter will be more difficult to achieve, since it involves a sacrifice of the interests of some, relative to the status quo, whereas the former does not. There is a case for not making the ideally just the enemy of the good.

[29] In a "pay-as-you-go" scheme, the pensions of retired workers are paid for by the contemporaneous pensions contributions of current workers. In a funded pension, by contrast, the pensions of retired workers are paid for by their own previous pensions contributions when in employment, along with subsequent investment returns. Whereas not all DB pensions are "pay as you go," since some of them are funded, by definition all DC pensions are funded.

In DB pension schemes, where employers bear most of the risks, it is inevitable that management will also insist upon extensive rights of governance of the pension scheme. Under CDC, by contrast, there will be a stronger case, and more scope, for workers to "take charge of" and "manage their own affairs." In this regard, CDC is analogous to traditional IDC pension schemes, where management leaves workers on their own to bear all the risks. Management doesn't claim control over IDC pension pots, in spite of the fact that they typically make substantial contributions into these pots. They value the fact that their responsibility extends no farther than the depositing of the promised sum into the pot each month. Just as management does not interfere with the investment decisions of individuals with IDC pots, but washes their hands of this and leaves it to workers (often outsourcing the pension fund to some outside organization), they shouldn't feel the need to interfere with CDC investments. The decision of workers, under CDC, to "make fair agreements with one another" to pool their funds among themselves does not transform the DC pension pot into a concern of management.

Workers should also be left free to run their CDC pension schemes as non-profit mutual societies with no external shareholders. In this way, they would not, as under a traditional IDC, be forced, upon retirement, to enter into a contract for an annuity or financial services with a for-profit corporation whose shareholders are other than the workers in the collective. Rather, they would remain invested members of their own mutual society, with pension income paid out of the pooled resources of the collective throughout their retirement. There would also be no need to attract outside investors to start and sustain their pension fund. Scheme members could instead draw upon the steady stream of small monthly pensions contributions from workers and their employers.[30]

The fact that CDC funds are under the autonomous control of workers, rather than management or external shareholders, might give rise to practices of ethical investment. Rather than everyone being bound by a majority decision of all members of the CDC collective regarding the ethical investment of a single fund, the arrangement could involve unanimous consent, whereby each person chooses from a range of different funds, each invested in accordance with a different set of ethical principles—including the null set, which would presumably be ordinary nihilistic investment, with no concern for anything other than financial returns. Apart from the constraint

---

[30] It would be a virtue to some, such as R. H. Tawney, who are associated with the idea of property-owning democracy, that the income-bearing assets in the pension fund derive, via such contributions, from labor income and in this respect are "related to genuine productive effort." See Jackson (2012, 41).

that one would require the company of enough like-minded others to gain the benefits of risk pooling and economies of scale, there needn't be any limit to the number, or the ideological orientation, of the funds.[31]

In arguing that Rawlsian property-owning democracy unjustifiably min- imizes the role of welfare state provision involving taxation and transfer, Ben Jackson writes:

> if the major forms of individual property ownership that could plausibly be equal- ized in contemporary capitalist societies are home ownership and shares in private companies, then, as the financial crisis of 2008 has made clear, this will inevitably involve the exposure of individuals to significant financial risk. It is therefore crucial to secure individuals against such risks through collective social welfare provision if the property-owning democracy strategy is to be pursued.   (2012, 48)

One of the main themes of this chapter, however, is that the mutual associ- ation of workers, and the pooling of their pensions contributions, is a means, beyond state transfers to the unfortunate, of protecting people against financial risk. Such risk pooling can provide a fairly high level of financial security even when pensions contributions are invested primarily in stocks and shares, thereby allowing workers to share in the proceeds of the growth of the economy. James Meade himself, from whom Rawls bor- rowed the very term "property-owning democracy," called for something closely resembling the investment approach of a CDC pension fund when he advocated "the encouragement of financial intermediaries in which small savings can be pooled for investment in high-earning risk bearing securities" (Meade 1964, 59).

Large, occupational, collective, funded pension schemes can give rise to the voluntary provision of primary goods that the state would otherwise need to step in to deliver, via tax and transfer. Especially where there are political constraints on the raising of such taxes, we should attend to the full range of instruments at our disposal for securing such goods through the private firms and voluntary associations that form civil society.[32] We should

---

[31] The funds would not necessarily have to possess the familiar leftist tilt into green and socially responsible investment. There is, for example, a Catholic Values Fund that restricts its investments to companies that are not at odds with the teachings of the Church. And there is a once infamously named Vice fund (since rebranded), which purchases stock in firms devoted to armaments, tobacco, gambling, alcohol, and pornography.

[32] There is a default tendency of some on the left to appeal too exclusively to the state to bring about social justice via public sector institutions funded out of general taxation. Obama's Affordable Care Act, for example, was strongly opposed by some on the left who wanted to hold out for a single payer system in which the state acts as the sole provider of health insurance on the model of Canadian Medicare. The British National Health Service is regarded by some on the left as better still, insofar as health care itself in the form of state-run hospitals and public sector physicians—and not merely insurance for it—is provided by the state. But the provision of health care via private insurance and

facilitate those voluntary collective schemes that most efficiently convert the pensions contributions of workers into income in retirement, without excessive profit-taking by the wealthy through management charges and shareholder earnings. The less of his wage or salary a worker needs to set aside in order to generate a good pension, the more income from labor will be available for taxation for purposes of redistribution to the least advantaged, who thereby also benefit from the well-designed collective occupational pensions of others.

References

Arrow, Kenneth (1963). "Uncertainty and the Welfare Economics of Medical Care," *The American Economic Review* 53: 941–73.

Bovenberg, Lans, Roel Mehlkopf, and Theo Nijman (2016). "The Promise of Defined Ambition Plans: Lessons for the United States." In Olivia S. Mitchell and Richard C. Shea, eds., *Reimagining Pensions: The Next 40 Years*. New York: Oxford University Press.

Brown, Robert, and Craig McInnes (2014). "Shifting Public Sector DB Plans to DC: The Experience so far and Implications for Canada." Canadian Public Pension Leadership Council.

Burke, Edmund (1835). "Reflections on the Revolution in France." In his *The Works of Edmund Burke: With a Memoir*, vol. 1. New York: George Dearborn.

Cannon, Edward, and Ian Tonks (2013). "The Value and Risk of Defined Contribution Pension Schemes: International Evidence," *Journal of Risk and Insurance* 80: 95–119.

Cohen, G. A. (2008). *Rescuing Justice and Equality*. Cambridge, MA: Harvard University Press.

Davis, Rowland, and David Madland (2013). "American Retirement Savings Could Be So Much Better." Center for American Progress.

Dworkin, Ronald (2000). *Sovereign Virtue*. Cambridge, MA: Harvard University Press.

Dworkin, Ronald (2002). "*Sovereign Virtue* Revisited," *Ethics* 113: 106–43.

Heath, Joseph (2006). "The Benefits of Cooperation," *Philosophy and Public Affairs* 34: 313–51.

Heath, Joseph (2014a). "Contractualism: Micro and Macro." In his *Morality, Competition, and the Firm*. New York: Oxford University Press.

Heath, Joseph (2014b). "Reasonable Restrictions on Underwriting." In his *Morality, Competition, and the Firm*. New York: Oxford University Press.

multiple payers in, for example, France has given rise to care in that country that the World Health Organization has deemed superior to the more complete state provision in the neighboring UK.

Jackson, Ben (2012). "Property-Owning Democracy: A Short History." In Martin O'Neill and Thad Williamson, eds., *Property-Owning Democracy: Rawls and Beyond.* Chicester: Wiley-Blackwell.

Marx, Karl (1970). "Critique of the Gotha Programme." In *Karl Marx and Frederick Engels: Selected Works in Three Volumes*, vol. 3. Moscow: Progress Publishers.

Meade, James (1964). *Efficiency, Equality and the Ownership of Property.* London: George Allen & Unwin.

Merton, Robert (2014). "The Crisis in Retirement Planning," *Harvard Business Review* July–August: 3–10.

Osborne, George (2014). "Forward" to "Freedom and Choice in Pensions: Government Response to the Consultation." Her Majesty's Treasury.

Otsuka, Michael (2002). "Luck, Insurance, and Equality," *Ethics* 113: 40–54.

Popat, Shamil, Chris Curry, Tim Pike, and Ciaran Ellis (2015). "Modelling Collective Defined Contribution Schemes." Pensions Policy Institute.

Rawls, John (1971). *A Theory of Justice.* Cambridge, MA: Harvard University Press.

Rawls, John (1993). *Political Liberalism.* New York: Columbia University Press.

Rawls, John (2001). *Justice as Fairness: A Restatement.* Cambridge, MA: Harvard University Press.

UK Department of Works and Pensions (2013). "Public Consultation: Reshaping Workplace Pensions for Future Generations."

Vallentyne, Peter (2002). "Brute Luck, Option Luck, and Equality of Initial Opportunities," *Ethics* 112: 529–57.

Wesbroom, Kevin, David Hardern, Matthew Arends, and Andy Harding (2013). "The Case for Collective DC." Aon Hewitt.

10

Authority and Harm

Jonathan Parry

This paper explores the connections between two central topics in moral and political philosophy: the moral legitimacy of authority and the ethics of causing harm. Each of these has been extensively discussed in isolation, but relatively little work has considered the implications of certain views about authority for theories of permissible harming, and *vice versa*.[1] As I aim to show, reflection on the relationship between these two topics reveals that certain common views about, respectively, the justification of harm and the moral limits of authority require revision. The paper proceeds as follows. Sections 1 and 2 clarify the question to be addressed and set out two main claims that I will defend. Sections 3–6 argue for the first claim. Sections 7–10 defend the second. Section 11 concludes.

1. THE CENTRAL QUESTION

The core concern within the ethics of harm is obvious. Though harming others is normally morally prohibited, under certain conditions it is intuitively permissible, or even required. Theories of harm aim to provide a systematic account of the factors that determine when these exceptions arise.

The theorist of authority, by contrast, is concerned with the fact that certain persons and institutions claim to possess the moral power to issue commands and, by doing so, place others under obligations to act in certain ways. Paradigmatic examples include a parent directing their child to 'Clean up your room!', a policewoman ordering a car driver to 'Stop right there!', and a colonel commanding his troops to 'Hold your positions!' At a more

---

[1] An exception being a recent pair of articles by Malcolm Thorburn (2008) and John Gardner (2010), though these focus primarily on the relevance of authority to criminal law defences for causing harm. David Estlund (2007) also provides an important discussion, which this paper builds upon.

general level, states and legal systems claim to create obligations by enacting laws and through the pronouncements of officials. In all these cases, the commander purports to create new 'content-independent' reasons for action, over and above the subject's pre-existing reasons for and against the action commanded. Furthermore, these new reasons claim a privileged status in the subject's practical deliberation. They are not simply to be weighed alongside all her pre-existing reasons, but are instead intended to silence or 'preempt' (at least some of) those reasons, preventing them from bearing on how she now ought to act.

Despite the ubiquity of authority claims, there is a clear puzzle as to how they could be true. Put simply: How can I acquire something as morally serious as an obligation just by someone communicating her intention that it be the case?[2] A theory of authority then faces two closely related tasks. The first is to identify the conditions, if any, under which this power is morally justified and obedience therefore required. The second is to provide an account of its moral limits, since obligations to obey are presumably neither unconditional nor absolute.

Despite their different objects of justification—harm vs obedience— these two topics are ultimately concerned with what moral reasons agents have; with what individuals all-things-considered ought and ought not to do. Given this, there is a range of cases in which answering these questions requires determining how our accounts of harm and of authority interact with one another. These are cases in which an authority's command requires its subject to cause, or refrain from causing, harm to others. Under what conditions, if any, do these commands give subjects all-things-considered reason to obey? This is no hypothetical question. For example, members of law enforcement and military organizations are routinely subject to such commands. The question is most striking in the case of command to perform acts of harming that would be morally prohibited in the absence of the command. Here, two putative sources of obligations require opposing actions. A theory of authority or harm will be incomplete unless it tells us how conflicts like this should be resolved, by providing an account of the extent (if any) to which authoritative commands can affect the moral status of harmful actions.

2. TWO CLAIMS

To demonstrate the relevance of authority I focus on two specific debates within the ethics of harm. The first is the very general question of identifying

---

[2] For a detailed discussion of the nature of these intentions, see Enoch (2011; 2014).

the *range* of considerations that are capable of justifying harm. On a fairly standard view, the stringent constraint on harming is explained in terms of individuals having basic rights against harm. Given this, justifications for harming are thought to take one of two basic forms. The first is that the individual harmed *lacks* their normal right against harm, and so harming them does not wrong them. For example, they may have waived their right (as in the case of boxing matches), forfeited their right in virtue of some prior wrongdoing (as in the case of punishment), or rendered themselves liable to harm in virtue of posing an unjust threat to others (as in cases of self- and other-defence). A second form of justification holds that individuals' rights not to be harmed can be *overridden* by weightier moral reasons. Most obviously, that harming a person directly prevents a much greater harm to others. In these cases, harm is justified as the (impartial) lesser evil.[3]

The above are often classified as agent-neutral justifications, in that they do not make essential reference to any particular agents to whom they apply.[4] For example, if John is liable to defensive killing, or if killing John will save many innocent lives, then any agent may potentially act on these justifications. In addition, some theorists defend the existence of agent-relative justifications, which apply only to particular agents.[5] These are typically grounded in considerations of permissible partiality. On this view, when certain agent-relative reasons—such as protecting oneself and one's loved ones—come into conflict with respecting others' rights not to be harmed, the agent-relative reason may sometimes be weightier. Given its structure, this can be understood as a distinct species of lesser-evil justification (Lazar, 2013).

While the precise range of justifications for harming is much debated, it is generally assumed that the above candidates exhaust the possibilities.[6] Term this view *Completeness*.

The second debate arises within discussions of defensive harm. It concerns the permissibility of using defensive force against individuals who threaten unjust harm to others, but possess an all-things-considered justification for doing so. This issue rests on a more general question regarding

---

[3] As Helen Frowe puts it, more precisely: 'Lesser-evil justifications obtain when one will prevent substantially more harm than one causes, such that the disparity between the harm and the good overrides the deontological presumption against causing harm' (Frowe, 2015, p. 274).

[4] For a lucid overview of the agent-neutral/agent-relative distinction, see Ridge (2011).

[5] See, for example, Davis (1984), Quong (2009), and Lazar (2013).

[6] For example, one of the most thorough recent discussions, which 'points tantalizingly' towards a 'grand unified theory' of permissible harming, consists almost entirely in an analysis of liability and lesser-evil justifications (Rodin, 2011, p. 110).

how different agents' reasons for causing harming *interact* with one another. While it seems plausible that an agent's justification gives others *some* reason not to defensively harm them, debate centres on the extent to which the justificatory burden is raised. On one prominent (but by no means universal) view there can be no justified defence against justified infringements of rights against harm.[7] Term this view *Immunity*.

I will argue that extending a certain view of the justification of authority into the domain of harm generates counter-examples to both *Completeness* and *Immunity*. To do so, I defend two specific claims. Firstly, I defend the strong claim that, under certain conditions, the command of an authority can provide an agent with a moral justification for causing harm, even in cases where the harm both transgresses rights and fails to bring about goods sufficient to override those rights. This claim thus denies *Completeness*, positing an additional 'authority-based' form of justification.[8]

With the first claim in place, I shift from the question of the normative situation of those *subject* to commands to cause harm, to those who are *threatened* with harm by authorized agents. In particular, I consider the permissibility of defensively harming such agents. I defend a second claim, which holds that an agent's having an authority-based justification for harming does not, in itself, raise the justificatory burden on defensively harming that agent, compared to if they lacked that justification. This claim thus denies *Immunity*.

3. OPPOSING THE FIRST CLAIM

I anticipate many will find my first claim highly unintuitive, even repugnant. To begin a defence of this claim, I will outline three broad views about authority that support this common-sense reaction.

---

[7] See, for example, Tadros (2011, ch. 9), McMahan (2014), and Frowe (2015). For further discussion, see Waldron (2000). Note that *Immunity* does not rule out cases in which two or more agents may be permitted to defensively harm one another as a result of *waiving* their rights against harm (as in boxing matches, for example) since these are not cases of rights infringements.

[8] It is worth distinguishing my first claim from an uncontroversial sense in which commands might seem to justify causing otherwise-unjustified harm. To demonstrate, consider a case in which failing to obey a command to cause unjust harm will result in a bad consequence occurring. Perhaps, if disobeyed, the commander will unleash their wrath on innocent people. If this bad consequence is sufficiently grave then the subject may well be justified in acting as commanded. However, in such cases, while the command *results* in reasons for action that justify causing harm, the command *itself* does not create those reasons. Rather, the existence of the command simply affects non-normative facts so as to activate an ordinary lesser-evil justification. For discussion of this distinction, see Estlund (2008, p. 118) and Enoch (2014).

At the most general level, one might endorse philosophical anarchism and deny that the commands of authorities *ever* create reasons for action. This challenge is often stated in the form of a paradox, starting from the plausible assumption that agents should always act in accordance with the balance of reasons that apply to them.[9] Given this, in cases where an authority commands acting against the balance of reasons, obeying the command seems to involve acting against reason. If, on the other hand, we are commanded to act as reason recommends, then we ought to do so, but not *because* we have been commanded. From the perspective of practical reason, commands are either redundant or pernicious.

However, endorsing anarchism simply in order to resist my first claim does seem a case of killing the baby to save the bathwater. Fortunately, a more moderate, and plausible, strategy is available. This accepts that there is some successful response to the anarchist's challenge—so that *some* authorities are capable of creating *some* obligations—and instead appeals to the moral limits of that power. This is a very natural position to take. It seems obvious that wherever the precise limits lie, commands to cause harm that would otherwise be morally unjustified surely exceed them, given the gravity of the wrongdoing involved. As Matthew Noah Smith puts it in a recent article,

> The first characteristic of the obligation to obey the law is that there are very few limits on what an obligation to obey the law can require a subject to do. There are, of course, some limits. *Presumably, if obedience to the law requires commission of serious moral wrongs, then one is not obligated to obey the law.* But this limit is at the moral extremes. (Smith, 2013, p. 349, my emphasis)

This common thought supports two distinct objections to my first claim, corresponding to two different ways in which the obligation to obey a legitimate authority is limited.[10] The *Invalidation Objection* holds that the obligation to obey is necessarily *voided* when the authority's commands require actions that would otherwise be seriously morally wrong.[11] These commands create no reasons to obey. By contrast, the *Pro Tanto Objection* grants that such commands may succeed in creating obligations, but holds that these obligations are necessarily *overridden* by the subject's weightier duty not to cause serious harm to others.[12]

---

[9] For the most influential formulation of the paradox, see Wolff (1970).
[10] On this distinction, see Christiano (2008, pp. 261–2).
[11] For explicit defence of this view, see Knowles (2007).
[12] For versions of this view, see McMahan (2009, p. 88) and Stilz (2014, p. 333 n. 22).

4. SERVICE JUSTIFICATIONS OF AUTHORITY

In order to defend my first claim, a plausible account of authority is needed that reveals all three objections to be mistaken. This requires two components. Firstly, in response to the anarchist, we need an account of how one person's authority over another—understood as the moral power to create content-independent and peremptory obligations—can be morally justified. Secondly, in response to the Invalidation and Pro Tanto objections, it needs to be shown that commands to inflict unjustified harm need not necessarily exceed the moral limits of authority. I will argue that 'service' accounts of authority are able to satisfy both these requirements. On this view, very roughly, one agent's having authority over another can be justified when, and to the extent that, the authority having this moral power serves the subject's ends.

Let me begin by outlining Joseph Raz's well-known argument for justifying authority in this way (Raz, 1986). This advances two main theses. The first ('preemption') thesis explains the peremptory character of commands in terms of a hierarchical account of practical reasons. On this view, an authoritative command to φ is intended to give its subject both an additional first-order reason for φ-ing and a second-order *exclusionary* reason not to act on the basis of (some of) the pre-existing first-order φ-related reasons. These reasons are supplanted by the command.

Of course, the fact that commands are intended to play this role does not show that they do so. This second step is provided by the second ('normal justification') thesis, according to which,

> the normal way to establish that a person has authority over another person involves showing that the alleged subject is likely better to comply with reasons which apply to him . . . if he accepts the directives of the alleged authority as authoritatively binding and tries to follow them, rather than by trying to follow the reasons which apply to him directly.   (Raz, 1986, p. 53)

On this view, authority is justified in virtue of the rational gains it provides its subject. An authority is entitled to create new obligations by issuing commands because, and to the extent that, its having this ability enables the subject to better achieve aims they have independent reason to achieve.[13]

---

[13] Some object that this way of justifying authority fails because it cannot account for the idea that having authority necessarily involves a claim right to rule that correlates with the subject's duty to obey (Darwall 2009; 2010). However, it is far from obvious that authority does require such a right, rather than a power to create duties. For (in my view) convincing refutations, see Raz (2010), Marmor (2011b), and Enoch (2014). As these authors point out, in many (perhaps most) cases it seems far more morally attractive to say that the duty to obey an authority is owed to those that the authority's powers are meant to benefit, rather than to the authority itself. To this, let me add that this seems

Authorities can satisfy this test in two main ways. Firstly, obeying a common authority may enable individuals to better coordinate their behaviour with one another, thereby resolving various collective action problems they may encounter in pursuing valuable aims. Secondly, an authority may possess greater expertise than the subject on certain morally important matters (where expertise is understood broadly, as the ability to issue directives that track right reason more reliably or efficiently than the subject is able to).[14]

The normal justification thesis thus offers a broadly instrumental account of authority, thereby responding to the anarchist's worry that obedience necessarily conflicts with reason.[15] Obeying an authority may simply be the optimal means of achieving one's ends and, when so, obedience is justified (Raz, 2010, p. 299).[16] This idea also explains the preemptive character of authoritative commands: The subject best conforms to reason by allowing commands to replace their own practical assessment of certain considerations. It is easiest to illustrate this point in cases of expertise-based authorities (another, though broadly parallel, story has to be told with respect to coordinative authorities.) To put things somewhat crudely, such authorities are less likely than the subject to make mistakes as to what reason requires within an identifiable class of cases. Under these conditions, if the subject assigns its commands a preemptive role, she will achieve an identical level of success that the authority achieves. Alternatively, she could adopt a non-preemptive strategy, in which she simply gives the reasons that favor the

especially plausible when it comes to the specific application of a service account that I argue for, in which the authority's purpose is to enable its subjects to better distribute harms.

[14] An authority may also serve its subject by reducing the burdens of deliberation (Raz, 2009, pp. 149–50). I will leave this possibility aside, since this ground of authority is unlikely to apply in the contexts I will be discussing.

[15] Though common, this characterization is an oversimplification, since service accounts can accommodate non-instrumental reasons to obey (see Viehoff, 2011). However, since the cases I discuss are not of this type, I will continue to characterize service accounts as instrumental.

[16] Some argue that the Normal Justification Thesis does not provide a sufficient condition for legitimate authority, because genuine authority must also be conferred by some institutional norm or practice (Marmor, 2011a; 2011b), or at least recognized by some informal social practice (Enoch, 2014). I am unsure whether this is true, but for the purposes of this paper we need not settle the matter, since my specific conclusions about harm do not require that the Normal Justification Thesis be sufficient. Each of these putative necessity conditions are compatible with the view that that service plays a significant role in the justification of authority, whether or not it is sufficient (Enoch, for example, is fairly explicit that his view can be understood as a friendly modification of the service conception). This is all that my argument requires. If it turns out that authority does require institutions or social practices, then my conclusions are accordingly limited to those contexts. However, given that the questions motivating this paper are most likely to arise in precisely those contexts, this doesn't seem particularly worrying.

action commanded some additional weight in her deliberations. In a sub-class of cases, this weight will tip the balance in favour of acting as commanded, and her rate of mistake will match the authority's. In the remaining cases the command will not tip the balance and she will act according to her own assessment. Here, her rate of mistake will exceed the authority's. Across the total class, then, the subject does worse than the authority. A weighing strategy can only serve to reduce her overall conformity with reason, compared to preemption. Instrumental reason thus dictates that commands have preemptive force (Raz, 1986, pp. 67–9).[17]

A service-based view also explains why mistaken commands—commands that fail to reflect the balance of reasons in a particular case—can still succeed in creating obligations. This is because authorities do not need to be infallible in order to serve their subjects. Provided the authority is better placed than the subject with respect to achieving conformity with reason, the subject still improves their overall performance by obeying. Crucially, subjects can only gain the benefits of authority if its commands remain binding even in certain cases where they fail to track right reason. For, in order to avoid acting against reason in such cases, the subject would have to rely on their own assessment of the relevant considerations. But such a policy requires forsaking the overall gains of obedience, since the authority meets the condition of normal justification despite its fallibility.

To demonstrate, consider a simple case of advisory (rather than practical) authority, in which A has authority over B within the domain of financial investment. B will overall better maximize his returns by following A's directives, rather than by acting on his own judgement. This is compatible with A, from time to time, mistakenly directing B to make poor investments, costing B 100 dollars each time. However, detecting these mistakes would require engaging in the same process of financial reasoning that B went through in each case. If B does so, and acts on his own judgement, he will overall do worse in terms of maximizing his returns, compared to a more general policy of obedience. B therefore has sufficient reason to act as A directs, including in cases where A errs.

However, this doesn't mean that all commands from a legitimate authority create reasons to obey. The validity of commands is limited in two respects on a service-based view (I discuss their limited weight in section 6). The first restricts the jurisdiction of authority. Given the value of autonomy, there will be a range of domains in which agents' overriding rational aim is to

---

[17] In addition, preemption can also be defended via an argument from double-counting. Since, on a service account, valid commands are wholly grounded in the reasons that apply to the subject, subjects cannot simultaneously be subject to a command and the reasons upon which it is based, because these reasons have already been accounted for in producing the command (Raz, 1986, pp. 58–9).

choose for themselves, rather than achieve the 'optimal' outcome. For example, one's choice of leisure activity, romantic partner, religious affili-ation, etc. Given the priority of autonomous choice in these areas, obeying an authority would be self-defeating. Such domains are just not 'authority-apt' and commands issued within them are void.[18]

Service accounts also limit authority at the level of specific commands, as well as domains. Though directives may remain binding even if they fail to reflect right reason, this doesn't mean that *all* mistaken directives bind. Service justifies obedience only to the extent necessary to optimize the sub-ject's overall conformity with reason. Commands that require obedience beyond this point are invalid. When disregarding a mistaken command does not incur a rational cost, the subject is free, in fact required, to do so. To illustrate, consider a variation on the financial advisor example, in which A mistakenly directs B to burn ten of his dollars. In this case, B can judge that the directive is mistaken without having to engage in any complex financial reasoning of the kind that A is superior to B at doing. He can therefore disregard it without forfeiting the benefits of generally following A's directives. To clarify, whether a command's departure from right reason serves to invalidate it does not depend on how large a mistake it is. In our pair of financial examples, B's conforming to the first directive loses him ten times as much money as conforming to the second. Yet only the first is reason-giving. Instead, validity depends on the *type* of mistake. As Raz (1986, p. 62) puts it, what matters is the *clarity* of a mistake, not its *gravity*. Only clear mistakes invalidate, because only disobeying clearly mistaken commands is compatible with optimizing one's conformity with reason.[19]

5. THE AUTHORITY VIEW OF HARM

My contention is that if we accept a service account of how the commands of authorities can *ever* create obligations, it is a relatively short step to accepting that the commands of authorities can give subjects sufficient reason to cause otherwise-unjustified harm, thus vindicating my first claim. I set out this argument below and discuss some of its intricacies in the next section.

[18] In his more recent writings, Raz (2009, p. 137) terms this restriction the 'independence condition'. For earlier statements, see Raz (1986, p. 57; 1989, p. 1180). For detailed discussion, see Tucker (2012).

[19] It is worth pointing out that commands can be invalidated as clear mistakes even if the subject only finds themselves in a position to form the relevant judgement by accident or good fortune.

A service-based view provides a very general account of the justification of authority: A has authority over B within domain X, if obeying A's commands enables B to better conform to the X-related reasons that apply to B. The argument from this general account to a defence of my first claim proceeds in four steps.

The first is to make one element of this three-place relation more specific: the domain of authority. Presumably, unless extreme pacifism is true, there are possible domains in which acting in accordance with reason may involve causing harm to others. Term such domains *harm-apt*. I mentioned two possible examples earlier—the domains of military service and law enforcement.

The second step simply notes that agents operating in harm-apt domains may be differently situated regarding their abilities to assess and successfully bring about conformity with the harm-related reasons. Term this 'agent-variability'.

The third step combines the first two. Harm-aptness and agent-variability open up the possibility that agents may better conform with the harm-related reasons by obeying the commands of another, rather than by trying to conform to those reasons directly. This shows how one agent may acquire authority over another regarding the distribution of harm. Put differently, domains can be both harm-apt and *authority-apt*. If an agent will better distribute harm by obeying the commands of an authority, it seems uncontroversial that this is what they all-things-considered ought to do.

A fourth and final step is required to support my first claim. This is provided by the fact that, as explained above, authorities can be legitimate despite their fallibility. Subjects can be all-things-considered required to obey commands that fail to reflect right reason. When an authority serves its subjects within a harm-apt domain binding, yet mistaken, commands may include those that require distributing harm in ways that are not justified on the basis of the authority-independent reasons.

Term this four-stage argument the *Authority View of Harm*. To illustrate it, consider the following example:

> **Volcano**: A volcano erupts in Nation A. In order to save as many lives as possible the lava flow needs to be diverted from areas of higher population density to lower. This requires Nation A's citizens to dig an integrated system of trenches, along which the lava can be redirected.

Assume that Nation A's citizens will do better in terms of saving lives by obeying their government on matters of lava redirection, compared to not obeying. This may be due to the government's ability to achieve coordination among its subjects (because whether any individual trench-digger contributes to successful lava redirection depends on what other trench-diggers do), or its expertise (it makes sufficiently good decisions regarding lava redirection), or a combination of both. According to the Authority View of Harm, Nation A's government thereby acquires authority over its subjects regarding the domain of lava redirection. Nation A's citizens have a duty to obey their government on matters of lava redirection, including certain commands that are mistaken and require harming innocents in the absence of a lesser-evil justification. Since this policy of obedience is their optimal means of distributing harm, they are morally required, all things considered, to do so.

In summary: I have argued that if a broadly service-based view is defensible, a common and intuitive view about the moral limitation of authority is mistaken. It is not true, as a general matter, that commands to perform seriously wrongful actions *necessarily* fail to generate all-things-considered obligations to obey. This result also denies the common assumption that justifications for harm fall into one of two categories, in which the reasons against harming are either vitiated or overridden. Instead, there exists an additional form of justification, in which these reasons are defeated by *exclusion*.

Before moving on, it is worth considering an objection to the Authority View.[20] The objection holds that the subject's reasons to obey are not of the right sort to justify causing harm. More specifically, it claims that if the reasons to obey an authority arise from its superior expertise, its commands only provide the subject with reasons to *believe* that their actions are justified, and not practical reasons to *act* as commanded. Hence, subjects are 'justified' in causing harm only in the 'evidence-relative' sense, which may furnish them with an excuse for harming, but not a moral permission. This specific worry echoes a more general objection that service accounts can only establish epistemic, and not practical, authority (see, for example, Darwall, 2010).

In response, it is not obvious that the reasons to obey an expertise-based authority can be straightforwardly reduced to reasons for belief, as the critic claims. This is because the subject's epistemic aim of forming true beliefs about the world can come apart from her practical aim of improving their conformity with reason by obeying an expertise-based authority. For example, it may be that within an identifiable range of cases, the subject will more successfully form true beliefs about the balance of reasons in each case by relying solely on her own assessment, compared to deferring to the authority. Yet she may still do better in terms of conforming her *behaviour* with right reason by obeying the very same authority. For example, although she may make fewer mistakes than the authority, the mistakes that she does make may be more serious, such that *acting* on her assessments will yield

---

[20] Thanks to an anonymous referee for pressing me to address this objection.

worse practical results than a policy of obeying the authority, including (at least some of) its mistaken commands. Cases such as this suggest that one can have reason to obey an expertise-based authority, even if its directives do not provide reasons for forming beliefs. If so, the commands of such authorities create reasons for action, and so are capable of justifying behaviour (including harmful behaviour) more robustly than the mere evidence-relative sense.

A more straightforward response is also available. This simply points out that the objection has very limited scope, since it applies only in the case of authorities that are justified solely on the basis of expertise. But expertise is not the only, or even the main, way of justifying authority in terms of service. In many (perhaps most) cases, authorities are legitimated on the basis of their ability to enable their subjects to coordinate their actions with one another, so that they can better achieve morally important goals.[21] In the *Volcano* case, for example, whether each citizen successfully contributes to saving lives depends on coordinating their actions with others. The Authority View claims that if obeying an authority enables the required coordination, then the citizens are required to do so, including in (at least some) cases where the authority issues mistaken commands. For present purposes, the point is that reasons to coordinate are clearly practical reasons, and not merely reasons for belief. Given this, even if we concede that expertise-based authorities are merely epistemic authorities,[22] this does not significantly undermine the Authority View. At most, it reduces the range of cases in which authority-based justifications for harm apply. However, given that right action in many paradigmatic harm-apt domains (such as law enforcement and military action) will depend on coordination, this doesn't seem especially troubling.

6. THE MODERATE OBJECTIONS REVISITED

This section refines the Authority View by explaining why the two moderate objections outlined above fail to refute my first claim. According to the Pro Tanto Objection, commands to cause unjustified harm are necessarily overridden by the duty not to transgress the basic rights of others. However, as

[21] Some have objected that achieving coordination does not require authorities with the power to impose duties, but only that one course of action be made salient (Green, 1983; 1985). However, as Raz (1989) points out, this seems true only in extremely specific kinds of coordination problems, in which the participants satisfy certain subjective conditions.

[22] In his most recent writings on the topic, Raz seems willing to concede this (Raz, 2010).

the Authority View reveals, it is a mistake to treat all such cases in terms of a straightforward competition of reasons. In order for authorities to successfully serve their subjects, their commands must have the status of preemptive reasons, excluding the reasons on which they are based. This is equally true in harm-apt domains as in any other.

However, this does not mean that valid commands cannot be overridden by weightier first-order reasons. This is perfectly admissible on a service account, provided that the reasons in question do not fall within the authority's jurisdiction (Raz, 2009, pp. 144–6). To demonstrate, imagine that Smith has the aim of acting rightly on some morally important matter. The correct course of action depends on a trade-off between three distinct variables, X, Y, and Z. Furthermore, imagine that an authority passes the test of normal justification regarding Smith within the domains of the X-related and Y-related reasons, but not the Z-related reasons. Under these conditions the authority's command excludes variables X and Y from Smith's practical reasoning. But the command may perfectly permissibly be weighed against the Z-related reasons. Furthermore, it is entirely possible that the non-excluded Z-related reasons are sufficiently weighty to override the obligation created by the command, giving Smith all-things-considered reason to disobey.

Given this, the Authority View is compatible with there being cases in which the Pro Tanto Objection gives an accurate picture of the normative situation. For example, in some contexts distributing harms correctly may require a trade-off between minimizing harm and distributing it equitably. In these cases, an authority might successfully serve its subjects regarding the (sub)domain of harm minimization, but not the (sub)domain of equity. Like all of us, authorities are typically better at some things than others. Under these conditions, commands to cause (or refraining from causing) harm only exclude reasons pertaining to harm-minimization. Equity-based considerations are not excluded and, in some cases, may be sufficiently important to outweigh the obligation created by the command. In cases like this, the subject will have both an obligation to inflict unjustified harm and a weightier countervailing reason not to do so. However, the important point is that while there may be many cases that have this structure, it is not true of *all* cases. This is what the Pro Tanto Objection requires if it is to refute my first claim.

The Invalidation Objection claims that an authority's commands only create obligations if their content does not significantly depart from the balance of moral reasons. Authorities that issue such commands necessarily exceed their legitimacy. Hence, commands to impose harms (or at least sufficiently serious harms) that are not independently justified are void. The problem with this objection is that service accounts provide a very general model of how the moral power to create content-independent obligations can be justified, which applies across different domains of reasons. Given this, it is hard to find a principled rationale for the localized denial of this power that the objection requires. If the aim of improving one's conformity with reasons can *ever* explain why commands that require acting against the balance of pre-existing reasons create obligations, why should it not also do so regarding the reasons that govern the distribution of harm? It is arbitrary to simply carve off this domain as immune from a service-based justification.

However, this may be too quick. On a service-based view there are certain domains in which commands *are* necessarily and non-arbitrarily invalid: those in which choosing autonomously is more important than achieving optimal outcomes. One might then resurrect the Invalidation Objection by claiming that agents have more reason to distribute harms autonomously than optimally. In other words, harm-apt domains are never authority-apt.[23] If so, commands to inflict unjustified harm *would* necessarily fail to create obligations.[24] But this is very hard to believe. If there is any domain in which improving one's conformity with reason trumps the value of exercising autonomy, it is surely that of harm distribution. Appealing to autonomy cannot rescue the Invalidation Objection from the charge of arbitrariness.[25]

The Invalidation Objection may also be revised in a different direction. As explained above, commands that are *clearly* mistaken create no reasons for action. Given this, one might argue that commands whose content seriously departs from the balance of moral reasons *also* constitute clear

[23] This version of the Invalidation Objection thus denies the third step in the four-stage argument for my first claim.

[24] The revised objection is actually broader than the original, since it would also invalidate commands to cause *justified* harm.

[25] I think this response also suggests how the Authority View can respond to a more general class of objections to service accounts. These objections maintain that service accounts fail to give a plausible general account of political authority, because they give insufficient attention to the role that *procedural* considerations play in justifying authority (such as fairness, democracy, public reason, etc.), focusing instead on the value of the *outcome* of following the authority's directives (see, for example, Waldron (1999); Hershovitz (2003); Christiano (2004); Quong (2011)). While I think these objections are mistaken and that service accounts are flexible enough to accommodate procedural values (see Viehoff, 2011; 2014), the point I want to highlight is that when it comes to the distribution of serious harms, considerations of outcome are intuitively paramount. So, when restricted specifically to harm-apt domains, the case for justifying authority in terms of service is at its most compelling. Some critics seem willing to concede this. For example, Jonathan Quong, who is otherwise critical of service accounts, agrees that they provide a convincing account of the justification of authority within fairly narrow domains of morally important reasons, such as those constituted by our basic rights and duties *vis-à-vis* one another (Quong, 2011, ch. 4). This will presumably include the moral reasons governing the distribution of harm.

mistakes. This would provide a non-arbitrary basis for the claim that commands to cause unjustified harm are invalid in virtue of their immoral content, since whether a command constitutes a clear mistake *is* determined by its content. However, on this revised view it is the clarity of a command's departure from right reason, and not its immorality *per se*, that accounts for its invalidity.

However, it is highly implausible that every command to cause otherwise-unjustified harm also constitutes a clear mistake. In order for a command to qualify as a clear mistake, the subject must be able to determine that the command fails to reflect right reason without engaging in the same reasoning that the authority went through in producing its commands. Importantly, whether or not the subject can form such a judgement depends not only on the command's content, but also on the particular domain in which the command is issued and the nature of the service that the authority provides. Given this contextual element, the very same command may constitute a clear mistake when issued in one domain, but not in another. Perhaps *some* commands constitute clear mistakes across all domains, such as those that require impossible actions ('Do X and not-X! Now!'). But the claim that *every* command to inflict unjustified harm constitutes a clear mistake is surely false. Harm-apt domains are precisely those in which determining that such commands are mistaken frequently (though not always) requires repeating the authority's deliberations.

Both the Pro Tanto and Invalidation Objections are thus unsuccessful in refuting my first claim. They do not fail because they misidentify ways in which authority is limited. Service accounts agree that the commands of authorities are limited in terms of both their weight and validity. Rather, they fail because they assume that the question of whether particular commands exceed those limits can be settled independently of a specific account of authority's justification. I have argued that this is a mistake. On a service-based view, the scope and limits of the obligation to obey are calibrated to what is required for the authority to provide the relevant service. When the service consists in enabling subjects to better distribute harm, subjects can be required, all-things-considered, to obey (at least some) commands to cause unjustified harm.

7. DEFENDING THE SECOND CLAIM

In what follows, I shift focus from the question of the *range* of reasons that are capable of justifying harm, to that of how different agents' reasons for harming *interact*. More specifically, if my first claim is defensible and authoritative commands can provide an independent source of justification, to what extent does an agent's possession of an *authority-based* justification for causing unjust harm affect whether other agents are permitted to defensively harm the authorized agent? Whereas the preceding discussion centred on those who are *subject* to commands to cause harm, the following concerns the normative situation of those who are *threatened* by authorized agents.

To recapitulate, within the literature on defensive harm several theorists defend the view I labelled *Immunity*, which holds that there is no justified defence against justified infringements of rights against harm. In opposition, I argue that authority-based justifications reveal *Immunity* to be mistaken. The fact that an agent is justified in causing unjust harm *in virtue of being commanded* does not, in itself, raise the justificatory burden on defensively harming that agent. Though denying *Immunity* is not an uncommon position in itself, the argument I offer is distinctive because it is compatible with certain commitments that are often taken to strongly support *Immunity*.

Discussions of the permissibility of harming justified threateners typically focus on cases in which the threatener possesses an (impartial) lesser-evil justification for harming others. These provide a useful starting point for assessing the case of authority-based justifications. A standard test case is the following:

> **Tactical Bombers**: A bomber crew is on a mission to destroy a munitions factory as part of a just war. Destroying the factory will result in the deaths of five innocent bystanders as a side-effect. However, the good achieved by bombing the factory is sufficient to justify doing so as the lesser evil. The five bystanders have access to an anti-aircraft gun and are able to shoot down the bombers before they drop their bombs.

The question here is whether the bystanders are permitted to defensively kill the bombers, given that the bombers are justified in causing their deaths. While many hold that the bystanders would be so permitted (Steinhoff, 2008; Mapel, 2010; Rodin, 2011; Hosein, 2014), others argue that the bombers' justification entails that defence is impermissible (Tadros, 2011, ch. 9; McMahan, 2014; Frowe, 2015).

The debate between these two views often turns on one's position on the *range* of justifications for harming. As explained above, justifications are standardly divided into agent-neutral and agent-relative. Agent-neutral justifications—such as defensive liability and (impartial) lesser-evil—apply to all agents, whereas agent-relative justifications—such as those grounded in permissible partiality—apply only to specific agents. If one takes the range of justifications to be thoroughly agent-neutral, then a commitment to *Immunity* follows quite naturally. If the reasons that determine how harm ought to be distributed in any particular case apply equally to all agents, then this gives every agent the common aim of seeing to it that that this distribution comes about, or at least not preventing it from coming about.[26] For the agent-neutralist, it is contradictory to hold that certain agents may be justified in bringing about one distribution of harm, while others are justified in bringing about an opposing distribution.[27]

Conversely, if one accepts the possibility of agent-relative justifications, then *Immunity* need not hold. If some forms of justification apply only to specific agents, there is no oddity in claiming that different parties can be simultaneously justified in harming one another. For example, while the bombers may possess a lesser-evil justification, the innocent bystanders may be justified in resisting on the basis of permissible self-partiality.

8. AUTHORIZED THREATENERS AND IMMUNITY

Let us now consider the permissibility of defence against authorized threateners. On first impression, it is tempting to endorse *Immunity* here and hold that the permissibility of violent resistance is precluded by their justification. This view is appealing because it generates the intuitively right result in a range of cases, such as the following:

> *Police Officer:* A police officer acts to arrest an individual as a result of a command to do so from a morally justified authority. However, the command is mistaken (but not clearly so) and the prospective arrestee is innocent.

In this case, it seems impermissible for the arrestee to use defensive force against the police officer. Combining the Authority View of Harm with *Immunity* provides a neat explanation of why this is so. The Authority View allows us to characterize the police officer as posing a justified threat to the innocent arrestee, despite the fact that the harm is not justified by the command-independent reasons. The addition of *Immunity* allows us argue that the police officer's justification for harming defeats the arrestee's normal

---

[26] For the characterization of agent-neutrality in terms of common aims, see Parfit (1984, p. 27).

[27] For example, Victor Tadros (2011, ch. 9) defends a thoroughly agent-neutral view of permissible harming in general and explicitly appeals to this view in order to reject the possibility of symmetrically justified harming (with the exception of cases in which the conflict is itself agent-neutrally valuable, such as in certain sporting contests).

permission to resist aggression.[28] Furthermore, this analysis also yields the intuitively right result in a variation on the case:

> ***Vigilante***: A private individual acts to carry out a citizen's arrest on the basis of a reasonable suspicion that the arrestee will otherwise commit a serious crime. However, they are mistaken and the prospective arrestee is innocent.

In this case it *does* seem intuitively justified for the arrestee to forcefully resist. Again, combining the Authority View with *Immunity* neatly explains this. Although, by hypothesis, both the police officer and the vigilante threaten an identical harm, only the police officer possesses a justification for doing so, because only the police officer threatens harm in conformity with an authoritative command. Though the vigilante may reasonably believe that they are justified in harming the arrestee, they in fact lack sufficient reason to do so. Since this analysis classifies the vigilante as a species of unjustified threatener, *Immunity* does not apply and resistance may then be justified (subject to the usual requirements of necessity and proportionality).

However, other cases strongly suggest that *Immunity* does not hold in the case of authority-based justifications. Consider the following:

> ***Combatants***: A group of combatants act to annex an area of territory belonging to a neighbouring state as a result of a legitimate command to do so. However, the command is mistaken (but not clearly so) and the invasion is unjustified.[29]

In this case it seems clearly permissible for those threatened by the authorized agents to resist (or for third parties to do so on their behalf). Yet applying *Immunity* to this case generates the opposite result. Surrender would be morally required, which is highly counter-intuitive.[30]

---

[28] This is not to deny that there are alternative explanations of the intuition that it is impermissible for the innocent arrestee to resist that are compatible with *Completeness*. For example, defence may be futile or counterproductive, given that other police officers will act to make the arrest even if the initial arresting officer is successfully resisted. In my view, such explanations are unsatisfactorily contingent. Thanks to James Lenman and Jeff McMahan for raising this point.

[29] See Estlund (2007) for further discussion of this sort of case.

[30] The right to resist all forms of military aggression has recently come under sustained criticism, so it is not necessarily counter-intuitive to claim that resistance may be unjustified in a case like the one described above (see, especially, Rodin, 2014). However, what is counter-intuitive, even on the most pacifistic views, is the conclusion that resistance may be unjustified *because* the aggressors act with justification. Hence, the oddity of the conclusion generated by applying *Immunity* in the *Combatants* case can be appreciated regardless of one's position on the right to resist military aggression.

The interaction question thus raises an important challenge for the idea of authority-based justifications, in the form of a dilemma. Since, by hypothesis, both the police officer and the combatants possess the same form of justification for harming, we cannot claim that *Immunity* applies to one but not the other. Either *Immunity* holds in both cases—giving the wrong result in the *Combatants* case—or fails to apply in both cases—giving the wrong result in the *Police Officer* case.

9. AUTHORIZED THREATENERS AND AGENT-RELATIVITY

I propose an account of interaction for authority-based justifications that aims to avoid the dilemma. The proposal has two parts. First, I argue that *Immunity* does not apply in the case of authority-based justifications for harming, thereby avoiding the first horn. Second, I provide an alternative and non-*ad hoc* account of why defence may be unjustified in cases such as *Police Officer*, thus avoiding the second horn. This section defends the first part; the following section argues for the second.

Recall the above discussion of the relationship between views about the range of reasons that are capable of justifying harm and views about how those reasons interact interpersonally. Those who take the range of justifications to be thoroughly agent-neutral are typically committed to *Immunity* as an account of interaction, whereas those who accept the existence of agent-relative justifications deny it. Given this, one strategy for denying that *Immunity* applies to authority-based justifications is to argue that the reasons that constitute the latter are agent-relative. Since agent-relative reasons need not affect the normative situation of other agents, the possession of an agent-relative justification for bringing about a certain distribution of harm does not mean that others also have reason to bring about that distribution.

The argument for this view is tentative, but fairly straightforward: authority-based justifications fit the standard characterization of agent-relative reasons. One can only give a full statement of the reason for action provided by a legitimate command by making explicit and ineliminable reference to a particular agent for whom it is a reason. When an authority issues a command to φ this is not intended to bring a new reason for φ-ing into existence for all agents generally, but only for the subject(s) of the command. Moreover, the agent-relativity of the reasons created by legitimate commands is particularly salient under service accounts of authority, which require the obligation to obey to be demonstrated anew with regard to each subject and their particular circumstances.[31] On the view that legitimate

---

[31] On the idea that authority is 'piecemeal' in this way, see Raz (1986, p. 71 and p. 80).

authorities are those that enable individuals to compensate for various deficiencies and shortfalls in their practical reasoning, the justification of an individual's obligation to obey must necessarily appeal to specific facts about *that* individual.

If this characterization of authority-based justifications as agent-relative is defensible, we have the beginnings of an explanation of why *Immunity* does not hold in cases such as *Combatants*, thus avoiding the first horn of our dilemma. Though, by hypothesis, the combatants possess sufficient reason for causing harm, these reasons do not affect the normative situation of others, and so do not count against resistance.

It may be objected that this claim is too strong.[32] The objection proceeds from the following assumption: that all agents have a *pro tanto* reason to promote others' conformity with reason, which includes enabling them to be served by authorities. Given this, one may claim that prospective victims (as well as third parties) do in fact have *some* reason not to resist authorized threateners, because resistance would prevent the authorized agent from conforming to reasons that apply to them: those provided by their authority's command. Hence, I am mistaken to claim that the authorized threatener's justification does not count against resistance on the part of their victims.

However, I don't think this conclusion follows from the assumption. It may well be true that I have reason to promote all other agents' conformity with reason, and that doing so may involve bringing it about that others *are subject* to authorities that serve them. But it does not follow from this that I necessarily have reason to promote others *obeying* authoritative commands, in cases where the command fails to reflect the balance of pre-existing reasons.[33] While *the subject* of the mistaken command may have sufficient reason to obey it, they do so only because a policy of obedience is an optimal, though imperfect, means *for them* to achieve greater overall conformity with their ultimate reasons. When the strategy goes awry in particular cases, I should be guided by the subject's ultimate reasons, not their instrumental reasons. Hence, in cases like *Combatants*, the victims' aim of promoting others' conformity with reason does not give them reason to refrain from resisting their attackers. If anything, it gives them reason to resist.

Though the preceding points go part of the way towards showing why defensively harming authorized threateners can be justified, they are not yet sufficient for this conclusion.[34] While they may show that the *reasons that justify* the authorized threatener do not count against violently resisting them, it might still be the case that the fact *that the threatener is justified* does so. More specifically, it might be objected that the authorized threatener's justification exempts them from liability to defensive harm. If so, this would impose a significant, perhaps even decisive, constraint on harming them.

The first point to note in response is that the doctrine 'justification defeats liability' is controversial.[35] One potential problem is that justification does not typically defeat other kinds of moral liability, such as liability to compensate *ex post* for causing harm.[36] The second, more substantial, point is that (as far as I am aware) those who endorse the doctrine have only explicitly defended it with respect to standard cases of impartial lesser-evil justifications, such as the *Tactical Bombers*. We should therefore be cautious in claiming that these arguments generalize to other forms of justification, and to authority-based justifications in particular. In fact, there are reasons to doubt that they do. Take, for example, the most sustained defence of the doctrine, put forward by Jeff McMahan. On McMahan's view, the doctrine is grounded in a specific account of the basis of liability, according to which 'the assignment of liability follows the distribution of harm in accordance with the demands of justice' (McMahan, 2008, p. 234). In the case of standard justified threateners, who have an impartial lesser-evil justification, 'there is no reason that justice would demand that unavoidable harm be distributed towards them' (p. 234), and so they are exempt from liability. While I find this view quite plausible, the rationale clearly does not apply to agents who possess authority-based justifications, since precisely what these justify is acting *contrary to* the just distribution of harm.[37] By the lights of McMahan's account, authorized threateners should be liable to defensive harm. What this shows, I think, is that justification *per se* does not defeat liability (if indeed it defeats it at all). Rather, it depends on the kind of reasons that provide the particular justification.

[34] Thanks to two anonymous referees for helping me see this.

[35] This slogan is Jeff McMahan's. Note that the doctrine is weaker than *Immunity*, since it is compatible with it being permissible to defensively harm justified threateners on grounds other than liability.

[36] An objection made by Steinhoff (2008) and Rodin (2011), who reject the doctrine. For responses, see McMahan (2008).

[37] Though I cannot argue for it here, I suspect that this may also be true of agent-relative justifications more generally, or at least those grounded in prerogatives to show partiality towards one's own interests (see Quong, 2009). These justifications can also be characterized as granting defenders a permission to act against the just distribution of harm. So if, as McMahan claims, liability tracks the just distribution of harm, the prerogative should not defeat liability.

This argument regarding liability completes my case for denying *Immunity* in the case of authorized threateners. If defensible, my second main claim can be vindicated: an agent's possession of an authority-based justification for causing harm does not, in itself, raise the justificatory burden for defensively harming that agent, compared to if they lacked that justification. Note that this is compatible with the possibility that independent factors *other than their justification* might constrain the permissibility of defence against authorized threateners. Most obviously, authorized agents seem clearly non-culpable for threatening unjust harm. Though few theorists hold that non-culpable threateners escape liability,[38] many accept that a lack of culpability can count against the permissibility of defensive harm to some degree.

Before moving on, it is worth highlighting two implications of the authority-based case for agent relativity sketched above. Firstly, it suggests that agent-relative reasons can be generated even if it is true that the authority-independent reasons, upon which authoritative commands are based, are entirely agent-neutral. Even in a world populated solely by agent-neutral reasons, authorities may still serve their subjects by issuing commands that enable them to achieve greater conformity with those reasons. But the instrumental reasons created by these commands will be agent-relative. Authoritative commands that are justified in this way may be understood as a species of 'derivative' agent-relative reasons. These are reasons for action that are specific to certain agents, but whose normative force is derived from their role in enabling that agent to conform to the ultimate, agent-neutral reasons.[39]

Secondly, the Authority View provides a novel argument for both the existence of agent-relative justifications for harm and for the possibility of cases of symmetrically justified harming. Unlike existing agent-relative accounts of permissible harm, the Authority View makes no appeal to considerations of partiality, and so may avoid the standard objections pressed against these accounts.

10. AUTHORITY AND CONSTRAINTS

The preceding section sought to show how we can avoid the first horn of our dilemma. An additional argument is required to avoid the second horn: that defensively harming authorized agents is straightforwardly justified in

---

[38] For a notable exception, see Lazar (2009).

[39] For discussion of this type of reason, see Hooker (2000, p. 110) and Gardner (2007, p. 65).

cases such as *Police Officer*, in which resistance seems intuitively impermissible. This conclusion seems forced on us if, as I claim, *Immunity* does not apply in the case of authority-based justifications. This final section aims to provide a plausible and non-*ad hoc* account of why resisting authorized threateners may be impermissible in such cases, which does not appeal to the fact that the threatener is justified (this would simply return us to the first horn of the dilemma).

In the paper so far, I have focused on one important normative consequence of authoritative commands: the creation of a justification for causing harm where none existed antecedently. In order to explain why resisting authorized threateners is sometimes impermissible we need to look at the wider range of normative consequences that authoritative commands can effect. In particular, in addition to providing agents with decisive reasons to perform actions that would otherwise be unjustified, commands may also create decisive reasons to *refrain* from performing actions that would otherwise be *justified*. If the idea of authority-based justifications for harming is defensible, the possibility of authority-based *constraints* should also be.

Once we recognize this additional possibility, we have the resources for explaining why, in cases like *Police Officer*, it may be impermissible to resist an authorized threatener. The key feature of such cases is that the command that harm be caused is addressed to *both* the agent who carries out the harmful action *and* the agent who will suffer the resulting harm. Given this, the command may affect the normative situation of both agents. In particular, the command [Joe be arrested!] may give the police officer a decisive reason to inflict the harm of arrest on Joe *and* give Joe a decisive reason not to exercise his normal right of self-defence. This additional moral power to constrain the use of force may also be justified on service-based grounds (though other forms of justification are possible). For example, an authority's having this power may enable subjects to achieve the coordinative and adjudicative benefits of a system of law.[40] It is this dual exercise of authority, I contend, which explains why resisting authorized threateners is impermissible in certain cases.[41]

---

[40] For a discussion of how authorities may serve their subjects on grounds of adjudication, see Viehoff (2011).

[41] Of course, authority-based constraints will not always be decisive. For example, in cases where the authority's power to impose this constraint is grounded in its enabling subjects to better comply with their reasons to coordinate with others and adjudicate disagreements impartially, the constraint may be overridden by countervailing considerations that fall outside this domain, such as the costs the subject would have to bear by obeying. My argument can thus accommodate the intuition that if the harm faced by Joe were more serious—long-term imprisonment, for example—then he may be morally justified in resisting, despite being commanded not to.

To clarify, the appeal to authority-based constraints is not a tacit reaffirmation of *Immunity*. It's true that both the authorized agent's justification for causing harm and their victim's lack of justification for resisting share the same origin: an authoritative command issued by a common authority. But these normative consequences are entirely independent of each other. We can see this by noting that agents can be subject to authority-based constraints on resistance even if the aggressors lack any justification. Consider the following:

> **Invasion**: Nation A is facing wholly and clearly unjustified annexation of part of its territory by a more powerful neighbour, Nation B. A's government has service-based authority over its citizens regarding the domain of national defence and, after assessing the expected costs and benefits, commands its citizens not to militarily resist B's agents.

Assume for the sake of argument that resistance by Nation A's citizens is rendered impermissible by the authority's command.[42] This prohibition is clearly not brought about by justification on the part of the aggressors, since they lack any justification whatsoever. Cases such as this demonstrate that authority-based constraints on defence are entirely separable from the moral status of the threatened harm.

11. CONCLUSION

Reflection on the relationship between the justification of harm and the justification of authority reveals that certain widely held views about the morality of harm and the limits of the obligation to obey require revision. A complete theory of permissible harm will need to make space for both authority-based justifications and authority-based constraints.

Acknowledgments

For written comments on versions of this paper, I am extremely grateful to Yitzhak Benbaji, Christopher Bennett, Cécile Fabre, Adil Ahmed Haque, Jamie Kelly, James Lenman, Jeff McMahan, Jonathan Quong, Massimo Renzo, Daniel Statman, Victor Tadros, and especially Daniel Viehoff. The paper also benefited from stimulating discussions at a workshop on Victor Tadros's *The Ends of Harm*; the Association for Legal and Social Philosophy Annual Conference; the Oxford War Discussion Group; the inaugural conference of the Stockholm Centre for the Ethics of War and

---

[42] For a different argument for the possibility of such cases, see Stilz (2014).

Peace; and seminars at the University of Sheffield and the University of Toronto. I would also like to thank two anonymous reviewers for *Oxford Studies in Political Philosophy* for their extremely perceptive and helpful comments. Work on this paper was supported by the Arts and Humanities Research Council (UK) and the Society for Applied Philosophy.

References

Christiano, T. (2004) 'The Authority of Democracy', *Journal of Political Philosophy*, 12(3), pp. 266–90.

Christiano, T. (2008) *The Constitution of Equality*. Oxford: Oxford University Press.

Darwall, S. (2009) 'Authority and Second-Personal Reason for Acting', in Sobel, D. and Wall, S. (eds) *Reasons for Action*. Cambridge: Cambridge University Press, pp. 134–54.

Darwall, S. (2010) 'Authority and Reasons: Exclusionary and Second Personal', *Ethics*, 120(2), pp. 257–78.

Davis, N. A. (1984) 'Abortion and Self-Defense', *Philosophy and Public Affairs*, 13(2), pp. 175–207.

Enoch, D. (2011) 'Giving Practical Reasons', *Philosopher's Imprint*, 11(4), pp. 1–21.

Enoch, D. (2014) 'Authority and Reason-Giving', *Philosophy and Phenomenological Research*, 89(2), pp. 296–332.

Estlund, D. (2007) 'On Following Orders in an Unjust War', *Journal of Political Philosophy*, 15(2), pp. 213–34.

Estlund, D. (2008) *Democratic Authority*. Princeton: Princeton University Press.

Frowe, H. (2015) 'Claim Rights, Duties and Lesser-Evil Justifications', *Proceedings of the Aristotelian Society*, 89(1), pp. 267–85.

Gardner, J. (2007) *Offences and Defences*. Oxford: Oxford University Press.

Gardner, J. (2010) 'Justification under Authority', *Canadian Journal of Law and Jurisprudence*, 23(1), pp. 73–98.

Green, L. (1983) 'Law, Coordination, and the Common Good', *Oxford Journal of Legal Studies*, 3(3), pp. 299–324.

Green, L. (1985) 'Authority and Convention', *The Philosophical Quarterly*, 35(141), pp. 329–46.

Hershovitz, S. (2003) 'Legitimacy, Democracy, and Razian Authority', *Legal Theory*, 9(3), pp. 201–20.

Hooker, B. (2000) *Ideal Code, Real World*. Oxford: Oxford University Press.

Hosein, A. (2014) 'Are Justified Aggressors a Threat to the Rights Theory of Self-Defense?', in Frowe, H. and Lang, G. (eds) *How We Fight*. Oxford: Oxford University Press, pp. 87–103.

Knowles, D. (2007) 'The Domain of Authority', *Philosophy*, 82(1), pp. 23–43.

Lazar, S. (2009) 'Responsibility, Risk, and Killing in Self-Defense', *Ethics*, 119(4), pp. 699–728.

Lazar, S. (2013) 'Associative Duties and the Ethics of Killing in War', *Journal of Practical Ethics*, 1(1), pp. 6–51.

Mapel, D. (2010) 'Moral Liability to Defensive Harm and Symmetrical Self-Defense', *Journal of Political Philosophy*, 18(2), pp. 198–217.

Marmor, A. (2011a) 'The Dilemma of Authority', *Jurisprudence*, 2(1), pp. 121–41.

Marmor, A. (2011b) 'An Institutional Conception of Authority', *Philosophy and Public Affairs*, 39(3), pp. 238–61.

McMahan, J. (2008) 'Justification and Liability', *Journal of Political Philosophy*, 16(2), pp. 227–44.

McMahan, J. (2009) *Killing in War*. Oxford: Oxford University Press.

McMahan, J. (2014) 'Self-Defense against Justified Threateners', in Frowe, H. and Lang, G. (eds) *How We Fight*. Oxford: Oxford University Press, pp. 104–37.

Parfit, D. (1984) *Reasons and Persons*. Oxford: Oxford University Press.

Quong, J. (2009) 'Killing in Self-Defense', *Ethics*, 119(3), pp. 507–37.

Quong, J. (2011) *Liberalism without Perfection*. Oxford: Oxford University Press.

Raz, J. (1986) *The Morality of Freedom*. Oxford: Clarendon Press.

Raz, J. (1989) 'Facing Up: A Reply', *Southern California Law Review*, 62, pp. 1153–235.

Raz, J. (2009) *Between Authority and Interpretation*. Oxford: Oxford University Press.

Raz, J. (2010) 'On Respect, Authority and Neutrality: A Response', *Ethics*, 120(2), pp. 279–301.

Ridge, M. (2011) 'Reasons for Action: Agent-Neutral vs. Agent-Relative', in Zalta, E. N. (ed.) *Stanford Encyclopedia of Philosophy*. http://plato.stanford.edu/archives/win2011/entries/reasons-agent/.

Rodin, D. (2011) 'Justifying Harm', *Ethics*, 122(1), pp. 74–110.

Rodin, D. (2014) 'The Myth of National Defence', in Fabre, C. and Lazar, S. (eds) *The Morality of Defensive War*. Oxford: Oxford University Press, pp. 69–89.

Smith, M. N. (2013) 'Political Obligation and the Self', *Philosophy and Phenomenological Research*, 86(2), pp. 347–75.

Steinhoff, U. (2008) 'Jeff McMahan on the Moral Equality of Combatants', *Journal of Political Philosophy*, 16(2), pp. 220–6.

Stilz, A. (2014) 'Authority, Self-Determination and Community in Cosmopolitan War', *Law and Philosophy*, 33(3), pp. 309–35.

Tadros, V. (2011) *The Ends of Harm*. Oxford: Oxford University Press.

Thorburn, M. (2008) 'Justifications, Powers, and Authority', *Yale Law Journal*, 117, pp. 1070–130.

Tucker, A. (2012) 'The Limits of Razian Authority', *Res Publica*, 18(3), pp. 225–40.

Viehoff, D. (2011) 'Procedure and Outcome in the Justification of Authority', *Journal of Political Philosophy*, 19(2), pp. 248–59.

Viehoff, D. (2014) 'Democratic Equality and Political Authority', *Philosophy and Public Affairs*, 42(4), pp. 337–75.

Waldron, J. (1999) *Law and Disagreement*. Oxford: Oxford University Press.

Waldron, J. (2000) 'Self-Defense: Agent-Neutral and Agent-Relative Accounts', *California Law Review*, 88, pp. 711–50.

Wolff, R. P. (1970) *In Defense of Anarchism*. New York: Harper.

Index